new inspiration

Judy Garton-Sprenger and Philip Prowse
with Amanda Bailey, Helena Gomm
and Peter Smith

Teacher's Book 1

Macmillan Education
Between Towns Road, Oxford OX4 3PP
A division of Macmillan Publishers Limited
Companies and representatives throughout the world

ISBN 978-0-230-41018-3
ISBN 978-0-230-41238-5 (pack)

First published 2011

Original design by Giles Davies and eMC
Page make-up by Expo Holdings, D&J Hunter Design
Illustrated by Kathy Baxendale (p183), Mark Davis (pp167 and 182), Gillian Martin (pp164, 168, 169, 172 and 184), Julian Mosedale (pp165, 176, 181), Julia Pearson (pp171 and 180), Simon Smith (pp166, 173 and 186) and Harry Venning (pp163 and 185).
Cover design by Designers Collective

For full photographic acknowledgements please refer to the Student's Book.

The author and publishers are grateful for permission to reprint the following copyright material:
Don't You Want Me – Words and Music by Philip Adrian Wright, Jo Callis and Philip Oakey, copyright © 1981, reproduced by permission of EMI Virgin Music, London W8 5SW; Hal Leonard Corporation & Music Sales Limited.
Rocket Man (I Think It's Gonna Be A Long Long Time) – Words and Music by Elton John and Bernie Taupin. Copyright © 1972 UNIVERSAL/DICK JAMES MUSIC LTD. Copyright Renewed. All Rights in the United States and Canada Controlled and Administered by UNIVERSAL – SONGS OF POLYGRAME INTERNATIONAL, INC. All Rights Reserved. Used with Permission. Reprinted by Hal Leonard Corporation;
Rocket Man – Words & Music by Elton John & Bernie Taupin © Copyright 1972 Dick James Music Limited. Universal/Dick James Music Limited. All rights in Germany administered by Universal Music Publ. GmbH. All Rights Reserved. International Copyright Secured. Used by permission of Music Sales Limited;
Together We Are Strong – Written by Sam Brown and Jools Holland. Copyright © 2002 BUG MUSIC (BMI). All Rights Reserved. Used by Permission. Reprinted by permission of Hal Leonard Corporation and Hornall Bros Music;
Raining In My Heart – Written by Boudleaux & Felice Bryant. Copyright © 1959 by House of Bryant Publications, and Sony Music Publishing, used with permission. All Rights Reserved.

Printed and bound in Thailand

2015 2014 2013 2012 2011
10 9 8 7 6 5 4 3 2 1

Contents

NEW INSPIRATION

New Inspiration is a four-level course designed to take teenagers from beginner to intermediate level (CEF A1–B1+). The course aims to appeal to the modern teenager through imaginative and exciting topics, introduces up-to-date language and expressions, increases confidence through learner independence activities, provides regular opportunities for revision and self-assessment, and caters for different learning styles. For the teacher it offers everything needed for successful lessons with full support at every stage.

The course offers a dual-entry possibility and those learners who have already made some progress in English can start with *New Inspiration 2*.

KEY IDEAS

A fundamental concept in the organisation of *New Inspiration* is that of *difference*.

Different ages

Teenagers are passing through a challenging period of their lives with great physical, social and psychological changes. A 13-year-old lives in a different world from a 16-year-old. In designing *New Inspiration* our aim has been to create a course which grows with its students.

Different abilities

Every class is a mixed-ability class. We see mixed ability not as a problem, but as a fact of life to which we need to respond in our teaching. Our response in creating *New Inspiration* has been to develop *flexible* materials which offer a variety of learning paths to success.

Different interests

One of the most striking findings of the research phase in preparing this course was the wide variety of different interests among students. We have therefore provided a broad range of materials to engage students in challenging but achievable tasks. The topic syllabus gives the opportunity for cross-curricular and cross-cultural work so that students learn about life and the world at the same time as learning English. Language learning also needs to be fun to be effective, so we have included lots of games, poems and puzzles, as well as a story in the Workbook and songs in the Teacher's Book.

Different backgrounds

Teenagers come to the language classroom with a wide range of backgrounds – not only in social and educational terms, but also because of different learning histories. Students in the same class may have had positive, negative or no language learning experiences at primary level; they may have started learning another language, or had private lessons or extra classes in English. Students who started learning English at primary level may have been exposed to predominantly oral activities, games and songs, and be surprised at the different demands of the class they are now in.

New Inspiration aims to provide a safe transition to the new level, and to revise and recycle language in fresh contexts.

Different learning styles

We believe that it is important for students to 'learn how to learn'. We have provided opportunities for students to experiment with different learning styles and develop language learning strategies which suit them. We have tried to make students aware that, while they may have a preferred learning style, they could benefit from experimenting with others.

Different aspirations

Within each teenager there is a young adult in the making, and all have differing goals and aspirations for the future. We have aimed to provide students with practical language skills and a positive attitude to learning. This will lead them to success in examinations and prepare them for using English in the real world.

Different class sizes and numbers of hours a week

The Teacher's Book provides lesson plans full of extra optional activities which can be given to less confident learners or to fast-finishers, and the Workbook exercises can all be used for self-study. Teachers with more hours at their disposal will find that they have material for considerably more than the 90–120 hours of the core course if they use the optional activities.

KEY FEATURES OF *NEW INSPIRATION*

Multi-syllabus

The course has a topic-led syllabus which integrates separate communicative, lexical, grammatical, pronunciation, skills and learner independence syllabi. This provides a principled approach to vocabulary acquisition and to the development of the four skills. The Contents pages of the Student's Book list the topics, lesson titles, communicative aims, language areas, pronunciation points, skills and learner independence training.

Reading

At Levels 1 and 2, students encounter new language in the first three lessons of each unit through dialogues and prose texts. The dialogues feature an international group of teenage characters with whom the students can identify, while the prose texts focus on topics of interest and relevance to the students' lives and studies. Dialogues and texts are preceded by pre-reading/listening tasks to develop predictive skills.

Vocabulary and grammar

The topic-led syllabus provides a firm basis for systematic coverage and development of vocabulary. Lessons contain Word Banks and activities to revise and extend lexical fields, and students are encouraged to maintain their own vocabulary notebooks. At the back of the Student's Book there is a unit-by-unit Word List with phonemic transcriptions.

There is a clearly structured approach to grammar, leading to fluency activities where students apply the target language in communicative situations. Language Workout boxes at the end of each lesson are cross-referenced to a comprehensive Language File at the back of the Student's Book, which provides full paradigms and explanations of grammatical points with controlled practice exercises.

Pronunciation

The first three lessons of each unit provide explicit work on pronunciation, stress and intonation arising from the lesson language. Phonemic symbols are given as support where relevant; these are intended for recognition only. There is a Pronunciation Guide at the back of the Student's Book.

Skills development

Careful attention is paid to the development of the four language skills in each unit, both in the first three lessons and in the fourth Integrated Skills lesson. Guided writing: a carefully staged programme of tasks, helps the growth of students' writing skills. There is further work on reading and writing skills in the Workbook, together with suggestions for extensive reading.

Learner independence

The Integrated Skills lessons in each unit offer work on the development of learner independence, and this is supported by parallel sections in the Workbook and advice in the Teacher's Book lesson notes.

Cognitive development, and language awareness and enjoyment

New Inspiration contains a range of activities, such as quizzes and questionnaires, which encourage students to think in English. 'Your response' activities after a text or dialogue also encourage the development of critical thinking and personal responses to reading.

Inspiration *Extra!* sections at the end of each Student's Book unit contain either a full project, or a Language Links activity focusing on plurilingualism and a sketch for students to act out. There are also word games, puzzles and limericks. Games can also be found in the Student's Book lessons, and the Workbook contains more puzzles, crosswords and brainteasers.

Mixed ability

The first three lessons of each unit contain Extension activities for fast-finishers. Inspiration *Extra!* also includes both a Revision and Extension section which caters for two different ability levels – revising and extending language from the preceding four lessons – and a Your Choice! section where students can choose between activities reflecting different learning styles. There are further Revision and Extension sections in the Workbook.

Recycling and reviewing

The syllabus regularly recycles new language. As well as the Revision and Extension sections, there are four Review sections at each level, providing further revision and learner independence self-assessment sections. There are further Review sections in the Workbook.

Culture and CLIL

Each level also features four Culture sections which build cross-cultural awareness, encourage discussion, develop vocabulary, and lead up to Mini-projects. The Workbook contains further Culture sections with reading, writing and vocabulary exercises. There is a wealth of CLIL material appropriate to the students' age and level throughout the course, including a dedicated section in each Workbook.

COURSE COMPONENTS

Student's Book

The Student's Book provides 90–120 hours of teaching material within eight units. Each unit has four lessons – each on two pages for ease of use – and an Inspiration *Extra!* section. The first three lessons in each unit present and practise new language, and the fourth is an Integrated Skills lesson. Each pair of units is preceded by a Preview, which gives the learner a taste of what is to come, and followed by a Review. At the back of the book there is a Language File, a Word List, a Pronunciation Guide and a list of Irregular Verbs.

Workbook

The Workbook offers exercises which can be done in class or as self-study. It mirrors the Student's Book in its organisation, providing a wealth of extra language practice material, integrated skills and learner independence work, mixed-ability Revision and Extension exercises, Culture pages and Review sections. It includes pronunciation exercises, brainteasers, crosswords and suggestions for follow-up work on the Internet. The Workbook also contains CLIL materials linked to other subjects studied at this level, and a unit-by-unit story for extensive reading with associated language practice activities.

Teacher's Book

The Teacher's Book features a practical approach to methodology with step-by-step lesson notes. There are stimulating ideas for warmers to start each lesson as well as optional activities throughout the lesson notes. There are follow-up activities at the end of each lesson and suggestions for homework. Useful cultural information is provided to help answer student queries, and downloadable songs with activities are also included. Full audioscripts are integrated within the notes, as are answers to all the Student Book exercises. There is also a complete Workbook Answer Key.

Tests CD

The editable Tests are designed to cater for mixed-ability classes by providing Standard and Higher Tests for each Student's Book unit. Teachers can use the test that best suits their students and adapt it as necessary. There is also a diagnostic test, three end-of-term tests and an end-of-course test. Tests include grammar, vocabulary, reading, listening and writing.

Class Audio CD

All the Student's Book dialogues, texts and pronunciation exercises are recorded. Recorded items are indicated by the symbol 1.04 in the Student's Book and Teacher's Book.

New Inspiration Digital

New Inspiration embraces the digital generation offering multi-media and interactive solutions for use in class and at home. *New Inspiration Interactive Classroom* for use with an Interactive Whiteboard or digital projector includes the Student's Book in digital format with integrated audio and answer key, interactive activities and cultural video clips. *New Inspiration Practice Online* (www.macmillanpracticeonline.com/newinspiration) provides self-marking interactive practice activities, videos and fun language games. The *New Inspiration Resource Site* (www.macmillanenglish.com/inspiration) provides the teacher with extra language practice materials, cross-curricular and culture lessons, webquests and a social networking section.

New Inspiration and the Common European Framework

The Common European Framework (CEF) is a widely used standard created by the Council of Europe. In the classroom, familiarity with the CEF can be of great help to any teacher in identifying students' actual progress and helping them to set their learning priorities.

New Inspiration offers a wide range of teaching materials in various components which give teachers the opportunity to develop all aspects of their students' language ability. The CEF can be used to follow their progress.

Below are the A1–A2 descriptors (description of competences) covered in *New Inspiration 1* which students are aiming to reach. A basic level of confidence with the A1-A2 descriptors is expected as students start using *New Inspiration* 2, and by the end of the course students should be able to accomplish more of the B1 level. Many of the B1 descriptors talk of greater confidence with the same kinds of ability already described at A2: others only emerge for the first time at B1.

On the teacher's website you will find a list of unit by unit descriptors with suggested targets which you can print out and copy for your students to assess themselves. Students can use these at any point to get a detailed picture of their own individual progress.

What is a CEF Portfolio?

If you are using portfolios as a way of evaluating your students' coursework over the year, you will find a wide variety of opportunities within each *New Inspiration* unit to provide material for the dossier.

A portfolio is a means to document a person's achievements. Artists, architects or designers collect samples of their work in portfolios. The basic idea is that students collect samples of their work in their portfolio. Most of the time, these samples will be texts created by the students, but they could also include photos of classroom scenes, wall displays, audio recordings and DVDs. All these documents provide evidence of a student's performance, e.g. during a discussion, an oral presentation or a role play.

The portfolio consists of three parts: the **Language Passport** with information about a student's proficiency in one or more languages i.e. qualifications, the **Language Biography** where students reflect their learning process and progress and say what they can do in their foreign language(s) and the **Dossier**, a collection of materials and data put together by students to document and illustrate their learning experiences.

Although it may be a demanding task to set up in the beginning, the overall aim is for students to be involved in planning, collecting and evaluating their own work – taking responsibility for their own learning. This in turn may lead to increased participation and autonomy on the learners' part.

	New Inspiration 1 TB Descriptors	Unit 1	Unit 2	Unit 3	Unit 4	Unit 5	Unit 6	Unit 7	Unit 8
Listening A1	I can understand when someone speaks very slowly to me and articulates carefully, with long pauses for me to assimilate meaning.	8							
	I can understand simple directions how to get from X to Y, by foot or public transport.								
	I can understand questions and instructions addressed carefully and slowly to me and follow short, simple directions.								
	I can understand numbers, prices and times.	9, 15, 16, 21, 22							
Listening A2	I can understand what is said clearly, slowly and directly to me in simple everyday conversation; it is possible to make me understand, if the speaker can take the trouble.			39					
	I can generally identify the topic of discussion around me when people speak slowly and clearly.	12, 14, 20	26, 31	38, 43	55, 56	66, 72	79, 82	93, 94	
	I can understand phrases, words and expressions related to areas of most immediate priority (e.g. very basic personal and family information, shopping, local area, employment).	14, 17, 19	24, 25	38, 41, 42, 43	51	64, 65, 72, 75		93 , 97	107
	I can catch the main point in short, clear, simple messages and announcements.				55			97	

	I can understand the essential information in short recorded passages dealing with predictable everyday matters which are spoken slowly and clearly.	14, 19	25, 26, 28, 29, 31	37, 38, 39, 40, 41, 42, 43, 46, 48, 49	51, 52, 54, 55, 56	63, 64, 66, 68, 70, 71, 75	76, 79, 81, 82, 83	88, 90, 93, 94, 97, 98	102, 105, 107, 108, 109
	I can identify the main point of TV news items reporting events, accidents etc. when the visual supports the commentary.								
Reading A1	I can understand information about people (place of residence, age, etc.) in newspapers.						76		
	I can locate a concert or a film on calendars of public events or posters and identify where it takes place and at what time it starts.								
	I can understand a questionnaire (entry permit form, hotel registration form) well enough to give the most important information about myself (name, surname, date of birth, nationality).								
	I can understand words and phrases on signs encountered in everyday life (for instance "station", "car park", "no parking", "no smoking", "keep left".	20		46		72		98	
	I can understand the most important orders in a computer programme such as "PRINT", "SAVE", "COPY", etc.		28						
	I can follow short simple written directions (e.g. how to go from X to Y).		28						
	I can understand short simple messages on postcards, for example holiday greetings.								
	In everyday situations I can understand simple messages written by friends or colleagues, for example "back at six o'clock".								108
Reading A2	I can identify important information in news summaries or simple newspaper articles in which numbers and names play an important role and which are clearly structured and illustrated.	18	34	40, 44	56	68	76, 78, 84, 86	92, 93, 94, 101	104, 106
	I can understand a simple personal letter in which the writer tells or asks me about aspects of everyday life.	16	32	45		64		96	
	I can understand simple written messages from friends or colleagues, for example saying when we should meet to play football or asking me to be at work early.							91	108, 109
	I can find the most important information on leisure time activities, exhibitions, etc. in information leaflets.				50, 58			96	
	I can skim small advertisements in newspapers, locate the heading or column I want and identify the most important pieces of information (price and size of apartments, cars, computers).								
	I can understand simple user's instructions for equipment (for example, a public telephone).		29						
	I can understand feedback messages or simple help indications in computer programmes.								
	I can understand short narratives about everyday things dealing with topics which are familiar to me if the text is written in simple language.		24, 30, 32	38, 40, 42, 44, 48, 49	52, 54, 60	65	80, 81, 82	90	102, 110
	I can introduce somebody and use basic greeting and leave-taking expressions.	8							

Spoken Interaction A1	I can ask and answer simple questions, initiate and respond to simple statements in areas of immediate need or on very familiar topics.	8, 9, 11, 13, 21	25, 27, 31	37, 41, 45	58, 59	64, 72	78	97	
	I can make myself understood in a simple way but I am dependent on my partner being prepared to repeat more slowly and rephrase what I say and to help me to say what I want.								
	I can make simple purchases where pointing or other gestures can support what I say.								
	I can handle numbers, quantities, cost and time.	15, 21							
	I can ask people for things and give people things.								
	I can ask people questions about where they live, people they know, things they have, etc. and answer such questions addressed to me provided they are articulated slowly and clearly.	8, 9	25, 28	49		67		95	104, 105
	I can indicate time by such phrases as "next week", "last Friday", "in November", "three o'clock".								
Spoken Interaction A2	I can make simple transactions in shops, post offices or banks.								
	I can use public transport: buses, trains, and taxis, ask for basic information and buy tickets.								
	I can get simple information about travel.				58			97	
	I can order something to eat or drink.								103
	I can make simple purchases by stating what I want and asking the price.								105
	I can ask for and give directions referring to a map or plan.								
	I can ask how people are and react to news.						83	97	
	I can make and respond to invitations.								103, 108, 109, 111
	I can make and accept apologies.					66	80, 83		109
	I can say what I like and dislike.	11	24, 31	37, 39, 45	51, 54	66		93, 97, 98	
	I can discuss with other people what to do, where to go and make arrangements to meet.								
	I can ask people questions about what they do at work and in free time, and answer such questions addressed to me.			41, 43, 45, 48		72	77	91, 98	
Spoken Production A1	I can give personal information (address, telephone number, nationality, age, family, and hobbies).	8, 9, 17, 19		43, 45				95	
	I can describe where I live.								
Spoken Production A2	I can describe myself, my family and other people.	16	25						
	I can describe where I live.				57				
	I can give short, basic descriptions of events.			42	53		81, 84	91	111
	I can describe my educational background, my present or most recent job.								
	I can describe my hobbies and interests in a simple way.		31	43, 45					

	I can describe past activities and personal experiences (e.g. the last weekend, my last holiday).						77, 78, 79, 81, 83		
Strategies A1	I can say when I don't understand.	19				75	83		
	I can very simply ask somebody to repeat what they said.					75			
	I can very simply ask somebody to speak more slowly.								
Strategies A2	I can ask for attention.					75			
	I can indicate when I am following.								
	I can very simply ask somebody to repeat what they said.								
Language Quality A2	I can make myself understood using memorised phrases and single expressions.	8, 9, 12	29, 31	45	57	71			109
	I can link groups of words with simple connectors like "and", "but" and "because".			39, 43, 49			83, 84, 85	91, 95	
	I can use some simple structures correctly.	9, 15, 17	25, 27, 29, 34, 35	39, 41, 43	51, 53, 55, 60	65, 69	79, 81, 84, 85, 86, 87	91, 93, 95, 99, 101	103, 105, 107, 112, 113
	I have a sufficient vocabulary for coping with simple everyday situations.	11, 13, 14, 16, 19, 20, 22	24, 25, 26, 29, 30, 33, 35	36, 39, 41, 42, 43, 44, 46, 47, 48, 49	50, 51, 53, 55, 56, 58, 61	62, 65, 66, 67, 69, 70, 71	77, 78, 80, 81, 83, 85, 86, 87	88, 89, 91, 92, 93, 99	102, 103, 105, 110, 112, 113
Writing A1	I can fill in a questionnaire with my personal details (job, age, address, hobbies).	9				71			
	I can write a greeting card, for instance a birthday card.								
	I can write a simple postcard (for example with holiday greetings).				59				
	I can write a note to tell somebody where I am or where we are to meet.								
	I can write sentences and simple phrases about myself, for example where I live and what I do.	13, 21	25,		51		85		
Writing A2	I can write short, simple notes and messages.		29, 33				84	91	
	I can describe an event in simple sentences and report what happened when and where (for example a party or an accident).						77, 84		107
	I can write about aspects of my everyday life in simple phrases and sentences (people, places, job, school, family, hobbies).	19, 21	31, 32, 33	39, 47	55, 57	65, 69, 73	77, 79, 85	91, 93, 99, 101	105, 107, 110, 111
	I can fill in a questionnaire giving an account of my educational background, my job, my interests and my specific skills.								
	I can briefly introduce myself in a letter with simple phrases and sentences (family, school, job, hobbies).		32	41, 43, 45	57				111
	I can write a short letter using simple expressions for greeting, addressing, asking or thanking somebody.								108, 109, 111
	I can write simple sentences, connecting them with words such as "and", "but", "because".	23		39, 45, 49		65	83	93	
	I can use the most important connecting words to indicate the chronological order of events (first, then, after, later).						83		

Using *New Inspiration*

There are four Preview sections at each level of *New Inspiration* giving students a brief introduction to the communicative aims and topic/vocabulary areas they will cover in the following two units.

Communicative Aims

Students match photographs with some of the items in the Topic and Vocabulary box. This activity introduces students to the topics they will cover in the next two units.

Topics and Vocabulary

Categorisation activities introduce students to some of the key vocabulary of the following two units, and they are also encouraged through brainstorming to identify other words that they already know for some of the topics.

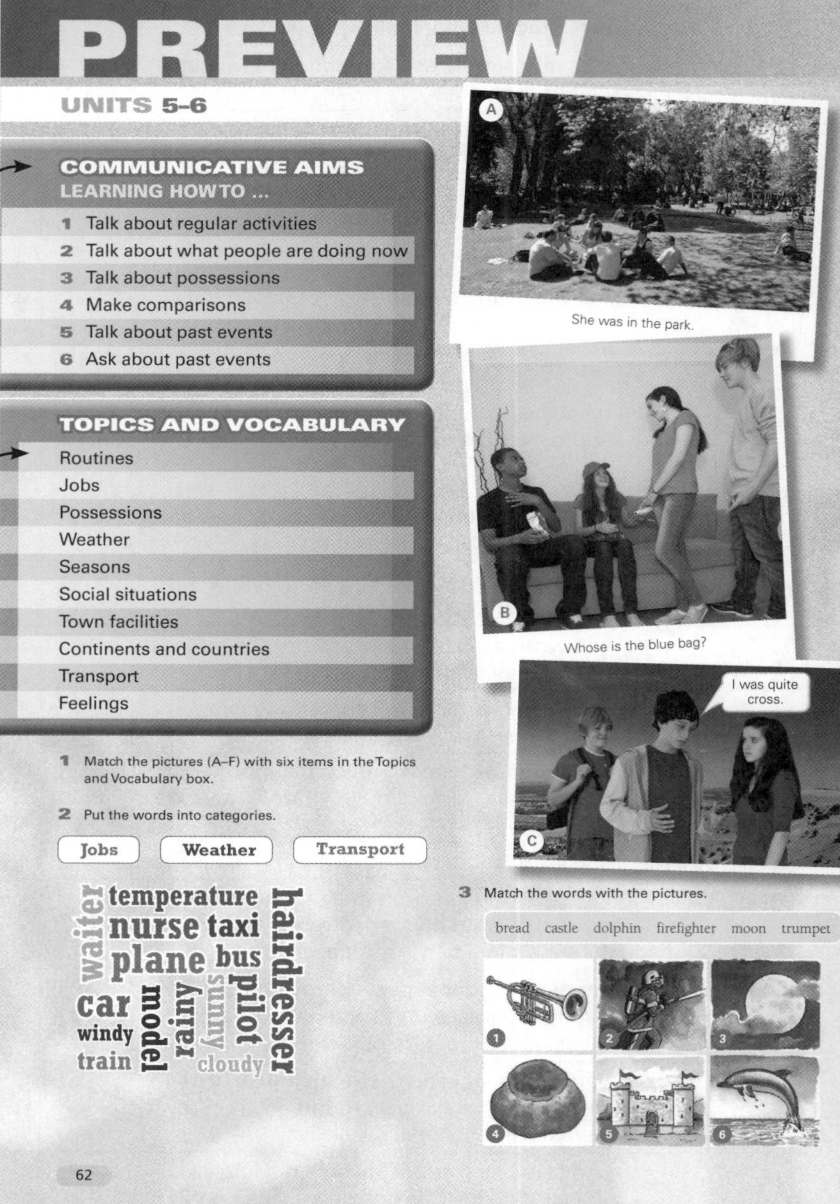

PREVIEW

UNITS 5–6

COMMUNICATIVE AIMS
LEARNING HOW TO ...

1 Talk about regular activities
2 Talk about what people are doing now
3 Talk about possessions
4 Make comparisons
5 Talk about past events
6 Ask about past events

TOPICS AND VOCABULARY

Routines
Jobs
Possessions
Weather
Seasons
Social situations
Town facilities
Continents and countries
Transport
Feelings

A — She was in the park.

B — Whose is the blue bag?

C — I was quite cross.

1 Match the pictures (A–F) with six items in the Topics and Vocabulary box.

2 Put the words into categories.

Jobs | Weather | Transport

waiter temperature nurse taxi plane bus car model rainy sunny pilot hairdresser windy train cloudy

3 Match the words with the pictures.

bread castle dolphin firefighter moon trumpet

1 2 3 4 5 6

62

PREVIEW
D
TODAY'S WEATHER
Amsterdam 17
Brighton 15°
London
It's rainier in London than in Mexico City.
E
My mother teaches maths and French.
F
Some Vikings went east through Europe to Asia.
4 2.30 Listen to extracts 1–3 from Units 5 and 6. Match them with these topics.
A Social situations
B Routines
C Weather
5 Do the Capital City Quiz with two other students.
CAPITAL CITY QUIZ
TRUE OR FALSE?
1 Mexico City is bigger than Geneva.
2 Madrid is higher than Amsterdam.
3 Rio de Janeiro is hotter than Moscow.
4 Rome is older than New York.
5 London is wetter than Cairo.
Answers to Quiz: All the facts are true.
Believe it or not!
Every year there are 16 million thunderstorms in the world! That's 1,800 thunderstorms every hour, and 6,000 flashes of lightning every minute!
63

Questionnaire
Students complete a quiz or questionnaire related to one of the topics of the following two units, to encourage them to personalise their knowledge of the topic.

Believe it or not!
Interesting facts related to one of the topics of the following units.

Listening Preview
Students listen to short extracts from the following units and identify what kind of passage the extracts are taken from or what topic they discuss.

The first three lessons in each unit present new language. While these lessons follow a similar pattern up to the After Reading exercise, the subsequent practice activities vary from lesson to lesson but always include pronunciation and end with writing and Language Workout. Lessons may also include Word Banks and vocabulary exercises, games and role plays as appropriate for the lesson aims. There are usually one or two Extension activities for fast-finishers. In every case there is a progression from controlled presentation and practice of new language to freer, more communicative activities.

Lesson heading

The heading shows the lesson topic – in this case *It's sunnier* – and the communicative aim(s) and target language of the lesson.

Warmers

The Teacher's Book suggests at least two warmers for each lesson. These may revise previously learnt language or prepare students for the lesson topic.

1 Opener

The aim of the Opener is to set the scene for the reading text or listening passage or to pre-teach vocabulary, or both.

2 Reading

The new language is usually presented in a text which is preceded by pre-reading tasks or prediction activities. Students then read the text. Teachers may then wish to play the recording, pausing to answer queries about language or content, or to ask students to close their books and listen without reading.

Weblink

The Teacher's Book provides at least one URL relevant to each lesson (in this case a website with weather forecasts for cities around the world. Teachers are advised to check these links before sharing them with the students as web addresses frequently change.

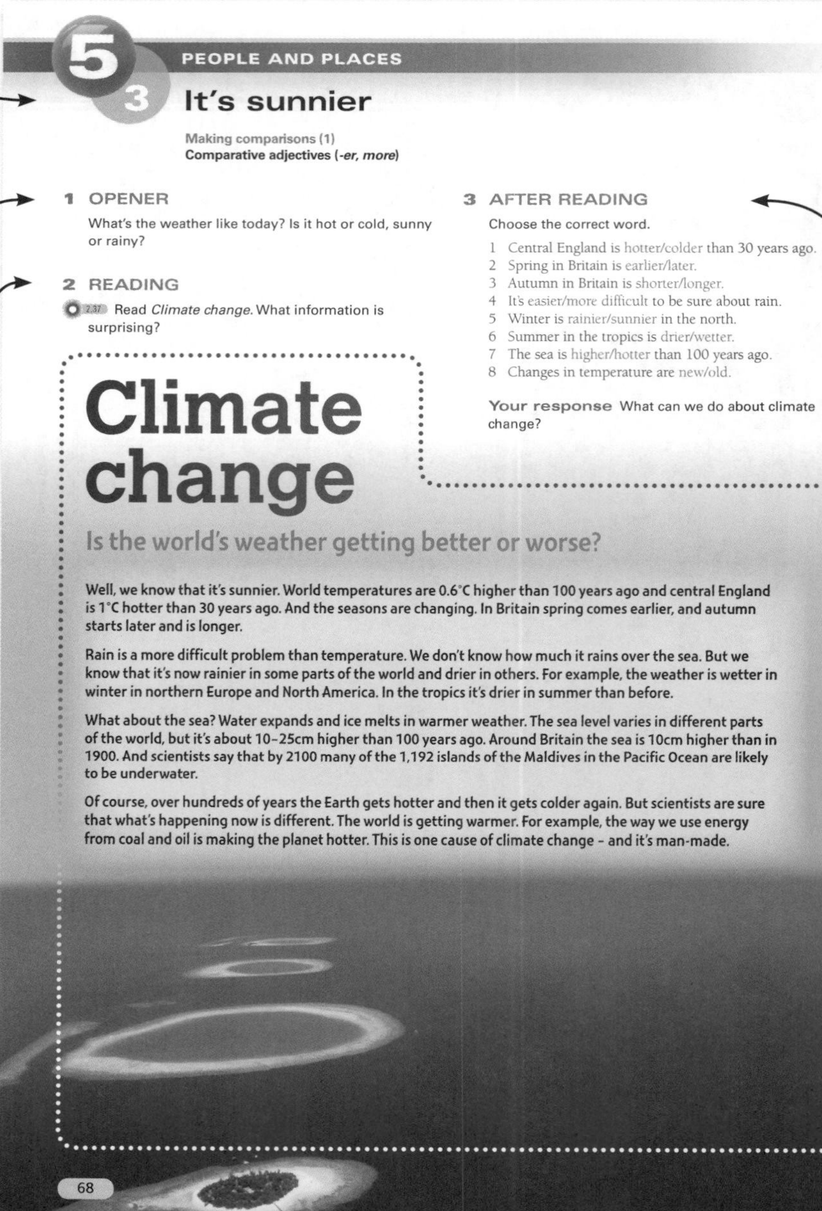

5 3 PEOPLE AND PLACES

It's sunnier

Making comparisons (1)
Comparative adjectives (*-er, more*)

1 OPENER

What's the weather like today? Is it hot or cold, sunny or rainy?

2 READING

2.37 Read *Climate change*. What information is surprising?

Climate change

Is the world's weather getting better or worse?

Well, we know that it's sunnier. World temperatures are 0.6°C higher than 100 years ago and central England is 1°C hotter than 30 years ago. And the seasons are changing. In Britain spring comes earlier, and autumn starts later and is longer.

Rain is a more difficult problem than temperature. We don't know how much it rains over the sea. But we know that it's now rainier in some parts of the world and drier in others. For example, the weather is wetter in winter in northern Europe and North America. In the tropics it's drier in summer than before.

What about the sea? Water expands and ice melts in warmer weather. The sea level varies in different parts of the world, but it's about 10–25cm higher than 100 years ago. Around Britain the sea is 10cm higher than in 1900. And scientists say that by 2100 many of the 1,192 islands of the Maldives in the Pacific Ocean are likely to be underwater.

Of course, over hundreds of years the Earth gets hotter and then it gets colder again. But scientists are sure that what's happening now is different. The world is getting warmer. For example, the way we use energy from coal and oil is making the planet hotter. This is one cause of climate change – and it's man-made.

3 AFTER READING

Choose the correct word.

1 Central England is hotter/colder than 30 years ago.
2 Spring in Britain is earlier/later.
3 Autumn in Britain is shorter/longer.
4 It's easier/more difficult to be sure about rain.
5 Winter is rainier/sunnier in the north.
6 Summer in the tropics is drier/wetter.
7 The sea is higher/hotter than 100 years ago.
8 Changes in temperature are new/old.

Your response What can we do about climate change?

68

3 After Reading

These exercises use a variety of different formats including true/false, open questions, matching questions and answers, and completion. The aim is intensive reading. After Reading ends with Your response: an activity which invites the student to respond personally to the text or dialogue.

Follow-up activities and homework

The Teacher's Book offers optional follow-up activities, usually including a game, to help with mixed-ability teaching and to cope with variable aptitude and amounts of time available. Homework suggestions (usually writing) are also provided for each lesson.

4 Vocabulary

Lessons may also offer explicit lexical development through Word Banks of lexical sets and vocabulary exercises.

UNIT 5

4 VOCABULARY

Complete the words for the four seasons.

sp____ su____ a____ w____

Match these words with photos 1–6.

Word Bank Weather

cloudy foggy rainy sunny snowy windy

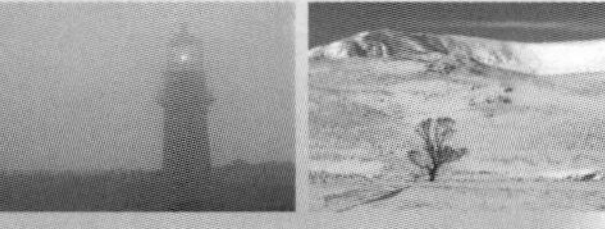

Now compare the weather in different seasons.

It's cloudier in spring than in summer.

5 SPEAKING

What about the weather in your country?

Think about these questions:

- Temperature: is it hotter in summer and colder in winter now?
- Rain: is it wetter or drier in the different seasons now?
- Seasons: are the times of the seasons changing?

Is it hotter in summer now?

Is it wetter in spring now?

Ask your teacher what he/she thinks.

Extension Write sentences about changes in temperature, rain and the seasons in your country.

6 PRONUNCIATION

Circle the /ə/ sound in these words.

/ə/

autumn Britain drier hotter hundred picture problem season summer than weather wetter

2.38 Now listen and check. Repeat the words.

7 SPEAKING

Look at the chart and compare the weather.

TODAY'S WEATHER

Amsterdam	17°
Brighton	15°
London	14°
Madrid	30°
Mexico City	27°
Moscow	25°
New York	24°
Zurich	21°

It's rainier in London than in Mexico City.

It's hotter in Madrid than in Moscow.

The weather in Brighton is worse than the weather in Zurich.

8 WRITING

Look at the chart in exercise 7 and write a paragraph comparing today's weather in your town/city and the cities in the chart.

Our weather is better/worse than London's.
It's hotter/colder in Madrid than here.

LANGUAGE WORKOUT

Complete.

Adjective	Comparative	Adjective	Comparative
cold	cold___	dry	dr**ier**
high	____	easy	____
short	____	sunny	____
late	lat**er**		
		difficult	**more** difficult
big	big**ger**	famous	____ famous
hot	hot**ter**	expensive	____ expensive
wet	wet___	popular	____ popular
Irregular			
good	**better**		
bad	**worse**		

▶Answers and Practice
Language File pages 118–119

69

7 Speaking

In the Speaking activity, students *use* the target language to communicate, in this case comparing the weather in different cities. This activity often also *personalises* the target language and students use it to talk about their own lives and opinions.

8 Writing

Each of the first three lessons in each unit ends with a writing activity. These typically have the dual function of writing skills development and reinforcement of the target language. In this lesson students write a paragraph comparing the weather in their town/city with one of the cities in the chart in exercise 7.

Language Workout

The Language Workout boxes highlight the target language with sentences from the reading text or paradigms for the students to complete. The bottom of the box refers students to the Language File at the back of the book where they can check their answers, find a fuller treatment of the grammatical point and do a practice exercise focusing on the form of the target language. The Teacher's Book provides suggestions for further practice activities and additional information about the target language.

Teachers may decide when to draw students' attention to the Language Workout, and the Teacher's Book gives suggestions for when it can be used. For example, it may be appropriate to refer to it before learners are expected to produce the target language, and/or for consolidation at the end of the lesson.

Extension

Lessons have one or more Extension activities offering more challenging practice for fast-finishers.

6 Pronunciation

Each of the first three lessons in every unit contains a pronunciation exercise focusing on particular sounds or stress and intonation. The Teacher's Book provides more information about the phonological area being treated and suggests further activities.

The fourth lesson in each unit is an Integrated Skills lesson. In these lessons the four skills support each other, usually moving from a reading text to a listening activity, then a speaking activity based on the listening or reading and concluding with a writing activity for which the reading, listening and speaking have prepared the students. The lesson ends with a Learner Independence section.

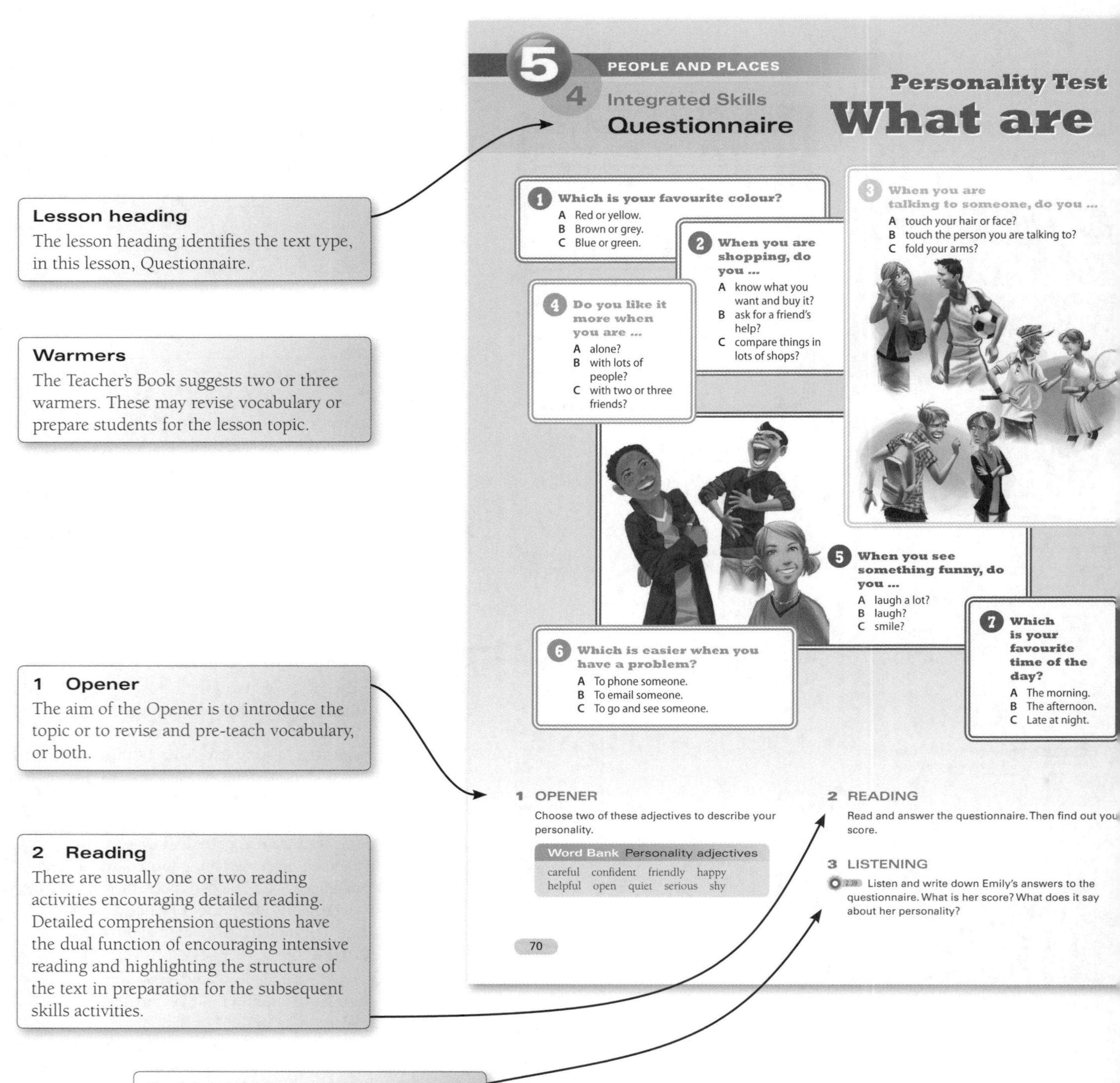

5 PEOPLE AND PLACES

4 Integrated Skills

Questionnaire

Personality Test

What are

1 Which is your favourite colour?
A Red or yellow.
B Brown or grey.
C Blue or green.

2 When you are shopping, do you ...
A know what you want and buy it?
B ask for a friend's help?
C compare things in lots of shops?

3 When you are talking to someone, do you ...
A touch your hair or face?
B touch the person you are talking to?
C fold your arms?

4 Do you like it more when you are ...
A alone?
B with lots of people?
C with two or three friends?

5 When you see something funny, do you ...
A laugh a lot?
B laugh?
C smile?

6 Which is easier when you have a problem?
A To phone someone.
B To email someone.
C To go and see someone.

7 Which is your favourite time of the day?
A The morning.
B The afternoon.
C Late at night.

1 OPENER

Choose two of these adjectives to describe your personality.

Word Bank Personality adjectives

careful confident friendly happy helpful open quiet serious shy

2 READING

Read and answer the questionnaire. Then find out you[r] score.

3 LISTENING

2.39 Listen and write down Emily's answers to the questionnaire. What is her score? What does it say about her personality?

70

Lesson heading
The lesson heading identifies the text type, in this lesson, Questionnaire.

Warmers
The Teacher's Book suggests two or three warmers. These may revise vocabulary or prepare students for the lesson topic.

1 Opener
The aim of the Opener is to introduce the topic or to revise and pre-teach vocabulary, or both.

2 Reading
There are usually one or two reading activities encouraging detailed reading. Detailed comprehension questions have the dual function of encouraging intensive reading and highlighting the structure of the text in preparation for the subsequent skills activities.

3 Listening
These activities develop intensive listening skills. Here students listen for Emily's answers to the questionnaire.

4 Speaking
Students then use their answers to the Listening activity to practise speaking. Here they compare their score with Emily's score and discuss what it says about their personality. The Teacher's Book offers further optional activities.

Learner Independence

Learner Independence sections typically include three activities, focusing on classroom English, vocabulary development, and idiomatic expressions.

you like?

8 Which is your favourite evening activity?
A Watching TV.
B Talking to a friend.
C Going to a party.

9 How often do you wear the same clothes the next day?
A Sometimes.
B Never.
C Very often.

10 When you are angry with people, do you ...
A shout at them?
B discuss the problem with them?
C say nothing?

Personality Test scores

1	A=6	B=2	C=4	**20–33 points**
2	A=6	B=4	C=2	You are quiet and careful. You are a serious person and think a lot
3	A=4	B=6	C=2	before you do something. You think a lot about other people too,
4	A=2	B=6	C=4	but are quite happy when you are alone.
5	A=6	B=4	C=2	**34–47 points**
6	A=4	B=2	C=6	You are a friendly, open, helpful person. Friends are important to
7	A=2	B=4	C=6	you and you always help them with their problems.
8	A=2	B=4	C=6	**48–60 points**
9	A=4	B=6	C=2	You are a confident person. You aren't at all shy and you enjoy life
10	A=6	B=4	C=2	a lot. You think quickly and often tell others what to do.

4 SPEAKING

Compare your score with other students' scores and Emily's score. What does your score say about your personality? Do you agree with your score? Is there anything you want to change in the description of your personality?

5 WRITING

Use your answers to the questionnaire and your score to write a paragraph about your personality.

My favourite colour is ...

UNIT 5

LEARNER INDEPENDENCE

6 Classroom English: Match the words with the punctuation marks.

Word Bank Punctuation

brackets capital letter comma exclamation mark full stop hyphen question mark

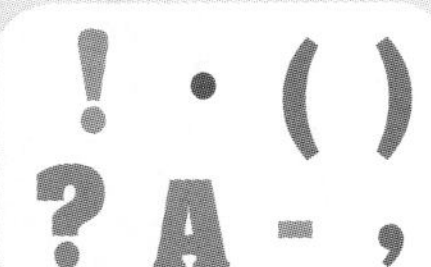

2.40 Now listen and write the punctuation marks you hear.

7 Add these sections to your vocabulary notebook.

Jobs Weather and seasons
Personality adjectives

8 2.41 **Phrasebook:** Find these useful expressions in Unit 5. Then listen and repeat.

I'm having a wonderful time.
It's a beautiful day.
It's time to ...
Well done!
Whose turn is it?
What's the problem?
Good idea.

Now write a three-line dialogue using one or more of the expressions.

A It's time to go home.
B Not now. I'm having a wonderful time.
A But it's three o'clock in the morning!

71

6

In this lesson students look at different punctuation marks. Discussion may take place in English or the mother tongue, as appropriate to the learner's level. The emphasis here is on giving the students the language they need in the classroom, so there is no need to use their native language. The Teacher's Book offers optional activities to further explore this area.

7

The aim here is to increase their vocabulary.

8 Phrasebook

This section occurs in every unit and helps students learn idiomatic expressions in context. Students find the expressions from within the unit, practise pronunciation and then complete a small follow-up activity, in this case writing a short dialogue with the idiomatic questions they have learned.

Follow-up activities and homework

The Teacher's Book offers optional follow-up activities, usually including a game, to help with mixed-ability teaching and to cope with variable aptitude and amounts of time available. Homework suggestions (usually writing) are also provided for each lesson.

Weblink

The Teacher's Book provides at least one URL relevant to each lesson (in this case a website giving personality information on the different signs of the zodiac). Teachers are advised to check these links before sharing them with the students as web addresses frequently change.

5 Writing

Here students use their answers to the questionnaire to write a paragraph about their personality. The Teacher's Book suggests that students check each other's work for grammar, spelling and punctuation, and also provides further optional activities.

Inspiration *Extra!* follows the Integrated Skills lesson in each unit and always includes, on the left-hand page, a Game, plus either a Project, Language Links or a Sketch. On the right-hand page there are mixed-ability activities giving opportunities for both revision and extension, and Your Choice!, which allows students to choose from two different activities.

Language Links
The aim of the Language Links section is to raise plurilingual awareness. Here, students are encouraged to see how knowing one or two languages can often help them to identify words in other languages.

Game
Here, students play a miming game to practise job vocabulary. There is always a game on this page, and there are also games throughout the book in the lessons and in the Teacher's Book optional activities.

5 PEOPLE AND PLACES

Inspiration EXTRA!

LANGUAGE LINKS

Many words in English are like words in other languages. Which of these words are like words in your language?

International words in English
banana camera chocolate cinema club drama football golf guitar jeans music photograph pizza sandwich stop television tennis video volleyball weekend

Find other words in Units 1–5 which are like words in your language. Make a section in your vocabulary notebook for these words. Notice the differences in spelling!

Baggage
Gepack
Equipajes
Bagagli

SKETCH *The Car*

2.42 Read and listen.

BUS

MAN Excuse me. This car – is it yours?
WOMAN Why?
MAN It's outside my house. I don't want it here.
WOMAN Why not?
MAN I want to have *my* car outside my house. Can you please drive the car away?
WOMAN No, I'm sorry, I can't.
MAN You can't?
WOMAN No.
MAN I don't understand. Can't you drive?
WOMAN Of course I can drive.
MAN Then why can't you drive the car away?
WOMAN I don't have the car keys.
MAN You don't have the keys? But it's your car.
WOMAN No, it isn't mine.
MAN It isn't yours? Then whose is it?
WOMAN I don't know. Oh, here's my bus. Bye!

Now act out the sketch in pairs.

Game *What's My Job?*

- Form two teams: Red and Blue.
- A Red Team student thinks of a job and mimes it for his/her team to guess. They ask questions using the present continuous and present simple.
- Then a Blue Team student thinks of a job and mimes it for his/her team to guess.
- Teams score a point for every job they guess in 60 seconds.

Q Are you driving a car?
A No, I'm not.
Q Do you travel a lot?
A Yes, I do.
Q Do you wear a uniform?
A Yes, I do.
Q Are you a train-driver?
A No, I'm not.
Q Do you go to lots of countries?
A Yes, I do.
Q Are you flying a plane?
A Yes, I am!
Q Are you a pilot?
A Yes, I am!

72

Sketch
The aim of the sketches is for students to enjoy using English while also getting valuable stress and intonation practice. The Teacher's Book has suggestions for using the recording and for acting out the sketches.

Revision

The Revision exercises provide further writing practice for less confident students in mixed-ability classes. In this unit, students write sentences about Cathy's typical day, make a list of vocabulary, write about the weather and write about Emily. They are always given sections of the unit to refer back to.

UNIT 5

REVISION

LESSON 1 Look at Cathy's email on page 64. Write a description of her typical day at sea.

Cathy gets up at 7am and she has breakfast at 7.15.

LESSON 2 Look at the photo on page 66. Make a list of all the clothes and other things that the people are wearing and holding.

grey sweatshirt, blue bag, ...

LESSON 3 Look at the weather chart on page 69. Write sentences about today's weather in the cities.

In Brighton it's very cloudy and it's windy. The temperature is 15 degrees.

LESSON 4 Look at Emily's answers to the questionnaire on pages 70–71. Write a paragraph about her.

Emily's favourite time of the day is ...

EXTENSION

LESSON 1 Choose four members of your family. Write sentences about what they do, and say what they're doing at the moment.

My mother is a teacher. She's having lunch at the moment.

LESSON 2 Look at the photo on page 66. Write questions and answers about people's things.

Whose is the red cap?
It's Emily's.

LESSON 3 Make true sentences using these comparative adjectives.

bigger more expensive more famous higher more popular smaller

Your shoes are bigger than mine.

LESSON 4 Write a paragraph about your best friend's personality. Use the questionnaire on pages 70–71 to help you.

YOUR CHOICE!

THINK OF A WORD!

- Work in pairs.
- Student A says a word for an object, for example, *wallet, photo, comb, guitar, camera, watch.*
- Student B says a word for each of these six categories:

something smaller
something bigger
something earlier in the dictionary
something later in the dictionary
a shorter word
a longer word

A Wallet.
B Earring, car, spring, windy, tea, sunglasses

WORLD WEATHER REPORT

- Work in a small group and find out information about weather in different parts of the world from newspapers or the Internet.
- Choose two places to write about and note down important information. For example:

What's the temperature in January and in July?
How much rain is there every year?
Is it often windy?
Does it snow in winter?

- Use your notes to write a *World Weather Report*. Show your report to other students.

73

Extension

The Extension exercises provide challenging writing activities for more confident students in mixed-ability classes. In this unit, students write sentences about their family, write questions and answers about a photo, write comparative sentences and write about their best friend's personality.

The Revision and Extension exercises are a flexible resource and may be done at the end of the unit or after the relevant lesson. Alternatively the students can do them as homework. The Teacher's Book provides possible answers.

Project

Projects provide a valuable resource for student creativity, self-expression and language consolidation. They also allow students of varying abilities to all contribute. Students are encouraged to save their projects to add to their portfolios. While intended for use with the whole class, the projects could also be used for homework or as supplementary material with more confident students in mixed-ability classes. The group size for projects will vary from class to class, but teachers may prefer to have groups of three to six members.

1. Projects require students to go back through part of the unit which models the writing they will do. Then students brainstorm ideas, choosing a few to write about.
2. There is then a research phase using reference books, libraries or the Internet to gather information for the project. This could involve interviewing people, for example, family members.
3. Finally the group work together to produce their project, reading each other's work, editing and illustrating it. The Teacher's Book offers suggestions for organisation.

Your Choice!

The aim here is for students to choose and do the activity they like best. The activities reflect different learning styles and the aim is to encourage awareness of learning styles and to foster learner independence. Your Choice! activities may involve individual, pair or group work.

There are four Culture sections at each level of *New Inspiration* providing both factual information and the opportunity for cross-cultural comparisons. The section illustrated here deals with the topic of gestures.

Opener
The aim of the Opener is to introduce the topic and stimulate discussion, often through a quiz.

Vocabulary
The Culture section texts provide a rich source of useful new vocabulary, and there are a variety of activity types here to give practice.

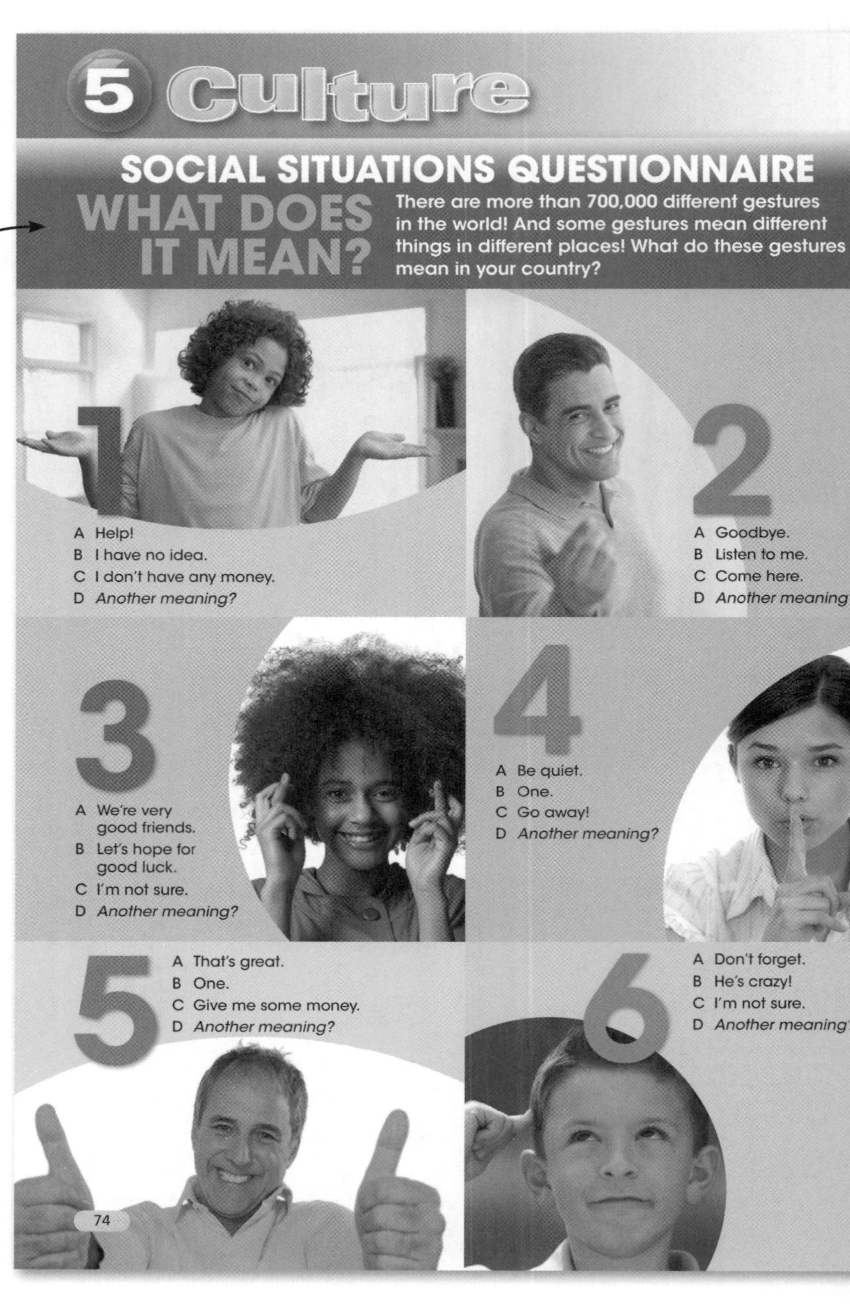

5 Culture
SOCIAL SITUATIONS QUESTIONNAIRE
WHAT DOES IT MEAN?
There are more than 700,000 different gestures in the world! And some gestures mean different things in different places! What do these gestures mean in your country?
1
A Help!
B I have no idea.
C I don't have any money.
D Another meaning?
2
A Goodbye.
B Listen to me.
C Come here.
D Another meaning?
3
A We're very good friends.
B Let's hope for good luck.
C I'm not sure.
D Another meaning?
4
A Be quiet.
B One.
C Go away!
D Another meaning?
5
A That's great.
B One.
C Give me some money.
D Another meaning?
6
A Don't forget.
B He's crazy!
C I'm not sure.
D Another meaning?
74

1 Reading

Here, students read and answer a questionnare about gestures.

Culture

READING

Read and answer the questionnaire.

LISTENING

2.43 Listen to Adam and Emily answering the questionnaire. What do the gestures mean in Britain? Are there any differences between Britain and your country?

READING

Read *What do you say at a party?* and choose the best responses.

2.44 Now listen and check.

4 SPEAKING

What do you say in these situations? Choose from the expressions below.

What do you say …

1 when someone sneezes?
2 when you want to talk to someone?
3 when you stand on someone's foot?
4 when you can't understand someone?
5 when someone doesn't look happy?
6 before someone goes on holiday?

a What's wrong?
b Can I have a word with you?
c Bless you!
d Have a fabulous time!
e Sorry? Can you say that again?
f I'm very sorry!

2.45 Now listen and check.

What do you say at a party?

1 *This is my friend, Tamara.*
A I don't know.
B What's your name?
C What's she called?
D Hi, nice to meet you.

2 *What do you do?*
A How do you do?
B I'm a model.
C I'm looking for my wallet.
D I'm going home.

3 *Do you want something to drink?*
A Thank you.
B Yes, please.
C Yes, thank you.
D Yes, I want.

4 *What's he like?*
A He likes football and swimming.
B He has brown hair and blue eyes.
C He's feeling ill.
D He's a great guy.

5 *Can I use your phone?*
A Never mind.
B Sorry, I can't.
C Yes, of course.
D I can't remember.

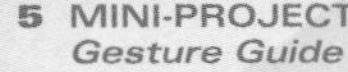

5 MINI-PROJECT
Gesture Guide

Work with another student and write a short guide to gestures in your country.

- Find four pictures of people making gestures. Look in newspapers and magazines or on the Internet. For example, look for gestures people make when they say goodbye, when they meet someone, or when they mean *Yes* or *No*.
- By each picture write the meaning of the gesture.

Read your work carefully and correct any mistakes. Then show your *Gesture Guide* to other students.

75

Weblink

The Teacher's Book provides at least one relevant URL (in this case a website with more information on gestures around the world). Teachers are advised to check these links before sharing them with the students as web addresses frequently change.

5 Mini-Project

The Mini-Projects in the Culture sections typically use the text as a model and invite the students to work in pairs and write about aspects of their own culture.

There are four Reviews at each level of *New Inspiration*. Each Review covers the new language of the preceding two units. The Teacher's Book contains the answers to all the exercises.

Review exercises are contextualised, often using information from the relevant lesson, so that students are creating meaningful sentences.

Language points reviewed include not only main verb tenses but problem areas such as pronouns and comparatives.

The Workbook offers a parallel Review with text and multiple-choice questions, examination-type exercises, and a self-assessment Progress Check consisting of 'I can do …' statements.

Exercise 1
Each review begins with a text covering the new language of both units with KET/PET examination-type objective test questions, usually multiple-choice cloze.

Weblink
The Teacher's Book provides at least one relevant URL (in this lesson a website with more activities for students to practise their English). Teachers are advised to check these links before sharing them with the students as web addresses frequently change.

REVIEW
UNITS 5-6

1 Read and complete. For each number 1–12, choose word A, B or C.

'I DIDN'T WAIT – I JUMPED IN!'

A teenager jumped into the River Thames in London yesterday and __1__ the life of a tourist. Jo Andrews was by the river when she __2__ a young man in the water.

18-year-old Jo, who started a new job at a swimming pool two weeks __3__, said, 'The tourist fell out of a boat into the water.'

'He shouted, but he __4__ speak any English. At first no one thought it was a problem. There __5__ lots of people there and they all laughed. Then I heard a shout of "Help!". It was the young man's father,' said Jo, who __6__ at Chelsea Sports Centre. 'The father jumped into the water too, but he __7__ know how to swim.'

'I asked a woman to help me,' Jo said. 'The woman jumped in and swam to the __8__ father. I swam out to the son. His head was underwater. I pulled him up, but then he __9__ down again. It became __10__ difficult to hold him. My jeans got wetter and wetter and they pulled me under the water. I thought I __11__ in the water for a long time, but it was really only two or three minutes.'

People __12__ Jo and together they pulled the young tourist out of the river. 'I didn't wait – I jumped in,' said Jo. Her mum, Jackie, said: 'I'm very pleased. She was wonderful.'

	A	B	C
1	A save	B saves	C saved
2	A saw	B see	C sees
3	A after	B ago	C before
4	A didn't	B doesn't	C don't
5	A was	B wasn't	C were
6	A is working	B work	C works
7	A didn't	B doesn't	C don't
8	A tourist	B tourist's	C tourists
9	A goes	B going	C went
10	A more	B many	C much
11	A am	B was	C were
12	A help	B helping	C helped

86

2 Complete with the correct form of the present simple or present continuous.

1 Pierre usually ______ to the cinema on Friday. (go)
2 It's 7.30 – Teresa and Katya ______ breakfast. (have)
4 Emily's cousin ______ on a boat this summer. (work)
5 She ______ to the news on the radio every day. (listen)
5 The exchange students ______ Brighton at the moment. (visit)
6 ______ you ______ the party? (enjoy)
7 I ______ your phone number. (not know)
8 How many languages ______ you ______? (speak)

3 Write questions and answers.

magazine/Adam
Whose magazine is this? It's Adam's.

1 cat/Teresa
2 sunglasses/Pierre
3 mobile phone/Mr Ward
4 jeans/Katya
5 umbrella/the teacher
6 CDs/my friend

4 Write sentences.

her — *They're her earrings. They're hers.*

1 his
2 our
3 their

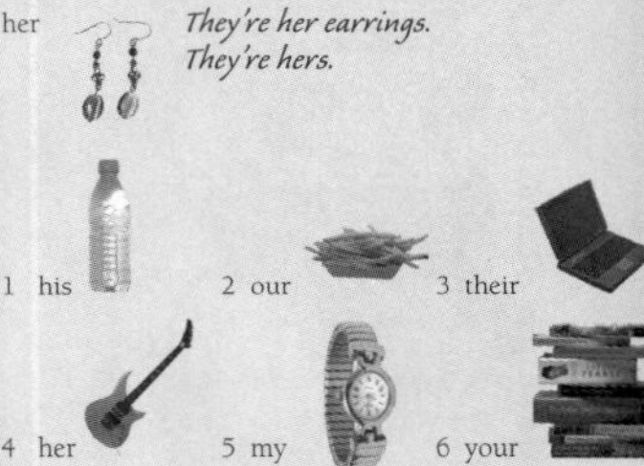

4 her
5 my
6 your

5 Write sentences using comparative adjectives.

Spain/hot/than Britain
Spain is hotter than Britain.

1 Florida/sunny/than New York
2 Japanese/difficult/than English
3 A Ferrari/expensive/than a Fiat
4 Mexico City/big/than Rio de Janeiro
5 Mount Everest/high/than K2
6 Tom Cruise/famous/than me

6 Ask and answer.

television/1920 ✗
Was there television in 1920? — No, there wasn't.

cars/1950 ✓
Were there cars in 1950? — Yes, there were.

1 computers/1940 ✗
2 email/1990 ✓
3 jeans/1890 ✓
4 mobile phones/1900 ✗
5 beer/1850 ✓
6 trainers/1930 ✗
7 radio/1890 ✗
8 cameras/1930 ✓

Write the past simple of these regular verbs under the correct sound.

answer ask check decide enjoy kiss listen repeat shout smile talk wait

/d/	/t/	/ɪd/
answered	*asked*	*decided*

2.58 Now listen and check.

Complete with the past simple of these verbs.

cook find know play run sail see visit

1 The Vikings ____ to America a thousand years ago.
2 Adam and Ruby ____ pasta for dinner last night.
3 We ____ a film about Dracula on TV a week ago.
4 Emily ____ five kilometres this morning.
5 Mr Ward ____ New York last year.
6 Jake ____ basketball yesterday.
7 I ____ 20 euros in the street a minute ago!
8 You ____ the answers to all the questions!

Ask and answer.

Did Teresa phone home? Yes, she did.
Did she phone Adam? No, she didn't.

1 Teresa/phone home ✓/Adam ✗
2 Pierre/write a letter ✗/an email ✓
3 Emily/wear a jacket✓/a dress ✗
4 Katya and Teresa/go the café ✗/the shopping centre ✓
5 Jake and Adam/play tennis ✓/basketball ✗
6 Diana/listen to CDs ✗/the radio ✓

Now write sentences.

Teresa phoned home. She didn't phone Adam.

VOCABULARY

Complete with eight of these words.

blood coast dress explorer hill news storm sun temperature train

1 It's a beautiful day and the ____ is shining.
2 She wore a nice ____ for the party.
3 It's very hot – what's the ____?
4 Christopher Columbus was a famous ____.
5 Vampires drink people's ____.
6 We walked up the ____ to the church.
7 I watched the ____ on TV.
8 You can go from London to Brighton by ____.

11 Match these words with their definitions.

apologise cross *adj* huge journalist noon nurse ship short terrible wet

1 midday
2 say sorry
3 opposite of *long* or *tall*
4 big boat
5 quite angry
6 opposite of *dry*
7 very bad
8 very big
9 someone who looks after people who are ill
10 someone who writes news stories

12 Match the verbs in list A with the words and phrases in list B.

A	B
1 ask	at someone
2 close	a boat
3 drive	maths
4 fly	your eyes
5 fold	for help
6 go	a plane
7 sail	to sleep
8 shout	a car
9 teach	your arms

REVIEW

LEARNER INDEPENDENCE
SELF ASSESSMENT

Look back at Lessons 1–3 in Units 5 and 6.

How good are you at ...?	✓Fine	? Not sure
1 Talking about regular activities Workbook p54 exercises 1 and 2	☐	☐
2 Talking about what people are doing now Workbook p54 exercise 3	☐	☐
3 Talking about possessions Workbook pp56–57 exercises 1, 2 and 5	☐	☐
4 Making comparisons Workbook pp58–59 exercises 1–5	☐	☐
5 Talking about past events Workbook p66 exercises 1–3, pp68–69 exercises 1–6 and p70 exercise 1	☐	☐
6 Asking about past events Workbook p67 exercises 4–6 and pp70–71 exercises 2–4	☐	☐

Not sure? Have a look at Language File pages 117–120 and do the Workbook exercise(s) again.

Now write an example for 1–6

1 Adam's father flies planes to South-east Asia.

87

Collocation

All the Review sections include an exercise to raise awareness of the importance of collocation.

Learner Independence: Self Assessment

This Self Assessment section for each two units lists the communicative aims and invites students to rate their confidence in each one. Students who are not sure about their ability in a particular area are referred to the Language File and the relevant Workbook exercises. The Teacher's Book offers guidance on handling this.

Follow-up activities and homework

The Teacher's Book offers optional follow-up activities, usually games. Homework suggestions (usually writing) are also provided.

Vocabulary

Vocabulary exercises include completion, matching words with their definitions, and collocation (in this case matching verbs and phrases).

Welcome!

Language	Communicative aims	Vocabulary	Optional aids	
Present simple: *be* Personal pronouns Questions: *What ...?* *Where ...? Who ...?*	Introducing yourself and others Talking about where you are from	Countries and nationalities Numbers 1–20	Warmer 1: a soft ball (or a ball of paper) Exercise 1: UK map; Optional activity: world map	Exercise 5: small cards with names of famous people and their countries

Useful information

Brighton is a popular tourist destination on the south coast of England. It is famous for the Royal Pavilion, which is a former royal palace, and Brighton Pier, which has a funfair, restaurants and arcade halls. In the photo the coursebook characters are standing on the pier and you can see the beach in the background.

WARMER 1

Introduce yourself to the class. Say *Hello, I'm .../My name is ... I'm from ...* Walk around the room introducing yourself to individual students and telling them where you are from. Use a soft ball to encourage students to introduce themselves. Throw the ball to a student who then introduces him/herself and says where he/she is from. He/She then throws the ball to another student who does the same. Continue until all the students have introduced themselves.

WARMER 2

Write the question *How are you?* on the board, then ask a student the question. Repeat with different students and elicit a response (*I'm fine, thanks*). Drill the pronunciation of *I'm* and establish that it is a contraction of two words (*I am*). Students go round the class asking each other how they are and responding in different ways.

1 READING

- The aim is to introduce the present simple of *be* and to introduce the students to the photo story that runs through the book. Ask students to look at the photo on pages 6–7. Ask *How many countries can you find?* Be prepared to explain that *Brighton* is a city. Ask *Where is Brighton?* Establish that Brighton is on the south coast of England and is a popular city for tourists and international students. Show students on a map of the UK if you have one.
- Play the recording, telling students to follow the words in their books while they are listening.

1.01 Recording

See text on pages 6–7 of the Student's Book.

- Ask *Who is from England?*

Answers

David Ward, Adam and Emily

- Play the recording again, for students to repeat.
- Write the words *What does ... mean?* on the board and ask students if they have any questions about the vocabulary from the text. Praise students who ask using a full sentence. Encourage other students to answer the questions asked.

Optional activities

- ♦ Nominate six students for a role play and act out the dialogue on pages 6–7. Correct any pronunciation errors by getting the whole class to repeat sections of the dialogue.
- ♦ Students find the countries mentioned in the recording on a map of the world.

2 AFTER READING

- Ask the students to complete the sentences with the correct word.
- Check the answers by asking different students to read each sentence. Write the sentences on the board.

Answers

1 Switzerland 2 Katya 3 the USA 4 Teresa
5 Emily, Katya, Teresa 6 David Ward

- Read the first sentence exaggerating the stress on *Pierre* and *Switzerland* slightly. Ask the students to identify the important words in the sentence. Explain the concept of stress and underline these two words.
- Invite students to come to the board and underline the stressed words in the other sentences.
- Drill the sentences in chorus for pronunciation and stress.

Optional activity

Students write three sentences about their classmates using sentences from exercise 2 as models.

3 LISTENING

- Hold up the book, point to the picture of Emily and ask *What's her name?* Elicit *Her name is Emily*. Repeat for Adam.
- Students listen and complete the missing information.
- Check the answers by asking two students to read the dialogue. Then ask the class to read the dialogue twice in pairs, each time reading a different role.

1.02 **Recording and answers**

ADAM *Who's she?*
EMILY *Her name is* ***Katya****.*
ADAM *Is she American?*
EMILY *No, she isn't.*
ADAM *Where's she from?*
EMILY *She's from* ***Russia****.*

4 SPEAKING

- Demonstrate the activity yourself by pointing at a student in the picture and asking the two questions. Elicit the full forms of *Who's* (*Who is*) and *Where's* (*Where is*). Drill the pronunciation of the contraction.
- Ask the students to work in pairs, taking turns to ask questions about the exchange students. Remind them to use contractions when speaking.
- To practise the possessive adjective form, ask various students *What's your name?* eliciting *My name is* ... Mix up the questions by changing the pronoun to *my*, *his* and *her* and pointing at different people. Ask the students to do the same in pairs.

5 ROLE PLAY

- Model the conversation between the three celebrities and then repeat it with two students giving the responses. Drill the sentences in chorus for pronunciation and stress.
- Distribute one card with a famous person's name and country to each student. Put the students in pairs. Ask them to go around the class meeting as many pairs as they can in four minutes. Then students return to their desks and write as many pairs as they can remember.

Useful information

(It's) Nice to meet you is usually followed by the reply *(It's) Nice to meet you, too*. This is only ever used on the first meeting. The word *pleased* could substitute *nice*. A second meeting could begin with *Hello again* or *Nice to see you again*.

6 SPEAKING

- Drill the words in the box in chorus for pronunciation.
- Ask students to find the countries for the nationalities from memory or by looking back at page 8.

Answers

American – the USA, English – England, Russian – Russia, Spanish – Spain, Swiss – Switzerland

- Write the answers on the board in two columns and mark the stress on the words with two syllables or more. Drill the words in chorus.
- Hold up the book and point at Miley Cyrus asking the two questions in the model. Explain that we never contract in short (*yes/no*) affirmative answers. Ask students to ask and answer questions about the exchange students by pointing at the pictures in the webpage article on page 8 and following the model.

Optional activity

Invite students to add new pairs of countries and nationalities to the list on the board.

7 PRONUNCIATION

- Ask students to look at the words.
- Play the recording, pausing after each word for students to repeat. Show students the position of the lips in /**w**/ and show them how they should be able to feel their breath when pronouncing the /**h**/ sound.
- Ask students if they know any other English words with these sounds.

1.03 **Recording**

/**w**/ *we welcome what where*
/**h**/ *he her his who*

8 VOCABULARY

- Play the recording, pausing after each word for students to repeat. Draw attention to the two options for 0 (*oh*, *zero*), and the stress on the words with *teen*.

1.04 **Recording**

See text on page 9 of the Student's Book.

Optional activity

Put students in two teams: one team counts from 1 to 19 in odd numbers, each member saying one number, and the other team from 2 to 20 in even numbers. If there is a mistake, they must start again. The first team to the end wins.

9 GAME BINGO

- Students draw their own 'Bingo cards' in their notebooks (a grid with three columns and three rows). Ask the students to choose nine numbers from 1 to 20 and write them on their Bingo card. Tell the students to cross off a number when they hear it. The first student to cross off three numbers in a line shouts out *Line*. The first to cross off all nine numbers shouts out *Bingo!*
- Play the recording and monitor the students.

1.05 **Recording**

eight eighteen twelve six eleven
seven fifteen two thirteen four
twenty fourteen three sixteen nine
nineteen one ten five seventeen

10 LISTENING

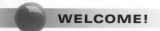

- Ask students to look at the chart. Ask *Where is Emily from? Where is Teresa from? What's Emily's telephone number? What's Adam's address?*
- Explain to the class that they are going to listen for the missing information. Elicit what type of information is missing (numbers, names and street names). Explain that it is important to relax when listening and focus on the information they need and that it is not necessary to understand every word.
- Play the recording twice. Check the answers.

1.06 Recording and answers

Now – information for our visitors. Here you are. Listen and check the addresses and phone numbers.
Teresa, you're with Emily. Her address is ***17*** *Park Road, Brighton, and her phone number is 291347.*
Pierre, you're with Adam. His address is 8 Hill Street, Lewes, and his phone number is ***837921****.*
Katya, you're with ***Emily****, too. Her address is 17* ***Park*** *Road, Brighton, and her phone number is 291347.*
And Jake, you're with me! My address is ***10*** *Market Lane, Hove, and my phone number is* ***790329****.*

11 WRITING

- Drill the two questions in chorus for pronunciation and stress.
- Ask students to meet three students that they have not spoken to today and ask them the questions and write down the answers.

LANGUAGE WORKOUT

- Ask students to look at the top half of the Language box and identify the personal pronouns. Ask the class to say which are singular and plural. Ask a volunteer to explain the difference between *he, she* and *it*.
- Explain contractions using the example *you are/you're*. Ask students to note down the examples of *pronoun + be* in the dialogues. Elicit which form is usually used when speaking – full forms or contractions (contractions).
- Ask students to complete the first chart in the Language box. Confident students can complete first and then check, while others can look back at pages 6–8 and then complete.
- Students turn to page 114 of the Language File to check their answers.

Answers
I'm *we're*

- Draw attention to the bottom half of the Language box and the reversal of the pronoun and the verb *be* in questions. Ask the class *Am I from China?* Continue by saying *I am not from China*. Write this on the board and elicit the contraction (*I'm not from China*). Ask students to complete the chart.
- Students turn to page 114 of the Language File to check their answers.

Answers
are you? *isn't* *aren't* *are they?*

PRACTICE

- Students do Practice exercises 1 and 2 on page 114 of the Language File. They complete the sentences and questions with the correct form of *be*.
- Check the answers by asking different students to say the completed sentences.

Answers
1
1 is, is *2 are* *3 are* *4 is, am* *5 is, is* *6 are*
2
1 Are, aren't *2 Is, isn't* *3 Are, am not* *4 Are, aren't*
5 Is, isn't

Follow-up activities

- ♦ In pairs, one student closes the book and the other asks questions about the characters, e.g. *Where is Pierre from?* The student with the closed book answers from memory. Students change roles.
- ♦ **Game** *Celebrity party* Redistribute the cards from the role play (exercise 5). Set a time limit of three minutes. Students move around introducing themselves and finding out who other students are and where they are from. They then have one minute to remember and write down in their notebooks the name and country or nationality of the people they have met. The student with the most names and nationalities wins.

HOMEWORK

Students cut out pictures of famous people from magazines and write two sentences about them, e.g. *Her name is Victoria Beckham. She's from England.*

WEBLINKS

For a webcam of Brighton see: www.bbc.co.uk/southerncounties/content/webcams/btn_seafront_webcam.shtml

Revision and Extension p21

Language File p114

Workbook Welcome! pp2–5

PREVIEW

Units 1–2

Activities
Identifying topics
Categorising vocabulary
Contextualising listening extracts

Project
Favourite things

Vocabulary
Clothes
Family
Music

Optional aids
Follow-up activities: slips of paper

WARMER 1

If students did the homework in the last lesson, ask them to show their pictures to the class and read out their sentences.

WARMER 2

Draw two female faces and two male faces on the board. Explain to students that they are the international exchange students from Welcome! Point at each face in turn, asking *What's his/her name?* and *Where's he/she from?* and eliciting the answers.

WARMER 3

Ask students to look at the photos and speech bubbles on pages 10–11 and to say what they can see.

1
- The aim is to introduce students to the main topics and vocabulary they will cover in the first two units.
- Explain to students that the two boxes at the top of the page show the communicative language and topics/vocabulary they will use in the first two units of *New Inspiration 1*.
- Go through the topics in the second box with the class and make sure everyone understands them. Then ask them to look at pictures A–F and match them with six of these topics.

Answers
A music B family C possessions
D numbers E colours F clothes

2
- Explain that words from each of the three vocabulary categories (clothes, family and music) are arranged in the word square. Give students two minutes to write the words in the correct category.
- Students check their answers in pairs and then as a whole class.

Answers
Clothes: jacket, trousers, skirt, pullover, T-shirt
Family: brother, sister, daughter, grandfather, mother,
Music: piano, rap, guitar, band, drums

3
- Students match the words with the pictures.

Answers
1 camera 2 jeans 3 phone 4 window 5 bag 6 cap

4
- The aim of this activity is for students to contextualise a short listening extract by working out what the topic is. Explain that they should listen for the main gist of the extract and that it doesn't matter if they don't understand every word.
- Play the recording. Students match each of the three extracts to the topics (A–C).

1.07 Recording
1 The city of Machu Picchu is on a mountain in Peru. It's 550 years old
2 My favourite band is Linkin Park. It has six members and they're from California, in the USA.
3 This is a photo of my family. My mother is on the right – her name is Valentina. It's her fortieth birthday today.

Answers
1 B 2 C 3 A

5
- Elicit or explain the meaning of *favourite*. Put students into groups of three and ask them to do the questionnaire, writing down their answers. Ask them to join other groups to share their answers.
- Point out the 'Believe it or not!' fact at the bottom of the page. Find out if there are any numbers in the students' own language(s) which have the same number of letters as the meaning.

Follow-up activity

In small groups, students brainstorm vocabulary for three other categories from the box on page 10. Give them an example for each category before they start and allow them to use dictionaries if they wish. Give them two minutes to write as many words as they can think of on slips of paper. When the time is up, ask them to shuffle their slips of paper so they are in jumbled order. They then swap slips with another group. Give them another two minutes to sort the slips they have received into the correct categories.

HOMEWORK

Ask students to interview family members or other students at the school to find out their favourite colours, numbers, months and musical instruments. They then present their findings to the class in the next lesson.

That's a great bag!

Communicative aims	**Language**	**Pronunciation**	**Vocabulary**	**Optional aids**
Talking about possessions	*this/that* Indefinite article	Alphabet and spelling	Possessions Alphabet and spelling	Warmer 1: cards with names of famous people Exercise 8 Optional activity: plastic bags Follow-up activities: box and cards, Blu-Tack

WARMER 1

Game *Pictionary* Students play in teams. One student from the class comes to the board, is given a card with a famous person's name on it and draws a picture of the famous person on the board. The first team to shout out *His/Her name is …* gets a point, as does the first team to say *He/She is from …* Someone from another team draws the next person.

WARMER 2

Game *First to 20* Divide the class into groups of four. The students take turns to say the numbers 1 to 20 in order. Each student can say one, two or three consecutive numbers, then the next student continues. The student who says *20* is the winner.

1 OPENER

- The aim is to recycle the questions and answers from the *Welcome!* lesson. Ask *What's his name? What's her name?* Elicit more information from the class about Teresa and Adam. If students cannot remember, tell them to look back at pages 6–7. Ask *What else is in the picture?* Be prepared to teach *rucksack* and *ID card.*
- Ask *What are they talking about?*

Answers

They are talking about what is in Teresa's bag.

2 READING

- Ask students to predict what is in Teresa's bag.
- Play the recording. Students read and listen. Encourage them to guess unfamiliar vocabulary from the context. Be prepared to translate *surname*, *guess*, *wallet*.

1.08 Recording

See text on page 12 of the Student's Book.

Answers

N-A-V-A-R-R-O. Look it's on my ID card.

3 AFTER READING

- Read through the questions with the students.
- Students read the dialogue again and answer the questions.
- Ask students to explain the full form of *What's* (*What is*). Drill the pronunciation of the questions.
- Check answers by having different students ask and answer the questions.

Answers

1 Navarro
2 Her ID card, a bottle of water, an MP3 player, a photograph of her family, her wallet
3 A photograph of her family

Optional activity

1.08 Play the dialogue again, sentence by sentence, for students to repeat for pronunciation and intonation practice.

Your response

Ask students to answer the question *What's in your bag?* for themselves. They could work in pairs if they wish. Go round the class eliciting answers and be ready to give help with vocabulary. Be sensitive about students who do not wish to reveal personal information about themselves and do not push them if they are embarrassed.

4 PRONUNCIATION

- Play the first part of the recording and have students follow in their book.
- Play the first part again, this time with the students repeating the letters aloud.
- Establish the meaning of *vowels/consonants*. Explain that many letters in English have the same vowel sound. Play the next part of the recording a group at a time and elicit the common vowel sound of each group.
- Play the second part again, this time with the students repeating the letters aloud.

- Ask the students to listen to the final part of the recording and write down the words they hear. Play each word twice if necessary.
- Invite students to spell the answers back to you for you to write up on the board.
- Drill the pronunciation of the words and ask students to mark the stress.

1.09 **Recording and answers**

A B C D E F G H I J K L M N O P Q R S T U V W X Y Z
A H J K B C D E G P T V F L M N S X Z I Y
O Q U W R
1 F-A-V-O-U-R-I-T-E
2 W-A-double L-E-T
3 R-U-C-K-S-A-C-K
4 P-H-O-T-O-G-R-A-P-H
5 B-O-Y-F-R-I-E-N-D

Optional activities

♦ **Game** *First to Z* Divide the class into groups of four. The students take turns to say the alphabet in order. Each student can say one, two or three consecutive letters, then the next student continues. The student who says *Z* is the winner.

♦ Students write down five words from the lesson and spell them to their partner, who writes them down.

5 SPEAKING

- Ask students to look back at the photo on pages 6–7. Point to the first person and elicit who it is and the spelling of his/her name.
- Students work in pairs and take turns to ask the name of the other people. Monitor, making sure they are using *his/her* correctly.

Extension Ask students to point at classmates and ask and answer the same questions.

LANGUAGE WORKOUT OPTION

If you want to pre-teach the language students will be using in the following activities, you may like to go to the Language Workout box now.

6 VOCABULARY

- Students match the words with the pictures individually then check with a partner.
- Students listen to the recording and check their answers.
- Drill the pronunciation of the words by playing the recording again and pausing for students to repeat the words.
- Ask students which words don't have the stress on the first syllable (*umbrella, MP3, alarm*).

1.10 **Recording and answers**

1	*a calculator*	9	*an umbrella*
2	*an mp3 player*	10	*an alarm clock*
3	*a pen*	11	*a bottle of water*
4	*an ID card*	12	*a digital camera*
5	*a packet of tissues*	13	*a wallet*
6	*a mobile phone*	14	*a photo*
7	*a comb*	15	*a key*
8	*a ticket*	16	*a passport*

7 LISTENING

- Play the recording. Students listen and write down the objects they hear. Confident students should tick the pictures while others tick the words in exercise 6.

1.11 **Recording**

TERESA *So what's in your bag? An MP3 player?*
ADAM *No.*
TERESA *A pen?*
ADAM *Yes.*
TERESA *A comb?*
ADAM *Yes.*
TERESA *A bottle of water?*
ADAM *Right.*
TERESA *A photograph of your girlfriend?*
ADAM *No. What else?*
TERESA *A mobile?*
ADAM *Yes, my new mobile phone.*

Answers

a pen, a comb, a bottle of water, a mobile phone

8 SPEAKING

- Model the first dialogue by pointing at a picture from exercise 6 and asking the questions and answering them yourself. If you haven't already looked at the Language Workout box with the class you could look at it now. Repeat with a different object but invite a student to answer the questions.
- Students work in pairs. Student B covers up the vocabulary list in exercise 6 while Student A points to one of the objects pictured, saying *What's this?* The students continue as in the dialogue. Student A can look at the words to check Student B's spelling. Pairs swap roles.
- Draw students' attention to the Language Workout box below and explain or elicit the difference between *this* and *that*.
- Model the second dialogue by pointing to something in the classroom saying *What's that called?* Invite the students to reply. Ask *How do you spell it?*
- Invite students to ask you questions about any classroom objects they want to know in English. Encourage them to write down the new words as you spell them.
- Students point at things in the classroom and ask a partner for the name and the spelling. Tell them that if they do not know what something is they should ask you. Encourage them to use *What's this/that in English?*

Optional activity

Students work in groups of five, each putting two items in a plastic bag. The first student takes out an item and the student to the left scores a point if they can say a true sentence about the object using a possessive adjective, e.g. *It's his/her pen, It's your pen, It's my pen*. If the student cannot make a sentence, the turn continues round the circle. Once a correct sentence has been said, that student takes out the next object. Continue until all the objects and their owners have been identified.

9 WRITING

- Ask students to identify Teresa's three favourite things. Invite three students to read out the short descriptions. Check pronunciation and any questions of vocabulary.
- Explain to students that they are going to write sentences about their three favourite things. Monitor, helping them with vocabulary. Write the expression *What's … in English?* on the board to encourage them to ask for new words.

Optional activity

Students draw three simple pictures of their three things. They point to each other's pictures and ask *What's this?* More confident students can speak without using their notes. Others can look back at their descriptions when necessary.

Extension Ask a confident pair to demonstrate the activity, with one reading out the question and the other using the sentences they wrote in exercise 9 to give their answers. Then ask the students to mingle and ask each other about their favourite things.

LANGUAGE WORKOUT

- Ask students to look at the top half of the Language box and explain that we use *this* for talking about things which are close and *that* for things which are not close. Demonstrate with familiar objects close to you and objects more distant in the room.
- Ask students to complete the sentences in the box. Confident students can complete first and then check, while others can look back at exercise 2 and then complete.
- Drill the examples in chorus for pronunciation and stress.

Answers
What's this in English?
That's my rucksack over there.

- Ask students to look at the bottom half of the Language box and point out that we use *a* with singular nouns that begin with a consonant and *an* with those that begin with a vowel (*a, e, i, o* and *u*). You could also point out that we say *an MP3 player* even though the word begins with a consonant because we spell out the letters at the beginning and *M* is pronounced /em/.

Follow-up activities

- ♦ **Game** *Alphabet race* Put students in teams of three. Each team has a secretary. Say a letter of the alphabet and give students one minute to write words that begin with that letter. Write all the words on the board. Give 2 points for an original word and 1 point for a word that two or more teams have written.
- ♦ **Game** *Label the classroom* Use classroom items and pictures to practise *What's ... in English?* Put students in teams and give them ten cards and some Blu-Tack. Students must write a word on the card and attach it to the item. Only one label per item! When a team has finished, they must all write ten words in their notebooks. This ensures the team works together!
- ♦ Students start a Vocabulary box. They can write new words from the lesson on one side of the card and an explanation, illustration or translation on the other side.

HOMEWORK

Students make a Favourite Things poster with sentences like *My favourite group is Coldplay. My favourite colour is blue.*

Students make ten new vocabulary cards of classroom objects or personal possessions. They find out the word using a dictionary or bring the cards to the next lesson to ask the teacher.

WEBLINKS

Students can practise the pronunciation of the English alphabet at www.learnenglish.de/basics/alphabet.htm

Revision and Extension p21

Language File p114

Workbook Unit 1 Lesson 1 pp6–7

Photocopiable notes p154, Worksheet p163

How old is it?

Communicative aims	**Language**	**Pronunciation**	**Vocabulary**	**Optional aids**
Telling the time Describing places	*these/those* Plural nouns Questions: *When …?* *How old …?*	Numbers	Numbers 21–10,000 Telling the time Prepositions of place	Warmer 1: a map of Britain Exercise 6, optional activity: a large adjustable clock

Useful information

The Royal Pavilion, see photo on page 14 of the Student's Book, was the seaside home of the Prince of Wales, later George IV. The building was started in 1787 and finished around 1822. Queen Victoria disliked Brighton and sold the pavilion to the city in 1850.

The London to Brighton Bike Ride is a charity event. The ride is 54 miles long. The money goes to the British Heart Foundation, a charity that helps people with heart disease.

WARMER 1

Ask students to name British cities and write them on the board. Draw a map of Britain on the board. Divide the class into four teams, each with their own coloured pen (or their own letter) who stand in lines at the back of the class. Call out a city. The first student runs to the board and puts a dot or a letter where they think it is. The remaining students can shout *up, down, left, right* to help their teammate. Allocate a point to the closest (have a map of Britain to hand) then call out the second place. A new student tries to locate the next place, and so on.

WARMER 2

If you set the vocabulary homework from Lesson 1, put the students in small groups to share the vocabulary they have discovered or to ask each other questions. Give students a short test on vocabulary from previous lessons. If you have started a Vocabulary box, choose words from the box.

WARMER 3

If you set the poster homework from lesson 1, put the posters up around the room with numbers on. Students work in pairs to identify who made each one.

1 OPENER

- The aim of the opener is to revise the questions and answers from the Welcome! lesson as well as providing a context for the dialogue.
- Hold up your book and point to David Ward. Ask *What's his name?* and elicit *His name is Mr Ward/David Ward.* Ask *Is he a student?* and elicit *No, he's a teacher.*

Ask students to identify the other people in the photo by asking and answering questions in pairs.

Answers

The six people are from left to right: David Ward, Pierre, Jake (at the back), Katya, Emily, Teresa (half hidden) and Adam.

- Check the answers by pointing at the photo and asking different students to identify the person. After each answer, ask the class *Where is he/she from?*
- Ask *Where are the students?* (Brighton).

2 READING

- Play the recording. Students read and listen. Be prepared to translate *programme, wow, beach, pavilion, welcome party*.

1.12 **Recording**

See text on page 14 of the Student's Book.

Answer

Katya is pointing at lots of bicycles.

Optional activity

Students practise the dialogue in groups of four, each student taking the part of one of the characters. Model the intonation of the exclamations and questions

3 AFTER READING

- The aim is to read the dialogue for specific information and to focus students' attention on the large numbers and the times.
- Read the sentences to the class.
- Students read and decide if sentences 1–5 are true or false. Ask them to note down the words in the dialogue that help them decide on their answers.
- Check the answers orally with the class before asking students to write the corrections for the false sentences.

Answers

1 False. The students are in the street next to the Royal Pavilion.
2 False. The Royal Pavilion is about 200 years old.
3 False. The number of people in the Bike Ride is about twenty-five thousand.
4 True
5 False. The welcome party is at quarter to seven (6.45).

Optional activity

Students write more true/false questions about the dialogue and test each other in small groups.

Your response

Students work in pairs and discuss which activity they think is the best. Then have class feedback.

4 VOCABULARY

- Students write the missing numbers in their notebook.
- Play the recording for students to check.
- Play the recording again for students to repeat the numbers.

1.13 Recording and answers

twenty *twenty-one* ***twenty-five*** *thirty*
forty *fifty* ***sixty*** ***seventy*** *eighty*
ninety *a hundred/one hundred* *two hundred*
five hundred *a thousand/one thousand*
two *thousand* ***ten thousand***

5 PRONUNCIATION

- Write the numbers 13–19 and 30–90 (in tens) in two columns on the board. Tell the students to copy them into their notebooks. Ask the students what problems they have with these numbers (they sound very similar).
- Drill the numbers in pairs (e.g. 13–30, 14–40, etc), drawing students' attention to the pronunciation of the last syllable (*teen* – long and stressed, *ty* – short and unstressed).
- Students listen to the recording and write the numbers they hear.
- Play the recording again and check the answers.

1.14 Recording and answers

30 14 15 60 70 18 90

6 LISTENING

- Ask the students to look at the clock face. Drill the times starting at o'clock. Ask the class *What time is it?* Write up the answer using the stem *It's ...*
- Play the first half of the recording. Ask students to match a name to each watch.
- Check the answers by asking different students. Drill the four times. Establish from the class the question each person was asked (*What time is it, please?*).

1.15 Recording

VOICE *Jake, what time is it, please?*
JAKE *It's half past twelve.*
VOICE *Katya, what time is it, please?*
KATYA *It's twenty-five past twelve.*
VOICE *Adam, what time is it, please?*
ADAM *It's quarter past twelve.*
VOICE *Emily, what time is it, please?*
EMILY *It's twenty-five to one.*

Answers

Jake D Katya B Adam C Emily A

- Play the second half of the recording. Ask students to write the times in numbers.
- Ask individual students to read out their answers. Ask students to write the five times in words in their notebooks.

1.15 Recording

1
VOICE 1 *Mr Ward, what time is it, please?*
MR WARD *It's twenty to one.*
2
VOICE *Katya, what time is it, please?*
KATYA *It's quarter to one.*
3
VOICE *Adam, what time is it, please?*
ADAM *It's ten to one.*
4
VOICE *Teresa, what time is it, please?*
TERESA *It's five to one.*
5
VOICE *Pierre, what time is it, please?*
PIERRE *It's one o'clock.*

Answers

1 12.40 2 12.45 3 12.50 4 12.55 5 1.00

Optional activities

- If you have a clock with movable hands, show five different times to the students who write down the times in words. If not, draw clocks on the board.
- **Game** *Clock race* Put students in threes, numbered 1, 2 and 3. Each numbered student is in a different corner of the room with pen and paper and the teacher is in the other corner. Draw a time on a clock face. Student 1 comes up and looks at it and writes down the time in a digital form, e.g. *5.20*. Student 1 tells student 2 who writes it down in the long form, e.g. *twenty past five*. Student 2 tells student 3 who draws the time on a clock face. Student 3 goes to the teacher to check the clocks are the same. Give 3 points for the first, 2 for the second and 1 for all teams with corect times. Ensure all students have a turn at drawing the final clock.

7 SPEAKING

- Ask students to look at the model question and answer. Drill the sentences in chorus for pronunciation.
- Students work in pairs and ask and answer questions about the times on the watches in exercise 6.
- Ask students to look at the Student Exchange programme on page 14. Establish the meaning of *tour*. Explain that *When* is used to ask what time something happens.
- Students take turns to ask each other about the Exchange programme. Monitor and help where necessary.

8 READING

- Ask students to look at the pictures in *Famous Places*. Ask if they recognise any of them.
- Invite four students to read the four descriptions. Draw students' attention to the *Prepositions of place* box to clarify the meanings of the prepositions.
- Ask students to match the photos with the descriptions.
- Play the recording for students to listen and check.
- Model the first question *Where is the Aya Sofya?* and elicit the answer. Ask *How old is it?* Elicit the answer, insisting on a full sentence with *It's*. Make sure students pronounce the 't' in *It's* clearly.
- Students ask and answer the other questions in pairs, taking turns. More confident students can cover the text and answer from memory.

1.16 Recording

1 The temple of Abu Simbel is in Egypt next to the River Nile. It's 3,200 years old.
2 Aya Sofya is in the centre of Istanbul in Turkey. It's 1,500 years old.
3 The Taj Mahal is near Delhi in India. It's 370 years old.
4 The city of Machu Picchu is on a mountain in Peru. It's 550 years old.

Answers

1 The temple of Abu Simbel 2 Aya Sofya
3 The Taj Mahal 4 The city of Machu Picchu

Optional activity

Students think of an object and describe where it is, e.g. *It's near the door, next to the table. It's on the floor.* The other students guess what it is, e.g. *Is it the bin?*

9 WRITING

- Ask students to think of three buildings in their country for which they can answer the three questions.
- Students write their three descriptions using the descriptions in exercise 8 as models.

Extension Students take turns to read out the descriptions they wrote in exercise 9 to the class, without saying the names of the buildings. The rest of the class guess what they are.

LANGUAGE WORKOUT

- Ask students to look at the top half of the Language box and complete the words.
- Drill the examples in chorus for pronunciation, drawing students' attention to the short vowel sound in *this* and *that* and the long vowel sound in *these* and *those*.
- Recap on the difference between *this* and *that*. Ask students to find examples of *these* and *those* in the text (*... these are copies of the programme, ... look at all those bicycles*).
- Invite a volunteer to explain the difference between *these* and *those*.
- Ask students to look at the bottom half of the Language box. Focus on the four ways of forming plural nouns and ask the students to complete the words.
- Students turn to page 114 of the Language File to check their answers.

Answers
that, these
visitors, years, watches, copies, parties

PRACTICE

- Students do Practice exercise 3 on page 114 of the Language File. They complete the sentences with *these* or *those*. Check the answers.

Answers

1 These 2 those 3 those 4 these 5 These 6 Those

Follow-up activity

Write *English lesson, lunch* on the board. Elicit *When is the English lesson? When is lunch?* Ask the questions and write the answers on the board. Elicit other subjects. Students choose five and go around the class asking different students a question.

HOMEWORK

Students write a short description of their rooms using prepositions, e.g. *My computer is on the desk.*

Students find photos of their family to bring in for the next lesson.

WEBLINKS

Students can learn more about the Royal Pavilion at www.royalpavilion.org.uk

Revision and Extension p21

Language File pp114–115

Workbook Unit 1 Lesson 2 pp8–9

Photocopiable notes p154, Worksheet p164

When's your birthday?

Communicative aims	Language	Pronunciation	Vocabulary	Optional aids
Talking about your family	Possessive adjectives	Syllable stress	Family members Ordinal numbers Months	Language Workout Optional activity: students' family photos

Useful information

The original Roman year had ten named months *Martius* (March), *Aprilis* (April), *Maius* (May), *Junius* (June), *Quintilis* (July), *Sextilis* (August), *September* (September), *October* (October), *November* (November), *December* (December). The last four months literally mean 7th, 8th, 9th and 10th months. At the time there were probably two unnamed months in winter when there was little happening in agriculture. Numa Pompilius, the second king of Rome circa 700BC, added the two extra months *Januarius* (January) and *Februarius* (February) and made January the first month of the year.

WARMER 1

Game *Teacher* Write _ _ _ _ _ _ _ on the board. Divide the class into two teams who take turns to guess a letter. Give one point for each letter they guess correctly. If one team guesses the word, they win all the remaining points. If they guess wrong they lose three points. Solution: *bicycle*. Play again with *pavilion* and *mountain*.

WARMER 2

Game *Vocabulary challenge* Put students in groups of three. One student has their book open and spells a word from a previous lesson. The other two students listen and say the word when they know it. Less confident students can write down the letters. Each student says five words. Monitor, making sure students are saying the letters correctly. Write any problematic letters on the board. Spell some words which include those letters at the end of the activity.

1 OPENER

- The aim is to prepare the vocabulary for the following exercises. Ask students to look at the photo on page 16 and identify what it is. Establish that it is a photo of Katya's family.
- Students work in pairs. One student says a word from the box, the other says the word that goes with it to make a masculine/feminine pair, e.g. *brother/sister*.

Answers

brother – sister, daughter – son, father – mother, grandfather – grandmother, husband – wife

2 READING

- Play the recording. Students read and listen. Encourage students to guess unfamiliar vocabulary from the context. Be prepared to translate *centre*, *birthday*, *can't believe*.
- Ask students to identify all the people in the photo. Ask *Who isn't in the photo? (Katya.)*

Katya Petrova 1.17 **Recording**

This is a photo of my family. My mother is on the right – her name is Valentina. It's her fortieth birthday today. I can't believe she's 40! The man next to Mum is my father. His name is Maxim and he's 42. My sister Anna is on the left and she's 18. The boy in the orange T-shirt is my brother – he's called Dima. The two people in the centre are my grandparents, Vera and Mikhail. Mum is their daughter. I'm not in the picture – I'm the family photographer.

Answers

From the left: Anna, Dima, Mikhail, Vera, Maxim, Valentina

3 AFTER READING

- Students read the text again and match the questions with the answers. Students can take turns to read a question to a partner to check answers.
- Check the answers with the whole class by inviting different students to ask the questions and others to answer.

Answers

1b 2h 3f 4e 5a 6g 7c 8d

Your response

Students work in pairs and tell each other the names of people in their family.

Optional activity

Students work in pairs. One student asks the questions from exercise 3 again and the other answers from memory. Pairs change roles and repeat.

4 VOCABULARY

- Ask students to match the ordinal numbers with the words.

1.18 Recording and answers

1st	*first*	*14th*	*fourteenth*
2nd	*second*	*15th*	*fifteenth*
3rd	*third*	*16th*	*sixteenth*
4th	*fourth*	*17th*	*seventeenth*
5th	*fifth*	*18th*	*eighteenth*
6th	*sixth*	*19th*	*nineteenth*
7th	*seventh*	*20th*	*twentieth*
8th	*eighth*	*21st*	*twenty-first*
9th	*ninth*	*22nd*	*twenty-second*
10th	*tenth*	*30th*	*thirtieth*
11th	*eleventh*	*31st*	*thirty-first*
12th	*twelfth*	*40th*	*fortieth*
13th	*thirteenth*		

- Play the recording, pausing after each word for the students to repeat.

Extension **Game** *Number tennis* Divide the class into two teams. Students 'serve' a number to the other team, who must 'return' the ordinal number. If the ordinal number is correct, the receiving student returns another number to a different student who converts it, and so on until a mistake is made. First team to six points wins a set.

5 PRONUNCIATION

- Play the recording. Students listen and mark the stressed syllable in each word.
- Play the recording again. Students listen and repeat the months.

1.19 Recording and answers

January, February, March, April, May, June, July, August, September, October, November, December

Optional activity

Game *First to December* Divide the class into groups of three. The students take turns in saying the months in order. Each student can say one, two or three consecutive months, then the next student continues. The student who says *December* is the winner.

6 LISTENING

- Students work in pairs, look at the photos and identify the famous people.
- Elicit the names from the class in the form *His/Her name is* ...
- Ask if anyone knows where the people are from (Usain Bolt, Jamaica; Scarlett Johansson, Johnny Depp, Christina Aguilera and George Clooney, the USA). Encourage the students to produce full sentence answers.
- Students listen to the recording and write the birthdays.

1.20 Recording and answers

1
That's Usain Bolt. When's his birthday?
It's on 21st August.
2
That's Johnny Depp. When's his birthday?
It's on 9th June.
3
That's Christina Aguilera. When's her birthday?
It's on 18th December.
4
That's Scarlett Johansson. When's her birthday?
It's on 22nd November.
5
That's George Clooney. When's his birthday?
It's on 6th May.

- Drill the first two speech bubbles in chorus for pronunciation and stress. Draw students' attention to the preposition *on* which is used for dates and *of* which is used between dates and months. Explain to the students that when the date is not given the preposition is *in*, e.g. *My birthday is in November*.
- Demonstrate by pointing at Usain Bolt and asking *When's his birthday?* Elicit the answer *It's on the twenty-first of August*.
- Ask students to work in pairs and to take turns to point at the people and ask and answer the questions.
- Students ask each other about their own birthdays.

Optional activity

Game *Birthday lines* Divide the class into teams which stand in lines. Tell the teams to arrange themselves in birthday order by asking the question *When's your birthday?* Check the teams have got the order correct by eliciting the birthdays of each student in turn in the form *My birthday is on the ___ of _____*.

7 SPEAKING

- Drill the two questions and elicit answers from a couple of students. Students then ask each other questions about their families.

8 WRITING

- Ask students to complete Katya's family tree with the correct family members. Remind students that the answers are all in relation to *Katya*.

Answers

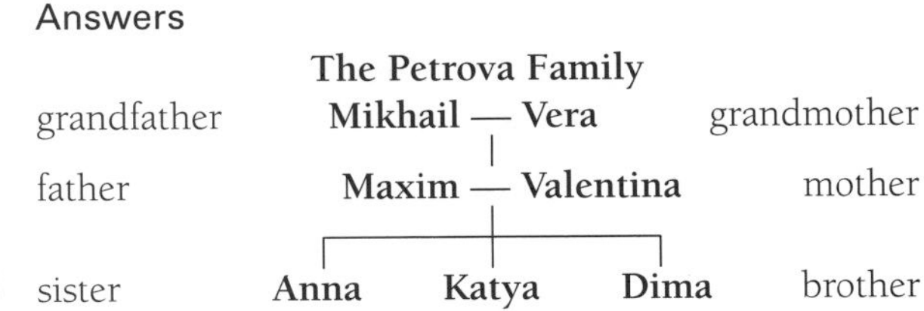

Extension Ask students to work in pairs and take turns to tell their partner about their family. Each student draws the family tree of their partner. Students swap partners and tell a new partner about the family tree they have drawn. This will practise the use of *his/her*.

Optional activity

Do a dictation of your family tree, e.g. *My name is Peter. Julie is my sister. Trevor is my father.*

LANGUAGE WORKOUT

- Ask students to look at the Language box and explain that we use possessive adjectives before nouns, e.g. *my book*.
- Ask students to complete the chart. Confident students can complete first and then check, while others can look back at exercise 2 and then complete.
- Students turn to page 115 of the Language File to check their answers.

Answers

Personal pronouns	*Possessive adjectives*
I	***my***
you	*your*
*he/**she**/it*	***his**/her/its*
we	*our*
you	***your***
they	***their***

- Drill the words in chorus for pronunciation.

Optional activity

Students who have brought in family photos show them to another student, who asks *Who is this/that?* The student with the photo points to the person, saying *This is my ...*

PRACTICE

- Students do Practice exercise 4 on page 115 of the Language File. They complete the sentences with possessive adjectives and check their answers in pairs, referring to the dialogue if necessary.

Answers

1 My 2 our 3 her 4 their 5 his 6 your, my

Follow-up activity

Students ask each other what their favourite month is and why. Elicit the question and the answer stem *I like ______ because ...* Help students to formulate their reasons in English, putting some examples on the board to support them.

HOMEWORK

Students draw their own family tree and then write a paragraph describing it.

WEBLINK

Students can find out who they share their birthdays with at www.famousbirthdays.com

Revision and Extension p21

Language File p115

Workbook Unit 1 Lesson 3 pp10–11

Photocopiable notes p154, Worksheet p165

Integrated Skills Personal information

Skills	Learner Independence	Vocabulary	Optional aids
Reading School Website *Listening* Noting down personal details *Speaking* Interviewing *Writing* Personal information	Classroom English Vocabulary notebook Phrasebook	Personal information Useful expressions	Exercise 6 Optional activity and Follow-up activities: magazines to make personal posters, ideally with famous people in them, cardboard, scissors, glue

WARMER 1

Write on the board jumbled questions asking for personal information from Unit 1. Students re-order the questions and then take turns to ask a partner.

WARMER 2

Elicit the months from the class and write them on the board with January at the top. Ask a volunteer to guess your birthday. Elicit the meaning of *guess*. Explain that after each guess you will point up or down. Pointing up means they must guess closer to January and down means they must guess closer to December. All guesses must follow the structure *I think your birthday is on the (ordinal) of (month)* which you can write on the board to support the students. Continue until a student successfully guesses the date. Students can repeat the game in pairs, playing with a student they don't usually work with.

1 OPENER

- The aim is to encourage students to predict before reading. Ask students to look at the photos on page 18 with their hand covering the text, and describe what they can see. Then ask them to guess where the places in the photos are.

Answers

Valencia, Geneva and Moscow

2 READING

- Ask students to explain the difference between *What* and *Who* questions (for things and people) and establish when we use *Where* (for places) and *When* (for times/ dates).
- Ask students to complete the questions with *How, What, Where, When, Who*. Check the answers by inviting students to read each question. Drill the questions with the whole class.
- Ask students to work in pairs to ask and answer the questions for Teresa, Pierre and Katya. More confident students can answer after listening to the recording while the others can refer to the text on page 18. Ask students the two possible ways of saying one's age, referring to the text if necessary. *(I'm 14 years old / I'm 15).*
- Play the recording and ask different students to ask the question and answers across the class first for Teresa, then for Pierre and Katya.

1.21 **Recording**

See text on page 18 of the Student's Book.

Answers

What is her/his surname?	*(Teresa) Navarro*	*(Pierre) Dubois*	*(Katya) Petrova*
What is her/his nationality?	*Spanish*	*Swiss*	*Russian*
Where is she/he from?	*Valencia, Spain*	*Geneva, Switzerland*	*Moscow, Russia*
How old is she/he?	*15*	*14*	*15*
When is her/his birthday?	*22nd April*	*2nd September*	*20th February*
Who is her/his favourite singer?	*Rihanna*	*Beyoncé*	*Mika*

Optional activity

Give students three minutes to memorise all they can from the texts. Students close their books. Read the texts including some false information, e.g. *Pierre's from Paris in Switzerland.* Students shout *Stop!* when they hear incorrect information and correct it.

3

- Ask students to match the answers for Jake to the questions in exercise 2.
- Check the answers across the class. One student asks the question and another student answers.

Answers

1 What is his surname? Turner.
2 What is his nationality? American.
3 Where is he from? Washington DC.
4 How old is he? 14 (years old).
5 When is his birthday? 11th of March.
6 Who is his favourite singer? Jay-Z.

4 LISTENING

- Ask students to look at the information profiles for Emily and Adam.
- Before you play the recording ask the class how many numbers they are going to write (two for each person – one cardinal and one ordinal).
- Play the recording. Students listen and complete the missing information.
- Allow the students time to check with a partner before listening again. Write *How do you spell it?* on the board to support the students.
- Play the recording again.
- Check the answers across the class.

1.22 Recording

Hi. I'm Emily. And my surname is Fry – F-R-Y – Fry. I'm English and I'm a student at Brighton High School. I'm fourteen and my birthday is on 25th January. And my favourite singer is Lemar. That's L-E-M-A-R.
Hello there. I'm Adam. Adam Campbell– that's C-A-M-P-B-E-L-L and I'm English too. I'm at Brighton High School and I'm fifteen years old. My birthday is on 10th August. And my favourite singer? It's Alicia Keys. That's A-L-I-C-I-A K-E-Y-S.

Answers

Fry, English, 14, 25th January, Lemar
Campbell, English, 15, 10th August, Alicia Keys

5 SPEAKING

- Explain to students that they are going to interview three other students and complete the information shown on the form.
- Ask students to look at the questions in exercise 2 and establish what changes they will have to make to the questions (*is his/her* → *is your, is he/she* → *are you*). Elicit the six questions from the class and answer them yourself.
- Put students in groups of four. More confident students begin the interviews. The others write down the questions before speaking.

Optional activities

- ♦ Elicit other questions with the stem *What is your favourite ...? e.g. football team, film, colour*. Allow students to ask these questions in their interview.
- ♦ **Game** *Noughts and crosses* Draw a grid of nine squares. In each square write a word that is the answer to a *What is your favourite ...?* question. Divide the class into two teams. Each team takes turns to choose an answer and attempt to ask the right question. If the team is successful, mark their respective 0 or X in the square. Make sure different students take turns. The first team to get a line of three noughts or crosses in any direction wins the game. This could also be played in smaller groups.

6 WRITING

- Students use the information from exercise 5 to write a paragraph about each student they interviewed. Less confident students can refer to the examples on page 18.

Optional activity

Students make a poster for one of the students they interviewed. They can cut out pictures from magazines to illustrate the student's 'favourite things'. The posters can be presented to the class and/or put up around the classroom.

7 LEARNER INDEPENDENCE

- The aim is to encourage students to use English when they have questions about vocabulary.
- Play the recording. Students listen and repeat.
- Ask students to give you some examples of the phrases in use by pointing at things and asking for the word in English or by asking for translations of words.

1.23 Recording

What's this/that?
What's it called?
What's the English word for ...?
What's ... in English?
How do you spell it?
Sorry, I don't understand.
How do you pronounce F-E-B-R-U-A-R-Y?
What does ... mean?

Optional activities

- ♦ Students close their books. Play the recording as a dictation for them to write the phrases in their notebooks.
- ♦ Give one phrase to each student to produce a poster with the phrase plus a picture that explains its usage, e.g. someone with a puzzled face, holding a giant object with a speech bubble saying *What's this in English?* Put the posters around the classroom and use them as reference when needed. After one month take down one of the phrases. On a subsequent lesson elicit which phrase is missing. Each day take down a different phrase until they are all gone.

8

- Ensure all students have a notebook to record vocabulary. Make sure they have four sections with the following headings: *Telling the time, Family, Months of the year, Classroom English.*
- At various stages during the course have a notebook inspection to see if all students are recording vocabulary effectively.

9 PHRASEBOOK

- Ask students to look through the unit, find the expressions, and notice how they are used. Help with translation where necessary. Students can add phrases they like in a Personal Phrasebook section of their notebooks.
- Play the recording for students to listen and repeat the expressions.

1.24 **Recording and answers**

Hello. (David Ward, Welcome!)
Hi. (Katya, Welcome!)
Sorry? (Teresa, Lesson 1)
Oh, I see. (Teresa, Lesson 1)
Guess! (Teresa, Lesson 1)
OK. (Adam, Lesson 1)
Right! (Teresa, Lesson 1)
Thank you very much. (Katya, Lesson 2)
Wow! (Katya, Lesson 2)
Great! (Adam, Lesson 2)
Excuse me. (Katya, Lesson 2)
Yes, please! (Adam, Lesson 2)

- Go through the example dialogue. Ask students to work in pairs to produce a short dialogue using one or more of the expressions. Students read their dialogues to the class.

Follow-up activities

- ♦ Students work in small groups and produce a fantasy family tree, cutting out the heads of famous people and making a family tree like the one on page 17. Students present their family trees to the class orally, e.g. *This is David Beckham – his sister is Rihanna and his father is Johnny Depp.*
- ♦ Choose five words that have been misspelled in written work over Unit 1. Say each word twice for students to write down. Students say and spell the words back to you.

HOMEWORK

Students make sure they have their vocabulary notebooks up to date. They find six new words related to family.

Students interview a family member and produce a short information sheet.

Students write an interview with a star using the questions from exercise 2.

WEBLINK

Students can go to www.onestopenglish.com for more activities and games that practise English.

Revision and Extension p21

Workbook Unit 1 Lesson 4 pp12–13

Inspiration EXTRA!

Optional aids

Game: Bingo cards, Extension, Lesson 3: a family photo

LANGUAGE LINKS

- Check that students understand the signs in the photo.
- Give students a few minutes to decide which of the words they can see in signs in their town.
- Ask students to report back to the class. Then elicit any other English words they see on signs in their country.

GAME WORD BINGO

- The aim is to revise vocabulary from Unit 1. Ask students to look at the pictures. Check they know what the things are. (All have been covered in Unit 1.)
- Distribute one Bingo card to each student. Ask them to choose nine things from the pictures and write them on the Bingo card. Tell the students to cross off a word when they hear it. The first student to cross off three words in a line shouts out *Line*. The first to cross off all nine numbers shouts out *Bingo!*
- Play the recording and monitor the students.

1.25 Recording

calculator MP3 player ID card comb ticket
umbrella clock camera pen wallet
photo key passport map watch

Optional activity

Play *Bingo* again. To reuse the cards, tell the students to cross off items heard in the first game with a diagonal line through each square. To play again, students cross off words they hear with a diagonal line from the other corner. Play again. Put students in groups of five. One student is the caller and the other four play the game.

SKETCH BACK TO FRONT

- The aim is for students to enjoy using their English while also getting valuable stress and intonation practice. Ask them to read and listen to the dialogue.
- With a more confident class, play the recording with books closed. Then play it again with books open. With a less confident class, play the recording once while the students follow in their books, and then once again with books closed.
- Ask the class to explain what *back to front* means. Elicit examples of things that are back to front in the text (*nine past twenty, Lirpa, Yam, kcab*).

1.26 Recording

See text on page 20 of the Student's Book.

- Students work in pairs. Play the recording again, with one student repeating A and the other B. Encourage them to exaggerate stress and intonation.
- Ask students to close their books, and play the recording again. Students work in pairs and read the sketch aloud. Choose several pairs to act out the sketch in front of the class.

Optional activities

♦ Make an audio or video recording of students performing the sketch.
♦ **Game** *Backwards* Spell some words from Unit 1 backwards. The students write the words and shout out the actual word when they know it. Students could also play this in small groups.

REVISION

Lesson 1

Answers

A a bottle of water
B a mobile phone
C an umbrella
D a (digital) camera
E a packet of tissues

Lesson 2

Answers

A It's half past three.
B It's ten to five.
C It's quarter to four.
D It's quarter past twelve.
E It's five to two.
F It's twenty-five to eight.

Lesson 3

Suggested answer

That's her sister on the left. Her name is Anna and she's 18. Next to Anna is her brother Dima. Next to Dima is her grandfather. His name is Mikhail. Next to him is her grandmother, Vera. Next to Vera is Katya's father. His name is Maxim. On the right is her mother, Valentina.

Lesson 4

Suggested answers
Emily's surname is Fry. She is English. She is 14 and her birthday is on 25th January. Her favourite singer is Lemar. Adam is English and his surname is Campbell. He is 15 years old. His birthday is on 10th August. His favourite singer is Alicia Keys.

EXTENSION

Lesson 1
Insist on full sentences, e.g. *In my bag I have a phone and three pens.*
Students' own answers

Lesson 2
Students' own answers

Lesson 3
Elicit the prepositions students might need here: *on the left/right, next to.*
Students' own answers

Lesson 4
Remind students of the third person subject pronouns and possessive adjectives.
Students' own answers

YOUR CHOICE!

The aim is to give students more learner independence and help them identify their preferred ways of learning. Encourage them to choose an activity that they feel less comfortable with if they want a challenge or are aware that they need practice in a particular area.
How do you spell it? gives students the opportunity to practise spelling and revise new words from Unit 1.
Count and clap gives students the opportunity to practise saying numbers aloud.

Language File pp114–115

Workbook Unit 1 Inspiration EXTRA! pp14–15

CULTURE

Countries around the world

Optional aids

Exercise 6, Optional activity: large pieces of paper, pictures of sights in different countries;
Exercise 7: map of the world

Useful information

The Hobo-Dyer Equal Aera Projection Map
The challenge for map makers has always been to represent a round earth on a flat piece of paper. The method most commonly used is the Mercator Projection which increases the size of areas according to their distance from the equator. The map on pages 22–23 is the Hobo-Dyer Equal Area Projection Map which attempts to represent areas of land as accurately as possible.

WARMER

Write the ten countries in the listening exercise on the board as anagrams. Students work in pairs to order the letters correctly. Check the answers with the whole class and drill the pronunciation. Ask the students to write down the capital city of each of the ten countries in three minutes. Students turn to pages 22–23 to check their answers.

1 OPENER

- Students look at the map of the world on pages 22–23 and identify what is interesting about it.

Answers

It has south at the top and north at the bottom, unlike most world maps which have north at the top. The size of the countries is also different from those shown on most maps.

2 LISTENING

- Go through the information on population and languages in the boxes and make sure students can pronounce them all.
- Play the recording. Students listen and complete the missing information.

1.27 Recording and answers

*Our first country is **Australia**. The capital of Australia is Canberra and the population is **22 million**. The main language in Australia is **English**.*
*The next country is **Brazil**. The capital of Brazil is Brasilia and the population is **193 million**. The main language in Brazil is **Portuguese**.*
*Brazil is big, but **Canada** is very, very big. Its capital is Ottawa and the population is **34 million**. The main languages are **English** and **French**.*
*And now another very big country: **China**. Its capital is Beijing and the population is **1,340** million. The main language in China is **Chinese**.*
*Our next country is **Germany**. The capital is Berlin and the population is **82 million**. The main language in Germany is **German**.*
*Next is **Mexico**. Its capital is Mexico City and the population is **111 million**. The main language in Mexico is **Spanish**.*
*And now **Russia**, another very big country. Its capital is Moscow and its population is **142 million**. The main language in Russia is Russian.*
*Then **Spain**. The capital of Spain is Madrid, and the population is **46 million**. The main language in Spain is **Spanish**.*
*Now **Switzerland**. The capital is Berne and the population is **8 million**. The main languages in Switzerland are **German**, **French** and **Italian**.*
*And the **USA** is last. Its capital is Washington, DC and its population is **310 million**. The main languages in the USA are **English** and **Spanish**.*

Optional activity

Before you play the recording, put the students in groups and ask them to guess where the population and language information should go in the boxes on the map.

3 PRONUNCIATION

- Students copy the countries and languages in order into their notebooks.
- Play the recording, pausing after each word for students to repeat.
- Play the recording again, this time students mark the stress on each word.
- Ask which countries and which languages don't have the stress on the first syllable (Australia, Brazil; Chinese, Italian, Portuguese).

1.28 Recording and answers

Australia Brazil Canada China
Germany Mexico Russia Spain
Switzerland the USA – the United States of America
Chinese English French German
Italian Portuguese Russian Spanish

4 SPEAKING

- Ask the example questions and elicit answers from the class.
- Students work in threes. One student has their book open and asks the other two students three questions. The first student to answer each question scores a point.
- Pre-teach expressions for reacting to guesses, e.g. *Almost, Nearly, Good guess!* Encourage the student asking the questions to use these expressions.
- Students take turns to ask the questions.

5 LISTENING

- Keep students in the same groups of three. Tell them to listen and say where the music is from.
- Play the recording. Students discuss and write down their answers. Check the answers by asking for volunteers. Put the expression *We think it's ...* on the board.
- Reveal the answers.

Recording

Six different types of music

Answers

1 Mexican 2 French 3 Italian 4 Chinese 5 Russian 6 Spanish

6 WRITING

- Ask students to work in pairs or small groups and brainstorm information about five of the countries.
- Students produce five short texts about their chosen countries.

Optional activities

- ♦ Students decorate their texts with pictures and drawings to make class posters.
- ♦ Pre-teach the expression *is famous for …* and give an example, e.g. *Spain is famous for paella.* More confident students can include similar statements in their texts.

7 MINI-PROJECT COUNTRIES AROUND THE WORLD

- Students work in pairs and find out information for five more countries. They then join other pairs and share their information.
- Ask the students to write their information neatly on a piece of paper. Attach these to a map of the world displayed on the wall, with arrows joining the information to the correct countries.

WEBLINK

Students can see maps of the world at www.multimap.com/world

Workbook Culture pp16–17

1 She has a lovely smile

Communicative aims	Language	Pronunciation	Vocabulary	Optional aids
Describing people	*have*: affirmative	/ð/ they /θ/ think	Colours Clothes	Exercise 8: copies of a blank email Follow-up activity: magazines with pictures of (famous) people, card and glue

WARMER 1

Elicit the names of the characters in Unit 1. Divide the students into groups and give them two minutes to write as many sentences as they can about the characters.

WARMER 2

Game *Word tennis* Divide the class into two teams. Students 'serve' a country to the other team who must 'return' the serve with the corresponding nationality. If the word is acceptable, this continues until one team makes a mistake or hesitates excessively. The returning team scores a point if they can think of the corresponding nationality. First team to six points wins a set. After the game, elicit any new country-nationality pairs from the class and write them on the board. Drill pronunciation and make sure students copy new words into their notebook.

1 OPENER

- The aim of the opener is to pre-teach colour vocabulary for the reading text and exercises to follow.
- Drill the words in chorus for pronunciation and stress.
- Establish that colours are adjectives and come before nouns in English or after the verb *be*, e.g. *I have brown hair. My hair is brown.*

Optional activity

In pairs, Student A thinks of something in the classroom and says, e.g. *Something brown.* Student B guesses what it is. Write the structures *Is it ...? / Yes, it is. / No, it isn't* on the board to support the students. Student B has ten guesses before student A reveals the answer. Students change tasks and repeat. Students note down new vocabulary in their notebooks.

2 READING

- Play the recording. Students read and listen. Encourage them to guess unfamiliar vocabulary from the context. Be prepared to translate new vocabulary.
- Students match the paragraphs 1–5 with the photos A–E. Then have students read the text again, look at the flags and decide where the people are from.

1.30 Recording

See text on page 24 of the Student's Book.

Answers

1 E 2 D 3 A 4 B 5 C
Laxmi is from India.
Daniel is from South Africa.
Kumiko is from Japan.
Pedro and Felipe are from Puerto Rico.
Hanna is from Germany.

3 AFTER READING

- Invite a student to read the sentences. Make sure students understand *true* and *false*.
- Students read the text again and decide if sentences 1–6 are true or false. Ask them to note down the words in the text that help them decide on their answers.
- Check the answers before students write corrections for the false sentences. Monitor and help where necessary. Ask students to read their answers to the class.

Answers

1 True
2 False. He has white shoes.
3 False. She has pink hair.
4 True
5 True
6 False. It has six colours.

Optional activity

Students write the sentences in exercise 3 using pronouns or possessive adjectives to replace the names. *(Answers: 1 She 2 He 3 She 4 Their 5 They 6 His)*

Your response

Ask students to say what they think of the clothes in the photos. Do they like them? Do they have any clothes like these? Establish that we use *I think* before we give our opinion.

4 VOCABULARY

- Drill the words in the Word Bank in chorus for pronunciation and stress.
- Read the two example sentences. Remind students that we use *I think* before we give our opinion.
- Students work in pairs and match the words with the clothes. Play the recording for them to check the answers. Elicit the answers from different students, checking pronunciation.

1.31 Recording and answers

1 a shirt	*6 a hat*
2 a pair of trousers	*7 a jacket*
3 a cap	*8 a top*
4 a pullover	*9 a skirt*
5 a pair of jeans	*10 a pair of shoes*

Optional activities

- ♦ Students cover the words and take turns to describe the clothes in the picture.
- ♦ Students tell each other about the clothes they have at home, e.g. *I have two pairs of trainers and six pairs of shoes*.

5 LISTENING

- Ask students to look at the chart, listen and complete it by writing how many of each item of clothing each person has.
- Play the recording of Teresa only. Give the students time to write and check with a partner. Elicit the answers from the class in the form *Teresa has a jacket. Teresa has three pairs of jeans*, etc.
- Play the rest of the recording, pausing after each speaker to allow students time to write and check. Play the whole recording again if necessary. Students compare answers in pairs.
- Invite different students to give the answers orally.

1.32 Recording

TERESA *I have a jacket and three pairs of jeans. I have one pullover and two shirts. I have two skirts and four tops. I have two pairs of trainers.*

PIERRE *I have two caps. I have two pairs of jeans. I have two pullovers and four shirts. I have two tops and three pairs of trainers.*

KATYA *I have a cap and a jacket. I have a pair of jeans and two shirts. I have four skirts and six tops. I have one pair of trainers.*

JAKE *I have a jacket and four pairs of jeans. I have five shirts and two pairs of trainers.*

Answers

	Teresa	*Katya*	*Pierre*	*Jake*
cap		*1*	*2*	
jacket	*1*	*1*		*1*
pair of jeans	*3*	*1*	*2*	*4*
pullover	*1*		*2*	
shirt	*2*	*2*	*4*	*5*
skirt	*2*	*4*		
top	*4*	*6*	*2*	
pair of trainers	*2*	*1*	*3*	*2*

Extension Go through the instructions and the example with the class. Then put students into pairs to play the game.

6 PRONUNCIATION

- Ask students to read the two columns silently. Establish the difference between the two columns (the pronunciation of *th*).
- Play the first half of the recording, pausing after each word for the students to repeat.

1.33 Recording

/ð/ ***they*** *there then father clothes*
/θ/ ***think*** *three thanks birthday fourth*

- Ask students to copy the chart into their notebooks, listen to the second half of the recording and write the words from the box in the correct column.
- Check their answers.

1.33 Recording

brother mother month thing third those

Answers

/ð/ ***they*** *brother mother those*
/θ/ ***think*** *month thing third*

Optional activities

- ♦ Students add more words to the two columns.
- ♦ Students write sentences using words with the same sound, e.g. *Her fourth birthday is next month*. Students practise saying the longest sentences.
- ♦ In pairs, students test each other's spelling of the words with these sounds.

7 SPEAKING

- Students look at the picture and listen to the recording. They match the names of the stars with the numbers. Check answers with the class.

1.34 Recording

Announcer: Ladies and gentlemen, please welcome: Rosie Raven!
F: Rosie Raven has green eyes and short black hair.
Announcer: Max Minster!
F: Max Minster has brown hair and grey eyes.
Announcer: Tara Tress!
F: Lovely Tara Tress has long blonde hair and blue eyes.
Announcer: Oscar Oldman!
F: And here is Oscar Oldman, with his white hair and brown eyes.
Announcer: Holly Hyde!
F: Now we have Holly – she has red hair and green eyes.
Announcer: Peter Punk!
F: Peter Punk has black eyes and today he has purple hair.

Answers

1 Rosie Raven 2 Holly Hyde 3 Peter Punk
4 Max Minster 5 Tara Tress 6 Oscar Oldman

- Read the question and answer to the class.
- Ask students to work in pairs and ask each other about the other stars.
- Write any new vocabulary on the board as it arises. Be ready to teach *medium-length hair*. If students want to describe the clothes the stars are wearing, make sure new vocabulary is put on the board and recorded in notebooks. Drill the words in chorus for pronunciation and stress.

Answers

Rosie Raven has green eyes and short black hair.
Max Minster has grey eyes and brown hair.
Tara Tress has blue eyes and long blonde hair.
Oscar Oldman has brown eyes and white hair.
Holly Hyde has green eyes and red hair.
Peter Punk has black eyes and purple hair.

8 WRITING

- If possible, photocopy a blank email with all the names/subject headings blank. Be sure to blank out any visible addresses.
- Distribute one copy of a blank email (or a blank sheet of paper) to each student. Ask them to write a paragraph describing themselves and their family. More confident students can add other information about themselves. Other students can write out their drafts in their notebooks first.

Optional activity

Students swap emails then go to meet another student. Students read the email to the other student who tries to guess who it is about.

LANGUAGE WORKOUT

- Ask students to look at the Language box and explain that we use the verb *have* for talking about possession. Demonstrate by holding up one of your own possessions and saying *I have a ...* Point to different students and say what they have. Draw attention to the use of *has* for *he/she*.
- Ask students to complete the sentences in the box.
- Students turn to page 115 of the Language File to check their answers.

Answers

have has has

- Drill the examples in chorus for pronunciation and stress.

Optional activity

Test the students by calling out a subject, e.g. *we* or *David and John*, to which the students must respond with the correct form of *have*.

PRACTICE

- Students do Practice exercise 5 on page 115 of the Language File. They complete the sentences with the correct form of *have*. Students check each other's work.

Answers

1 has 2 has 3 have 4 has 5 have 6 have

Follow-up activities

- Distribute magazines which include pictures of famous people. Students cut out a famous person and write a description. Students could add more sentences for homework.
- Write the following sentences on the board and tell students to copy the sentences including a colour.
  I have ___ hair. I have ___ eyes. I have a ___ house.
  I don't a have a ___ dog.
  The sky is ___ today.

HOMEWORK

Students write sentences about their possessions using seven different colours.

WEBLINK

Students may enjoy playing the game Hangman at www.learnenglish.de/Games/Hangman/HangmanClothes.htm

They click on the letters to guess the word.

Revision and Extension p33

Language File p115

Workbook Unit 2 Lesson 1 pp18–19

Photocopiable notes p155, Worksheet p166

I can play the guitar

Communication aims	Language	Pronunciation	Vocabulary	Optional aids
Talking about ability	*can* and *can't* Linking words: *and, but, or*	Weak and strong forms: *can/can't*	Possessions Musical instruments Skills	Follow-up activities: small cards

WARMER 1

Game *The long sentence game* Student A says a sentence, e.g. *I have a blue skirt*. Student B says *I have a blue skirt and a green top*. Continue round the class adding new items of clothing and colours until someone repeats a colour or an item of clothing; then start again.

WARMER 2

Game *Who is it?* Students play in groups of three. One student describes someone in the class to the other two students. The one who guesses who it is describes the next person.

1 OPENER

- The aim is to pre-teach the vocabulary for the exercises to follow. Drill the pronunciation of the words in the box. Establish the meaning of *can* in the question.
- Ask students to look at the picture and decide what they can see. Students do the task individually and then compare answers in pairs.
- When all the groups have found seven or eight items check the answers.

Answers

an alarm clock, a bed, books, jeans, a photo, a red cap, a saxophone

Optional activity

Write the word BEDROOM on the board vertically. Students write words for things they have in their bedroom that include each letter, e.g.

						B	E	D				
C	O	M	P	U	T	E	R					
						D	E	S	K			
			A	L	A	R	M	C	L	O	C	K
				P	H	O	T	O				
				B	O	O	K	S				
				L	A	M	P					

Allow students to use dictionaries or ask you for help with words.

2 READING

- Ask students to look again at the photo on page 26. Point at the girls in turn asking *What is her name? Where is she from? Can you describe her?* Prompt the students by pointing at your hair and clothes.
- Play the recording. Students read and listen. Encourage them to guess unfamiliar vocabulary from the context. Be prepared to translate *two-girl band* and *behind*.

1.35 **Recording**

See text on page 26 of Student's Book.

Answers

English, Spanish, German, French, Italian

3 AFTER READING

- Students match the questions with the answers.

Answers

1f 2a 3c 4b 5d
Answer e is not used.

Your response

Have students work in pairs and talk about what instruments they can play. Have a class vote to see which instrument is the most popular.

4 PRONUNCIATION

- Explain to students that there are two pronunciations for *can*: one weak /kən/, and one strong /kæn/, depending on the type of sentence – affirmative, question or short answer. *Can't* is always strong and has a long sound like *car*, /kɑːnt/.
- Play the first part of the recording (to *I can't play the guitar*) pausing after each line. Students listen and repeat. Ask *When is can weak? In affirmative sentences? (Yes) In questions? (Yes) In short answers? (No)*
- Ask students to look at the four sentences and decide if the pronunciation of *can/can't* is weak or strong. Play the recording twice. Check the answers with the whole class. Play the recording again if necessary. Drill the sentences in chorus for pronunciation and stress.

1.36 Recording

/kən/
She can play the guitar.
Who can speak French?
/kæn/ *and* /kɑːnt/
Yes, I can.
No, I can't.
I can't play the guitar.
1 We can sing in lots of languages.
2 I can't see.
3 Yes, I can.
4 What can you play?

Answers
1 weak 2 strong 3 strong 4 weak

5 SPEAKING

- Ask students to read through the first part of the questionnaire. Be prepared to translate: *programme (v), send, burn a CD, create, download (v), use a social networking site.*
- Ask students to do the questionnaire and compare their answers with two other students.
- Invite some feedback from different students about each question.
- Ask students to read through the second part of the questionnaire. Be prepared to explain *mend a bicycle puncture, cook a meal, iron(v), underwater, ride a horse.*
- Ask students to do the questionnaire and compare their answers with two other students as before.
- Invite some feedback from different students about each question. Ask *Who can do six things on the questionnaire? eight things? ten things? twelve?*

Extension Ask students to mingle and ask each other the questions in the Life Skills Questionnaire. Every time they get a *Yes* answer, they should note down the name and move on to a new question. The first student to get a name for each question is the winner.

6 WRITING

- Ask students to make their own Life Skills Questionnaire like the one on page 27 using some of the prompts given. Read through the prompts and be ready to explain *tell jokes, remember dates, read music, make a cake, sew on a button, lift 20 kilos, walk on your hands.* Drill the words for pronunciation.
- Model an example question from the first section *Memory*. Tell students to choose six questions. Advise them to write their questions in a column down the left-hand side of the page with five vertical columns to the right for each of the five students.
- Tell students to give their questionnaire to five students to complete. The five students write their short answers in the corresponding boxes, e.g. *Yes, I can. No, I can't.*
- Each student writes a paragraph about the answers. Pre-teach the word *no one.*
- Write the following sentences on the board to support the students:
  Five students can tell jokes.
  One student can read music.
  No one can sew on a button.

Optional activity

Students present their paragraphs in small groups beginning with the introduction: *Here are the results of my Life Skills Questionnaire.*

Extension Ask students to complete their Life Skills Questionnaire for a member of their family. They could present an oral summary of the results, comparing them with their own answers, in the next lesson. Alternatively, you could ask them to write a paragraph about their family member's answers, again comparing them with their own.

LANGUAGE WORKOUT

- Ask students to look at the top half of the Language box and explain that we use the verb *can* for talking about ability. Demonstrate by speaking English very fast and fluently, saying *I can speak English.* Continue by singing very badly and gesturing to the class to give an opinion – *You can't sing.*
- Ask students to complete the sentences in the box. Drill the sentences, eliciting the missing words as you go.

Answers
can can't Can can can't can't

- Ask students to read the dialogue in exercise 2 again and note down examples of sentences with *and, but* and *or.*
- Ask students to look at the sentences and decide when we use *and, but* and *or.* To help them, elicit whether each part of the sentences is affirmative or negative. Draw a + where the part is affirmative and a – where it is negative.
- Ask students to look at the second half of the Language box and complete the sentences with *and, but* and *or.* They check each other's work.

Answers
and but or

PRACTICE

- Students do Practice exercises 6 and 7 on page 116 of the Language File. They write questions and answers with *can* and *can't*, and complete sentences with *and, but* and *or.* Students check each other's work.

Answers

6

1 Can Emily speak Spanish? No, she can't.
2 Can Emily play the sax? Yes, she can.
3 Can Teresa sing? Yes, she can.
4 Can Emily play the piano? Yes, she can.
5 Can Teresa find the light switch? No, she can't.
6 Can Emily find the light switch? Yes, she can.

7

1 and 2 but 3 and 4 or 5 but 6 or

Optional activities

- Ask students to make more *can* questions about Emily and Teresa for their partners. Students ask and answer the questions.
- Students write five sentences, three true and two false, about themselves using *can* and *can't*. Students read their sentences and their partner says *true* or *false*.
- Students work in groups of three and ask questions about languages with *can*, e.g. *Can you speak Russian?* They then write sentences using *and*, *but* and *or* about their group, e.g. *John can speak Russian but Alicia can't speak Russian.*

Follow-up activities

- **Game** *Vocabulary game* Students write on cards new vocabulary from this lesson associated with abilities. Collect the cards and divide the class into teams of two or three. One student from each team comes to the front of the class. Choose a card for each student. Show Student 1 a card. He/She mimes the meaning of the word to his/her team which wins a point for a correct guess. Students 2 and 3 then take turns to mime their words. Continue with different team members and words.
- Add the cards to the Vocabulary box. Students can write new words from the lesson on one side of a card and an explanation, illustration or translation on the other side of the card.
- Survey: *The can challenge* Write the following on the board:
  ... can say the alphabet in English with no mistakes
  ... can count to 30 in 15 seconds
  ... can jump very high
  ... can sing
  ... can spell *Questionnaire*
  Elicit each question from the class, e.g. *Can you say the alphabet in English with no mistakes?* Say *Yes, I can* and demonstrate it. Repeat for the other tasks. Tell the students they have five minutes to ask as many questions as possible to other students. If someone says they can do one of the tasks, then they must demonstrate it. After five minutes, students write sentences, e.g. *Carlos and Mary can jump high. Nobody can sing.*

HOMEWORK

Students think of five new *Can you ...?* questions to ask at the beginning of the next class.

WEBLINK

For another exercise using *can* or *can't* go to www.englishexercises.org/makeagame/viewgame.asp?id=1518

Revision and Extension p33

Language File pp115–116

Workbook Unit 2 Lesson 2 pp20–21

Photocopiable notes p155, Worksheet p167

3 Keep still

Communicative aims	Language	Pronunciation	Vocabulary
Giving instructions	Imperatives Definite article	Syllable stress	Communication technology Text message abbreviations

WARMER 1

If students have written questions with *can* for homework, they can ask and answer them in pairs.

WARMER 2

Write jumbled sentences/questions with *can* and *can't* on the board, e.g. *can't the play teacher our saxophone / sew a on you can button?* Students write the sentences in their notebooks and ask their partner the questions.

WARMER 3

Game *The easy game* Arrange the whole class in a circle. Each student must say a word in English, any word (except numbers), without hesitation or repetition of a previous word. Play one round to demonstrate. After the demonstration round, each student who hesitates or repeats a word steps in the circle and becomes a judge. Once six students are in the middle, they leave the circle and start a new game of their own. Continue in this way until you have a main winner and some winners among the losers!

1 OPENER

- The aim of the opener is to pre-teach the vocabulary for the lesson topic. Drill the words in the box and tell students to ask another student to explain any words they don't know. Check any remaining doubts with the whole class.
- Elicit from different students which words they think will appear in the lesson. Ask *What other words are also connected to these? (Possible answers: phone, screen, button, enter, image, receive.)* Ask students to find the words quickly in the lesson to check.

Answers

These appear in the User Guide and the dialogue: computer, menu, microphone, select, webcam. Code, dial and number appear in exercise 4.

2 READING

- Students read the User Guide. Then have them read and listen to the dialogue. Encourage them to guess unfamiliar vocabulary from the context.
- Ask the students to say what Pierre's problem is and the solution.

1.37 Recording

See text on page 28 of the Student's Book.

Answers

Pierre's mum can't see him on the screen as the picture isn't very good. The solution is for Pierre to move so there is light on his face.

3 AFTER READING

- The aim is to read the dialogue and the User Guide for specific information and to introduce the imperatives *go to* and *select* in context.
- Invite different students to read the sentences. Check pronunciation.
- Students read the dialogue and the User Guide and decide if sentences 1–5 are true or false. Ask them to note down the words that help them decide on their answers.
- Check the answers orally with the class before asking students to write the corrections for the false sentences.

Answers

1 False. Make sure there is light on your face.
2 True
3 False. Don't speak a long way from the microphone.
4 False. Adam has a new laptop.
5 True

Your response

Ask the students to discuss the questions in pairs. Then conduct class feedback to see how many people make video calls from their computer.

4 LISTENING

- The aim is to introduce more vocabulary related to phones and for students to listen for specific information. Ask the students to read the pairs of possible answers. Establish the difference between *area code, national code* and *international code*.
- Play the recording. Students tick what Mrs Fry says. Play the recording again if necessary. Students compare answers in pairs. Invite different students to read out the sentences they heard. As they do so, elicit the imperative from each sentence.
- Ask the students if they know the international code for their country. Drill the pronunciation *zero-zero* then the number.
- Students tell their partner how to make an international call using the correct answers from the exercise as support.

1.38 Recording

SARAH *Katya – you have a message: 'Please phone your parents.'*
KATYA *Thanks a lot, Mrs Fry.*
SARAH *You can call me Sarah!*
KATYA *Oh, OK! Er, now where's my mobile?*
SARAH *No, don't use your mobile for international calls – it's very expensive! You can use our phone.*
KATYA *Oh, thank you.*
Sarah *First, dial the international code for the country. What's the international code for Russia?*
KATYA *It's 007.*
SARAH *OK. Dial 007, then the area code – what's the number for Moscow?*
KATYA *It's 0495.*
SARAH *Don't dial the first number of the area code. So for Moscow, just dial 495.*
KATYA *Right.*
SARAH *Then dial your parents' number. Easy.*
KATYA *Thank you very much, Mrs Fry, er, Sarah.*
SARAH *The phone is over there. And don't forget to ask me for help!*

Answers

1 *Don't use your mobile.*
2 *You can use our phone.*
3 *First, dial the international code.*
4 *Dial 007.*
5 *Don't dial the first number of the area code.*
6 *Then dial your parents' number.*

LANGUAGE WORKOUT OPTION

If you want to pre-teach the language students will be using in the following activities, you may want to look at the top half of the Language Workout box now.

Optional activity

1.38 Play the recording from *First, dial ...* to *Easy*. Ask the class to dictate the dialogue back to you and write it on the board. Play the recording again if necessary. Remove one word from each sentence. The class reads the dialogue to you. Students practise the dialogue in pairs as you keep removing words. Eventually remove the whole dialogue. Students practise one more time with a new partner.

Extension Ask students to work in pairs and tell each other how to make a call from Britain to their home. This will be easier if you have already done the optional activity described above with them.

5 PRONUNCIATION

- Ask students to read the words in the box silently and check the meaning of any they don't know. Ask how many syllables the words have (two). Tell the students to look at the two columns under the box and establish the difference between the two columns (the position of the stressed syllable).
- Ask students to copy the chart into their notebooks. Play the first part of the recording, pausing after each word to give students time to write the word in the correct column. They check their answers in pairs.
- Play the second part of the recording for students to check and correct if necessary. Draw the table on the board and invite students to write the words in the correct column. Play the second part of the recording again. Students repeat the words.

1.39 Recording and answers

about address around hello menu message mobile number parent picture select today tonight webcam

■ ▪ *menu message mobile number parent picture webcam*
▪ ■ *about address around hello select today tonight*

6 READING

- Ask students to close their books. Write the following on the board:
  _ _ _ / _ _ _ _ / _ / _ _ _ / _ _ _ _ / _ _ _ _ _ _ _
- Divide the class in two teams who take it in turns to guess a letter. Give one point for each letter that appears in the sentence. If one team guesses the sentence, they win all the remaining points. If they guess wrongly, they lose five points. Solution: *You have a new text message.*
- Ask the students if they send text messages. Ask if they are the same as writing a letter. Elicit the differences (abbreviations, missing grammar words, special text words, e.g. GR8). Elicit suggestions for how they could abbreviate the sentence on the board. (U HV A NU TXT MSG)
- Ask the students to look at the three examples on page 29. Ask the class if they use abbreviations like this.
- Ask the students to read the text message abbreviations with a partner. Students match the abbreviations to the words. Check the answers by asking different students to read a pair.

Answers

2DAY – today 2MORO – tomorrow ABT – about B4N – bye for now BF – boyfriend CU – see you EZ – easy GF – girlfriend GR8 – great IC – I see ILUVU – I love you L8 – late L8R – later 2NITE – tonight NE – any PLS – please RUOK – Are you OK? SOME1 – someone

7

- Ask students to work out the meaning of the messages individually and put them in the right order. Students compare in pairs.
- Invite two students to read the dialogue.

Answers

A, E, C, B, D

8 WRITING

- Ask students to read the text message and write it out in full sentences, paying attention to the punctuation. Students check their answers in pairs.

Answers

Hi! Thanks for the CD. I love it. Are you OK? See you tomorrow about six (o'clock). Please don't be late. Bye for now.

Optional activity

Game *Word Tennis* See Unit 2, Lesson 1 Warmer for instructions. Play with letters.

LANGUAGE WORKOUT

- Ask students to look at the top half of the Language box. Explain that the verbs *go, keep* and *don't move* are examples of the imperative in English. Ask if the students can see a difference between an imperative sentence and a normal sentence. Establish that there is no subject before the verb.
- Ask students to complete the sentences by looking back at the text. Confident students can complete first and then check, while others can look back at exercise 2 and then complete.
- Students turn to page 116 of the Language File to check their answers.

Answers

Check *Don't*
don't

- Write the following on the board:
  a) an international call – *the* international code
  b) Think of a number – What is *the* number?
  c) *The* first number
- Ask students to look at the bottom half of the Language box and discuss why the definite article *the* is used and why the indefinite article *a/an* is used. Establish that we use *the* for specific or unique things whereas *a/an* is used for unspecified things.
- Draw a picture of the sun, the moon and the earth. Establish that we use *the* for these because there is only one of each. Ask students to think of other things or people of which there are only one (e.g. *the Pope, the Queen of England, the sky, the sea*).

PRACTICE

- Students do Practice exercise 8 on page 116 of the Language File. They use the imperative to turn requests into commands and check their answers in pairs. Monitor to make sure students are omitting the question mark. Ask different students to read their answers to the class.

Answers

1 Phone your parents.
2 Don't use mobile phones in class.
3 Give me the number.
4 Spell your name.
5 Don't tell people my phone number.

Follow-up activities

- ♦ **Game** *Text race* Students write their own text messages in large letters on individual sheets of paper. Stick the text messages up around the classroom. Students play in pairs. They have five minutes to write down as many text messages as they can. After that they return to their seats to write out the messages in full.
- ♦ In pairs, Student A writes a text message to Student B, who replies to the message on the same sheet of paper. Allow students to keep 'texting' each other for four minutes. Give the text conversations to another pair who write them out in full. Each pair acts out their new dialogue.

HOMEWORK

Students think of other text abbreviations and write five text sentences.

Students find ten more words to add to their two-syllable word lists in exercise 5.

WEBLINK

Students may like to see a comprehensive list of texting terms at www.life123.com/technology/home-electronics/text-messaging/text-message-abbreviations.shtml

Revision and Extension p33

Language File p116

Workbook Unit 2 Lesson 3 pp22–23

Photocopiable notes p155, Worksheet p168

2 4 *Integrated Skills* Favourite band

Skills
Reading My favourite band article
Listening Noting down details of a band
Speaking Interviewing
Writing Description of a band

Learner Independence
Classroom English
Vocabulary notebook
Phrasebook

Vocabulary
Music
Useful expressions

WARMER 1

If students have written text messages for homework, they can exchange them and write them out in full sentences.

WARMER 2

Write the words MY FAVOURITE BAND on the board. Students work in groups. Allow them a limited time to see how many words they can make using the letters. They may not use a letter more than once unless it appears more than once in the words above. The team with the most words wins. Possible words include: *a, an, as, am, at, is, it, on, of, or, and, but, out, in, are, arm, art, team, name, not, no, from.*

1 OPENER

- The aim of the opener is for students to predict vocabulary based on the topic before reading the text. Drill the words in the box and ask students to ask each other about words they don't know.
- Elicit from different students which words they think will appear in the lesson. Ask *What verbs are connected to these?* Possible answers: *sing (a song), play (the guitar, the drums, CDs), wear (a jacket), buy/listen to (CDs).* Ask students to find the words quickly in the lesson to check.

Answers
CDs drums friends gigs guitar members song website

2 READING

- Students read the questions first. Help with any questions asked. Students complete the chart for Jake. To check, ask one student to read the question and then choose another student to answer it. Be prepared to explain *download.*

Answers
Linkin Park
Six
California
Leave Out All the Rest
Three members are school friends.
www.linkinpark.com
Pictures of the band; a place to download videos of their gigs

Optional activities

- ♦ 1.40 Students could read and listen to complete chart.
- ♦ Give students three minutes to memorise all they can from the text and then close their books. Read the text including some false information, e.g. *San Diego, California.* Students shout *Stop!* when they hear incorrect information and correct it.

3 LISTENING

- Ask students if they know anything about The Black Eyed Peas. Help with vocabulary and write any new words on the board.
- Play the recording. Students listen for specific information and complete the chart. Play the recording again. Pause to check the answers for each question.

1.41 **Recording**
My favourite band is The Black Eyed Peas. It's a hip-hop band with four members: william, apldeap, Taboo and Fergie. They're from Los Angeles, California. My favourite song is 'Where is The Love?'. What's special about the band? That's easy. They're all really good friends. Their website address is www.blackeyedpeas.com - that's W-W-W-dot-B-L-A-C-K-E-Y-E-D-P-E-A-S-dot-C-O-M. It's a great site with lots of photos and it also has videos of the band.

Answers
Black Eyed Peas
Four
Los Angeles, California
Where Is The Love?
They're all really good friends.
www.blackeyedpeas.com
Photos and videos of the band

4 SPEAKING

- In pairs students interview each other about their favourite band, taking turns to ask and answer questions and noting down the answers. Students find a new partner and do a second interview. Fast finishers can ask additional questions. If students don't have internet access, they could replace the last two questions with *What clothes do the band wear? Who is your favourite band member? Why?*

5 WRITING

- The aim is to write a paragraph about another student's favourite band using Jake's model on page 30 for guidance. Tell students to read Jake's text again.
- Students write a similar paragraph/three-paragraph text based on the answers from one of their interviews in exercise 4 – the one which was the most interesting or complete. Write the subject pronouns *he, she, they* on the board and elicit the correct forms of the verbs *have* and *be* for these subjects. Remind students to use the correct form of *have/be* as you monitor. Students then give their texts to another student to check.

Optional activity

Ask students to tell the class something interesting about the band they wrote about.

6 LEARNER INDEPENDENCE

- Drill the questions in chorus for pronunciation and stress. Drill the two answers in the book. Invite different students to ask you some of the questions.
- Students work in pairs and answer the questions. Monitor, helping with pronunciation and intonation.
- Drill the questions and answers under the box. Invite different students to ask you if they can borrow things.
- Students work in pairs to make and reply to requests using the words in the box.

Optional activity

Less confident students write a dialogue in pairs using some of the expressions. Students read their dialogues to another pair.

7

- The aim is to encourage students to get into the habit of recording vocabulary in English in an organised way. Ask if any students already have pages or sections in their vocabulary notebooks for Clothes or Musical instruments. Praise students who already have these and encourage them to think of more words to add. Other students add the new sections and look back through the unit and find words to write down.
- Ask the class which is the best way of recording the words they find. Establish some techniques the students could use, e.g. grouping by word type: verb, noun, adjective; drawing a word map; writing true personalised sentences including the vocabulary; drawing pictures.
- Students add new words using their preferred method.

Optional activity

Students choose five words that they find difficult to spell. Students ask each other *How do you spell ...?*

8 PHRASEBOOK

- Students look back through the unit to find the expressions.
- Play the recording for students to listen and repeat the expressions.

1.42 Recording and answers

Never mind! (Teresa, Lesson 2)
Any questions? (Emily, Lesson 2)
See? (Emily, Lesson 2)
Lucky you! (Pierre, Lesson 3)
Yes, of course you can. (Adam, Lesson 3)
There's something wrong. (Pierre, Lesson 3)
Don't worry. (Adam, Lesson 3)
Thanks a lot. (Pierre, Lesson 3)
No problem. (Adam, Lesson 3)
It's really cool. (Jake, Lesson 4)

- Read through the four questions, checking that the students understand the words. In pairs, students decide which expression goes with each question.

Answers

a Yes, of course you can
b There's something wrong.
c It's really cool.
d No problem.

Optional activity

Test if the students remember the expressions by saying the first word or two. Students have to finish the expression.

Follow-up activity

Write jumbled questions and sentences from Unit 2 for the students to re-order.

HOMEWORK

Students make a wordsearch of ten words related to their favourite band.

WEBLINK

Students may like to find out more about Jake's favourite band, Linkin Park at www.linkinpark.com

Revision and Extension p33

Workbook Unit 2 Lesson 4 pp24–25

Inspiration EXTRA!

Optional aids

Project: photos of students, their homes, families

PROJECT PERSONAL WEB PAGE

1

- Explain to students that the aim of this project is to make a personal web page. Read Merel's web page.
- Put students into pairs and ask them to match the list of information with the correct items in Merel's web page.
- Give students time to make a list of their own personal information.

2

- Ask students to use their list of personal information to write their own text, using Merel's as a model. Monitor and give help where needed.
- Encourage students to check their own work carefully.
- Let students read each other's texts to offer suggestions and for correction.

3

- Each student decides how they would like their web page to look. They read their texts through carefully again to correct any mistakes and then write them out neatly and choose pictures to illustrate them.
- Students put their work together and show their personal web pages to other students. Display them in the classroom if you can.

GAME NOUGHTS AND CROSSES

- Read through the instructions in the Student's Book. Check students understand by asking a volunteer to explain the game in their own language.
- Divide the class into two teams and play the game. Make sure different students take turns. If a student says a word but spells it incorrectly, the other team can spell the word to win the square or say and spell a different word.

PUZZLE

- Students work out the puzzle in pairs. Explain that they must find one letter for each line of the puzzle. The letters spell a word.

Answer

guitar

REVISION

Lesson 1
Students' own answers

Lesson 2
Student's own answers

Lesson 3
Students brainstorm words in pairs. Write all words on the board for students to add to their lists.

Lesson 4

Suggested answer

Emily's favourite band is called The Black Eyed Peas. It has four members. They're from Los Angeles in California. Her favourite song is called Where Is The Love? *What's special about the band? They're all really good friends. Their website address is www.blackeyedpeas.com. It has lots of photos and videos of the band.*

EXTENSION

Lesson 1
Students' own answers

Lesson 2
Students' own answers

Lesson 3
Elicit a few examples from the whole class. Then students work in pairs. Set a time limit and write up all the expressions on the board for students to copy.

Lesson 4
Students prepare a text of the lyrics of a song they know, leaving out some familiar words. They could bring in the song to play while other students fill in the missing words.

YOUR CHOICE!

The aim is to give students more learner independence and help them to identify their preferred ways of learning. Encourage students to choose an activity that they feel less comfortable with if they want a challenge or are aware that they need practice in a particular area.
Star Profile gives students the opportunity to write about their favourite celebrity.
Dictionary Search gives students the opportunity to practise using a dictionary and to expand their vocabulary.

You may now like students to do the song *Together We Are Strong*. See p162 for the notes and p187 for the worksheet.

Language File pp115–116

Song – photocopiable notes p162, worksheet p187

Workbook Unit 2 Inspiration EXTRA! pp26–27

Units 1–2

Optional aids

Follow-up activity: vocabulary from Units 1–2 on slips of paper

1 Give the students two minutes to read the text and say what different things you can download to a mobile phone. Students read the text again and choose the appropriate word for each space. Do the first one together as an example. Encourage students to read the whole sentence both before and after the space. This can be done in pairs or individually as a short test.

Answers
1 B 2 B 3 A 4 C 5 C 6 B 7 C 8 C 9 A 10 A

Optional activity

Confident students can first attempt the task without looking at the word options.

2 Students write questions using the words given and then answer them. Look at the examples first. Do the first one together. Note: warn students to be careful about items 3 and 7 (plural subjects). Monitor, making sure students are using the correct pronouns. If this seems to be a weak area, elicit the subject pronouns from the class and write them on the board. Check the answers by asking one student to read the question and then choose another student to answer. Students then ask and answer the questions in pairs.

Answers
1 Is Emily 14? Yes, she is.
2 Is Jake from Spain? No, he isn't.
3 Are Adam and Emily English? Yes, they are.
4 Is Machu Picchu in Switzerland? No, it isn't.
5 Is Katya from Russia? Yes, she is.
6 Is Pierre from Brighton? No, he isn't.
7 Are Emily and Teresa sisters? No, they aren't.
8 Is October the tenth month? Yes, it is.

3 Elicit from students which verb form is missing from all the sentences (*be*). Do the first one together. Students complete the questions with the correct form of the verb *be* and an appropriate word if necessary.

Answers
1 is, name 2 are, from 3 are 4 is 5 are

4 Tell students they need to complete the sentences and questions with *this*, *that*, *these* or *those*.

Answers
1 that 2 this 3 these 4 those

5 Students write the plural forms of the nouns.

Answers
1 friends 2 streets 3 cities 4 watches 5 people
6 photos 7 addresses 8 families 9 months
10 countries 11 cameras 12 tissues

Optional activity

Students divide the answers into four categories according to the formation of the ending (+*s*, +*ies*, +*es*, irregular). Students add two more words to each category.

6 With a less confident class elicit the possessive adjectives first. Students complete with the correct possessive adjective.

Answers
1 my, Her 2 His 3 her 4 Our 5 their 6 its

7 Students complete the sentences with the correct form of *have*.

Answers
1 has 2 have 3 have 4 have 5 has 6 has

8 Students write questions using the words given and then answer them. Go through the example with the class. Draw students' attention to the use of the pronoun in the second question. Check the answers by asking one student to read the question and then choose another student to answer. Students then ask and answer the questions in pairs.

Answers
1 Can Emily play the guitar? Yes, she can.
Can she play the drums? No, she can't.
2 Can they swim 5km? No, they can't.
Can they run 5km? Yes, they can.
3 Can Pierre ride a horse? Yes, he can.
Can he iron a shirt? No, he can't.
4 Can you send a text message on a mobile? Yes, I can.
Can you burn a CD on a mobile? No, I can't.
5 Can Katya speak French? No, she can't.
Can she understand French? Yes, she can.
6 Can she read a book? Yes, she can.
Can she read music? No, she can't.

9 Ask students to look at the example. Remind students to pay attention to the correct form of the possessive adjective.

Answers
1 Can I close the window?
2 Can I phone my parents?
3 Can I see the photos?
4 Can I borrow your jacket?
5 Can I listen to your MP3 player?
6 Can I use your camera?

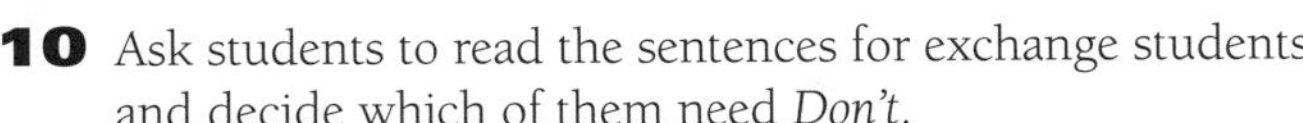

10 Ask students to read the sentences for exchange students and decide which of them need *Don't*.

> Answers
> *1 - 2 - 3 Don't 4 - 5 Don't 6 Don't*

VOCABULARY

11 Students complete the sentences with the words. More confident students could cover the words and complete from memory.

> Answers
> *1 sister 2 past 3 meet 4 address 5 favourite 6 surname 7 birthday 8 message*

12 Drill the pronunciation of the words in the box. Students match the words with the definitions individually, then compare with a partner.

> Answers
> *1 grandmother 2 brother 3 January 4 December 5 German 6 London 7 bicycle 8 century 9 clock 10 population*

13 Remind students that it is very helpful to learn common verb + noun phrases of this kind. Elicit the type of words in column A (verbs) and column B (nouns).

> Answers
> *1 cook a meal 2 dial a number 3 go home 4 iron a shirt 5 lift ten kilos 6 play the drums 7 ride a horse 8 send a text message 9 spell your name 10 tell a joke*

Optional activity

Students think of other words that go with column A, e.g. *cook a chicken, go to school*.

14 Students choose the word in each group which is different from the others in some way. Point out that they should be able to explain their choices. Do the first one together as an example.

> Answers
> *1 button (the others are numbers)*
> *2 trainers (the others are for the body not the feet)*
> *3 umbrella (the others use batteries)*
> *4 new (the others are colours)*
> *5 Spain (the others are nationalities or languages)*
> *6 camera (the others are musical instruments)*
> *7 boyfriend (the others are relatives/family members)*
> *8 comb (you can put things in the others)*

LEARNER INDEPENDENCE SELF ASSESSMENT

- Explain to students that the aim of the self assessment is to encourage them to check their own progress and to take any necessary action to improve. Point out that the list 1–8 covers language from Units 1 and 2. Students tick the 'Fine' box for functional language that they feel confident using, but put a question mark in the 'Not sure' box for functional language that they have difficulties with or still cannot use confidently.
- Encourage students to look at the Language File and re-do exercises from the Workbook in areas where they have problems. They may also like to re-do exercises from the lessons and from the Revision and Extension sections in Units 1 and 2.
- Students write an example sentence for each language area in the list. You may like to elicit the grammar needed for each example, e.g. *Introducing yourself and others – My name is ... / This is ...* before students write sentences. Students can refer to the relevant lessons and the Language File for support.
- Ask students to compare their sentences with a partner's, and to discuss and correct any mistakes they may find. They then evaluate their own performance for each language area in terms of *Fine* and *Not sure*.
- Check their sentences so that you can note down language areas for future practice where students are uncertain.

Follow-up activity

Game *Don't say the word* Students play in groups. Select one student from each group and give them five slips of paper that you prepared earlier with vocabulary from Units 1 and 2. That student has one minute to explain to his/her group as many of those words as possible without using the words themselves. For every word that the group manages to guess within the minute, they get one point.

HOMEWORK

Students bring their vocabulary notebooks up to date.

Students write a paragraph about a person they like (celebrity, pop star, friend) including personal information, description and abilities.

WEBLINKS

Students can practise their English with different games at www.onestopenglish.com

Language File pp114–116

Workbook Review Units 1–2 pp28–29

PREVIEW

Units 3–4

Activities
Identifying topics
Categorising vocabulary
Contextualising listening extracts

Project
Food and sport survey

Vocabulary
Food
Sport and the gym
Parts of the body

Optional aids
Follow-up activities: slips of paper

WARMER 1

If students did the homework in the review, ask them to read out their texts about a person they like. If they do this without saying the person's name, the other students could guess who it is.

WARMER 2

Ask students to look at the photos and speech bubbles on pages 36–37 and to say what they can see.

1

- The aim is to introduce students to the main topics and vocabulary they will cover in Units 3 and 4.
- Remind students that the two boxes at the top of the page show the communicative language and topics/ vocabulary they will use in the next two units of *New Inspiration 1*.
- Go through the topics in the second box with the class and make sure everyone understands them. Then ask them to look at pictures A–F and match them with six topics.

Answers
A parts of the body
B school subjects
C tourist attractions
D food
E sport and the gym
F leisure activities

2

- Explain that words from each of the three vocabulary categories (food, sport and parts of the body) are arranged in the word square. Give students two minutes to write the words in the correct category.
- Students check their answers in pairs and then as a whole class.

Answers
Food: banana, cheese, egg, fish, tomato
Sport: basketball, tennis, swimming, football, golf
Parts of the body: hand, mouth, ear, leg, eye

Optional activity

In small groups, students think of as many different words as possible to add to the three categories. Give them a time limit and then get the groups to read their words aloud to the class.

3

- Students match the words with the pictures.

Answers
1 magazine 2 shop 3 face 4 octopus 5 volleyball 6 car

4

- The aim of this activity is for students to contextualise a short listening extract by working out what the topic is. Explain that they should listen for the main gist of the extract and that it doesn't matter if they don't understand every word.
- Play the recording. Students match each of the three extracts to the topics (A–C).

2.01 Recording

1
DIANA *Come inside, everyone – dinner is ready. Pierre, I hope you like fish.*
PIERRE *Yes, I love it. I like everything except octopus. I really don't like octopus.*
DIANA *Don't worry – octopus isn't on the menu!*
2
Brighton is on the south-east coast of England, about 90km from London. Come and visit this exciting city – it has something for everyone.

There are lots of attractions for teenagers, including the Brighton Museum & Art Gallery, with information about the city and its history, and the Sea Life Centre, a fantastic aquarium with sharks and an underwater tunnel.

3

EMILY *I usually go running on Monday – but I hate it! I always go swimming on Tuesday. I often go shopping after school on Wednesday, but I never go shopping on Sunday. I usually play tennis on Thursday after school. I love dancing and I sometimes go dancing on Friday night. I also love movies and I always go to the cinema on Saturday night, after the gym.*

Answers

1 B 2 C 3 A

5

- Elicit or explain the meaning of *Do you like ...?* Put students into groups of four and ask them to do the survey, writing down their answers.
- Ask them to join other groups to share their answers.
- Point out the 'Believe it or not!' fact at the bottom of the page. Find out if there are any words in the students' own language(s) which you can read upside down.

Follow-up activities

- ♦ In small groups, students brainstorm vocabulary for three other categories from the box on page 36. See Follow-up in Preview 1–2 for further instructions.
- ♦ Students make lists of all the sports that they know. Give them two minutes and see who can produce the longest list.

HOMEWORK

Ask students to interview family members or other students at the school to find out what foods and sports they like. They then present their findings to the class in the next lesson.

LIFESTYLE

1 I really don't like octopus

Communicative aims	**Language**	**Pronunciation**	**Vocabulary**
Talking about likes and dislikes	Present simple: affirmative and negative	/tʃ/ cheese /k/ carrot /s/ CD	Food Colours

WARMER 1

Write the colours from Unit 2, Lesson 1, page 24 as anagrams on the board. In pairs students order the words. Fast finishers can find examples of the colours in the classroom.

WARMER 2

Write the headings *meat, vegetables, fruit, drink* on the board. Establish the meanings and invite students to give you a couple of examples for each column. Ask students to copy the table into their notebooks and add five words to each group. The winner is the first to finish. Fast finishers can continue adding words. Write up all the vocabulary generated for students to copy.

1 OPENER

- The aim is to introduce the context for the dialogue in exercise 2. Students answer the questions orally as a class.

Answers

Pierre, Adam, Ruby and Diana. They're in the garden of the Campbell's cottage in Lewes, Ruby/Adam's home.

2 READING

- Students read and listen to the dialogue to answer the question. Encourage them to guess unfamiliar vocabulary from the context. Be prepared to translate *cottage, flat, garden, chicken, eggs, inside, dinner.*

2.02 Recording

See text on page 38 Student's Book.

Answer

Fish

- Ask the students if they think that Ruby and Adam have a good relationship. Why not? Ask the class if it is normal for brothers and sisters to be like this.

3 AFTER READING

- Students complete the sentences with the correct answers.

Answers

1 cottage 2 house 3 eggs 4 Adam 5 Ruby 6 fish

- Ask students to read their answers to the class.

Your response

Encourage students to discuss foods they really don't like.

Optional activity

Students act out the dialogue in groups of three and change roles until they have been each character.

4 VOCABULARY

- Ask students to look at the pictures on page 39. Drill the pronunciation of the food items. Students work in pairs and match the words with the pictures, using the colour clues. Play the recording for students to check.

2.03 Recording and answers

1 cheese 2 eggs 3 ice cream 4 chocolate 5 carrots 6 fish 7 chips 8 pizza 9 mushrooms 10 octopus 11 cucumber 12 garlic 13 tomatoes 14 bananas

Extension **Game** *Word tennis* Divide the class into two teams. Students 'serve' a letter to the other team who must 'return' the serve with a food beginning with that letter. First team to six points wins a set. No item may be repeated. After the game elicit any new words from the class and write them on the board. Drill pronunciation and make sure students copy new words into their vocabulary notebooks.

5 PRONUNCIATION

- Ask students to look at the words *cheese, carrot, CD* in the chart and tell their partner the difference in pronunciation. Invite a student to explain to the class. Drill the three sounds and the three words.
- Ask students to copy the chart into their notebooks and write the words they hear in the correct column.
- Play the recording, pausing after each word so that students can check each word. Play the recording again, pausing after each word for students to repeat. Elicit the answers from the class.

2.04 Recording and answers

/tʃ/ cheese chicken chip chocolate
/k/ carrot cottage cream cucumber
/s/ CD centre century city

6 LISTENING

- Play the recording. Students identify the food items they hear. Elicit the answers from the class. Play the recording again. Students listen and complete the four sentences.

- Elicit the sentences from individual students, checking pronunciation and intonation.

2.05 Recording

RUBY *I love ice cream and I love chocolate. Mmm! I like pizza – that's my favourite meal. But I don't like bananas – or carrots. And I hate mushrooms – ugh!*

ADAM *My favourite meal is fish and chips. I love fish and chips. And I really like cheese. But I don't like … I don't like cucumber or tomatoes. And I hate garlic.*

Answers *(numbers of the pictures in brackets)*

Ruby likes ***icecream*** *(3),* ***chocolate*** *(4) and* ***pizza*** *(8). She doesn't like* ***bananas*** *(14),* ***carrots*** *(5) or* ***mushrooms*** *(9). Adam likes* ***fish*** *(6),* ***chips*** *(7) and* ***cheese*** *(1). He doesn't like* ***cucumber*** *(11),* ***tomatoes*** *(13) or* ***garlic*** *(12).*

Optional activity

2.05 Play the recording in small sections for students to repeat, imitating the intonation they hear.

7 SPEAKING

- Read the examples out loud. Recap the meaning of *and, but* and *or*. Students move around the class telling people about the food they like and don't like.

8 WRITING

- In pairs, students brainstorm possible things to ask questions about. Students decide on five things. The pairs separate and show their list to as many people as possible who say whether they *love, like, don't like* or *hate* the item. After five minutes tell the students to get back in pairs and tell their partner what the people they interviewed said. Remind students to use the third person *s*, e.g. *Sonia likes Johnny Depp*.
- Students write up their results using full sentences.

Extension Students write short texts about the things they love, like, don't like and hate. Encourage them to use complex sentences with *and, but* and *or*.

LANGUAGE WORKOUT

- Ask students to look at the Language box and to complete the chart. Confident students can complete first and then check, while others can look back at exercises 2 and 3 and then complete.
- Students turn to page 116 of the Language File to check their answers.

Answers

Affirmative	*Negative*
you ***like***	*I* ***don't*** *like*
they ***like***	*he/she/it* ***doesn't*** *like*
	we ***don't*** *like*

don't *= do not*

- Highlight that:
  - we add *s* for *he/she/it* in the affirmative form
  - we form the negative with *don't/doesn't* + verb.

PRACTICE

- Students do Practice exercise 9 on page 117 of the Language File. They write sentences using the present simple. Remind students not to forget the third person *s*.
- Remind students to use contractions and check punctuation.
- Check the answers by asking different students to say the completed sentences.

Answers

1 *Ruby likes Pierre.*
2 *He doesn't have a sister.*
3 *We love music.*
4 *They don't like octopus.*
5 *You don't speak Chinese.*
6 *Diana loves fish.*
7 *I don't want eggs for breakfast.*
8 *Sometimes Ruby hates Adam.*

Follow-up activities

- Ask three or four students to spell words from the lesson. Use *How do you spell … ?* Divide the class into pairs or teams and have them test each other on other words from the lesson.
- **Game** *The last letter game* One student says a food or drink item and the next student says a word that begins with the last letter of the previous word, e.g. *ice cream – m – meat.*

HOMEWORK

Students interview one of their family members about their food likes and dislikes and write a paragraph about them.

WEBLINK

Students can play hangman with fruit and vegetables at www.1-language.com/eslhangman/fruitveg1.htm

Revision and Extension p47

Language File pp116–117

Workbook Unit 3 Lesson 1 pp30–31

Photocopiable notes p156, Worksheet p169

Does she study in the evening?

Communicative aims	**Language**	**Pronunciation**	**Vocabulary**	**Optional aids**
Talking about regular activities	Present simple: questions and short answers	Syllable stress	School subjects Days of the week Prepositions of time	Exercise 7 Optional activity: card and coloured pens

WARMER 1

Check students' memory of the food vocabulary from the last lesson. Describe a food using type, colour, meals and whether you like it or not, e.g. *It is yellow. It is a fruit. I eat it for breakfast. I like it.* (Banana.) *They are brown. They are vegetables. I don't like them.* (Mushrooms.)

WARMER 2

Game *Teacher* See Unit 1 Lesson 3 Warmer for instructions. Use the names of school subjects.

1 OPENER

- The aim is to elicit vocabulary for the students to use in the following exercises as well as setting the context for exercise 2. Ask the students to look at the photos and to say what they can see. Ask *What country do you think they are in?* (India.)
- Students work in pairs to generate a list of school subjects in their vocabulary notebooks. Elicit ideas, write them on the board and drill the words in chorus for pronunciation and stress.
- Ask students to predict what school subjects the children in the photos study.

Optional activity

Write the words *love, like, don't like, hate* on the board in a column. Students go through the list and tell their partner about each school subject they have listed in the opener, e.g. *I like history, I don't like maths*. Students see how many opinions they have in common. Students write five sentences about their partners. Remind the class of the third person singular *s* and the auxiliary *doesn't*. Invite different students to read their sentences.

2 READING

- Play the recording. Students read and listen. Encourage them to guess unfamiliar vocabulary from the context. Be prepared to translate *headmaster, poor, backyard, outdoors, local language.*
- Ask students to say what information in the article they find surprising.

2.06 Recording

See text on page 40 of the Student's Book.

3 AFTER READING

- Students read the questions and the answers. Play the recording again for them to read and listen.
- Students match the questions and answers on their own. Set a short time limit and allow a minute to compare with a partner.
- Check the answers by asking one student to read the question and then choose another student to answer. Write the questions and answers on the board. Draw students' attention to the way the same auxiliary used in the question appears at the end in the short answer in an affirmative or negative form depending on the answer. Tell students to listen carefully to questions with auxiliaries because they always need the same auxiliary in the answer. Drill the questions and short answers in chorus for pronunciation and stress.

Answers

1 b 2 g 3 h 4 f 5 e 6 a 7 d 8 c

Your response

Elicit the students' responses to Babar Ali's story. Could something like that happen in their country?

Useful information

Babar Ali
Since the magazine article in this lesson was published, Babar Ali and his team of teachers have continued their work teaching poor children for free. Babar Ali himself has now graduated from high school and is studying English at college. He has a Facebook page where you can learn more.

4 LISTENING

- Tell students they are going to listen to Adam talking about his school timetable.
- Point out that there are some spaces which are blank in the timetable. Ask students to look at the first space. Ask *What time is this lesson? (At five past ten or from five past ten to ten past eleven.) What day is it? (Monday.) Is it before geography or after geography? (Before.) Is it in the*

morning or in the afternoon? (In the morning.)
- Elicit the answers from different students.

Optional activity

A less confident class could prepare for the listening by describing the other spaces in the same way *(day, time: from ... to, before/after, at)* using different time expressions, referring back to the table.

2.07 Recording and answers

We start school at nine o'clock in the morning. The first lesson is from nine to five past ten, and the second from five past ten to ten past eleven. Then we have twenty minutes' break and lessons start again at half past eleven. The fourth lesson is from five past twelve to ten past one and then we have lunch. After lunch we have one lesson from ten past two to quarter past three. On Mondays I have maths and ***French*** *before break, geography and art after break and science after lunch. On Tuesdays I start with science and then have computer studies. The third lesson is* ***English*** *and then I have maths before lunch. In the afternoon we have geography. Wednesday starts with English and* ***science****. After break we have history and German, and after lunch, my favourite – PE. On Thursday the first lesson is* ***history*** *and the second is geography. The third and fourth lessons are English and German, and after lunch we have art. On Friday I have English and science before break. It's science again after break and* ***maths*** *before lunch. And in the afternoon we have French and then it's the weekend!*

LANGUAGE WORKOUT OPTION

If you want to pre-teach the language students will be using in the following activities, you may like to go to the Language Workout box now.

5 SPEAKING

- Ask students to look at the prepositions of time in the Word Bank. Check they understand the meanings. Ask confident students to produce sentences using these prepositions.
- Read through the model questions and answers. Drill them all.
- Put students into pairs and have them take turns asking and answering questions about Adam's timetable in the same way.

Extension Go through the example dialogue with the class, then put students into pairs and ask them to compare their timetables with Adam's.

Optional activity

Divide the class into two teams and ask a series of questions, e.g. *When does Adam have English?* Insist on full sentences with correct preposition use for the teams to get points.

6 PRONUNCIATION

- Ask students to look at the stress patterns of *evening* and *history*. Ask the class to discuss the next word *languages* in pairs. Ask *Does it have two syllables or three?* Many students may guess incorrectly. Tell them to listen to the sound of each word rather than look at the letters. Play the recording and tell students to decide if the words have two or three syllables.

2.08 Recording and answers

■ ▪	*evening*	*history*	*subject*	*Wednesday*
■ ▪ ▪	*Saturday*	*languages*	*timetable*	*physical*

- Students listen and check. Play again for students to repeat the words.

Optional activity

Students put a line through the silent or unstressed letters in *diff~~e~~rent, hist~~o~~ry* and *We~~d~~n~~e~~sday*.

7 WRITING

- Ask students to interview each other using the prompts provided. Students note down their answers.
- Before students write their paragraph, elicit the verbs listed in the third person singular *(gets, has, goes, comes, has, goes)*.
- Students write a paragraph describing their partner's day. Students exchange their work for correction and to see if the information is similar.

Optional activity

Divide the class into six groups, each of which has one of the questions in exercise 7. Each group has five minutes to ask as many people as possible their question. Afterwards each group can draw a bar chart to represent the information and present it to the class, e.g. *In our survey two students get up at 7 o'clock*. They could use large card and pens if available.

Extension Students write a paragraph describing their day. Make sure they understand that this is to be a typical day and they are to describe regular activities or routines. As they work, go round and make sure they are using the present simple correctly.

LANGUAGE WORKOUT

- Ask students to look at the Language box and to complete the questions and short answers.
- Students turn to page 116 of the Language File to check their answers.

Answers
Does
do doesn't

PRACTICE

- Students do Practice exercise 10 on page 117 of the Language File. They complete questions with the correct form of *do*. Remind them that *does* is only for *he*, *she* and *it*.
- Check the answers by asking different students to read the completed questions.
- Students ask and answer the questions in pairs. Less confident students write the short answers to the questions in their notebooks first.

Answers
1 Do 2 Does 3 Do 4 Do 5 Does 6 Do

Optional activity

Students change one word in each question to make a new question, e.g. *Does your school have a break in the ~~morning~~ afternoon?* In pairs, students ask and answer their new questions.

Follow-up activity

Game *The long sentence game* See Unit 2 Lesson 2 Warmer for instructions. Use sentences e.g. *I like playing football. I like playing football and studying English.*

HOMEWORK

Students organise daily activities in their vocabulary notebooks ready for a test in the following class.

Students write six true sentences about themselves. Each sentence must include a different preposition of time.

Students make a wordsearch of ten school subjects. They can write the words across, down, forwards or backwards.

WEBLINKS

Students can play Hangman with school subjects at www.manythings.org/hmf/hm-subjects.html

Revision and Extension p47

Language File pp116–117

Workbook Unit 3 Lesson 2 pp32–33

Photocopiable notes p156, Worksheet p170

3 I never lift weights

Communicative aims	Language	Pronunciation	Vocabulary	Optional aids
Saying how often you do things	Adverbs of frequency	/ŋ/ danc<u>ing</u>	The gym Leisure activities Sport	Follow-up activity: one set of cut-up sentences per pair, one set of cut-up sentences on large pieces of card, Blu-Tack

Useful information

Hip-hop is an art form that includes deejaying, break-dancing and graffiti art. These art forms originated in the South Bronx area of New York City in the 1970s. Hip-hop dancing is an acrobatic style of dance, which includes headspins and backspins.
Jive is a rhythmical and swinging dance which was influenced by rock and roll, boogie and the African-American swing. It originated in New York around the 1940s. The dance involves kicks and flicks as well as use of the body and hips.

WARMER 1

If students have made school subject wordsearches for homework, they can swap them with a partner. Less confident students can see a list of the words they are looking for, while more confident students find the words before they see the list.

WARMER 2

Give definitions of eight words from the previous lesson. Students write the word.

WARMER 3

Students write five sentences about activities and subjects they like and don't like. Students include one false sentence. In pairs students swap their sentences and guess their partner's false sentence.

1 OPENER

- The aim is to pre-teach the vocabulary for the dialogue.
- Ask students to look at the picture and ask *Where are Katya and Emily?* (In the gym.) Write the words *go to the gym* and *do exercise* on the board. Establish the meanings. Ask if anybody goes to the gym. Ask students who do, *What activities do you do at the gym?*
- Ask the other students *Do you do exercise?* Elicit other types of exercise.
- Ask students to look at the words. Drill the pronunciation. Ask students to look at the picture with a partner and point to the words they can see. Elicit answers from individual students and check the meanings of the words not in the picture.

Answers
exercise bike, running machine

2 READING

- The aim is to introduce the adverbs of frequency *usually, sometimes, always, never, often* in context.
- Play the recording. Students read and listen. Encourage them to guess unfamiliar vocabulary from the context. Be prepared to translate *How often ...?, training session, lift (v), busy, it depends, hip-hop, jive*. If the students ask about any of the adverbs of frequency, write them at one side of the board. Once you have explained the other vocabulary, write all five adverbs of frequency on the board (*always, usually, often, sometimes, never*).

2.09 Recording
See text on page 42 of the Student's Book.

Answer
Yes

Optional activity

Ask *What is Emily wearing?* (A T-shirt, trainers, trousers.) Explain that the top is called a sports top and the trousers are called tracksuit trousers or bottoms. Ask *What is Katya wearing?* (Tracksuit bottoms, trainers, T-shirt.) Tell students to note down these words in the clothes section of their vocabulary notebooks.

3 AFTER READING

- Students read the dialogue again and correct the sentences.

Answers

1 *Emily usually comes to the gym on Monday* ***after*** *school.*
2 *Emily* ***always*** *starts on the running machine.*
3 *Emily* ***never*** *lifts weights.*
4 *Katya often goes to the gym* ***before*** *school.*
5 *The gym near Katya's flat is* ***always*** *busy in the afternoon.*
6 *Katya* ***usually*** *starts on the rowing machine.*
7 *Katya* ***always*** *goes to dance classes on Wednesday.*

Optional activity

Explain the idea of compound nouns. Ask students to find and note down examples of compound nouns in exercises 1 and 2 (*exercise bike, rowing machine, running machine, swimming pool, tennis court, training session, dance classes, dance routines*).

Your response

Encourage students to talk about whether or not they go to the gym and what they do there.

LANGUAGE WORKOUT OPTION

If you want to pre-teach the language students will be using in the following activities, you may like to go to the Language Workout box now.

4 LISTENING

- Drill the pronunciation of the phrases in the box. Ask students to match them to the pictures.
- Ask students to listen and note down how often Pierre and Emily do each activity. Play the recording. Pause after ... *I don't go swimming then.* Allow students to compare the first answer with a partner and check it as a class. Play again if necessary.
- Play the whole section for Pierre. Students compare answers in pairs. Play more than once if necessary. Elicit the first answer (*On Monday Pierre always goes swimming*). Drill this sentence in chorus for pronunciation and stress. Check the answers by asking individual students to say the answers in the same way.
- Repeat for Emily in the same way.

2.10 Recording

PIERRE *What do I do in my free time? Well, on Monday I always go swimming. On Sunday hundreds of people go to the pool and I never go swimming then. I usually play basketball on Tuesday and I sometimes play football on Wednesday evening. I often go running on Thursday morning. On Friday I usually go to the cinema after school – and on Saturday I often play volleyball.*

EMILY *I usually go running on Monday – but I hate it! I always go swimming on Tuesday. I often go shopping after school on Wednesday, but I never go shopping on Sunday. I usually play tennis on Thursday after school. I love dancing and I sometimes go dancing on Friday night. I also love movies and I always go to the cinema on Saturday night, after the gym.*

Answers

	Pierre	*How often?*	*Emily*	*How often?*
Monday	*swimming*	*always*	*running*	*usually*
Tuesday	*basketball*	*usually*	*swimming*	*always*
Wednesday	*football*	*sometimes*	*shopping*	*often*
Thursday	*running*	*often*	*tennis*	*usually*
Friday	*cinema*	*usually*	*dancing*	*sometimes*
Saturday	*volleyball*	*often*	*cinema*	*always*
Sunday	*swimming*	*never*	*shopping*	*never*

- Students work in pairs and talk about Pierre and Emily.
- Tell the class about how often you do these activities. Invite five students to do the same. Students tell a partner about their week using the nine activities.

Optional activities

- Less confident students could write down their sentences first.
- Fast finishers can talk about how often they do other activities, e.g. listen to music, watch television.

Extension Students write six sentences about their week, saying how often they do the various activities.

5 PRONUNCIATION

- Check if the students understand the words in the box.
- Play the recording, pausing for students to repeat the words.

2.11 Recording

/ŋ/ *dancing evening morning ring rowing running shopping something song swimming wrong*

Optional activity

Students think of other words with the /ŋ/ sound and note them down.

6 SPEAKING

- Ask students to look at the *Lifestyle Survey*. Check if they understand the words. Invite different students to ask you the questions so you can demonstrate the task using full sentence answers. Put the questions to individual students and ask the class which letter to write, e.g.
  T: *Do you go to bed late at the weekend?*
  S1: *I sometimes go to bed late.*
  T: *(to class) Which letter?*
  Class: S.
- Students complete the survey by asking the questions to three classmates. Listen for problems with intonation and pronunciation. Give feedback after the activity.

Extension Students use the information in their surveys to make comparisons. These can be done orally or in writing.

7 WRITING

- Students write an email to a friend about their weekend. Encourage them to add extra information where they can.

Optional activities

- ♦ Students read each other's emails to see how many things they do are the same.
- ♦ Students read their emails to another student but change one piece of information. Their partner guesses which piece of information is not true.

LANGUAGE WORKOUT

- Ask students to look at the Language box. Explain that we use adverbs of frequency to say how often we do things.
- Ask them to read the information and complete the two sentences in the box.
- Students turn to page 117 of the Language File to check their answers.

Answers
after before

PRACTICE

- Students do Practice exercise 11 on page 117 of the Language File. They rewrite sentences with the adverb in the correct position. Less confident students can note down the verbs in each sentence first.

Answers
1 *Emily **sometimes** goes to the gym at the weekend.*
2 *She **always** gets on the exercise bike after the running machine.*
3 *The training session for teenagers is **usually** great fun.*
4 *I **often** lift weights.*
5 *The gym is **never** busy in the evenings.*
6 *We **usually** swim in the pool after the gym.*

Optional activities

- ♦ Ask students to read the dialogue again and note down how often Emily and Katya go to the gym. (Emily usually goes on Monday and sometimes at the weekend. Katya often goes in the morning before school and always goes to the dance classes on Wednesday.) Ask *Who goes to the gym more – Katya or Emily?* Be prepared to translate *more*.
- ♦ Students tell each other in small groups how much exercise they do using adverbs of frequency.

Follow-up activities

- ♦ Write the dialogue from exercise 2 on the board, blanking out all the prepositions of time. Complete as a whole class.
- ♦ Cut up the following sentences and give them to students in pairs. Tell them to make two sentences that are true, e.g. *My partner never/usually does his/her homework. Our teacher is never/usually very happy.* Have the words on large pieces of cards for students to stick on the board. Invite different students to make different sentences by moving the words and have some extra cards with other activities, e.g. *goes to the gym, plays football, speaks English.*

HOMEWORK

Students interview a friend or family member using the questions from the *Lifestyle Survey* and write a paragraph about them.

Students write a paragraph about their own exercise habits.

WEBLINK

Students can learn to dance jive and salsa by copying the moves at www.jiveoholic.org.uk and www.salsa-dancing-addict.com

Revision and Extension p47

Language File p117

Workbook Unit 3 Lesson 3 pp34–35

Photocopiable notes p156, Worksheet p171

4 Integrated Skills Personal profiles

Skills

Reading Let's meet ... Lewis Hamilton! article
Listening Checking details in an email
Speaking Exchanging information
Writing Email to an epal

Learner Independence

Classroom English
Vocabulary notebook

Vocabulary

Personal information
Useful expressions

WARMER 1

Game *Back to the board* Divide the class into two teams. One person from each team sits with their back to the board facing their team. Write a word from Unit 3 on the board. The teams define the word to their teammate who guesses the word. The first person to say the word gets a point. Teams must not say the word or mime. After each word the guesser changes.

WARMER 2

Write *net, goal, ball, racket, skate* on the board. Students discuss in pairs what the connection is between the words (sport). Invite suggestions and elicit the meanings of the words.

1 OPENER

- The aim is to pre-teach the vocabulary for the following exercises. Books closed, ask students *Do you know Lewis Hamilton?* Elicit any information the students know.
- Students look at the photo on page 44 and read the words in the box. In pairs they decide which are most likely to be in the text. Establish the meaning of *race*.
- Ask students to scan the text about Lewis Hamilton to confirm their guesses.

Answers

boat car fitness gym holiday race routine star

2 READING

- The aim is to read for specific information and detail and to review expressions for giving personal information. Set a short time limit. Students note down answers individually and then compare with a partner.
- Check the answers by asking one student to ask a question and choose another student to answer it.
- Check any words in the text that students don't understand.

2.12 Recording

See text on page 44 of the Student's Book.

Answers

1 His age depends on the current year.
2 He is from Britain.
3 He has short black hair and brown eyes.
4 At race weekends he gets up early.
5 He enjoys pool, ten-pin bowling, golf and swimming.
6 He likes hip-hop, R&B, reggae, jazz, blues and rap.
7 Yes, he does.
8 He usually goes to his family's holiday home in Portugal.

3 LISTENING

- Students read the task and the letter. Check that they know what to do by asking a student to explain the instructions back to you. Ask them to predict what the incorrect information is. Suggest that they note down the mistakes as they listen. Tell them not to worry about correcting the mistakes at this stage.
- Play the recording. Students listen and note down the mistakes. They compare their answers in pairs.
- Play the recording again for students to correct the mistakes. They check their answers in pairs. Play the recording again if necessary.

2.13 Recording and answers

Hello! This is an email from your new epal. I'm ***14*** *years old and I'm from Brighton in the south of England. I have curly brown hair and blue eyes.*
I go to Brighton High School. On weekdays, I get up at 7.30 and go to school from ***9****am to 3.15pm. My favourite subject is science, but I hate* ***maths****!*
My favourite sport is ***tennis****, but I also like swimming. At weekends, I play the* ***saxophone*** *and I listen to music with my friends – we like rock and hip-hop. My friends and I always go to the cinema on Saturday, and my favourite films are* Twilight *and the Harry Potter films. We often go to the beach in the summer, and every August I go to* ***Spain*** *with my parents for a holiday.*
Please write and tell me about you and your life. Do you have a boyfriend?! I hope to hear from you soon.
Best wishes, Emily.

Optional activity

In pairs, Student A covers the text and tells Student B everything he/she remembers about Emily. Student B listens and checks in the book.

4 SPEAKING

- Students complete the questions with *How, What, When* and *Where*. Students can check their answers by looking back at page 44.

Answers
1 How 2 Where 3 What 4 When 5 What
6 What 7 What 8 What 9 Where

- Check the answers by asking individual students to say the question. Drill pronunciation of the questions for intonation and pronunciation.
- In pairs, students ask each other the questions.

5 WRITING

- The aim is to write an email to an epal using Emily's email as a model.
- Students write the first paragraph based on the answers they gave in exercise 4. After they have written it they can give it to a partner to check.
- Students write the second paragraph. Remind them that they need to end the email with something. Ask *What does Emily write?* (I hope to hear from you soon. Best wishes, Emily)
- After students have written their ending, give them a few minutes to check their email for grammar, spelling and punctuation. Then have them give it to a different student to read and check.

Optional activity

Write five incorrect sentences that you have seen on the board. Ask students to work in pairs to correct them.

6 LEARNER INDEPENDENCE

- The aim is to raise students' awareness of the fact that they can ask for help with vocabulary in English.
- Students look at the questions and match them with the answers.
- Check answers and point out that all the questions are good ways to ask for help with vocabulary in English.

Answers
1 racket 2 net 3 goal 3 skate

Optional activity

Students think of other questions they can use in the classroom. Write all good ideas on the board.

7

- The aim is to encourage students to get into the habit of recording vocabulary in English in an organised way. Ask if any students already have pages in their vocabulary notebooks with any of the following: *Food, Sport and the gym, Leisure activities, School subjects*. Praise students who have already done so and elicit different ways that students use to record the words they find. Revise the methods, e.g. by word type: verb, noun, adjective; drawing a word map; writing true personalised sentences; drawing pictures. Demonstrate a different method with each of the four categories listed in exercise 7. Elicit examples from the students until they get the idea, then let them continue in their notebooks.
- Students look back at the unit for more words to add.

8 PHRASEBOOK

- Ask students to find the expressions in Unit 3.
- Play the recording for students to listen and repeat the useful expressions.

2.14 Recording and answer
Go away! (Adam, Lesson 1)
Stop it! (Diana, Lesson 1)
How often do you come here? (Katya, Lesson 3)
Why not? (Katya, Lesson 3)
What about you? (Emily, Lesson 3)
It depends. (Katya, Lesson 3)
That sounds great! (Emily, Lesson 3)

- Read the example dialogue with a confident student. Ask students to work in pairs and write another three-line dialogue using expressions in the box.
- Ask confident pairs to act out their dialogues for the rest of the class.

Follow-up activity

Game *Word game* This can be played in teams. Say a topic word, e.g. sport or food. Give students a minute to write as many words as they can related to that topic. One point for each word, two points for an original word.

HOMEWORK

Students create a page in their vocabulary notebooks for classroom English and write the questions in exercise 6.

Students write a paragraph about a brother, sister or friend using the questions from exercise 4 as a guide.

WEBLINK

Students can discover more about Lewis Hamilton at www.lewis-hamilton-f1-driver.co.uk/lewis-hamilton-history

Revision and Extension p47

Workbook Unit 3 Lesson 4 pp36–37

Inspiration EXTRA!

LANGUAGE LINKS

- The aim of this exercise is to compare words in different languages.
- Ask students to look at the four groups of signs and decide which ones have the same meaning. Check answers and then get students to say which words seem similar.

Answers

Closed: Fermé, Geschlossen, Cerrado
Entrance: Entrée, Eingang, Entrada
Exit: Sortie, Ausgang, Salida
Open: Ouvert, Offen, Abierto

GAME WORD RACE

- Students work in pairs to answer the questions. Set a flexible time limit of five minutes.

SKETCH THE SURVEY

- The aim is for students to enjoy using their English while also getting valuable stress and intonation practice. Ask students to read and listen to the dialogue. Ask *When does the man work?* (at night).
- With a more confident class, play the recording with books closed. Then play it again with books open. With a less confident class, play the recording once while the students follow in their books, and then once again with books closed.
- Elicit possible jobs that people do at night, translating if needed, e.g. *hospital worker, security guard, taxi-driver.*

2.15 **Recording**

See text on page 46 of the Student's Book.

- Students work in pairs. Play the recording again, with one group repeating A and the other B. Encourage students to exaggerate stress and intonation.
- Ask students to close their books and play the recording again. Students work in pairs and read the sketch aloud. Choose pairs to act out the sketch in front of the class.

Optional activity

Make an audio or video recording of students performing the sketch.

REVISION

Lesson 1
Students' own answers

Lesson 2
Read through the example and tell students to use the prompts to write questions. Fast finishers can write their own questions. Students ask and answer the questions with a partner.

Answers

Do you walk to school every day? Yes, I do. / No, I don't.
Do we have a short break in the morning? Yes, we do. / No, we don't.
Do you do drama after school? Yes, I do. / No, I don't.
Do we have maths on Monday? Yes, we do. / No, we don't.
Do you go to bed at ten o'clock? Yes, I do. / No, I don't.

Lesson 3
Students' own answers

Lesson 4
Remind students to use the information from the corrected email in exercise 3 on page 45, not the original one.

Answers

1 *I'm 14 years old.*
2 *I'm from Brighton.*
3 *I have curly brown hair and blue eyes.*
4 *On weekdays, I get up at 7.30.*
5 *My favourite subject is science.*
6 *My favourite sport is tennis, but I also like swimming.*
7 *I like rock and hip-hop music.*
8 *My favourite films are* Twilight *and the* Harry Potter *films.*
9 *I often go to the beach in the summer, and every August I go to Spain with my parents for a holiday.*

EXTENSION

Lessons 1–4
Students' own answers

YOUR CHOICE!

The aim is to give students more learner independence and help them to identify their preferred ways of learning. Encourage students to choose an activity that they feel less comfortable with if they want a challenge or are aware that they need practice in a particular area.
Sports Star Poster gives students the opportunity to write about their favourite sports star and produce an illustrated poster.
Food Memory Chain gives students the opportunity to practise food vocabulary and improve their memories.

Language File pp116–p117

Workbook Unit 3 Inspiration EXTRA! pp38–39

Take two teenagers ... north and south

Useful information

Tallinn is the capital and the largest city of Estonia. It has a population of around 415,000 people and is situated in the north-west of the country on the Gulf of Finland. The main tourist attractions are the medieval old town with its ancient city wall, cobblestone streets and gothic church spires and the Estonian Open Air Museum.
Buenos Aires is the capital and the largest city of Argentina. It is situated in the east of the country on the shores of the Rio de la Plata estuary. The city was founded in 1536 by Spanish explorer Pedro de Mendoza. It is a centre for culture with a famous opera house and numerous museums, arts centres and galleries.

1 OPENER

- The aim is to arouse the students' interest in the context of the two texts. Ask students to look at the maps and to say which country is in the north and which in the south.

Answers
Estonia is in the north and Argentina is in the south.

2 READING

- Ask students to cover the texts and look at the photos. Ask if anybody knows the places (Tallinn, Estonia; Buenos Aires, Argentina). Invite students to describe the appearance of the two teenagers.
- Read through the instructions. Elicit possible ideas for each topic, e.g. *school* – favourite subjects, *leisure activities* – play tennis, go shopping.
- Play the first part of the recording. Students listen and read about Piret, and match the topics with the four paragraphs. They compare with a partner.
- Check the answers orally as a whole class.
- Play the second recording. Students listen and read about Emiliano, and match the topics with the four paragraphs. Again, they compare with a partner.
- Check the answers orally as a whole class.

2.16 Recording
See texts on pages 48 and 49 of the Student's Book.

Answers
Piret: Paragraph 1: Family, Paragraph 2: School, Paragraph 3: Food, Paragraph 4: Leisure activities
Emiliano: Paragraph 1: Family, Paragraph 2: School, Paragraph 3: Food, Paragraph 4: Leisure activities

3

- Check that the students understand all the questions. They read the text and note down their answers. They then compare answers in pairs.
- Check the answers orally, inviting volunteers to say the answers. Insist on full sentences, e.g. *Who lives in Argentina? Emiliano lives in Argentina.* Make sure students are pronouncing the third person *s*.

Answers
1 Emiliano 2 Piret 3 Emiliano 4 Piret
5 Emiliano 6 Piret 7 Emiliano 8 Piret
9 Emiliano 10 Emiliano 11 Piret 12 Emiliano

Optional activity

Game *45-second Challenge* In groups of four, students take it in turns to speak about one of the topics in exercise 2 for 45 seconds without excessive hesitation. Less confident students can make notes before speaking but they must not read their notes.

4 VOCABULARY

- Ask students to look at the compass. Explain that we use a compass to find the direction. Explain that the four directions are called compass points. Ask students to find the four directions in the text. Check the answers orally with the class.

Answers
Clockwise: north, east, south, west

Optional activities

- Suggest a way of remembering the compass points. Write *No English Studies at Weekends.* Invite students to work in pairs to think of a similar way of remembering the compass points. Put students' sentences on the board. Students vote for their favourite sentence.
- Draw a compass on the board and elicit the four points. Ask a student to come to the board and show you where *south-east* is. Tell the students to guess the other three half-points (*clockwise: north-east, south-west, north-west*). Invite students to write the answers on the board.

5

- Students could find the words individually or you could make it a team game where the first team to write down all the words wins.

Answers
- *rollerblading, tennis, skiing (text 1); gymnastics, football (text 2)*
- *jeans, sweatshirt, pullover, trainers (text 1); shorts, trousers, T-shirt (text 2)*
- *soup, potatoes, meatballs (text 1); meat, salad, fruit, pizza (text 2)*
- *biology, art, music, German, Estonian (text 1); science, Spanish, geography, computer studies, gymnastics (text 2); maths, English, history (both texts)*

Optional activity

Students add new words to their vocabulary notebooks.

6 SPEAKING

- Read the model sentence *They both live in flats* and elicit the meaning. Ask which word means the information is the same (*both*).
- Read the second sentence *Piret lives in a small flat*, but *Emiliano lives in a big flat* and elicit the meaning. Ask which word means the information is different (*but*).
- Drill the pronunciation of the two sentences.
- In pairs students compare the teenagers' lives. For a less confident class, elicit some examples orally from the more confident students before they speak in pairs.

Optional activity

Ask students to write sentences comparing the two teenagers. Set a 15-minute time limit.

7 MINI-PROJECT LIFESTYLE

- Students write sentences comparing their own lives with that of either Piret or Emiliano. Go through the example sentence first and ask students to complete it. Then ask them to write further sentences. Remind them to use *both* if the information is the same and *but* if it is different. Go round, monitoring and assisting where necessary.

WEBLINK

For maps and satellite images of Estonia and Argentina visit www.intute.ac.uk/worldguide/worldmap.html

Workbook Culture pp40–41

How many ghosts are there?

Communicative Aims	Language	Pronunciation	Vocabulary	Optional aids
Describing places and facilities	*there is/are*	Intonation in questions	Tourist attractions Classroom	Follow-up activities: cards for Vocabulary box

WARMER 1

Game *Teacher* See Unit 1, Lesson 3 Warmer for instructions. Play with words connected to school or use the list in exercise 7 on page 51.

WARMER 2

Draw students' attention to the title of Unit 4: *Sightseeing*. Establish the meaning of *sightseeing* (visiting the famous places in a city) and the meaning of *sight* (the famous places themselves). Ask *What are the famous sights in London/Paris/New York?* In pairs, students think of interesting places in their town, city (or a city nearby). Write them on the board. Students decide which three places in their town/city would be interesting for a visitor.

1 OPENER

- The aim is to encourage students to predict before reading. Ask students to look at the photos on page 50 with their hand covering the text. Ask if anyone knows what place is in the photo (Brighton). Ask them to describe what they can see.
- Ask students to look at the words in the box. Drill the pronunciation and check comprehension. Students note down the words they expect to find in the text.

Answers

aquarium, attractions, beach, history, museum, sea, sharks, (paragraph 2)
ghosts (paragraph 3)
pier, tourists (paragraph 4)

2 READING

- The aim is to introduce vocabulary for tourist attractions and the expressions *there is/there are* in context.
- Play the recording. Students read and listen. Encourage them to guess unfamiliar vocabulary from the context. Be prepared to explain *something for everyone, underwater tunnel, narrow, scary, funfair, rides*.
- Establish which of the words listed in the opener were used and ask students to match the attractions (in bold in the text) with the photos.
- Ask the class how Brighton is different from their town/city.

2.17 **Recording**

See text on page 50 of the Student's Book.

Answers

Main picture: Palace Pier
Clockwise from top left: water sports, ghost walk, The Lanes, Sea Life Centre, Brighton Museum and Art Gallery

Optional activity

With a more confident class, play the recording twice with books closed. The first time they listen, students check which of the words listed in the opener were used. The second time they listen, students take notes of things to see and do in Brighton and match them with the photos. Check the answers after each stage with the whole class.

3 AFTER READING

- Students match the questions and answers. Make sure they understand that one answer is not needed.
- Check the answers by inviting one student to ask the question and another to give the answer. Ask students to give you extra information where appropriate, e.g. *Is there an aquarium in Brighton? Yes, there is. It is called the Sea Life Centre.*

Answers

1 g 2 e 3 b 4 a 5 f 6 d
Extra answer: c

Optional activity

Give students three minutes to memorise all they can from the text, then close their books. Read the text including some false information, e.g. *Brighton is in the north of England*. Students shout *Stop!* when they hear incorrect information and correct it.

Your response

Ask students to discuss in pairs whether they would like to visit Brighton or not. They then report to the class. Encourage them to give reasons, citing attractions in the text they would or would not like to visit.

LANGUAGE WORKOUT OPTION

If you want to pre-teach the language students will be using in the following activities, you may like to go to the Language Workout box now.

4 SPEAKING

- Ask students to look at the photos on page 50. Drill the first pair of example sentences for pronunciation and stress.
- In pairs students identify which of the items in the box are in the photos and how many there are of each. Invite students to say an affirmative sentence about the photos.
- Drill the second pair of sentences in chorus for pronunciation and stress.
- Students tell their partners what isn't in the photo using *there isn't/there aren't*. Remind students to use the article *a/an* for singular items and *any* for plural items.
- Invite different students to say a negative sentence.

Answers

There's a beach. There are lots of chairs. There are lots of people. There's a museum. There are lots of shops. There are bags.
There isn't a bicycle. There aren't any boats. There isn't a café. There aren't any cars. There isn't a cinema. There aren't any ghosts. There isn't a restaurant. There isn't a school. There aren't any trees. There isn't an umbrella.

Extension Go through the example questions and answers with the class. Then ask them to close their books. Put them in pairs and get them to take turns asking and answering about the things in the photos.

5 PRONUNCIATION

- Students listen to the intonation and decide if it is rising or falling.

2.18 Recording and answers

1 There's a famous pier. ↓
2 Are there any tourists? ↑
3 Is there a restaurant? ↑
4 There isn't a school. ↓
5 How many shops are there? ↑

- Play the recording again for students to practise copying the speaker's intonation.

6 LISTENING

- The aim is to listen for specific information. The text also contains the expressions for making suggestions *Let's ..., What about ...* and ways to respond and give opinions: *I think x is/isn't (really) boring, I want to ..., I really don't like ..., Great!* For suggested ways to exploit these see the Follow-up activities.
- Ask students to read the sentences and check the meaning of *boring*.
- Play the recording. Students listen and complete the sentences with the names. Allow students time to compare with a partner before playing it again.

2.19 Recording

MR WARD *Right everyone, can you listen please? Here are four great Brighton attractions. There isn't time to see them all, so let's choose two. So first, this is the Brighton Museum & Art Gallery. As you can see there are lots of pictures there, and you can find out about the history of the city ... Er, yes Teresa?*
TERESA *I'm sorry, Mr Ward, but I think museums are really boring.*
MR WARD *Thank you, Teresa. I see. Well, ghosts aren't boring and the Brighton ghost walks are really popular. What about an evening walk and some stories about the city's ghosts?*
PIERRE *Great! Yes, please.*
MR WARD *Right, Pierre. Then this is a picture of the Sea Life Centre. It's the oldest aquarium in the world! There are all kinds of fish, and of course there are huge sharks. Yes, Jake?*
JAKE *I really don't like sharks, Mr Ward – I think they're scary.*
MR WARD *OK, Jake. Well, let's see. There's one place here I know you'll like, and that's the Palace Pier. Here's a picture of it. And you can go on the rides at the funfair – it's a great place to visit.*
KATYA *Yes, let's go there!*
MR WARD *OK, Katya! That's the Ghost Walk tonight and the pier tomorrow.*

Answers

1 Teresa 2 Pierre 3 Jake 4 Katya

7 VOCABULARY

- The aim is for students to practise using the grammar structures learned in this lesson.
- Read the instruction and drill the words in the box in chorus for pronunciation and stress. Check the meaning of any unknown words. If you have dictionaries, allow students to look up the words and tell each other the meanings.
- Model the two questions inviting answers from the class. Drill the questions and answers.
- Students ask and answer questions about their classroom. Remind the students to include extra information about size and colour.

8 WRITING

- Students write a short paragraph describing their classroom. They exchange their paragraphs for correction.

Extension Go through the example with the class. Then ask students to work in pairs and take turns choosing things in their classroom and saying how many there are. Their partner has to complete the sentence with the name of the item.

LANGUAGE WORKOUT

- Ask students to look at the Language box and explain that we use *there is/are* for describing things that are in a place. Give examples of things in the classroom, e.g. *There is a teacher; There are some students.*
- Ask students to complete the sentences in the box. Confident students can complete first and then check while others can look back at exercise 2 and then complete.
- Students turn to page 117 of the Language File Summary to check their answers.

Answers
There are isn't There there many, are there

- Highlight that:
  - we use *there is* before singular nouns and *there are* before plural nouns
  - after *there is* we use the singular article *a/an*.
  - after *there are* we use plural expressions, e.g. *five, lots of, some*
  - in *yes/no* questions and negatives with plural objects we use *any*
  - we do not contract *there are* to *there're*.
- Drill the examples in chorus for pronunciation and stress.

Optional activity

Describe a place familiar to the students using *there is/are*, e.g. *There is grass, there are students playing, there are two goals.* Students guess the place (*football pitch*). Once the students have guessed, write the place on the board and elicit the description back from the class. Students can continue playing in pairs.

PRACTICE

- Students do Practice exercises 12 and 13 on page 117 of the Language File.
- Students complete the sentences in exercise 12 with *there is/are* or *there isn't/aren't*. Students check their answers in pairs.

Answers
1 isn't 2 are 3 aren't 4 is 5 are

- Students complete the questions in exercise 13 with *Is/Are there* and answer them. They check their answers in pairs.

Answers
1 Is there; Yes, there is. / No, there isn't.
2 Are there; Yes, there are. / No, there aren't.
3 Are there; Yes, there are. / No, there aren't.
4 Is there; Yes, there is. / No, there isn't.
5 are there; There are ...

Optional activity

Students write five questions about their partner's *bedroom/living room/house*. Students ask and answer the questions. Students write a paragraph about their partner using the replies from the questions.

Follow-up activities

- ♦ Students write a similar dialogue in threes with three characters: one teacher and two students. The dialogue could be based around the students' town/city or one that they know.
- ♦ **Game** *Twenty questions* Students play in groups of four. One student thinks of a place and the other three take it in turns to ask *Is there/Are there ... in this place?* e.g. *Is there a famous building in this place? Are there English people in this place?* Put the four short answers on the board *Yes, there is/are, No, there isn't/aren't.* Students have up to 20 questions to guess the place and win a point. If they don't guess correctly, the student thinking of a place wins a point and thinks of another place.
- ♦ If you have a Vocabulary box, ask students to choose ten new words from the lesson and write a vocabulary card for each word.

HOMEWORK

Students write a paragraph about their town/city in the style of an information leaflet, decorating it with drawings and pictures if possible.

Students organise vocabulary from the lesson in their vocabulary books for a test in the following class.

WEBLINKS

Students can visit all the sites mentioned in this lesson and other attractions in Brighton at www.visitbrighton.com

Revision and Extension p59

Language File p117

Workbook Unit 4 Lesson 1 pp42–43

Photocopiable notes p157, Worksheet p172

She's wearing a long grey coat

Communicative aims	Language	Pronunciation	Vocabulary
Describing what's happening now (1)	Present continuous: affirmative	/ʌ/ come /əʊ/ home	Activities

Useful information

A ghost called the Grey Lady is said to haunt the Theatre Royal in Brighton. She is said to make regular appearances in the dressing room and occasionally in the theatre itself. The story goes that it is the ghost of the famous actress Sarah Bernhardt. One day a cleaner working in the building saw the ghost walk past her and disappear into a blank wall. It was later discovered that this was the location of an old doorway, now bricked-up, which led to the original ticket office for the cheaper seats. Many actors and actresses have seen this ghost, yet none of the sightings seem to be scary; the general opinion is that she is harmless.

WARMER 1

Give students a short test on vocabulary from the last lesson. If you have a Vocabulary box, choose words from the box. Give students definitions and ask them to write down the word. Check their answers and spelling.

WARMER 2

Game *Verb race* Divide the class into three teams. Divide the board into three columns. One person from each team runs to the board and writes a verb in their column and passes the pen to a different teammate who thinks of another verb, runs to the board and writes it, and so on. No team may repeat a verb already on the board. The team with the most correctly spelled verbs after two minutes is the winner.

1 OPENER

- The aim is to introduce the context for the dialogue in exercise 2. Students describe the photo. Help with vocabulary if necessary.

2 READING

- The aim is to introduce the present continuous affirmative in context.
- Play the recording. Students read and listen. Be prepared to translate *scared*, *learning lines*.
- Ask them to say why Adam is scared.

2.20 Recording

See text on page 52 of the Student's Book.

Answer

He thinks the woman coming out of the theatre is a ghost.

Optional activity

Students act out the dialogue in groups of five. Encourage them to be dramatic.

3 AFTER READING

- Students read and listen to the dialogue again and decide if the sentences are true or false. More confident students can answer the questions from memory before checking with the text. Ask them to note down the words in the text that helped them to decide on their answers.
- Check the answers before students write the corrections for the false sentences. Ask students to read their answers to the class.

Answers

1 False. The ghost at the theatre is called the Grey Lady.
2 True
3 False. She is holding a red book.
4 False. She is speaking.
5 True

Optional activity

Ask more comprehension questions about the dialogue. *Is there a ghost in the picture? What is the actor doing?*

Your response

Take a vote to see how many people believe in ghosts.

LANGUAGE WORKOUT OPTION

If you want to pre-teach the language students will be using in the following activities, you may like to go to the Language Workout box now.

4 GAME

- Demonstrate the game with an object that the students are familiar with. If a student guesses correctly, allow him/her to come to the front and choose an object. Drill the example questions and answers with the whole class. Students play in groups of four taking it in turns to mime holding an object.

5 PRONUNCIATION

- Say *come* and *home*. Ask *What's the difference in the pronunciation of the letter 'o'?*
- Play the first part of the recording, pausing after each word for students to repeat.

2.21 Recording

/ʌ/ ***come*** *colour* *love* *mother* *worry*
/əʊ/ ***home*** *coast* *coat* *ghost* *hold*

- Students copy the two columns into their notebooks. Play the second part of the recording and have them write the words in the correct column and compare their answers in pairs.
- Check by asking individual students to put the words in the right column.

2.21 Recording

brother *comb* *hope* *month*
old *one* *photo* *son*

Answers

/ʌ/ ***come*** *brother* *month* *one* *son*
/əʊ/ ***home*** *comb* *hope* *old* *photo*

LANGUAGE WORKOUT OPTION

If you want to pre-teach the language students will be using in the following activities, you may like to go to the Language Workout box now.

6 SPEAKING

- Ask students to look at the two pictures and describe the differences using the words in the box. Point out that when we describe what is happening in a picture we use the present continuous.
- Students continue saying sentences in pairs until they have found the ten differences.
- Check the answers by asking different students to say each pair.

Answers

1 *In picture A the man is wearing a white shirt. In picture B he's wearing a blue shirt.*
2 *In picture A the man's wearing brown shoes. In picture B, he's wearing black shoes.*
3 *In picture A the man's drawing the woman. In picture B he's painting a picture of the woman.*
4 *In picture A the woman is wearing a dark blue skirt. In picture B she's wearing a purple skirt.*
5 *In picture A the woman is wearing a red jacket. In picture B, she is wearing a dark green jacket.*
6 *In picture A the woman is singing. In picture B she's playing the piano.*
7 *In picture A the ghost is holding a book. In picture B he's holding his head.*
8 *In picture A the ghost is wearing white clothes. In picture B, he's wearing grey clothes.*
9 *In picture A the ghost is standing to the left of the window. In picture B he's standing to the right.*
10 *In picture A the ghost is looking at the man. In picture B he's looking at the woman.*

7 WRITING

- Ask students to look back at the photo on pages 6–7 and read the description of Teresa on page 53. Ask students to write sentences describing the other characters.

Answers

Teresa is standing on the right. She's wearing a pink top, blue jeans and gold sandals.
Mr Ward is standing on the left. He's wearing a red, blue and black (checked) shirt and black jeans.
Emily is standing next to Mr Ward. She's wearing a red top, blue trousers and white trainers.
Adam is standing next to Emily. He's wearing a purple T-shirt, blue jeans and brown shoes.
Katya is standing between Adam and Pierre. She's wearing a pink top, blue jeans and white shoes.
Pierre is standing next to Katya. He's wearing a blue T-shirt, blue jeans and black trainers.
Jake is standing between Pierre and Teresa. He's wearing a green T-shirt, black jeans and black trainers.

Extension Students read out their sentences from exercise 7 for the other students to guess from memory who the person being described is. They can look back at the book to check.

LANGUAGE WORKOUT

- Ask students to look at the Language box and explain that we use the present continuous for talking about things that are happening *now*. It is also often used to describe what is happening in pictures. Explain that the present continuous is formed with an auxiliary verb *be* (present simple) and the *-ing* form of the verb. Give some examples, e.g. *I am speaking. You are listening.* Explain that we can use the present continuous to describe what people are wearing. Elicit what you are wearing from the class.
- Ask students to complete the sentences in the box. Students turn to page 117 of the Language File to check their answers.

Answers
are *I'm*
is *He's*
are *speaking*

- Drill the sentences in chorus for pronunciation and stress.

PRACTICE

- Students do Practice exercise 14 on page 118 of the Language File.
- Go through the example sentence with the class. Students write sentences using the affirmative form of the present continuous, paying careful attention to the punctuation marks in each sentence.
- Check the answers by asking different students to read out their sentences.

Answers
1 *The guide is talking to the group.*
2 *The girls are watching the woman.*
3 *She is walking out of the theatre.*
4 *Katya is laughing at Adam.*
5 *I am doing this exercise.*
6 *We are learning English.*
7 *You are wearing a nice top.*
8 *The phone is ringing.*

Optional activities

- ♦ Ask the students to write the answers again, this time using contractions.
- ♦ Individually, students write two sentences using the present continuous about what two people in the class are wearing. Tell students to use the pronouns *he/she* instead of the name. Students give their sentences to another student who guesses the identity of the two people.
- ♦ Ask students to look back at the dialogue on page 52 and find other examples of the present continuous.

Follow-up activity

Individually, students write two sentences using the present continuous about people in the class. They then mix up the word order and give the sentences to a partner, who must re-order them. Write an example on the board, e.g. *board looking David at is the.*

HOMEWORK

Students find a photo or picture in a magazine with several people doing different things and write three sentences about three people: where they are, what they are wearing and what they are doing. E.g. *He is at the beach. He's wearing brown shorts, a red T-shirt and sunglasses. He's running on the sand.* Other students guess which person in the picture is being described in the next class.

WEBLINK

Students could visit: http://website.lineone.net/~frankparker/sussex_ghosts.htm for more stories about ghosts in Brighton.

Revision and Extension p59

Language File pp117–118

Workbook Unit 4 Lesson 2 pp44–45

Photocopiable notes p157, Worksheet p173

3 What's she doing?

Communicative aims	Language	Pronunciation	Vocabulary	Optional aids
Describing what's happening now (2)	Present continuous: negative, questions and short answers	Silent letters	Parts of the body	Warmer 1: small cards Follow-up activity: Pictionary: cards with words for people/ animals and actions

WARMER 1

Game *What am I doing?* Prepare some cards with activities, e.g. *drinking a cup of tea, swimming* written on. Tell the students they have to guess what you are doing. Mime one of the actions and elicit guesses. Write the full answer on the board, e.g. *You're swimming.* Different students come to the front and mime the other cards for the class to guess.

WARMER 2

If the students did the homework from the previous lesson, they can work in pairs taking it in turns to read a description while their partner guesses which person it is about.

1 OPENER

- The aim is to prepare the vocabulary for the following exercises. Ask students to look at the words in the box. Drill the words for pronunciation and stress. Ask students to look at the photos on page 54 and to identify as many of the words as they can. After they have compared answers in pairs, check any vocabulary questions. Elicit the answers from the students in the form *There is/There are* … Afterwards, ask about the words they didn't say, eliciting *There isn't a … There aren't any …*

Answers

There are arms in photos A, B and C.
There aren't any books in the photos.
There are feet in photos A, B and C.
There isn't a football in the photos.
There are hands in photos A, B and C.
There is a helmet in photo B.
There is a menu in photo A.
There isn't a phone in the photos.
There are shorts in photo C.
There are two signs in photo A.
There isn't a television in the photos.

Optional activities

- More confident students could be asked to tell you *where* the things are in the pictures.
- Students tell you what the people are doing in the pictures using the present continuous.

2 READING

- The aim is to introduce the present continuous question and short answer forms in context.
- Play the recording. Students read and listen. Encourage them to guess unfamiliar vocabulary from the context. Be prepared to translate *in the air, yoga, hungry*.
- Play the recording again. This time students match the dialogues with the pictures. Ask them to point at the things as they hear them.

Answers

1 B 2 C 3 A

2.22 Recording

See text on page 54 of the Student's Book.

Optional activities

- With a less confident class, elicit descriptions of the three pictures before playing the recording.
- With a more confident class tell the students to cover the text, listen to the recording and then match the conversations with the photos.

3 AFTER READING

- Put students in pairs. Ask them to take turns asking and answering about what the people in the photos are doing.

Your response

Ask students to discuss the questions in pairs and to report back to the class.

4 VOCABULARY

- Drill the words in the Word Bank in chorus for pronunciation and stress.
- Ask students to match the words to the numbers on the picture. They then compare answers in pairs.
- Play the recording for students to check their answers.

2.23 Recording and answers

1 head 2 hair 3 eye 4 ear 5 nose 6 face
7 mouth 8 teeth 9 arm 10 hand 11 thumb
12 finger 13 knee 14 leg 15 foot 16 toe

Optional activities

- **Game** *Teacher says* Tell students to touch parts of their body when you say *Teacher says*, e.g. *Teacher says touch your elbow*. If you don't say *Teacher says* first, e.g. *Touch your foot*, and they do so, they are out and become a judge. For more confident students you can include other instructions, e.g. *stand up, sit down, put your right hand up/down*.
- Ask the students to tell a partner how many of each body part they have. Ask *Which part is difficult to count?* (Hair.) This could be a good moment to explain the concept of an uncountable noun.

5 SPEAKING

- Hold up the book, point to one of the body parts on the picture of the boy and ask *What am I pointing at?* Repeat with two other parts. Drill the question. Students take turns pointing at the picture and asking their partner the question.

Extension Students match the parts of the body with the relevant verbs. Accept any answers that students can justify; for example, they may point out that you can hold something in your mouth and some people can walk on their hands.

Answers

mouth/teeth – eat
ear – hear
hand/finger/thumb – hold
finger/thumb – point
leg/feet – run
eye – see
nose – smell
head – think
leg/feet – walk

6 PRONUNCIATION

- Ask students to look at the words in the box. Ask if anyone can remember where in the book they came across the first word *comb*. (In Unit 1 Lesson 1.) Write the word *comb* on the board and elicit the pronunciation. Elicit which letter is not pronounced, ie silent *b*.
- Play the recording, stopping after each word for students to repeat. Ask students to think about the silent letters in each word.
- Students cross out the silent letters in each word. Play the recording again for students to check. Write the words on the board and invite students to cross out a silent letter.

2.24 **Recording and answers**

comb ghost guide knee right sign
talk thumb walk

7 LISTENING

- Ask students to read through the possible answers. Invite more confident students to demonstrate any unknown vocabulary using a mime.
- Ask students to listen to the recording and identify what the people are doing. Students compare answers in pairs. Elicit the answers in full sentences.

2.25 **Recording**

Sound effects:
1 Saxophone
2 Typing on a keyboard
3 Playing tennis
4 Cleaning teeth
5 Swimming
6 Eating

Answers

1 Emily is playing the saxophone.
2 Jake is using a computer.
3 Pierre and Adam are playing tennis.
4 Katya is cleaning her teeth.
5 Mr Ward is swimming.
6 Mr and Mrs Fry are having lunch.

Optional activity

Less confident students write down a complete sentence about each person before giving the answers.

- Ask students to look at the two model questions and say how they are different (the first starts with an auxiliary and the second starts with *What*).
- Ask the questions and write the two answers on the board. Elicit the difference between the answers (the first is a short *yes/no* answer and the second is a full sentence). Elicit the equivalent questions and answers for question 3 (*Are Pierre and Adam singing? No, they aren't. What are Pierre and Adam doing? They are playing tennis*).
- In pairs, one student asks the *yes/no* question and the other asks the open *What ...?* question. After three questions they swap and repeat.

8 WRITING

- Students write sentences about the people in exercise 7, following the example given.

Optional activity

Fast finishers write sentences about other students in the class.

Extension Demonstrate the activity first. Then invite students in turn to come to the front and mime a sports activity. The rest of the class have to guess what it is, using *Are you ...ing?* The miming student replies with *Yes, I am* or *No, I'm not.*

LANGUAGE WORKOUT

- Ask students to look at the Language box and elicit the use of the present continuous (for talking about things that are happening *now*). Draw attention to the position of *not* between auxiliary and verb as well as the reversal of subject and auxiliary to make the question.
- Ask students to complete the sentences. Students turn to pages 117–118 of the Language File to check their answers.

Answers
is *aren't* *aren't*
Are *I'm* *are* *is*
Are

- Drill the sentences in chorus for pronunciation and stress.

Optional activity

Ask students to write three more questions about the pictures on page 54. Students exchange sentences and write the short answers.

Follow-up activities

- Write jumbled questions on the board about students in the class using the present continuous, e.g. *Maria is tennis playing? Stephan doing homework is his?* Students order them in their notebooks and ask their partner the questions, writing short answers.
- **Game** *Pictionary* See Unit 1 Lesson 1 for instructions. Here have combinations of a person or an animal plus an action in the continuous form, e.g. *a horse jumping, an elephant swimming.*

PRACTICE

- Students do Practice exercise 15 on page 118 of the Language File. They complete the sentences with the present continuous. Remind students to notice the subject of each sentence. Students compare in pairs.
- Ask different students to read out a sentence.

Answers
1 *Where are we going?*
2 *Are you feeling hungry? Yes, I am.*
3 *Is the man cooking? No, he isn't.*
4 *Is he selling fish and chips? Yes, he is.*
5 *What is the girl doing?*
6 *She isn't running.*
7 *Is she going fast? Yes, she is.*
8 *The people aren't dancing.*

HOMEWORK

Students find some family photos and write sentences about them, e.g. *In this photo I'm sitting next to my sister. She is wearing a blue top and holding a blue bag. We are sitting in a park. My father is taking the photo.* Students can also do this with pictures from magazines.

WEBLINK

Students may enjoy playing the game hangman at this site: www.manythings.org/hmf/8972.html

Revision and Extension p59

Language File pp117–118

Workbook Unit 4 Lesson 3 pp46–47

Photocopiable notes p157, Worksheet p174

Integrated Skills Describing places and activities

Skills

Reading The Treasure of Tutenkhamun article
Listening Phone calls: describing rooms
Speaking Describing a room
Writing Email to an epal

Learner Independence

Classroom English
Vocabulary notebook
Phrasebook

Vocabulary

Furniture and fittings
Useful expressions

Optional aids

Warmer 3: pieces of paper with sticky tape

WARMER 1

If you set the homework in the previous lesson, stick the students' photos on the board and write a number next to each one. Students take it in turns to read out a sentence describing what the people in the photo are doing and what they are wearing. Other students listen and guess which photo is being described. This could be played as a team game.

WARMER 2

Give students a short test on vocabulary from Units 1–4. If you have a Vocabulary box, take words from the box. Give students definitions and ask them to write down the word. Check their answers and spelling.

WARMER 3

Game *Label me* Put students in groups of five. Nominate one student as the model. All the models stand at the front of the class. Give each group 15 pieces of paper with sticky tape. The team writes a part of the body on each piece of paper and sticks the label onto their model's relevant body part. Provide dictionaries if necessary.

1 OPENER

- The aim is to pre-teach the vocabulary for the activities to follow.
- Drill the pronunciation of the words in the box. Ask students to look at the pictures and find the things listed. If they don't know a word, they can use a dictionary or ask. Students compare answers in pairs. Hold up the book and point at different things asking *What's this?/What are these?* to check the answers.

Optional activity

Tell the class that some of the things in the box are in your room at home. Put the prompts *Is/Are there a/an/any ...?* on the board. Invite students to ask you questions. Then, in pairs, students talk about their own rooms and answer questions. Remind students to use *a/an* for singular objects and *some* or a number for plural objects. Less confident students can write down their sentences and questions before speaking.

2 READING

- Tell the students to read the text before reading the statements. Play the recording for students to listen while they read.
- Ask students to read the text again and decide if sentences 1–5 are true or false. Ask them to note down the words in the text that help them decide on their answers.
- Check the answers orally with the class before asking students to write the corrections for the false sentences.

2.26 Recording

See text on page 56 of the Student's Book.

Answers

1 *True*
2 *False. There are clothes and everyday objects and there is jewellery.*
3 *No information. There are objects which are over 5,000 years old, but we don't know if these are beds and chairs.*
4 *No information. There are games and musical instruments in the museum. It is highly unlikely that you would be able to play them, but the text doesn't actually say whether you can or not.*
5 *True*

Optional activity

Students write more true/false questions about the text and test each other in small groups.

3 LISTENING

- Ask students to look at pictures A, B and C and explain that Teresa and Pierre are in two of the rooms. Ask students to read the questions.
- Play the first conversation once. Allow students a minute to discuss possible answers. Play the recording again. Students listen and note down the answers to the questions. They compare their answers in pairs. Do the same with the second conversation. Finally play both conversations again to check the answers.
- Ask students to justify their answers by repeating lines from the conversation that they remember. Put these on the board to help support less confident students in exercise 4.

2.27 Recording

Phone Call 1

TERESA *Hello.*
JAKE *Hello. Is that Teresa?*
TERESA *Speaking.*
JAKE *Hi, Teresa. It's Jake. How are you?*
TERESA *Fine, thanks. And you?*
JAKE *Yes, great. Where are you and what are you doing?*
TERESA *I'm at Emily's house and I'm reading a magazine on my bed. I'm sharing a bedroom with Katya.*
JAKE *Oh, what's your room like?*
TERESA *It's a lovely big room – there are two beds and a red wardrobe. There's a laptop computer. And there are lots of pictures on the walls.*
JAKE *What kind of pictures?*
TERESA *There are pictures of flowers, and there's a big picture of a horse …*
JAKE *Oh, sorry, Teresa. It's time for dinner. Mrs Ward is calling me.*
TERESA *OK – see you tomorrow. Bye.*
JAKE *Bye!*

Phone Call 2

PIERRE *Hello?*
EMILY *Hi, Pierre! It's Emily. How are things?*
PIERRE *Fine – and with you?*
EMILY *I'm OK yeah. We're cooking a meal.*
PIERRE *Great!*
EMILY *What are you doing?*
PIERRE *I'm listening to music in Adam's bedroom – it's my bedroom too now.*
EMILY *Really? What's it like?*
PIERRE *Well, there are two beds and there's a TV. We can watch TV when we go to bed. Adam has lots of books and magazines. There's a wardrobe and there are posters of whales and other animals on the walls. Oh yes, and there's a desk where Adam does his homework. Oh! Wait a minute … OK, I'm coming. Sorry, Emily. I can't talk any more now. Adam's mum wants me to help her. See you.*
EMILY *OK. See you, Pierre.*

Answers
1 *Jake*
2 *She is reading a magazine on her bed.*
3 *C*
4 *Emily*
5 *He is listening to music in his (and Adam's) bedroom.*
6 *A*

4 SPEAKING

- Ask the students to look at the picture of the room which Teresa and Pierre did not describe (B). Elicit some phrases to describe the room, e.g. *There is/are …* In pairs, students take turns to say a sentence about the room. Prompt them to use colour, opinion and size adjectives as well as the vocabulary from exercise 1.
- Put the students into threes. One student describes one of the rooms and the other two guess which one it is. Monitor, noting down any common errors. Put these on the board at the end of the activity for class correction.

Optional activity

Students describe a room in their house. Their partner guesses which one it is.

5 WRITING

- Tell students they are going to write an email to an epal describing their room at home and what they are doing. Explain that they will need to imagine they are at home.
- Establish the difference between an epal and a penfriend. Ask students if they have epals or penfriends.
- Invite three students to read the questions. Explain that they should include the answers to these questions in their email. Remind them to start with a greeting and to put a suitable ending. During the activity help students with vocabulary and put new words on the board. Once there are five new words on the board stop the class to drill pronunciation. The students who asked for the words can explain their meaning to the class.
- Push more confident students to use adjectives to describe the things in their room.

6 LEARNER INDEPENDENCE

- The aim is to remind students of the expressions to use in English when they need help and to encourage them to use them.
- Students put the words in the right order to make sentences. Remind students to use the correct punctuation. Play the recording for them to check their answers.

- Ask individual students to write the sentences on the board. Check punctuation with the class. Ask *Which sentence is different?* (The first – it is not a question.)

2.28 Recording and answers

1 Sorry, I don't understand.
2 Excuse me, is this right?
3 How do you say this word?
4 What does that mean?
5 Can you say that again?
6 Can you help me, please?
7 Which exercise are we doing?
8 What is the right answer, please?

7

- The aim is to encourage students to group words in lexical sets (or categories) in their vocabulary notebooks rather than randomly or alphabetically. This process means that students review the meanings of words and it also helps storage and retrieval of words from memory.
- Tell students to write each category in their notebooks on separate pages. Ask students to mark the stress on the words *facilities, attractions* and *furniture*. Drill the pronunciation of these words.
- Students work individually and add to each group from memory. They then compare their list with a partner and add any extra words. Finally, they look back through the unit and add any other words they find.

Optional activities

- ♦ Students mark the stress on words of two or more syllables.
- ♦ Students tick the words they feel they know and put a question mark next to the ones they are still learning.

8 PHRASEBOOK

- Ask students to look through the unit, find the expressions and notice how they are used. Help with translation where necessary. Students can add expressions they like to their Personal Phrasebooks.
- Play the recording for students to listen and repeat the expressions.

2.29 Recording and answers

No, there isn't time (Lesson 1, exercise 2)
Oh, this is silly. (Adam, Lesson 2)
It's raining. (Adam, Lesson 2)
I'm going home. (Adam, Lesson 2)
Wait! (Teresa, Lesson 2)
Look! (Pierre, Lesson 2)
Oh no! (Adam, Lesson 2)
You're scared! (Katya, Lesson 2)
What's she doing? (Emily, Lesson 3)
I don't know. (Adam, Lesson 3)

- Ask students to work in pairs to make up a short dialogue following the instructions. Ask more confident students to write longer dialogues. Ask some pairs to act out their dialogues in front of the class.

Follow-up activities

- ♦ **Game** *Word game* This can be played in teams. Say a topic, e.g. *things in a bedroom* and give students a minute to write as many words as they can related to that topic.
- ♦ **Game** *What's in my perfect room?* Students draw a picture of their perfect bedroom and sit in pairs facing each other. Student A asks Student B about their room, e.g. *Is there a bed?* If Student B says yes, then Student A scores one point. The students continue until each student has asked ten questions. Students tell their partners any items not guessed, e.g. *There's a plant.*

HOMEWORK

Students organise new vocabulary from the lesson in their notebook and learn it for a quick test in the next lesson.

Students write a paragraph about a different room in their house.

WEBLINK

Students can look at more photos of the treasures of Tutankhamun at www.bbc.co.uk/history/ancient/egyptians/tutankhamun_gallery.shtml

Revision and Extension p59

Workbook Unit 4 Lesson 4 pp48–49

Inspiration EXTRA!

Optional aids

Project: pictures of local leisure facilities, card, scissors, glue

PROJECT LEISURE ACTIVITIES

1

- Explain to students that the aim of the project is to write about the leisure facilities in their town for a tourist information leaflet, decorated with pictures if possible. (Note: this could be their home town or a town where they are studying at the moment.)
- Divide the students into groups and appoint an 'editor' for each group. Ask them to make a list of the leisure facilities in their town.

2

- Give students two minutes to choose two or three leisure activities to write about. Draw their attention to the questions. Students answer the questions in as much detail as they can, as well as brainstorming to generate other ideas to write about. If students don't have access to specific information, e.g. opening times and prices, allow them to invent their own.

3

- Each person in the group writes a short text about one of the leisure facilities for a tourist information leaflet.
- In their groups, students exchange and read each other's texts and correct any mistakes. Monitor for any common mistakes and write them on the board to correct as a class. Students then copy their texts out neatly. The editor decides on the order of the texts while the others work on illustrating their leaflet with drawings or photos from magazines, newspapers, local brochures or the Internet.
- Students show their *Leisure activities leaflet* to other groups. Display them in the classroom if you can.

GAME OUTSIDE THE ROOM

- Books closed, students brainstorm leisure activities in pairs, listing them in their Vocabulary notebooks. Remind students to use the *-ing* form for activities. Elicit students' ideas and write them on the board, e.g. *watching TV, playing tennis*. Ask students to open their books and read the first list on page 58, adding any new items to their list. Check comprehension and drill the words in chorus for pronunciation and stress.
- Ask students to look at the second list and elicit the difference (the first list is things to do for fun).
- Read the instructions in the Student's Book with the class. Demonstrate the game with a confident student. Point out that it is better to guess general things first, e.g. the position of the person, the parts of body they are using, the objects they need, rather than simply guessing the activity. Demonstrate the game as many times as is needed for students to get the idea.
- Divide the class into two teams and play the game.

Optional activity

For less confident classes, write the questions from the demonstration on the board.

REVISION

Lessons 1–4
Students' own answers

EXTENSION

Lessons 1–4
Students' own answers

YOUR CHOICE!

The aim is to give students more learner independence and help them to identify their preferred ways of learning. Encourage students to choose an activity that they feel less comfortable with if they want a challenge or are aware that they need practice in a particular area.
Back to Back gives students a chance to practise speaking using the present continuous.
Describe and draw a room gives students the opportunity to practise describing a room.

You may now like students to do the song *Raining In My Heart*. The notes are on p162 and the worksheet on p188.

Language File pp117–118

Song – photocopiable notes p162, worksheet p188

Workbook Unit 4 Inspiration EXTRA! pp50–51

Units 3–4

Optional aids

Follow-up activity *Don't Say the Word*: vocabulary from the units on slips of paper.

1 Give the students two minutes to read the text, then ask *Why doesn't Mike Roots ride a real bicycle?* (He doesn't like the roads because they are dangerous.) Students read the text again and choose the appropriate word for each space. Do the first one together as an example. This can be done in pairs or individually as a short test.

Answers
1 C 2 B 3 B 4 A 5 C 6 A 7 B 8 B 9 C 10 A

Optional activities

- Confident students can first attempt the task without looking at the word options.
- Give students three minutes to memorise the text, then close their books. Then in threes, one student reads the text including some false information, e.g. *Mike Roots is from Manchester.* Students shout *Stop!* when they hear incorrect information and correct it. A different student reads each paragraph.

2 Students complete the sentences with the correct present simple form.

Answers
1 Teresa likes pizza.
2 Adam doesn't have a brother.
3 They hate chocolate.
4 Emily doesn't want an ice cream.
5 I don't speak Italian.
6 Ruby doesn't like bananas.
7 You don't want eggs.
8 We love fish.

3 Students complete the questions with the correct form of *do*. Do the first question together. Students then write the answers to the questions. Students refer to Unit 3 for the answers they don't know. Check the answers by asking one student to read the question and then choose another student to answer. Students then ask and answer the questions in pairs.

Answers
1 ***Does*** *Ruby like Pierre? Yes, she does.*
2 When ***do*** *you come home from school? (Depends on student.)*
3 What time ***do*** *they have lunch at Brighton High School? They have lunch at 1.10/from 1.10 to 2.10.*
4 ***Does*** *Emily lift weights? No, she doesn't.*
5 When ***does*** *Katya go to dance classes? On Wednesday.*
6 What ***does*** *Pierre always do on Monday? He always goes swimming.*
7 ***Does*** *Emily play basketball on Thursday? No, she doesn't.*
8 How often ***do*** *you go to the cinema? (Depends on student.)*

4 Read through the examples. With a less confident class, do the first two questions with the whole class. Students write questions and short answers using the prompts given. Students compare with a partner. Students look back in the book to find the answers. Check the answers by asking one student to read the question and then choose another student to answer.

Answers
1 Does Teresa play football? Yes, she does.
2 Does Pierre like octopus? No, he doesn't.
3 Do Adam and Ruby live in a cottage? Yes, they do.
4 Does Katya come from Switzerland? No, she doesn't.
5 Does Jake love sport? Yes, he does.
6 Does Ruby play tennis? No, she doesn't.
7 Do Adam and Ruby live in Geneva? No, they don't.
8 Does Adam have geography on Thursday? Yes, he does.

5 Ask students to complete the sentences with *at, in, on, from* or *to*.

Answers
1 at, in 2 from, to 3 on 4 at 5 at, in 6 from, to 7 at

Optional activity

Students write true sentences for themselves about their routines and timetable.

6 Tell students they need to include the adverb of frequency in the correct place and change the form of the verb if necessary.

Answers

1 Jake often goes to the cinema on Saturday.
2 I never watch TV in the morning.
3 Emily usually goes running on Monday.
4 We are always busy at the weekend.
5 They sometimes go shopping after school.

7 Students write questions and answers about Teresa's bedroom using the correct form of *there*. With a less confident class, do the first two questions with the whole class. Draw attention to the use of *any* before plural nouns.

Answers

1 Are there any posters? Yes, there are.
2 Is there a desk? No, there isn't.
3 Are there any curtains? Yes, there are.
4 Is there a TV? No, there isn't.
5 Are there any books? Yes, there are.
6 Is there a wardrobe? No, there isn't.
7 Is there an alarm clock? Yes, there is.
8 Are there any flowers? No, there aren't.

8 Students write sentences using the correct present continuous form.

Answers

1 Ruby is holding a mobile phone.
2 Adam and Jake are playing basketball.
3 Mr Ward is standing on the left.
4 We are watching TV.
5 They are cooking Chinese food.
6 Teresa is talking to Pierre.
7 The actor is learning her lines.
8 I am having breakfast.

Optional activity

Students rewrite the sentences in the negative form.

9 Read through the example and do the first one together. Check the answers by asking one student to read the questions and then choose another student to answer.

Answers

1 Is Teresa wearing a blue top? Yes, she is.
2 Are Jake and Adam playing tennis? Yes, they are.
3 Are Katya and Teresa eating ice creams? No, they aren't.
4 Is Mr Ward talking to the group? No, he isn't.
5 Is Jake staying with Adam? No, he isn't.
6 Is Katya writing an email? Yes, she is.
7 Are the boys playing football? Yes, they are.
8 Is Jake playing the guitar? No, he isn't.

10 Students complete the sentences with the verbs in the correct form of the present continuous. They then compare answers with a partner.

Answers

1 is/'s happening 2 are/'re waiting 3 are we waiting 4 is/'s making 5 isn't making 6 is/'s talking 7 are they talking 8 are/'re laughing 9 are/'re leaving 10 are you going 11 are/'re going 12 are/'re running

Optional activity

Ask students to close their books. Write the dialogue on the board but only the names and the verbs and a few helpful words, e.g.

JAKE *happen*
EMILY *wait*
JAKE *Why wait?*

Students reconstruct the dialogue from memory. Check with the whole class. Students practise the dialogue in pairs.

VOCABULARY

11 Drill the words and check the meaning. Students complete the sentences with the words.

Answers

1 cottage 2 flat 3 break 4 sports 5 late 6 subjects 7 beach 8 hands 9 restaurant 10 smell

12 Confident students can first cover the words and think of the answer.

Answers

1 breakfast 2 gym 3 theatre 4 weekend 5 timetable 6 lunch 7 egg 8 museum 9 umbrella 10 exciting

13 Remind students that it is a good idea to learn words that go together, e.g. *do + homework*. Elicit the type of words in column A (verbs) and column B (nouns).

Answers

1 go to bed 2 lift weights 3 listen to music 4 pay for something 5 play a game 6 smell food 7 visit a city 8 wear a uniform

Optional activity

Students add more nouns to the verb stems, e.g. *go to school, listen to the radio.*

LEARNER INDEPENDENCE SELF ASSESSMENT

- Explain to students that the aim of the self assessment is to encourage them to check their own progress and to take any necessary action to improve. Point out that the list 1–5 covers language from Units 3 and 4. Students tick the 'Fine' box for functional language that they feel confident using, but put a question mark in the 'Not sure' box for functional language that they have difficulties with or still cannot use confidently.

- Encourage students to look at the Language File and re-do exercises from the Workbook in areas where they have problems. They may also like to re-do exercises from the lessons and from the Revision and Extension sections in Units 3 and 4.
- Students write an example sentence for each language area in the list. You may like to elicit the grammar needed for each example before students write sentences. Students can refer to the relevant lessons and the Language File for support.
- Ask students to compare their sentences with a partner's, and to discuss and correct any mistakes they may find. They then evaluate their own performance for each language area in terms of *Fine* and *Not sure*.
- Check their sentences so that you can note down language areas for future practice where students are uncertain.

Follow-up activities

♦ **Game** *Noughts and crosses* See page 32 of the Student's Book for instructions. Draw this grid on the board:

Food	*present simple*	*leisure activities*
/ʌ/ come */əʊ/ phone*	*furniture*	*present continuous*
adverbs of frequency	*parts of the body*	*prepositions of time*

♦ **Game** *Don't say the word* See Review 1–2 Follow-up activity for instructions.

HOMEWORK

Students bring their vocabulary notebooks up to date.

Students write a paragraph about their weekends (routines, activities, places they go to).

WEBLINK

If your students are interested in some really adventurous cycling routes they can look at www.adventure-cycling-guide.co.uk/wheretogo.htm

Language File pp116–118

Workbook Review Units 3–4 pp52–53

Units 5–6

Activities
Identifying topics
Categorising vocabulary
Contextualising listening extracts

Project
Capital city quiz

Vocabulary
Jobs
Weather
Transport

Optional aids
Follow-up activities: slips of paper

WARMER 1

If students did the homework in the review, ask them to read out their paragraphs. Vote on who had the most exciting weekend.

WARMER 2

Divide the class into two teams and ask students questions about Units 3–4 to see how much they can remember. Encourage students to look back through Units 3–4 to find the answers if necessary.

WARMER 3

Ask students to look at the photos and speech bubbles on pages 62–63 and say what they can see.

1

- The aim is to introduce students to the main topics and vocabulary they will cover in the next two units.
- Remind students that the two boxes at the top of the page show the communicative language and topics/vocabulary they will use in the next two units.
- Go through the topics in the second box with the class and make sure everyone understands them. Then ask them to look at pictures A–F and match them with six topics.

Answers
A town facilities
B possessions
C feelings
D weather
E jobs
F continents and countries

2

- Explain that words from the three vocabulary categories jobs, weather and transport are arranged in the word square. Students write the words in the correct category.
- Students check their answers in pairs and then as a whole class.

Answers
Jobs: hairdresser, model, nurse, pilot, waiter
Weather: cloudy, sunny, windy, rainy, temperature
Transport: taxi, train, bus, plane, car

Optional activity

In small groups, students think of as many different words as possible to add to the three categories. Give them a time limit and then get the groups to read their words aloud to the class.

3

- Students match the words with the pictures.

Answers
1 trumpet 2 firefighter 3 moon 4 bread 5 castle 6 dolphin

4

- The aim of this activity is for students to contextualise a short listening extract by working out the topic. Explain that they should listen for the main gist of the extract and that it doesn't matter if they don't understand every word.
Play the recording. Students match each extract 1–3 to the topics A–C.

2.30 Recording

1
What's a typical day like at sea? Well, I get up at 7am and we have breakfast at 7.15 – we have coffee and toast. At 9am I go on watch for three hours. At midday I start cooking lunch and we have lunch at 12.30.

2
Well, we know that it's sunnier. World temperatures are 0.6°C higher than 100 years ago and central England is 1°C hotter than 30 years ago.

3
SUSANA *This is my friend Tamara.*
JOHN *Hi, nice to meet you.*
TAMARA *Nice to meet you too.*
JOHN *Do you want something to drink?*
TAMARA *Yes, please.*

Answers

1 B 2 C 3 A

5

- Remind students of the meaning of *capital city*. Put them into groups of three and ask them to do the quiz, writing down their answers.
  Ask them to join other groups to share their answers. Check with the class.

Answers

1 True 2 True 3 True 4 True 5 True

- Point out the 'Believe it or not!' fact at the bottom of the page. Find out if there are often thunderstorms in the students' countries.

Follow-up activities

- ♦ In small groups, students brainstorm vocabulary for three other categories from the box on page 62. See Preview 1–2 Follow-up activity for further instructions.
- ♦ Students make lists of all the personal possessions that are in the classroom today. Give them two minutes and see who can produce the longest list.

HOMEWORK

Ask students to interview family members or other students at the school to find out what are their favourite seasons and why. They then present their findings to the class in the next lesson.

I'm having a wonderful time

Communicative aims	**Language**	**Pronunciation**	**Vocabulary**	**Optional aids**
Talking about regular activities Talking about what people are doing now	Present simple and present continuous	/ə/ assistant	Routines Jobs	Exercise 6 Optional activity: pictures of different jobs Exercise 8: photos of famous people, a photo of Kate Moss

WARMER 1

Game *Shout it out* Organise the students into four groups. Give each group a vocabulary category from the previous four units, e.g. family members, clothes, music. Give each group two minutes to write down as many words as possible relating to their category. They then hand their list in. For each category, the rest of the class then has 30 seconds to call out as many related words as possible. If they say a word on the group's list, it is crossed out. The winning group is the one with the most words left on their list (not crossed out).

WARMER 2

Game *Clock Arms* Revise telling the time in preparation for the exercises in this unit. Ask *What's the time now?* Use your arms as clock hands. Put them in different positions and elicit the time. Then say different times and get the students to put their arms in the right position. Make the game challenging by using both systems of telling the time, e.g. *seven thirty and half past seven.*

1 OPENER

- The aim is to set the scene for the email and pre-teach some vocabulary for the following exercises. Ask students to look at the photo and say what they can see. Ask students to predict which words will be in the email and to justify their ideas. Be prepared to teach *dolphin, ocean, sailing, stars.*

2 READING AND LISTENING

- Explain that Emily's cousin is working on a boat this summer and that this is an email from her.
- Ask students to read the email first and predict the times. Encourage them to guess the meaning of unfamiliar vocabulary from context. Check comprehension by asking students what they think she looks for when she goes '*on watch*' (other boats, icebergs, land).
- Students listen to the recording and complete the email with the correct times.

2.31 Recording

Hello from the middle of the Atlantic Ocean!

We're sailing from Spain to Barbados in the Caribbean Sea and I'm having a wonderful time. I'm writing this on my laptop. It's a beautiful day, the sun is shining and dolphins are playing around the boat at the moment!

What's a typical day like at sea? Well, I get up at 7am and we have breakfast at 7.15 – we have coffee and toast. At 9am I go on watch for three hours. At midday I start cooking lunch and we have lunch at 12.30. In the afternoon, we read and sunbathe. At 6pm I write emails and at 6.45 we make a video call to our base in Brighton. Then we listen to the news on the radio. We have dinner at 7.30, and I go on watch again at 9pm – I sit outside and look at the stars. And at midnight I go to sleep!

Now it's time to make the video call.

Love

Cathy

- Play the recording again and check the answers.

Answers

1 7am 2 7.15 3 9am 4 12.30 5 6pm 6 6.45
7 7.30 8 9pm 9 midnight

3 AFTER READING AND LISTENING

- Students read and listen to the email again and decide if the sentences are true or false. Ask them to note down the words in the email that help them decide on their answers.
- Check the answers before students write corrections for the false sentences. Monitor and help where necessary. Ask students to read their answers to the class.

Answers

1 False. She is sailing from Spain to Barbados in the Caribbean.
2 True
3 False. They have coffee and toast.
4 True
5 False. In the afternoon, she reads and sunbathes.
6 True

Your response

Students discuss the questions in pairs.

Optional activity

Students find examples of the present simple and present continuous in the email in preparation for the next exercise.

LANGUAGE WORKOUT OPTION

If you want to pre-teach the language students will be using in the following activities, you may like to go to the Language Workout box now.

4 SPEAKING

- Read the first question and answer aloud to the class. Point out that the question uses the present simple because it is about Cathy's routine on the boat. A short answer, as given in the speech bubble, would be the most natural way to respond but insisting on a complete sentence will give students more practice with the form of the present simple.
- Students continue the exercise in pairs, taking it in turns to ask the questions.
- Demonstrate the second type of question and answer with a confident student. Ask *Why is this present continuous?* (Because it is happening now.) Students continue in pairs. Monitor and help where necessary.
- Check students' understanding by choosing different students to ask and answer some of the questions in front of the class.

Answers

1 *What time does Cathy get up? She gets up at 7am.*
2 *What time do they have breakfast? They have breakfast at 7.15.*
3 *What time does Cathy go on watch? She goes on watch at 9am and 9pm.*
4 *What time do they have lunch? They have lunch at 12.30.*
5 *What time does she write emails? She writes emails at 6pm.*
6 *What time do they make a video call? They make a video call at 6.45.*
7 *What time do they have dinner? They have dinner at 7.30.*
8 *What time does Cathy go to sleep? She goes to sleep at midnight.*

It's 7am now. What's Cathy doing? She's getting up.
It's 7.15 now. What's Cathy doing? She's having breakfast.
It's 9am now. What's Cathy doing? She's going on watch.
It's 12.30 now. What's Cathy doing? She's having lunch.
It's 6pm now. What's Cathy doing? She's writing emails.
It's 6.45 now. What's Cathy doing? She's making a video call.
It's 7.30 now. What's Cathy doing? She's having dinner.
It's midnight now. What's Cathy doing? She's going to sleep.

5 READING

- Cover the text and ask students to predict who is Teresa's parent, Pierre's parent, etc.
- The aim is to read for general comprehension. Play the recording for students to listen while they read. Set a short time limit to encourage students to do the matching exercise using key words only.

2.32 Recording

See text on page 65 of the Student's Book.

Answers

Teresa – Manuel, Pierre – Christine, Katya – Valentina, Jake – Ray, Emily – Sarah, Adam – Steven

6 VOCABULARY

- Check students understand the words in the box. Show pictures of people doing these jobs and elicit/teach the words. Monitor pronunciation.
- Demonstrate the question and answer with a confident student. Students continue in pairs.
- Check the answers by choosing different students to ask and answer the questions.

Answers

What does Steven Campbell do? He's a pilot.
What does Manuel Navarro do? He's a musician.
What does Ray Turner do? He's a police officer.
What does Valentina Petrova do? She's an interpreter.
What does Christine Dubois do? She's a teacher.
What does Sarah Fry do? She's a doctor.

- Students look back at the photos and text and choose the correct option. Do the first one together as an example.

Answers

1 Japan 2 Russian 3 trumpet 4 maths
5 isn't 6 woman

Optional activity

In groups of three or four, one student takes a card and mimes the job written on it and the others identify it.

Extension Explain that students are going to ask and answer questions about their family. Drill the two questions and elicit some alternatives, e.g. *What does your mother do? What are your grandparents doing now?* Demonstrate the activity by getting students to ask you the questions and answering about your family. Give students a few minutes to think about their family and their answers, and to look up/ask for any vocabulary they need. Students move around the classroom asking different students their questions. Set a time limit of five minutes. Ask a few students to report back on something interesting they learnt.

7 PRONUNCIATION

- Write *assistant, doctor, firefighter* on the board. Ask *What sound is in all these words?* Highlight and model the /ə/ sound. Students repeat the sound. Tell students that this is the most common sound in English. Many different spelling combinations can produce the /ə/ sound, as shown in the examples. Ask *Is the /ə/ sound stressed?* (No.)

- Play the recording, pausing after each word for students to repeat.
- Students copy the words into their notebooks and circle the /ə/ sound. Play the recording again if necessary.
- Check by nominating students to put their answers on the board.

2.33 Recording and answers

/ə/ assistant doctor firefighter hairdresser interpreter journalist model musician pilot police officer taxi-driver teacher waiter

8 WRITING

- If possible, use a photo of Kate Moss and elicit her name and what she does. Students read the example.
- Explain that they are going to write two similar paragraphs about famous people. Brainstorm famous people with the students, using photos if possible. Ask the students to choose two and write about what they do and what they think they are doing now. Tell them to use the example in the book as a guide. Set a ten-minute time limit. Monitor and help as necessary.
- Students exchange their paragraphs and say whether or not they agree with their partner's comments.

Optional activity

Ask students to write *This person* ... and not the name of the famous person on the paper. When they have finished, students read out their texts for the class to identify the famous person.

LANGUAGE WORKOUT

- Ask students to look at the Language box. Ask *Are the sentences the same as in the email?* (Not exactly.) *What's different?* (The person: *she/they* instead of *I/we*.)
- Drill the examples in chorus for pronunciation. Listen for problems particularly with the weak form of the verb *to be* in the present continuous.

Answers

read sits looks
is having are playing

Optional activity

With a less confident group, review the forms of the two tenses before asking students to complete the Language Workout box. Use examples from the email, e.g. *I get up, You get up, He/she gets up.*

PRACTICE

- Students do Practice exercise 16 on page 118 of the Language File.
- They choose the present simple or the present continuous to complete the sentences
- Check students' understanding by choosing different students to read out their sentences to the class.

Answers

1 is playing 2 do you go 3 have 4 I'm doing
5 is shining 6 starts 7 are working 8 Do you like

Follow-up activities

- ♦ **Game** *Mime the sentences* Divide students into two teams. Show one student from each team the same sentences. These students can mime or draw on the board but must not speak. The rest of their team has to say or write the correct sentences before the other team to win a point. Explain that the first part of the sentence is always a job and the second an activity. Possible sentences: *I am a teacher. I am teaching history* or *I am a pilot. I am flying to Australia* or *I am a musician. I am playing the guitar.*
- ♦ Give different pictures of places to each pair of students. Students imagine this is where they are. They write a short email to their friends saying what they are doing now and what they do every day in this place. Set a ten-minute time limit. Remind them to sign off with their names. Collect in the pictures, shuffle them, put them on the board and number them. Collect in the students' writing and put it up around the walls of the classroom. Students move around, read the emails and decide who is where.

HOMEWORK

Students write about one or two members of their family using the Kate Moss text as a model. They write about what they do and what they think they are doing at the moment.

WEBLINK

Students may like to visit this website where they can do a quiz related to the topic of jobs: http://a4esl.org/q/h/fb-bd-occupations.html

Revision and Extension p73

Language File p118

Workbook Unit 5 Lesson 1 pp54–55

Photocopiable notes p158, Worksheet p175

Whose turn is it?

Communicative aims	Language	Pronunciation	Vocabulary	Optional aids
Talking about possessions	Possessive pronouns Possessive *'s* Question: *Whose ...?*	Contrastive stress	Possessions	Warmer 2: 10 small objects Exercise 6, Extension activity: photos of famous people which can be cut up, blank paper

WARMER 1

Ask students to close their eyes and think of someone they know who is not in the room. Ask *What do you think they are doing now?* Students write down what that person is doing without showing anyone else. They tell their partner who the person is and their partner has five chances to guess what they are doing now.

WARMER 2

Game *Kim's game* Place ten small everyday objects on your table, e.g. purse, keys, watch, sunglasses, bottle of water. Hold up the objects and ask the students to tell you the names of them. Give students one minute to memorise all the objects. Remove or cover the objects. In pairs, students have two minutes to write down all the hidden objects. Ask the pair with the longest list to read their answers and confirm or correct. The winning pair is the one with the most correct objects.

1 OPENER

- The aim is to set the scene for the conversation and pre-teach some vocabulary for the following exercises. Ask students to look at the photo and identify the four people. Ask *What are they wearing? What are they doing?* Be prepared to teach *games console*.
- In pairs, students look for the objects. Ask one student to read out what they can see and ask everyone to point to that object if they can see it in their picture.

Answers

In the photo there is: a bag, a cap, a packet of crisps, a silver earring, a remote, a pair of sunglasses and a sweatshirt.

2 READING

- Ask students to close their books. Explain that they are going to listen to the conversation and decide what the problem is.
- Play the recording and check the answer. With less confident students, allow them to read the conversation on page 66 to check their ideas.

2.34 **Recording**

See text on page 66 of the Student's Book.

Answer

Jake wants to play next because he wants to play with Teresa.

3 AFTER READING

- Students match the questions and answers. Point out that one of the answers is not necessary. Encourage students to work out the meaning of *get cross* from the context. Check by asking for a similar expression (*get angry*) or translation.
- Students then listen, read and check their answers.
- Ask which answer is not used before checking the rest of the answers.

Answers

1 f 2 c 3 a 4 g 5 e 6 b
d is not used

Optional activity

2.34 Play the recording again, sentence by sentence, for students to repeat. Monitor pronunciation of words, e.g. *whose*, and intonation carefully. Students then act out the dialogue in groups of four.

Your response

Encourage students to talk in pairs or groups about video games. If they like them, get them to talk about their favourite games.

4 SPEAKING

- Ask students to cover page 67 and look at the photo on page 66 again. Ask the two example questions and elicit the answers. Elicit the two questions from the students and write them on the board. Highlight the use of *is/it* with singular nouns and *are/they* with plural nouns.
- With a less confident class, students divide the words in the box into singular and plural nouns.
- Students continue asking and answering questions in pairs using the words in the box. Monitor and help where necessary.

Answers

Whose is the black T-shirt? It's Jake's.
Whose is the blue bag? It's Emily's.
Whose are the crisps? They're Jake's.
Whose is the blue top? It's Emily's.
Whose is the grey sweatshirt? It's Adam's.
Whose is the pink top? It's Teresa's.
Whose is the red cap? It's Emily's.
Whose are the black jeans? They're Jake's and Emily's.
Whose is the silver earring? It's Teresa's.
Whose are the sunglasses? They're Adam's.
Whose is the watch? It's Teresa's.

Optional activities

- Students work in pairs. One student closes the book and asks the questions from memory. Students then swap roles.
- Students work in pairs. They study the photo on pages 6–7 for one minute. One student then closes the book. The other one asks *Whose …?* questions and the first student answers from memory. They then reverse roles using the photo on page 12. This could also be played as a team competition for the whole class.

Extension Each student borrows an item from three students. Student A holds up an object and asks *Whose is this?* Student B replies e.g. *It's Pedro's* and A answers *Yes, it is* or *No, it isn't. It's (name)'s.* Then they swap roles.

5 PRONUNCIATION

- The aim is to make students aware of how sentence stress is used to convey meaning. This exercise shows how stress is used to correct a statement.
- Students listen and repeat the question and answer.
- Write the answer on the board. Underline the stressed words.

2.35 Recording

Is it Adam's watch.
No, it isn't his. It's Teresa's.

- Students practise saying the example question and answer before continuing with the further questions.
- Play the recording for students to check.
- Ask some pairs to demonstrate the questions and answers in front of the class.

2.35 Recording and answers

Is it Adam's watch? No, it isn't his. It's Teresa's.
1 *Is it Teresa's cap? No, it isn't hers. It's Emily's.*
2 *Is it Adam's earring? No, it isn't his. It's Teresa's.*
3 *Are they Jake's sunglasses? No, they aren't his. They're Adam's.*
4 *Are they Teresa and Adam's crisps? No, they aren't theirs. They're Jake's.*
5 *Is it Emily's sweatshirt? No, it isn't hers, it's Adam's.*
6 *Is it Teresa's bag? No, it isn't hers. It's Emily's.*

Optional activity

Fast finishers can improvise further questions and answers using the objects in the box in exercise 4.

6 SPEAKING

- Focus on the photos and the example dialogue.
- Ask two confident students to read the dialogue. Check *What do you say if you agree with your partner's idea? (Yes, I think you're right.)*
- Students continue in pairs or groups of three. Tell them not to look through the Student's Book at other photos but remember. Set a five-minute time limit.
- Students listen and check their answers. With a less confident class, pause after each section to allow students to note the answer, and check the answers with the class at the end. Find out which pair or group had the most correct.

2.36 Recording and answers

1 *It's Emily's hair.*
2 *It's Adam's mouth.*
3 *It's Teresa's ear.*
4 *They're Pierre's eyes.*
5 *It's Teresa's hand.*
6 *It's Adam's nose.*
7 *It's Jake's foot.*
8 *It's Katya's arm.*

Extension Students cut up pictures of famous people and their possessions from magazines or the Internet. They paste them onto a blank piece of paper but keep a record of what item or body part belongs to each person. They then ask other students to identify whose they are. Alternatively, they could create a photo montage of the different items and write the names of the famous people at the bottom of the piece of paper. Students then exchange montages and guess whose hair, house, guitar, etc, it is. By numbering the photos and keeping a record of decisions, this could be set up as a class competition.

7 WRITING

- Students read the introduction. Check *How many bags are there? Whose are they? Where's Jake/Teresa/Emily from? What do they like/dislike?* Ask two students to read the dialogue aloud. Point out or elicit that all the apostrophes are missing from the dialogue. Ask students to say when we use apostrophes (for possession or to indicate a missing word).

- Students complete the dialogue with apostrophes.
- Write the correct dialogue on the board for them to check their answers.

Answers

PIERRE	*Is this Jake's bag?*
KATYA	*I don't know. Let's see what's inside. Whose magazines are these?*
PIERRE	*They aren't Jake's. They're in Spanish. I think they're Teresa's.*
KATYA	*Yes, that's Teresa's bag. But what about the blue bag?*
PIERRE	*I think it's Emily's – I'm sure she likes blue.*

Optional activity

Students write more mini-dialogues about the bags. Explain that they need to give a reason why they think each bag is Jake's, Teresa's or Emily's. Students exchange writing and correct each other's work for spelling, grammar and punctuation. In pairs, students choose one of their dialogues, memorise it, rehearse it and then perform it for the class.

LANGUAGE WORKOUT

- Ask students to look at the Language box and to complete the chart. Confident students can complete first and then check, while others can look back at exercises 2 and 3 and then complete.
- Students turn to page 118 of the Language File to check their answers.
- Point out that
  - possessive adjectives are always used with nouns, e.g. *my book, her CDs*
  - possessive pronouns are used without nouns, e.g. *it's mine, they are hers*
  - apart from *mine*, the possessive pronoun is formed by adding an *s* to the possessive adjective (*his* stays the same as it already ends in *s*)
  - when you use the person's name, there is no change: *It's Adam's book* or *It's Adam's*.

Answers

mine yours his

PRACTICE

- Students do Practice exercise 17 on page 118 of the Language File.
- Ask a student to read the example aloud. Point out that the choice of pronoun depends on the person who has the object and not the object, ie in the first sentence, the pronoun relates to *Pierre* not *trainers*.
- Students complete the sentences with the correct possessive pronoun.
- Check the answers by asking different students to say the completed sentences.
- Ensure students are pronouncing the final *s*. If necessary, model and then drill the sentences chorally.

Answers

1 mine 2 ours 3 yours 4 his 5 theirs 6 hers

Optional activities

- ♦ Point to objects that belong to you and ask *Is this Monica's?* Elicit *No, it's yours.* Say *Yes, it's mine*. Pick up students' objects and ask *Is this/Are these …?* and elicit appropriate answers. Students continue in pairs.
- ♦ Fast finishers can make their own sentences orally using objects in the room. One student says *The bag is the teacher's*. The other one then finishes *It's his/hers* and so on.

Follow-up activity

Game *Whose is this?* Ask each student to give you an object secretly so the rest of the class can't see it. Place all the objects in a bag. Take one object out at a time. In pairs, students note down the name of the object and who they think the owner is. When there are no more objects left in the bag, pick up each object in the same order and ask *Whose is this?* Elicit guesses. Get one pair to ask the person they think is the owner: *Is it yours, Stefan?* The students answer *Yes, it's mine* or *No, it isn't mine. Is it yours, … ?* and so on until the owner is found.

HOMEWORK

Ask students to write a similar dialogue to the one in exercise 7. This time their mother is trying to tidy the living room and she finds lots of things belonging to members of the family. Remind students to give a reason why they think the objects belong to which person.

WEBLINK

Students may like to visit this website to practise English sounds: www.bbc.co.uk/worldservice/learningenglish/multimedia/pron/index.shtml

Revision and Extension p73

Language File p118

Workbook Unit 5 Lesson 2 pp56–57

Photocopiable notes p158, Worksheet p176

3 It's sunnier

Communicative aims	Language	Pronunciation	Vocabulary	Optional aids
Making comparisons	Comparative adjectives (*-er, more*)	/ə/ autumn	Weather Seasons	Exercise 7 Optional activity: a map of the world Follow-up activities: a copy of the table per team

WARMER 1

Write the following five pairs of sentences on the board:
Who's is that bag? It's hers.
Here are your books. Where are mine?
Whose sunglasses are they? It's Adam's.
Is it my turn? No, I think it's Teresa.
I don't think this book is your. It's in Spanish.
Students work in pairs and have one minute to decide which one is correct (the second one) and correct the others.

WARMER 2

Game *Months Race* Divide students into teams. Students can either run up to the board and write the answer or write it on a sheet of paper and hold it up. Say *Write the name of this month. Write the name of a very short month. Write the name of the month when school starts. Write the name of the month when we celebrate Christmas*, etc. Check spelling. Give a point to the quickest team each time. Then get students to order the months.

1 OPENER

- Students answer the questions orally as a class. Lead into the topic of the lesson by asking *What about 200 years ago? Do you think the weather was the same?*

2 READING

- Students read and listen to the text.
- Encourage students to guess the meaning of unfamiliar vocabulary from the context. Be prepared to teach *earlier, later, the tropics*.
- Ask them to say what information is surprising.

2.37 Recording
See text on page 68 of the Student's Book.

3 AFTER READING

- Students choose the correct word first and then check by reading or listening to the text.
- Check the answers by asking different students to read the sentences aloud.

Answers
1 hotter 2 earlier 3 longer 4 more difficult 5 rainier 6 drier 7 higher 8 old

- Ask students to underline two pieces of information in the text which are new for them and tell their partner.
- Students ask and answer the question at the beginning of the text with their partner. Take a class vote on whether they think the weather is getting better, worse or not changing.

Your response

Brainstorm ideas from the class about what we can do about climate change. Write their ideas on the board.

Optional activity

With a more confident class, write the correct options from the exercise on the board and then get students to close their books. In pairs, students recreate the original sentences orally.

4 VOCABULARY

- Students complete the words for the four seasons. If they need more help, they could either look back at the text in exercise 2 or you could give them the letters mixed up to reorder.

Answers
spring, summer, autumn, winter

- Students match the words in the box with the photos. Model and drill the six words.

Answers
1 windy 2 cloudy 3 rainy 4 sunny 5 foggy 6 snowy

- Ask students to compare two seasons using the weather words. Do one or two with the whole class before students continue in pairs.

Optional activities

- Fast finishers can make more sentences comparing seasons using *long, short, hot, cold, wet, good, bad*.
- Make the speaking activity more challenging by getting students to say some true and some false sentences. Their partner should listen and say whether their comment is true or false.
- Mime an activity, e.g. sunbathing, putting up an umbrella, making a snowman, and ask the students *What's the weather like?* or *What season is it?* Students do the same in pairs.

5 SPEAKING

- Students think about changes in the weather in their country.
- In pairs, students can discuss the three questions. You might be able to prompt them with specific weather events in the country.
- Get students to ask you questions. Tell students about how the weather has changed since you were young and any facts you have learnt.

Optional activity

Ask students to close their books. Read *climate change* aloud. Change some of the facts, e.g. *World temperatures are lower than 140 years ago*. Students listen and shout out *Stop!* when they hear a mistake and correct it.

Extension Students write sentences about changes in temperature, rainfall and the seasons in their own country.

6 PRONUNCIATION

- Ask students to recall the sound /ə/ (from lesson 1). Elicit some examples of words with this sound, e.g. *doctor, model, pilot*.
- Students look through words and circle where they think there is a /ə/ sound.
- Play the recording for students to check. Write the answers on the board. Play the recording again, pausing after each word for students to repeat.

2.38 Recording and answers

/ə/ *autumn Britain drier hotter hundred picture problem season summer than weather wetter*

Optional activity

Give the students a list of words taken from previous lessons. Students divide them into words which do have the /ə/ sound and those which don't. If you have a Vocabulary box, use these cards. Students could mark the /ə/ sound in the correct place above the word.

7 SPEAKING

- Ask students what the symbols in the chart mean (*cloudy*, *rainy*, etc). Go through the examples with the class, then ask students to compare two of the cities using as many different adjectives as possible. Students continue in pairs.

Optional activities

- Students find the places on a map and make five predictions about the weather, e.g. *It's hotter in Madrid than in Warsaw*. They then look at the chart to see how many of their predictions were correct.
- Fast finishers can compare the weather in their town to the cities in the chart.
- Say *I'm thinking of a city* (one on the chart). Students should guess *Is it Brighton?* Answer *No, it's bigger/smaller/hotter/colder/windier than Brighton*. Students continue guessing until they find the correct answer. Students play the game in groups of three.

8 WRITING

- Focus on the weather chart again. Ask students some questions, e.g. *Is it hotter in London than here?* Make sure they answer in complete sentences.
- Explain that they should write about five sentences comparing their town to the cities in the chart. They should use different adjectives in each sentence. Set a time limit.
- Students exchange writing and compare and correct each other's work.

Optional activity

Students choose one of the cities on the chart and describe the weather there in comparison to five other cities, e.g. *The weather there is worse than in Zurich*. When they have finished they read their sentences to a partner or the class. The listener has to work out which city they are describing.

LANGUAGE WORKOUT

- Ask students to look at the Language box and to complete the chart. Point out that the comparative form for all the short adjectives and one of the long adjectives can be found in exercise 3.
- Students turn to page 118 of the Language File to check their answers.

Answers

colder higher shorter easier
sunnier wetter
more famous more expensive
more popular

- Highlight that
  - one-syllable adjectives ending in one vowel + one consonant double the final consonant in the comparative. (But we do not double *-w, -x, -y* at the end of words.)
  - adjectives ending in *-y* change the *y* to *i* and add *-er*.
  - most two-syllable adjectives and all adjectives of three or more syllables form the comparative with *more*.

Optional activities

- ♦ Get the students to cover the comparatives in the chart and remember them.
- ♦ Fast finishers can add more adjectives and comparatives to the correct group in the chart. You could provide a list, e.g. *cheap, happy, pretty, dangerous, tall*.

PRACTICE

- Students do Practice exercise 18 on page 119 of the Language File.
- Write *The tropics / sunny / Antarctica* on the board. Elicit the complete sentence *The tropics are sunnier than Antarctica*.
- Explain to students they have to compile sentences by choosing the words that go together. Set a five-minute time limit.
- Check answers by asking different students to read their sentences aloud. Check the spelling of *bigger*.

Answers

The tropics are sunnier than Antarctica.
Chinese is more difficult than English.
London's population is bigger than Zurich's.
Jake's hair is shorter than Ruby's.
The Arctic is colder than Brazil.
A mobile phone is smaller than a calculator.
Angelina Jolie is more famous than Jennifer Lopez.
Katya's bag is more expensive than her rucksack.

Optional activity

Students make other sentences using the comparative adjectives in the chart, e.g. *Spain is bigger than Portugal, English is easier than Chinese*. Students could then give each other prompts like *Spain / big / Portugal* or *English / easy / Chinese* to elicit sentences from their partner.

Follow-up activities

- ♦ **Game** *Comparisons* Ask students to name two film stars. Put students in pairs or small groups and ask them to write a sentence comparing the two film stars. The first group with a correct sentence wins a point. Continue the game using singers, countries, the students from *New Inspiration 1*, food, and so on. Tell students they are not allowed to repeat adjectives.
- ♦ Students write a comparative quiz in groups to give to other groups. Give an example question, e.g. *Who is taller, Tom Cruise or Nicole Kidman?* You could give them topics such as geography, famous people, animals.
- ♦ **Game** *Think of a word* Divide the students into teams. Hand out one table per team.

The word is ______.
Something smaller ______.
Something bigger ______.
Something earlier in the dictionary ______.
Something later in the dictionary ______.
A shorter word ______.
A longer word ______.

You provide the word and teams have to think of a different word for each of the six categories. Possible words to start: *wallet, photo, comb, guitar, camera, watch*. Don't allow students to repeat words from one round to the next.

HOMEWORK

Students imagine they are on holiday and are writing a postcard to their grandparents. Their grandparents are most interested in the weather and how it compares to the weather at home. Tell students to start their postcard *Dear Grandma and Grandpa* or *Granny and Grandad*, and finish *Lots of love*. Ideally, it should have a picture of where they are. Students may be able to get this from the Internet. They should write about six or seven sentences. Encourage more confident students to include other information about the food and the people.

WEBLINKS

Today's weather and a five-day forecast for towns and cities worldwide and can be found at http://weather.yahoo.com

Revision and Extension p73

Language File pp118–119

Workbook Unit 5 Lesson 3 pp58–59

Photocopiable notes p158, Worksheet 177

Integrated Skills Questionnaire

Skills
Reading Personality test
Listening Noting down answers
Speaking Comparing scores
Writing Describing character

Learner Independence
Classroom English
Vocabulary notebook
Phrasebook

Vocabulary
Personality adjectives
Punctuation
Useful expressions

Optional aids
Follow-up activity: pictures of different people

WARMER 1

Give students a short test on vocabulary from previous lessons.

WARMER 2

Write on the board:
What is he like? *He likes watching football.*
What does he like doing? *He's friendly.*
Students match the questions and answers. Elicit some adjectives to describe personality by referring to people the students know, e.g. TV personalities, soap opera characters, singers. Use the question *What is … like?* Write all the ideas on the board.

1 OPENER

- Check students understand the words in the box. Check pronunciation especially for *quiet* and *serious*.

Optional activity

Students write down three adjectives to describe themselves and three to describe their partner. After they have done the questionnaire they can check to see if the results are the same.

2 READING

- The aim is to read for detailed understanding and provide a context to use the adjectives of personality.
- Ask what the people are doing in the pictures and elicit *touch your hair, touch the person you are talking to, fold your arms, laugh a lot, laugh, smile, shout at someone, discuss, say nothing.*
- Students read and choose the best answer for them. Set a five-minute time limit.
- Students then work out their score and read about their personality type.

Optional activities

- ♦ With a more confident class, get students to interview each other and note down their partner's answers. They can then work out the score for their partner and tell them what personality type they are.
- ♦ Students look back at their choice of personality adjectives for themselves and their partner in exercise 1 and see if they were correct.
- ♦ Students look back at the questionnaire and decide what each question is testing, e.g. 2 – *confident, open*, 3 – *confident, shy, friendly.*

3 LISTENING

- Students listen and write down Emily's answers to the quiz.
- With less confident classes, pause after each question is answered and get students to check their answers with their partner. If necessary, play that section again.
- Students work out Emily's score and what it says about her personality.

2.39 Recording

EMILY *Hey, Jake, let's do this questionnaire.*
JAKE *OK. You go first – I ask the questions and you answer.*
EMILY *Ready when you are.*
JAKE *Right. Question 1: which is your favourite colour?*
EMILY *Well, look at my clothes and you know the answer. It's B and today I'm wearing a brown top.*
JAKE *And brown shoes! Question 2: what do you do when you are shopping – A, B or C?*
EMILY *C – compare things in lots of shops. I go into hundreds of shops!*
JAKE *Next question – that's number 3. When you are talking to someone, do you A) touch your hair or face, B) touch the person you are talking to, or C) fold your arms? I know your answer to this one!*
EMILY *Why?*
JAKE *Because you're doing it now. You're touching your hair.*

EMILY That's right! A.
JAKE Question 4 – do you like it more when A) you're alone, B) with lots of people, or C) with two or three friends?
EMILY It depends. I like it when I'm alone but my answer is C – with two or three friends.
JAKE Question 5. When you see something funny, do you A) laugh a lot, B) laugh C) smile?
EMILY B – laugh.
JAKE Next question – number 6. Which is easier when you have a problem? A, B or C?
EMILY B – to email someone. The good thing about email is that you can think about what you want to say.
JAKE Question 7. Which is your favourite time of the day?
EMILY That's easy. A – the morning.
JAKE Question 8. Which is your favourite evening activity?
EMILY I like TV and I like parties. But my answer is B – talking to a friend.
JAKE Question 9. How often do you wear the same clothes the next day? Sometimes, never or very often?
EMILY A – sometimes – when I can't find anything new!
JAKE And the last question – question 10. What do you do when you are angry with people?
EMILY Nothing. I say nothing – that's C. And now you – what are your answers?

Answers
1 B 2 C 3 A 4 C 5 B 6 B 7 A 8 B 9 A 10 C
Emily's score is 30.
This shows she is quiet and careful. She is a serious person and thinks a lot before she does something. She thinks a lot about other people but is quite happy when she is alone.

Optional activity

Students ask you the ten questions and work out your score and personality.

4 SPEAKING

- Demonstrate by saying what was right and wrong about the description of your personality when you did the test. Justify your points, e.g. *I agree that I am friendly. I like meeting new people and I usually say hello to everyone.*
- In groups, students should take it in turns to speak about their results. Tell them to justify their points. The group should then decide whether it was a good or a bad test. Get feedback on their ideas.

5 WRITING

- The aim is for students to write a paragraph describing their habits and personality using the questions in the personality test as prompts. Encourage students to use adverbs of frequency (Unit 3, Lesson 3), e.g. *When I go shopping, I usually know what I want and buy it.* Do a few sentences together as a class to demonstrate. Set a ten-minute time limit.

Optional activities

- ♦ Fast finishers can exchange their writing and check for grammar, spelling and punctuation. They could also comment on whether they agree with the description.
- ♦ Write some examples of good language and some examples of common errors on the board. In pairs, students identify which are good and which need correcting and then correct the mistakes.
- ♦ Collect the pieces of writing in and read some of them to the class (without mistakes). Students listen and identify the author.

6 LEARNER INDEPENDENCE

- The aim is to provide the students with the terminology to refer to punctuation. This makes instruction and correction of punctuation easier.
- Students match the words and the punctuation marks. With a less confident class, give students more help: say *You finish a sentence with a full stop, The names of countries in English begin with a capital letter, When you write something exciting you need an exclamation mark at the end.*

Answers
brackets ( )
capital letter A
comma ,
exclamation mark !
full stop .
hyphen -
question mark ?

- Students listen to the recording and write the correct punctuation mark. Choose a student to write the answers on the board and ask the rest of the class if they agree.

2.40 Recording and answers
1 . 2 ? 3 ! 4 , 5 -

Optional activity

Dictate a list of words to the students. Ask them to write them and use a capital letter if it is necessary in English, e.g. *Spain, Tuesday, mobile phone, Atlantic, German, weekend, winter, birthday, March, photograph, Jake, London, computer*. Check answers and highlight any differences in use of capital letters between their native language and English.

7

- The aim is to encourage students to group words in lexical sets in their vocabulary notebooks rather than randomly or alphabetically. This process means that students review the meanings of the words and it also helps storage and retrieval of words from memory.
- Write the three categories on the board. Elicit an example for each.
- Students work individually and add to each category from memory. They then compare their list with a partner and add any more. Finally they look back through the unit and add any others that they find. Set a minimum of eight words per category.

Suggested answers

Jobs	*Weather and seasons*	*Personality adjectives*
cleaner	*spring*	*careful*
doctor	*summer*	*confident*
electrician	*autumn*	*friendly*
firefighter	*winter*	*happy*
hairdresser	*cold*	*helpful*
interpreter	*hot*	*open*
journalist	*rainy*	*quiet*
nurse	*cloudy*	*serious*
pilot	*sunny*	*shy*
police officer	*windy*	
shop assistant		
taxi-driver		
teacher		
waiter		

Optional activities

- ♦ With less confident students, write the words on the board for students to categorise.
- ♦ Students mark the stress on words of two or more syllables.
- ♦ Students tick the words they feel they know and put a question mark next to the ones they are still learning.
- ♦ Fast finishers can test each other. One student gives a definition and the other says the word.

8 PHRASEBOOK

- Ask students to look through Unit 5 and find the expressions, and notice how they are used. Help with translation where necessary.
- Play the recording for students to listen and repeat the expressions.

2.41 **Recording and answers**

I'm having a wonderful time. (Cathy's email, Lesson 1)
It's a beautiful day. (Cathy's email, Lesson 1)
It's time to … (Cathy's email, Lesson 1)
Well done! (Emily, Lesson 2)
Whose turn is it? (Adam, Lesson 2)
What's the problem? (Adam, Lesson 2)
Good idea. (Teresa, Lesson 2)

- Students can add expressions they like to their Personal Phrasebooks.
- Read the example dialogue. Ask students what the relationship is between the two speakers (friends) and where they are (a party). Read the dialogue with a confident student.
- Ask students to work in pairs to make up three-line dialogues. Ask some pairs to act out their dialogues in front of the class. Other students should listen and say what the relationship between the two people is and where they might be.

Follow-up activity

Game *Speed-dating* Give each student a photo of a person. Make sure you have an equal number of pictures of men and women. They then decide on the following information for their person: *How old is he/she? What is his/her job? What does he/she like doing? What is he/she like?* Organise students in two circles, one inside the other, facing towards each other with those students with men in one circle and those with women in the other. Tell students that their person is single and looking for a boyfriend/girlfriend. They ask about the person opposite them and decide if they are a suitable boyfriend/girlfriend. They must not show their photos. When pairs have finished, get one circle to move round one place and interview their new partner. At the end, ask if anyone found a perfect match and then let them see the photos.

HOMEWORK

Students write a paragraph describing someone they know well, either a member of their family or a friend. They describe their personality and give examples, e.g. *He is confident. He is always sure he knows the answer.* Students can use the writing they did in exercise 5 as a guide.

WEBLINKS

Students may like to visit this website: www.fun4birthdays.com/horoscope to find out the personality traits of different star signs. They click on the word 'Personality' under the relevant star sign. Students may need help with some of the vocabulary.

Revision and Extension p73

Workbook Unit 5 Lesson 4 pp60–61

Inspiration EXTRA!

LANGUAGE LINKS

- The aim is to raise students' awareness of the fact that they probably already know many words in English and may be able to guess meanings through words in their own language.
- Students look at the words in the box and note down those which are similar to words in their own language. Elicit answers as a class.
- Ask students, in pairs or small groups, to look back over Units 1–5 for other words similar to words in their own language. The first team to find six words writes their words on the board.
- Students make a section in their vocabulary notebooks for words which are similar in their own language.

Optional activity

Students think of other words they know that are similar to their own language. Write all good ideas on the board and get students to copy them into their vocabulary notebooks. Make sure they are aware of spelling differences.

GAME WHAT'S MY JOB?

- The aim is to review the vocabulary of jobs and the present simple and continuous, particularly the question form.
- Explain the rules of the game. Check that the students have understood by demonstrating with the class, doing the mime and answering the questions yourself. Make sure that the students know that they can mime the job but can only say *Yes* or *No*. Ask *What can you say? How much time do you have to guess the job?*
- Divide the students into two teams. Teams play one at a time. The other team can time 60 seconds.

Optional activities

- ♦ With a more confident group, don't allow the students to mime the job.
- ♦ With a less confident group, go through possible questions first.
- ♦ If the team fails to guess, you could award a bonus point to the observing team if they can name the job.
- ♦ To make the game more competitive, both teams play at the same time and give the two students who are miming the same job. The first team to identify the job wins.

SKETCH THE CAR

- The aim is for students to enjoy using their English while also reviewing language presented in this unit and getting valuable stress and intonation practice.
- With a more confident class, play the recording with books closed. Then play it again with books open.
- With a less confident class, play the recording once while the students follow in their books, and then once again with books closed.
- Check comprehension by asking *Why doesn't she move the car?* (It isn't hers.)

2.42 Recording

See text on page 72 of the Student's Book.

- Divide the class into two equal groups and play the recording again, with one group repeating in chorus as the woman and the other group as the man. Encourage students to exaggerate stress and intonation and use gestures where appropriate.
- Ask the students to close their books and play the recording again. Then ask the students to work in pairs and read the sketch aloud. Choose several pairs to act out the sketch in front of the class.

Optional activity

Make an audio or video recording of students performing the sketch.

REVISION

Lesson 1

Encourage more confident students to read the email again once and then write the description from memory.

Suggested answer

Cathy gets up at 7am and she has breakfast at 7.15 – she has coffee and toast. At 9am she goes on watch for three hours. At noon she starts cooking lunch and she has lunch at 12.30. In the afternoon, she reads and sunbathes. At 6pm she writes emails and at 6.45pm she makes a video call to their base in Brighton. She has supper at 7.30, and she goes on watch again at 9pm – she sits outside and looks at the stars. At midnight she goes to sleep.

Lesson 2

Suggested answers

grey sweatshirt, sunglasses, blue jeans, pink top, silver earring, remote, watch, red cap, blue bag, blue top, crisps, black T-shirt, black jeans, sofa

Lesson 3

Suggested answers

In Amsterdam it's cloudy, sunny and very windy and the temperature is 17 degrees.
In Brighton it's very cloudy and windy and the temperature is 15 degrees.
In London it's very rainy and very windy and the temperature is 14 degrees.
In Madrid it's very sunny and hot. The temperature is 30 degrees.
In Mexico City it's sometimes rainy but very sunny and the temperature is 27 degrees.
In Moscow it's very sunny and the temperature is 25 degrees.
In New York it's sometimes rainy and it's windy. The temperature is 24 degrees.
In Zurich it's sometimes cloudy and sometimes sunny and the temperature is 21 degrees.

Lesson 4

Suggested answer

Emily's favourite time of the day is the morning. Her favourite evening activity is talking to a friend. She sometimes wears the same clothes the next day. Her favourite colour is brown. When she is shopping, she compares things in a lot of shops. When she is talking to someone, she usually touches her hair. She likes it more when she is with two or three friends. When she sees something funny, she laughs. When she has a problem, she emails someone. When she is angry with someone, she says nothing. She is quiet and careful. She is a serious person and thinks a lot before she does something. She thinks a lot about other people but she is quite happy when she is alone.

EXTENSION

Lesson 1
Students' own answers

Lesson 2

Suggested answers

Whose is the silver earring? It's Teresa's.
Whose is the packet of crisps? It's Jake's.
Whose are the sunglasses? They're Adam's.
Whose is the sweatshirt? It's Adam's.
Whose is the blue bag? It's Emily's.

Lesson 3
Students' own answers

Lesson 4
Students' own answers

YOUR CHOICE!

The aim is to give students more learner independence and help them to identify their preferred ways of learning. Encourage students to choose an activity that they feel less comfortable with if they want a challenge or are aware that they need practice in a particular area.
Think of a Word! gives students practice with vocabulary and comparatives.
World Weather Report gives students the opportunity to do some research about weather on the Internet and to write a report.

Language File pp118–119

Workbook Unit 5 Inspiration EXTRA! pp62–63

Social situations

1 READING

- Focus on the photos in the questionnaire. Ask *What are all these?* (gestures) *How many gestures are there in the world?* (more than 700,000)
- In pairs, students discuss what the gestures in the photos mean in their country.

2 LISTENING

- Explain that Emily and Adam are talking about what the gestures mean in Britain. Play the recording. Students listen and choose the correct option. Play the recording, or parts of the recording, again if necessary.
- Check answers. Ask *Which of the gestures mean something different in your country? Which are the same?*

2.43 Recording

EMILY	*OK, so what's happening in picture one?*
ADAM	*Well, she isn't saying 'Help'!*
EMILY	*No, she's saying 'I have no idea'.*
ADAM	*Yes, that's right.*
EMILY	*And picture two – what about this one? What's the man saying?*
ADAM	*It's not 'Goodbye'. I think he's saying 'Come here'.*
EMILY	*Yes, he is.*
ADAM	*Now picture three – she's saying 'Fingers crossed'!*
EMILY	*That's 'Let's hope for good luck'.*
ADAM	*Yep. And picture four?*
EMILY	*She's putting her finger to her lips– it means 'Sh, don't say anything.'*
ADAM	*Yes. It means 'Be quiet!'.*
EMILY	*And picture five – thumbs up...*
ADAM	*That means 'That's great' in Britain.*
EMILY	*Right. And the last picture ...*
ADAM	*Well, he's saying someone has mad ideas.*
EMILY	*So it means 'He's crazy'.*
ADAM	*That's right!*

Answers

1 B 2 C 3 B 4 A 5 A 6 B

Optional activity

In pairs, one student says the answer and their partner makes the appropriate gesture. Afterwards, they can change to making the gesture and saying what it means.

3 READING

- Focus on the party photo and ask students what they can see, what the people are doing and what they are wearing.
- In pairs, students read *What do you say at a party?* and choose the best option.
- Play the recording for them to listen and check their answers.

2.44 Recording

1

SUSANA	*This is my friend, Tamara.*
JOHN	*Hi, nice to meet you.*
TAMARA	*Nice to meet you too.*

2

JOHN	*What do you do?*
TAMARA	*I'm a model.*

3

JOHN	*Do you want something to drink?*
TAMARA	*Yes, please.*

4

TAMARA	*What's he like?*
SUSANA	*He's a great guy.*

5

JOHN	*Can I use your phone?*
TAMARA	*Yes, of course.*

Answers

1 D 2 B 3 B 4 D 5 C

Optional activities

- ♦ With a more confident class, elicit other possible responses, e.g. *Pleased to meet you, He's quite serious, I'm sorry I don't have any credit on it.*
- ♦ Students practise the conversations in pairs. When they have memorised the dialogues, tell them to imagine they are at a party and they should practise these short conversations with different people. Students move around the class practising the dialogues.

4 SPEAKING

- Focus on the situations. Check students understand *sneeze, stand on someone's foot.*
- With a more confident class, students can predict what to say before looking at the options. With a less confident class, students match the situations and expressions.
- Play the recording for students to check their answers.
- Confirm answers by choosing different students to answer the questions. Monitor for pronunciation of words and appropriate intonation.

2.45 Recording

1

JOHN *[Sneezes.]*
TAMARA *Bless you.*

2

TAMARA *[talking to someone else]*
JOHN *Can I have a word with you?*

3

TAMARA *Ouch – that's my foot!*
JOHN *I'm very sorry!*

4

TAMARA *Do you want something to eat?*
JOHN *Sorry? Can you say that again?*
TAMARA *Do you want something to eat?*

5

JOHN *You don't look very happy. What's wrong?*
TAMARA *I don't like this music.*

6

TAMARA *I'm going on holiday tomorrow.*
JOHN *Have a fabulous time!*

Answers

1 c 2 b 3 f 4 e 5 a 6 d

Optional activities

- Students practise these expressions in pairs, giving each other cues, e.g. one student sneezes, says *Ouch!* or *I'm going to Italy tomorrow*.
- With a more confident class, give students more expressions and they work out when you say them and put them in short dialogues, e.g. *Sleep well, Have a good weekend, See you tomorrow, Excuse me, Really!*

5 MINI-PROJECT GESTURE GUIDE

- Go through the instructions with the class. Students work in pairs to discuss and write their guide to gestures in their country.
- Allow plenty of time for them to do the necessary research and collect their pictures.
- Encourage them to do a first draft of their guide and to read it carefully and correct any errors before copying it out neatly and adding the pictures and captions.
- Display the completed guides in the classroom for everyone to read and enjoy.

WEBLINKS

Students may like to visit www.everythingesl.net/inservices/body_language.php for more information on gestures around the world.

Workbook Culture pp64–65

LOOKING BACK

1 Was he the first president?

Communicative aims	Language	Pronunciation	Vocabulary	Optional aids
Talking about past events (1)	Past simple: *be*	Weak and strong forms: *was*	Countries Places in a town	Exercise 4: pictures/ photos of places, e.g. a park Follow-up activities: a grid for each student; large pieces of paper

WARMER 1

Game *Chinese whispers* Arrange the students in two or three lines. Invite the first student in each line to come to you. Whisper to them *I like bananas and I love chocolate, but I hate mushrooms*. Tell each student to whisper the sentence to the second person in their team once only. The second whispers to the third and so on. The last person in each line comes to the front of the class and either (a) says what they heard or (b) writes it down. Give points to the team who was closest and repeat with a different combination. Use a sentence, e.g. *Mike Roots likes cycling, but he doesn't like cycling on dangerous roads.*

WARMER 2

Game *Last letter game* See Unit 3 Lesson 1 Follow-up activity for instructions.

1 OPENER

- Focus on the quiz. Ask *Are you good at quizzes? Do you watch quiz shows on TV? What type of questions are easier – music, history, film or sport?*
- Students look at the pictures in the quiz and discuss what they show.

Optional activity

Students write down all the things they can see in the pictures.

2 READING

- The aim is to provide a context for the introduction of the past simple of *be*.
- Ask students to work in pairs to do the quiz.
- Play the recording for them to listen and check their answers.
- Draw their attention to the use of *was* and *were* in the quiz. These are the singular and plural past simple forms of *be*.

2.46 Recording and answers

1 *The first president of the USA was* ***George Washington****.*
2 *The first people on the moon were* ***Armstrong and Aldrin****.*
3 *The artist Salvador Dalí was from* ***Spain****.*
4 *The first woman to win a Nobel Prize was* ***Marie Curie****.*
5 *At the age of 17,* ***Maria Sharapova*** *was a Wimbledon Tennis Champion.*
6 *The host country of the 2008 Olympic Games was* ***China****.*
7 *The Incas were from* ***Peru****.*
8 *Pompeii was a Roman* ***town****.*

3 AFTER READING AND LISTENING

- Students match the questions with the answers.
- Check answers and draw their attention to the use of *was/wasn't* and *were/weren't* in short answers.

Answers

1 b 2 g 3 a 4 c 5 d 6 f 7 h 8 e

Optional activities

- ♦ Students write more questions and short answers about items in the quiz and test each other.
- ♦ Students write false sentences, e.g. *The 2000 Olympic Games were in Greece.* They then read their sentences to their partner who has to correct the error. *No, the 2004 Olympic Games were in Greece* or *No, the 2000 Olympics weren't in Greece. They were in Sydney*.
- ♦ In pairs or small groups, students think of sentences about other famous people or events using the past tense of *be*. These sentences can be true or false. They write the sentences on a piece of paper, omitting the verb, e.g. *Louis Armstrong ______ the first man to walk on the moon.* They then exchange sentences with another group who have to choose the correct form for each sentence: *was, wasn't, were, weren't*, e.g. *Louis Armstrong wasn't the first man to walk on the moon.* (Neil Armstrong was the first man to walk on the moon.)

Your response

Ask students to say which questions were easy and which were difficult.

Extension Students write one or two more similar quiz questions (using the past simple of *be*). Remind them that they have to know the right answers and to provide two wrong answers as well. Monitor and give help with vocabulary. Collect the students' questions and have a class quiz.

4 VOCABULARY

- Ask students to name places in a town/city. (They should know some from Unit 4.) Alternatively, use pictures to elicit places. Check comprehension by asking *What do you do there? What can you buy there?*
- Students read the clues and work out who was where. Don't go through the answers yet.
- Read the model question. Ask a confident student to answer the question. Students continue in pairs and, in this way, check their answers.
- Check the answers as a class by nominating pairs to ask and answer the questions.

Answers

Name	*Place*
Adam	*in a café*
Emily	*on the beach*
Jake	*on the beach*
Katya	*at the shopping centre*
Pierre	*at the cinema*
Ruby	*in the park*
Teresa	*at the shopping centre*

Optional activities

- ♦ Instead of students reading the nine clues in exercise 4, you dictate them. Read naturally, including weak forms, but repeat each one up to three times if necessary. The aim is to give students listening, writing and grammar practice. Copy the names and places on the board and students work out the puzzle.
- ♦ In pairs, students invent their own logic puzzle. They use the same people and places but have different answers and so provide different clues.

5 PRONUNCIATION

- Focus on the Pronunciation box. Students listen to the pronunciation of the sentences. Tell them to listen carefully to the pronunciation of *was/wasn't*. Ask *Do you hear a difference?* Play the recording again, pausing after each sentence for students to repeat. Pronunciation of strong and weak forms tends to occur quite naturally when there is good sentence stress and rhythm so concentrate on this.

2.47 Recording

Weak form /wəz/
/wəz/ *Where was Adam's sister? She was in the park.*
Strong form /wɒz/
/wɒz/ *Was she on the beach? No, she wasn't.*

- Students read the four sentences and predict whether the pronunciation is strong or weak. They then listen and check.
- Check answers by nominating students to read the sentences using either the strong of weak form of *was*.

2.47 Recording and answers

1 It was five o'clock. /wəz/
2 Was he in a café? /wɒz/
3 Yes, he was. /wɒz/
4 Who was at the cinema? /wəz/

Optional activity

With a confident class, elicit/teach the rules of strong and weak pronunciation of *was* that are illustrated here: it is weak in positive sentences, e.g. *Adam was in a café*, and strong in questions beginning with *Was …?* and short answers, e.g. *Yes, he was.*

6 SPEAKING

- Read the dialogue aloud with a student. Ask *What can you change in the first question?* (the time) Elicit a possible question, e.g. *Where were you yesterday at 7pm?* Ask two confident students to demonstrate this dialogue. Encourage students to answer truthfully.
- Students continue in pairs.
- Ask pairs to perform their dialogues for the class.

Optional activity

Confident students can talk about last Saturday, Sunday, Monday, etc (especially the weekend where the routines are less predictable).

7 WRITING

- Go through the example with the class. Students write similar sentences about where they were and who they were with. Set a ten-minute time limit.
- Students compare their work.

LANGUAGE WORKOUT

- Ask students to look at the Language box and to complete the chart. Confident students can complete first and then check, while others can look back at exercise 3 and then complete.
- Students turn to page 119 of the Language File to check their answers.
- Highlight that
  - *was* is the past of *am/is* and *were* is the past of *are*
  - *was/were* are used in exactly the same way as *is/are*, ie they are inverted to make questions and *not (n't)* is added to make negatives.
- Model and drill the example sentences.

Answers
weren't
Was *Were*
Yes, he/she/it ***was****. No, he/she/it* ***wasn't****.*
Yes, they ***were****. No, they* ***weren't****.*
wasn't *were not*

Optional activity

Ask students questions, e.g. *Were you at the cinema last night? Was I late this morning? Was Mario in class yesterday?* Students respond with short answers.

PRACTICE

- Students do Practice exercises 19 and 20 on page 119 of the Language File. They complete the sentences, questions and answers with *was/wasn't* or *were/weren't*.

Answers
20
1 were 2 was 3 weren't 4 wasn't 5 was
21
1 Was, was 2 Was, wasn't 3 Were, weren't 4 weren't
5 Were, weren't

Follow-up activities

- ♦ **Game** *Bingo* Give each student a 4-by-4 grid with past simple statements in each square, e.g. *He/She was at the cinema last night. He/She wasn't late this morning. He/She knows where the painter Picasso was from.* Students move round and ask, e.g., *Were you at the cinema last night?* If they find a student who gives the answer in the box, they write that student's name there. They continue until one student makes a line, either vertically, horizontally or diagonally.
- ♦ Draw a word map on the board. Write *Places in town* in the centre. Elicit possible categories and write them on the word map, e.g. *tourist attractions, places to eat.* In small groups, students draw their own word map on a large piece of paper or card. They can use the categories on the board or some of their own and add as many words as they can. Set a time limit and give dictionaries if available. Display the word maps in the classroom.

HOMEWORK

Students interview their families about where they were at different times yesterday and write sentences using exercise 7 as a guide.

WEBLINK

Students can do another history quiz at www.eslcafe.com/quiz/whistory1.html

Revision and Extension p85

Language File p119

Workbook Unit 6 Lesson 1 pp66–67

Photocopiable notes p159, Worksheet p178

The Vikings liked music

Communicative aims	Language	Pronunciation	Vocabulary	Optional aids
Talking about past events (2)	Past simple: affirmative	/d/ discovered /t/ crossed /ɪd/ started	Countries Continents Food	Warmer 2 and Opener: a world map Follow-up activity: slips of paper

WARMER 1

Students choose six words from the previous lesson and make anagrams. In pairs, they exchange lists and see who can rewrite all the words correctly first.

WARMER 2

Game *The alphabet game* Ask students to write the letters A–Z down the margin of a piece of paper. In pairs or small groups, give students two minutes to think of a country for each letter. Do an example, e.g. *A, Austria*. Use this example to show that students shouldn't write continents, e.g. *Africa*, or cities, e.g. *Amsterdam*. After two minutes, ask the group with the most countries to read out their list. Check spelling and pronunciation. Use the countries to elicit/teach the continents, e.g. *Which continent is Spain in?*

1 OPENER

- The aim is to pre-teach these countries and continents so that the students understand the Viking history text better. Ask students to find and point to France on the map. Students continue in pairs.
- Check answers with a large world map or by pointing to the different countries/continents on the map in the book and eliciting the name. Check pronunciation.

Answers

Continents: Africa, Asia, Europe, North America, South America

Useful information

There are either six or seven continents depending on whether you count the Americas as one or two. They are: Africa, Antarctica, Asia, Australasia/Oceania, Europe, North America, South America.

2 READING

- Students read and listen to the story of the Vikings. Ask them to tick the countries and continents in exercise 1 that they hear (Africa, Asia, Denmark, Europe, Greenland, Iceland, North America, Norway, Sweden).
- Ask them to say what information they find most surprising. (Many may think that Christopher Columbus was the first European to visit North America.)

2.48 Recording

See text on page 78 of the Student's Book.

3 AFTER READING

- Students read and listen to the text again and decide if sentences 1–8 are true or false. Encourage them to guess the meaning of unfamiliar vocabulary from the context. Be prepared to explain *sail* (v), *steal* (v), *board games, dice games*.

Answers

1 *True*
2 *False. They went to Britain over 1,200 years ago.*
3 *False. The ships were big – they carried up to 200 people.*
4 *True*
5 *False. They drank beer.*
6 *False. They wore shirts and trousers.*
7 *True*
8 *False. They went to North America.*

Your response

Brainstorm any further information students know about the Vikings and find out if they were in their country.

LANGUAGE WORKOUT OPTION

If you want to pre-teach the language students will be using in the following activities, you may like to go to the Language Workout box now.

4 PRONUNCIATION

- Focus on the three pronunciations of the *-ed* ending. Model and drill the examples. Tell students that the difference between the /d/ and /t/ endings is minimal. It is easier to hear if the verb is followed by a word beginning with a vowel sound, e.g. *crossed out, discovered us*.
- Students could predict which column the words go into before listening. Play the recording once. Students compare their ideas with a partner. Play the recording again for students to confirm their ideas. Pause after each word to check answers. Drill each word chorally and individually.

2.49 Recording and answers

crossed discovered liked played sailed started visited wanted watched

/d/ *discovered played sailed*

/t/ *crossed liked watched*

/ɪd/ *started visited wanted*

Optional activity

You may wish to teach the students the rules: *-ed* is pronounced /t/ after unvoiced sounds, /d/ after voiced sounds and /ɪd/ when the word ends in *-ied* or when /t/ or /d/ is the last sound of the infinitive verb, e.g. *need, decide, hate, wait*. The rules for when to use /ɪd/ are the most useful for students.

5 GAME

- Nominate a student to read the first sentence aloud. Ask if it is true or false. Do the same with the second sentence.
- With a less confident class, students prepare their true/false sentences in pairs before changing partners and testing their new partner. With a more confident class, students can continue this speaking game without preparation.

Optional activity

Confident students can continue the game using other verbs, e.g. *wear, drink, eat, live*, and the information in the text 'The Vikings'.

6 LISTENING

- Ask students to copy the chart into their notebooks.
- Students look at the phrases and the verbs and predict the answers. Play the recording and students listen to check. Allow students to compare answers. Find out if any student guessed all the answers correctly.

2.50 Recording

KATYA *Yesterday I wore a dress. I went to the cinema, and I had an ice cream. And then I played computer games and I watched TV. And then I phoned my sister.*

PIERRE *Yesterday I wore a shirt and jeans. I went to a café and I had a pizza. And then I played tennis and I watched a DVD. And then I phoned my parents.*

Answers

Yesterday ...	Katya	Pierre
wore	*a dress*	*a shirt and jeans*
went to	*the cinema*	*a café*
had	*an ice cream*	*a pizza*
played	*computer games*	*tennis*
watched	*TV*	*a DVD*
phoned	*her sister*	*his parents*

- In pairs, students make sentences using the information in the chart.

Optional activity

Student A closes his/her book. Student B talks about Katya and Pierre but includes some false information. Student A listens and corrects the false information.

7 SPEAKING

- Explain to students that they are going to tell their partners about what they did yesterday, using the verbs in the chart in exercise 6. Give them a couple of minutes to think about what they are going to say.
- In pairs, one student describes what he/she did yesterday and his/her partner makes a note of what he/she says. Students then reverse roles.
- Ask students to tell you something interesting about their partners.

Optional activity

Fast finishers can talk about last Saturday and Sunday.

Extension Students play *Past simple challenge* in pairs. One student says a verb and the other one has to give the past simple of the verb. They can take turns to give verbs and keep a record of correct answers to see who wins.

8 WRITING

- Ask students to read the instructions. Check *Are you writing a postcard?* (No, an email.) *Who are you writing to?* (A friend.) *Are you writing about today?* (No, yesterday.)
- Elicit some alternatives to *Yesterday was a busy day!*, e.g. *Yesterday was a quiet day, Yesterday was a normal day at school.* Set a 15-minute time limit.
- Monitor and note examples of good language and errors. Put these on the board and ask students to identify and correct the errors.

Optional activities

- ♦ Students exchange writing and correct each other's work for spelling, grammar and punctuation.
- ♦ Collect in the pieces of writing and read some of them aloud in class. Students listen and guess who the writer is.
- ♦ If you have a computer room with Internet access, this activity could be done there. Students can either write to you at your email address (or an email address you have created for the purpose of this activity) or write to each other and then respond. You may wish to teach them some useful responses, e.g. *Wow! That sounds very tiring!* or *Your day sounds very similar to my day*. Print a copy of each email for the students to keep in their notebooks/files.

Extension Students write three true and two false sentences in their email. Then they show their sentences to their partner who has to guess which sentences are false.

LANGUAGE WORKOUT

- Ask students to look at the Language box. Read through the rules for the past simple with the students. Ask students to complete the examples of regular past tense verbs. Point out that they are all in the text on page 78. Students then find the irregular past tense verbs in the text.
- Students look at page 119 of the Language File and the irregular verb list on page 127 to check their answers.

Answers
crossed discovered played sailed
visited
liked lived
came drank ate found went had
made wore

- Highlight that the past form is always the same in the affirmative – there is no third person change.

PRACTICE

- Students do Practice exercise 21 on page 120 of the Language File
- Students read the sentences and decide which verb goes in each space. They then put the verb in the past tense. Point out that the first six are regular verbs and the second six are irregular.
- Check answers by choosing different students to say the completed sentences.

Answers
1 sailed 2 visited 3 liked 4 lived 5 carried 6 played
7 had 8 wore 9 found 10 went 11 came 12 made

Follow-up activities

- **Game** *Past tense bingo* Student make their own 'bingo cards' in their notebooks (a grid with three columns and three rows). Write 20 infinitives, some regular and some irregular, on the board and on slips of paper. Students choose nine and write them in the boxes in their grid. Put the slips of paper in a bag. Go round the class asking students to pick one out without looking and say the past tense aloud to the group. Students who have the infinitive cross it out. The first student to cross out all nine boxes shouts *Bingo!* and wins the game. Repeat the game, changing the verbs or writing the past tense on the board and slips of paper to check that students know the infinitive.
- Brainstorm leisure activities with the class, e.g. *go shopping, go to the gym, watch television.* Write them on the board and ask students to change the present to the past tense, e.g. go → *went, watch* → *watched.* Ask a confident student *When was the last time you …* (an activity on the board)? Then write the question on the board and ask two students to demonstrate the question and answer with a different activity. Students continue in pairs.

HOMEWORK

Students write an email similar to that in exercise 8, but this time they imagine they are someone famous, e.g. a singer, an actor or actress, a sports star, a politician. They write about what they did yesterday.

WEBLINK

Students may like to visit this website where they can find out more about the Vikings: www.bbc.co.uk/schools/vikings/index.shtml

Revision and Extension p85

Language File pp119–120

Workbook Unit 6 Lesson 2 pp68–69

Photocopiable notes p159, Worksheet p179

Did he say sorry?

Communicative aims	Language	Pronunciation	Vocabulary	Optional aids
Asking about past events	Past simple: negative, questions and short answers	Silent letters	Feelings Activities	Warmer 3: pictures of people showing different feelings Follow-up activities: chart for each student

WARMER 1

If you set the homework in the previous lesson, ask students to read their emails to each other. Their partner listens and gets one point for guessing the job of the person and a second point if they can name the person. Students can change partners and continue, keeping count of their score.

WARMER 2

Write anagrams of irregular past tense verbs on the board, e.g. *meca, dha, roew* (*came, had, wore*). Students race to re-order the letters and write the infinitive of each one next to it.

WARMER 3

Use pictures, mime or scenarios, e.g. *How do you feel when you see a ghost?* to elicit feelings – *happy, sad, angry/cross, scared, worried,* (*bored, interested, excited*). Ask students to tell their partner what makes them feel like each of these.

1 OPENER

- The aim is to set the scene for the conversation and to get students to predict what Pierre and Teresa are talking about and how Pierre feels.
- Students look at the photo and describe what they can see: who's in the photo, what they are wearing, what they are doing.
- Focus on Pierre and ask *How is he feeling?* Students choose one adjective from the box.

2 READING

- Tell students they are going to hear the conversation and need to note how Pierre feels.
- With a more confident class, do this as a listening exercise. With a less confident class, students read and listen. Check how Pierre feels.

2.51 Recording

See text on page 80 of the Student's Book.

Answer

Pierre is cross because Adam says he lost Pierre's camera but doesn't apologise. It turns out it's a joke.

LANGUAGE WORKOUT OPTION

If you want to pre-teach the language students will be using in the following activities, you may like to go to the Language Workout box now.

3 AFTER READING

- Students read the conversation again and answer the questions. You may want to pre-teach *lend* as the opposite of *borrow*.
- They then listen and/or read again to check their ideas. Encourage students to guess the meaning of unfamiliar vocabulary from the context and ignore words that are not necessary to complete the exercise.
- Check the answers by choosing different pairs to ask and answer the questions.

Answers

1 Pierre lent Adam his camera.
2 No, he didn't.
3 He went back to the bus.
4 Pierre
5 On the minibus
6 No, she didn't.
7 Pierre did.
8 She wanted to go to a Dracula movie.

Your response

Ask the students to say whether they think Adam's joke was funny or not.

4 READING

- Focus on the photo and ask what it is (a street). Tell them that this is a street in a part of Brighton called The Lanes. Ask *Who is in the picture* (a girl).
- Set a time limit of two minutes for students to read the text and answer the questions *Who did Pierre think he saw? Was it really her?* Check the answers (Teresa, no).
- Students then read again and decide which words are best. Don't check the answers at this point.
- Ask *Who do you think the girl is?*

5 LISTENING

- Tell students they are going to listen and check the words in exercise 4.
- Pause before the end of the recording and tell them they are going to find out who Pierre really saw. Check the answer.
- Focus on the example questions and answers. Tell students that they are going to check their answers to exercise 4 by asking and answering the questions like this. Make sure that they don't look at each other's notes. Students continue in pairs. If students are unsure of a final answer, they can ask you the question.

2.52 Recording

See text on page 81 of the Student's Book.

Answers

dinner walked window wore shouted
turned eyes called cinema
Pierre saw the ghost of a girl who lived there a long time ago.

Optional activity

Act out the story. Organise students into groups of three. Set a time limit of 15 minutes for students to prepare their performance. This will require careful re-reading of the story to see what happens when and who says what. Students watch each other's performances and decide which one is closest to the story in the book.

Extension Students close their books and take turns to tell a partner the story of what happened to Pierre in The Lanes. With less confident classes, write the answers to exercise 4 on the board. Students close their books, but use these prompts to recreate the story.

6 PRONUNCIATION

- Check students understand the words by asking e.g. *Which word is the past of think? Which word is the opposite of right?*
- Tell students that some English words have 'silent' letters, e.g. *ghost*. Students say the words in the box aloud and guess which letters are silent. Play the recording. Students listen and repeat. They then cross out the silent letters. Play the recording again if necessary. Check the answers on the board.

2.53 Recording

high honest knew thought tonight two
white wrong

Answers

high honest knew thought tonight
two white wrong

- Highlight that in words that begin *kn-* (e.g. *knee*) or *wr-* (*wrong*) the *k* and *w* are always silent. Encourage students to cross out silent letters with a different coloured pen whenever they learn new words.

Optional activity

Students make a sentence using as many of the words as possible. (They can use words not in the box as well.) The student who fits the most words into one correct sentence wins.

7 SPEAKING

- Read the example question and answer. Elicit examples of further questions, using the prompts. Tell students they should answer truthfully. Students continue in pairs.
- Ask some students to tell the class something that their partner did.

Optional activities

- ♦ Students ask you the questions.
- ♦ Encourage confident students to ask follow-up questions, e.g. *What did you watch? Did you see …?* and provide more information, e.g. *I didn't listen to the radio last night. I don't usually listen to the radio in the evening.*

Extension Students make notes of other students' answers to the questions. They then write sentences about five of them.

8 WRITING

- Students read the instructions. Check *What did you see?* (A ghost.) *Is your friend surprised?* (Yes.) With a less confident class, brainstorm questions the friend could ask, e.g. *When did you see it? Was it big? Was it white? Did it speak to you?* Set a ten-minute time limit.
- Note examples of good language and errors. Put these on the board and ask students to identify and correct the errors.

Optional activities

- ♦ Students do the writing in pairs. They both write the first line of the dialogue, then exchange papers and write their response, exchange again and respond and so on, reflecting a real conversation.
- ♦ In pairs, students choose one dialogue, memorise it, rehearse it and then perform it for the class.

LANGUAGE WORKOUT

- Ask students to look at the Language box and to complete the sentences. The answers for the negative past simple are in the dialogue in exercise 2. The answers for the questions and short answers are not in the text but can be worked out easily from the completed examples.
- Students turn to page 119 of the Language File to check their answers.

Answers
didn't didn't
Did Did
didn't did did

- Highlight that
  - *did* is the past of *do/does* and *didn't* is the past of *don't/doesn't*
  - the infinitive is used after *did/didn't*, not the past
  - the form is the same for all persons (I, you, he, she, etc)
  - the word order in negatives and questions is the same as in the present simple *Do you go …? → Did you go …? I don't have … → I didn't have …*
- Drill the examples in chorus for pronunciation and stress.

PRACTICE

- Students do Practice exercise 22 on page 120 of the Language File
- Students complete the sentences. Do the first one as an example with the class. Point out that the answer must be true.
- Check the answers by asking different students to say the completed sentences. When the answer is no, encourage students to explain, e.g. Teresa didn't get angry. Pierre got angry.

Answers
1 *Did the group go to Devil's Dyke? Yes, they did.*
2 *Did Teresa ask Pierre a question? Yes, she did.*
3 *Did Emily borrow Pierre's camera? No, she didn't.*
4 *Did Teresa and Pierre talk about Adam? Yes, they did.*
5 *Did Adam say sorry? No, he didn't.*
6 *Did Jake find the camera? No, he didn't.*

Optional activities

- ♦ In pairs, one student closes his/her book and the other tests his/her memory of the conversation by asking some questions from this exercise and exercise 3. They then change roles.
- ♦ Students write three sentences in the past, one positive, one negative and one question. They then jumble up the word order in each and give the sentences to a partner, who must re-order them. Write an example on the board, e.g. *games the Adam night on played console last* (Adam played on the games console last night).

Follow-up activities

- ♦ *Find Someone Who …* Hand out a copy of the following to each student:

Find someone who …	***Name***
had a *big breakfast/a cold shower/ a coffee* this morning.	
played *a musical instrument/ football/tennis* last weekend.	
went *to the cinema/to the gym/ shopping* yesterday.	
phoned *someone in their family/ a friend* last night.	
wached *a film/the news/the weather* on TV last night.	

Students choose one alternative for each sentence. They then move around the classroom, asking the appropriate question until they find someone who says yes. They write that student's name next to the sentence. Elicit how to change the sentence into a question, e.g. *went to bed after midnight → Did you go to bed after midnight?* and demonstrate the activity.
- ♦ Dictate five sentences from the lesson, e.g. *Adam borrowed my new camera and then he lost it, Teresa was here in a long white dress but now I can't find her.* Students exchange their sentences and correct each other's spelling, grammar and punctuation.

HOMEWORK

Students write a paragraph about their encounter with a ghost. They should say when it was, where they were, what it wore, etc.

WEBLINK

Students may like to visit this website: http://mikeperris.com/brighton/the-lanes-bt-neolithic.html for more information on ghosts in The Lanes. They may need help with some of the language.

Revision and Extension p85

Language File pp119–120

Workbook Unit 6 Lesson 3 pp70–71

Photocopiable notes p159, Worksheet p180

Integrated Skills Telling a story

Skills
Reading Dracula story
Listening Ordering pictures
Speaking Retelling a story
Writing Completing a text with conjunctions

Learner Independence
Irregular verbs
Vocabulary notebook
Phrasebook

Vocabulary
Useful expressions

Optional aids
Exercise 2 Optional activity: copies of introduction on page 82 of Student's Book
Follow-up activities: cards for Vocabulary box

Useful information

Bram Stoker was born in Dublin, Ireland in 1847. He was bed-ridden for much of his early childhood due to ill health. In 1878 he moved to London with his wife to become theatre manager at the Lyceum Theatre. He began writing a novel about vampires which developed into *Dracula* after spending time in Whitby in the north of England. *Dracula* is his most famous work but he also wrote several other novels, including a collection of short stories. He died in 1912.

WARMER 1

If you set the homework in the previous lesson, ask students to read their stories to each other.

WARMER 2

Game *Me too!* Each student writes down five things they did last weekend, e.g. *I went to the cinema*. The aim is to find other students who did the same things. They need to move round the class, asking the appropriate questions, e.g. *Did you go to the cinema last weekend?* They only need one match for each activity but each match must be with a different student. Students race to match all five.

WARMER 3

Game *Twenty Questions* See Unit 4 Lesson 1 Follow-up activity for instructions. Students guess the famous person, using questions e.g. *Are you dead or alive? What's/was your job?* You could choose to be Dracula to activate students' knowledge for the following exercises.

1 OPENER

- The aim is to encourage students to predict before reading. Pre-teach some essential vocabulary, e.g. *vampire, prince*. Look at the book cover picture and ask students to make predictions or say what they know about Dracula.

2 READING

- The aim is for students to read for detailed information and review the past simple. Ask students to read the questions and predict the answers.
- Set a short time limit for students to read the introduction and the start of the story and find the answers. Play the recording for them to listen while they read.

2.54 Recording
See text on page 82 of the Student's Book.

Answers
1 *In a castle in Transylvania.*
2 *Blood.*
3 *1897.*
4 *1875.*
5 *He didn't eat and he didn't sleep at night.*
6 *He was scared.*
7 *Mina.*

Optional activities

- Use the introduction as a running dictation. Students work in pairs (A and B). Copy the introduction text onto several pieces of paper and place them at the front of the class at a distance where the students cannot read them. Student A runs up to the text, remembers as much as they can, runs back and dictates it to B. B listens and writes it down as accurately as possible. Student A runs back to the text and remembers more, and so on. When one pair has finished, stop the activity. Give the pairs a moment to correct their version. Pairs exchange their pieces of writing and mark it against the original. They start with 50 points but lose a point for every incorrect/missing word, incorrect spelling, incorrect/missing punctuation, etc. The winning pair is the one with the highest score. You could then get students to reverse roles and do the same for the start of the story.
- To provide more practice with past simple question forms, give the students the answers instead of the questions and ask them to write the questions.

3 LISTENING

- Ask students to say what they can see in the pictures. Be prepared to teach *crash*.
- In pairs, students predict the order of the pictures and the story. Nominate a few students who have some ideas to tell their version of the story to the class.
- Students listen and order the pictures. Check the answers.

2.55 Recording

Meanwhile, Mina was on holiday with her friend Lucy. At first, Mina and Lucy enjoyed their holiday by the sea. But then Mina became worried.

'There's no news from Jonathan,' she said to Lucy. 'I hope he's all right.'

'Don't worry, Mina,' said Lucy. 'I'm sure he's fine.

One night there was a terrible storm and a boat crashed onto the beach. There was no one on the boat. But a huge dog jumped out of the boat and ran up the hill to the church.

Three nights later, Lucy got up in the middle of the night. She walked out of the house and went up the hill to the church. Mina found Lucy's bed was empty. 'Lucy isn't in her bed!' Mina thought. 'Where is she?'

Mina went up the hill to the church. She saw Lucy with someone tall and dark. Mina was scared and shouted 'Lucy! Lucy!' But when Mina ran up, Lucy was alone and there was no one else there.

Answers

1 C 2 A 3 D 4 B

4 SPEAKING

- Tell students that they are going to use the pictures to retell this part of the story. Give them the opportunity to listen again to hear the extra details on the recording.
- Do the first picture with the class. Prompt students with information not in the picture, e.g. *She was worried*. Remind students to use the past tense. Students continue in pairs.

Optional activities

- ♦ With a less confident class, do the activity as a class and write all the verbs on the board as you go. Then ask the students to do the activity in pairs using the verbs on the board as prompts.
- ♦ Fast finishers talk about what they think happened next.

5 WRITING

- The aim is to review these conjunctions to develop awareness of text cohesion. For students to be able to do this, they have to understand the text. So, first, ask them to predict the end of the story *Who lives? Who dies?* and then read to see if they were right. Ask *Was it a happy ending?*
- Then, focus on the completion exercise. Check if students know how to use the words by doing the first four together as a class.
- Students complete the text and then compare in pairs. Play the recording for students to listen and check their answers.

2.56 Recording and answers

Mina and Lucy went back to London, ***but*** *Lucy became very ill* ***and*** *died. She was now a vampire!*
Finally, Harker escaped from Dracula's castle ***and*** *he came back to England.* ***Then*** *he saw Dracula in London! Harker* ***and*** *Mina asked a friend, Professor Van Helsing, for help. Van Helsing guessed that Dracula was a vampire. The men decided to find* ***and*** *kill Dracula.* ***But*** *where was he?*
One night Dracula visited Mina ***and*** *kissed her neck. She started to change into a vampire!* ***Then*** *Van Helsing found out that that Dracula was on a boat to Transylvania.*
Harker, Van Helsing ***and*** *Mina went to Transylvania by train. Now Mina was very ill* ***and*** *there wasn't a lot of time. They found Dracula outside his castle – it was almost dark! They killed the vampire* ***and*** *saved Mina's life. Dracula was dead!*

Optional activities

- ♦ Students write true/false sentences about the story and then test each other on the story using their sentences.
- ♦ Students choose one character, Dracula, Harker, Mina, Lucy or Van Helsing and tell their partner something that they did or that happened to them, e.g. *I visited Castle Dracula*. Their partner listens and identifies the character.

6 LEARNER INDEPENDENCE

- The aim is to review some irregular past forms and present some new ones. Ask students how to form the regular past (*-ed*). Point out that these irregular verbs don't add *-ed* but change their form. This change can be just one or two letters, e.g. *drink* → *drank*, or it can be a completely new word, e.g. *go* → *went*. Students simply need to learn these changes.
- More confident students can guess first and then check their answers in the text. Less confident students can look back at the text and find the past forms.

Answers

became, came, drank, found, went, saw, thought, wrote

- Students look at the irregular verb list on p127. Ask e.g. *What's the past of win?* Students continue in pairs. More confident students can answer from memory rather than looking at the list. You could set students a regular homework task of learning ten irregular past tense forms and keep testing them on these. In this way, they will gradually build up the number of past tense forms they can understand and use.

7

- The aim is to encourage students to group words in lexical sets (or categories) in their vocabulary notebooks rather than randomly or alphabetically. This process means that students review the meanings of the words and it also helps storage and retrieval of words from memory.
- Write the three categories on the board. Elicit an example for each.
- Students work individually and add to each category from memory. They then compare their list with a partner and add any more. Finally they look back through the unit and add any others that they find. Set a minimum of six words per category.

Optional activities

- ♦ Students mark the stress on words of two or more syllables.
- ♦ Students tick the words they feel they know and put a question mark next to the ones they are still learning.
- ♦ Fast finishers can test each other. One student gives a definition and the other says the word.

8 PHRASEBOOK

- Ask students to look through the unit, find the expressions and notice how they are used. Help with translation where necessary. Students can add expressions they like to their Personal Phrasebooks.
- Play the recording for students to listen and repeat the expressions.

2.57 Recording and answers

What's the matter? (Teresa, Lesson 3)
Everything OK? (Teresa, Lesson 3)
Not really. (Pierre, Lesson 3)
To be honest … (Pierre, Lesson 3)
Here he comes! (Teresa, Lesson 3)
What do you mean? (Pierre, Lesson 3)
Let's forget about it. (Teresa, Lesson 3)

- Ask students to work in pairs to make up a short dialogue following the instructions. With a more confident class, ask students to include as many of the expressions as they can in their conversation. The winning pair is the one with the most expressions included in an understandable dialogue. Ask some pairs to act out their dialogues in front of the class.

Suggested answers

Everything OK?
Not really.
What's the matter?
To be honest, I feel really bad. I made a mistake – I'm really sorry.
Don't worry. Let's forget about it.

Follow-up activities

- ♦ Divide students into groups of six to eight. Each group prepares to act out the story. There are five main characters: Dracula, Harker, Mina, Lucy and Van Helsing. You also need a narrator to move the story along and you could have one or two villagers to comment on the boat crashing onto the beach and the dog. Students vote on the best performance at the end.
- ♦ Students write new vocabulary from this lesson on cards (to add to the Vocabulary box if you have one). Collect the cards and divide the students into teams of two or three. Show one student from each team the same card. These students mime the word or draw a picture of it on the board. Their team shouts out their guesses. The first team to say the right word wins a point.

HOMEWORK

Students choose one character, Dracula, Harker or Lucy, and write the Dracula story from his/her perspective, in the first person, e.g. *I visited Castle Dracula …*

WEBLINK

Students may like to visit: bramstoker.org for more information on the author of Dracula.

Revision and Extension p85

Workbook Unit 6 Lesson 4 pp72–73

Inspiration EXTRA!

Optional aids

Project: books on and pictures of famous explorers, scissors, glue

PROJECT FAMOUS EXPLORERS

1

- Explain to students that the aim of the project is to write file pages about famous explorers. Divide the students into groups of five and appoint an 'editor' for each group.
- Ask them to look back at Unit 6 Lesson 2. They should then make a list of famous explorers and expeditions. Draw their attention to the different types of expeditions listed in the book and ask them to choose one or two explorers or expeditions that they are interested in. Draw their attention to the text about Amy Johnson.

2

- Encourage students to use books and the Internet to find out more information. Tell them to use the questions for ideas on what kind of information to make notes of.

3

- Students work together in their group to write about their explorers and expeditions. They could use the Amy Johnson text as a model. Encourage them to produce a first draft, which they can all read and correct. They should then copy the corrected text out neatly. The editor selects the order of the texts while the others work on illustrating their file with photos from the Internet or drawings.
- Display the finished work in the classroom for everyone to read and enjoy.

GAME THREE IN A LINE

- Divide students into three teams. Students read the rules of the game. Check comprehension by asking *What do you do first?* (Choose a square.) *How do you win a square?* (Ask a correct question.) *What happens if your answer is wrong?* (You miss a turn.) *How do you win the game?* (You win three squares in a line.)
- Demonstrate the activity once using the verb *send*. Students then play the game. When teams answer questions, ask them to spell the past form of the verb.

Optional activities

- ♦ Replace the verbs in this box with verbs that your particular students find difficult to remember.
- ♦ Repeat the game with more verbs from the irregular verbs list on page 127.

REVISION

Lesson 1

Answers

Adam was in a café.
Emily was on the beach.
Jake was on the beach.
Katya was at the shopping centre.
Pierre was at the cinema.
Ruby was in the park.
Teresa was at the shopping centre.

Lesson 2

Suggested answers

Yesterday Katya wore a dress, went to the cinema, had an ice cream, played computer games, watched TV and phoned her sister.
Yesterday Pierre wore a shirt and jeans, went to a café, had a pizza, played tennis, watched a DVD and phoned his parents.

Lesson 3

Suggested answers

Pierre didn't look in a shop door. He looked in a shop window.
The girl didn't carry a long white dress. She wore one/a long white dress.
Pierre didn't laugh. He shouted.
The girl didn't dance. She turned.
Pierre didn't close his hands. He closed his eyes.
Teresa wasn't in The Lanes. She was outside the cinema.
Pierre didn't see Teresa. He saw a ghost.

Lesson 4
Students' own answers

EXTENSION

Lesson 1
Students' own answers
Make sure students know the answers to their own questions.

Lesson 2
Students' own answers

Lesson 3
Students' own answers
Elicit/Provide a starting line and response, e.g. *Hi! How was your weekend? Great!/Not bad./So so./Tiring.*

Lesson 4

Suggested answers

At first, Lucy and I enjoyed our holiday by the sea. But then I became worried. There was no news from Jonathan. Then one night there was a terrible storm and a boat crashed onto the beach. There was no one on the boat but a huge dog jumped out and ran up the hill to the church. Three nights later, Lucy got up in the middle of the night. She walked out of the house and went up the hill to the church. I saw that Lucy was not in her bed and I decided to look for her. I went to the church and I saw Lucy with someone tall and dark. I was scared and shouted her name. When I ran up, Lucy was alone and there was no one else there.

YOUR CHOICE!

The aim is to give students more learner independence and help them to identify their preferred ways of learning. Encourage students to choose an activity that they feel less comfortable with if they want a challenge or are aware that they need practice in a particular area.
Which Country is It? gives students the opportunity to write factual information about a country.
Consequences gives students the opportunity to work together to write stories in a fun format.

You may now like students to do the song *Don't You Want Me, Baby*. See p162 for the notes and p189 for the worksheet.

Language File pp119–120

Song – photocopiable notes p162, worksheet p189

Workbook Unit 6 Inspiration EXTRA! pp74–75

Units 5–6

1 Check general comprehension: look at the photo and headline and ask students to predict the story. *Why did she jump in?* Give students one minute to read the story and find the answer. Students read the text again and choose the appropriate word for each space. Do the first one together as an example. This can be done in pairs or individually as a short test.

Answers

1 C 2 A 3 B 4 A 5 C 6 C 7 A
8 B 9 C 10 A 11 B 12 C

Optional activity

Confident students can attempt the task before looking at the word options.

2 Students complete the sentences with the correct present tense form. Do the first one together as an example.

Answers

1 goes 2 are having 3 is working 4 listens
5 are visiting 6 Are, enjoying 7 don't know 8 do, speak

3 Students use the prompts to write questions and answers. Point out the plural nouns *sunglasses, jeans, CDs*. Check answers by asking one student to read the question and then another student to answer.

Answers

1 Whose cat is this? It's Teresa's.
2 Whose sunglasses are these? They're Pierre's.
3 Whose mobile phone is this? It's Mr Ward's.
4 Whose jeans are these? They're Katya's.
5 Whose umbrella is this? It's the teacher's.
6 Whose CDs are these? They're my friend's.

4 Focus on the pictures. Check students know all the words by pointing and asking *What's this? What are these?* Students write two sentences as in the example.

Answers

1 It's his (bottle of) water. It's his.
2 They're our chips. They're ours.
3 It's their computer. It's theirs.
4 It's her guitar. It's hers.
5 It's my watch. It's mine.
6 They're your books. They're yours.

5 Students complete the sentences as in the example.

Answers

1 Florida is sunnier than New York.
2 Japanese is more difficult than English.
3 A Ferrari is more expensive than a Fiat.
4 Mexico City is bigger than Rio de Janeiro.
5 Mount Everest is higher than K2.
6 Tom Cruise is more famous than me.

Optional activity

Ask students to close their books. Write the adjectives from this exercise on the board and ask students to recall the complete sentences.

6 Nominate students to read out the examples. Check *How do you know if the answer is yes or no?* (Tick or cross.) Students complete the questions and answers. Check answers by asking one student to read the question and then another student to answer.

Answers

1 Were there computers in 1940? No, there weren't.
2 Was there email in 1990? Yes, there was.
3 Were there jeans in 1890? Yes, there were.
4 Were there mobile phones in 1900? No, there weren't.
5 Was there beer in 1850? Yes, there was.
6 Were there trainers in 1930? No, there weren't.
7 Was there radio in 1890? No, there wasn't.
8 Were there cameras in 1930? Yes, there were.

7 Students put the verbs in the past form and then decide how they are pronounced. Encourage students to say them to themselves to help. Tell them there are four in each category. Play the recording for them to check their answers.

2.58 Recording and answers

/d/ *answered enjoyed listened smiled*
/t/ *asked checked kissed talked*
/ɪd/ *decided repeated shouted waited*

8 Students complete the sentences with the past forms of the verbs. Less confident students start by matching the verb and sentence, and then focus on changing the verb into the past.

Answers

1 sailed 2 cooked 3 saw 4 ran 5 visited
6 played 7 found 8 knew

9 Nominate students to read out the examples. Students write two questions and two answers for each point. Check answers by asking one student to read the questions and another student to answer.

Answers

1 *Did Teresa phone home? Yes, she did.*
Did she phone Adam? No, she didn't.
2 *Did Pierre write a letter? No, he didn't.*
Did he write an email? Yes, he did.
3 *Did Emily wear a jacket? Yes, she did.*
Did she wear a dress? No, she didn't.
4 *Did Katya and Teresa go to the café? No, they didn't.*
Did they go to the shopping centre? Yes, they did.
5 *Did Jake and Adam play tennis? Yes, they did.*
Did they play basketball? No, they didn't.
6 *Did Diana listen to CDs? No, she didn't.*
Did she listen to the radio? Yes, she did.

VOCABULARY

10 Students complete the sentences with the words in the box. Confident students could cover the list of words and guess which words are missing from the sentences before checking against list.

Answers

1 *sun* 2 *dress* 3 *temperature* 4 *explorer* 5 *blood*
6 *hill* 7 *news* 8 *train*

11 Students match the words with their definitions.

Answers

1 *noon* 2 *apologise* 3 *short* 4 *ship* 5 *cross*
6 *wet* 7 *terrible* 8 *huge* 9 *nurse* 10 *journalist*

Optional activity

Students write definitions of other words from Units 5 and 6. They exchange definitions and guess each other's words.

12 Remind students that it is often more useful to learn words that go together like this than single words.

Answers

1 *ask for help* 2 *close your eyes* 3 *drive a car*
4 *fly a plane* 5 *fold your arms* 6 *go to sleep*
7 *sail a boat* 8 *shout at someone* 9 *teach maths*

Optional activity

In pairs, one student says a word or phrase from list B and their partner recalls the verb.

LEARNER INDEPENDENCE SELF ASSESSMENT

- Explain to students that the aim of the self assessment is to encourage them to check their own progress and to take any necessary action to improve. Point out that the list 1–6 covers language from Units 5 and 6. Students tick the 'Fine' box for functional language that they feel confident using, but put a question mark in the 'Not sure' box for functional language that they have difficulties with or still cannot use confidently.
- Encourage students to look at the Language File and re-do exercises from the Workbook in areas where they have problems. They may also like to re-do exercises from the lessons and from the Revision and Extension sections in Units 5 and 6.
- Students write an example sentence for each language area in the list. You may like to elicit the grammar needed for each example before students write their sentences. Students can refer to the relevant lessons and the Language File for support.
- Ask students to compare their sentences with a partner's, and to discuss and correct any mistakes they may find. They then evaluate their own performance for each language area in terms of *Fine* and *Not sure*.
- Check their sentences so that you can note down language areas for future practice where students are uncertain.

Follow-up activity

Game *Noughts and crosses* See page 32 of the Student's Book for instructions. Draw this grid on the board:

Irregular past tense	Feelings	Character adjectives
Jobs	Comparative adjective	Weather
Silent letters	Present continuous	Past simple: *be*

HOMEWORK

Students bring their vocabulary notebooks up to date.

Students write a paragraph about a place they have visited and what they did when they were there.

WEBLINK

Students can visit the website http://www.manythings.org to practise their English.

Language File pp119–120

Workbook Review Units 5–6 pp76–77

Units 7–8

Activities
Identifying topics
Categorising vocabulary
Contextualising listening extracts

Project
Animal facts quiz

Vocabulary
Animals
Food and drink
Possessions

Optional aids
Follow-up activities: slips of paper

WARMER 1

If students did the homework in the review, ask them to read out their paragraphs about a place they have visited. If they do this without saying the name of the place, the other students could guess where it is.

WARMER 2

Ask students to look at the photos and speech bubbles on pages 88–89 and to say what they can see.

1

- The aim is to introduce students to the main topics and vocabulary they will cover in Units 7–8.
- Remind students that the two boxes at the top of the page show the communicative language and topics/ vocabulary they will use in the next two units.
- Go through the topics in the second box with the class and make sure everyone understands them. Then ask them to look at pictures A–F and match them with six topics.

Answers

A invitations and thanks
B accident and emergency
C food and drink
D travel
E leisure activities
F possessions

2

- Explain that words from the three categories animals, food and possessions are arranged in the word square. Give students two minutes to write the words in the correct category.
- Students check their answers in pairs and then as a whole class.

Answers

Animals: cat, dog, horse, whale, cow
Food: egg, potato, cake, rice, fruit
Possessions: computer game, camera, phone, skateboard, blu-ray disc, games console

Optional activity

In small groups, students think of as many different words as possible to add to the three categories. Give them a time limit and then get the groups to read their words aloud to the class.

3

- The aim of this activity is for students to contextualise a short listening extract by working out what the topic is. Explain that they should listen for the main gist of the extract and that it doesn't matter if they don't understand every word.
- Play the recording. Students match each of the three extracts to the topics A–C.

3.01 **Recording**

1
PIERRE *Hiya – wow, I'm really thirsty!*
DIANA *Would you like some tea?*
PIERRE *No, thanks – I'd like a cold drink.*
DIANA *There's some apple juice in the fridge. And there's some milk.*
PIERRE *Apple juice is fine. Are there any bananas?*
2
We're all scared of sharks, but they don't kill many people. And hippos kill more people than lions. In India and Sri Lanka the most dangerous animal is a snake – the Indian cobra. This snake kills over 50,000 people a year.
3
ADAM *What else do you like doing?*
KATYA *I enjoy swimming.*
ADAM *Hm, I don't mind swimming. When the water is warm!*
KATYA *And I like dancing – salsa, samba, you know.*
ADAM *Oh, I really hate dancing. I can't dance.*
KATYA *Of course you can! Everyone can dance!*
ADAM *Not me!*

Answers

1 B 2 C 3 A

4

- Put students into groups of three and ask them to do the quiz, writing down their answers.
- Ask them to join other groups to share their answers.

Answers

All the facts are true.

- Point out the 'Believe it or not!' fact at the bottom of the page. Find out if the students have ever seen a pet looking in a mirror.

Follow-up activities

♦ In small groups, students brainstorm vocabulary for three other categories from the box on page 88. See Preview 1–2 for further instructions.

♦ Students make lists of all the animals that they know. Give them two minutes and see who can produce the longest list.

HOMEWORK

Ask students to interview family members or other students at the school to find out what leisure activities they like. They then present their findings to the class in the next lesson.

1 What are you going to do?

Communicative aims	Language	Pronunciation	Vocabulary	Optional aids
Talking about future plans and intentions Asking for and giving reasons	*going to* *Why? because …*	Syllable stress	Accident and emergency	Follow-up activity: photos/pictures of different holidays

WARMER 1

Divide the class into teams. Teams race to write five true and grammatically accurate sentences about what has happened in the lives of the Student's Book characters recently. Do an example with the class, e.g. *Emily and Jake played on the games console, Pierre was angry with Adam.*

WARMER 2

Game *The long sentence game* Start the sentence by saying *Yesterday I got up early*. Nominate a student who repeats what you said and then adds another activity, e.g. *Yesterday I got up early and had a shower*. They nominate the next student who repeats this and adds another activity, and so on. The game continues round the class. To finish the game, get the whole class to say the final sentence together.

1 OPENER

- The aim is to set the scene and to get students to predict the topic of the conversation.
- Students look at the photo and describe what they can see.

2 READING

- Tell students they are going to hear the conversation and need to note what Pierre is talking about.
- With a more confident class, do this as a listening exercise. With a less confident class, students read and listen.
- Ask students to say what the problem is.

3.02 Recording

See text on page 90 of the Student's Book.

Answers

Pierre's dad had an accident at work and Pierre needs to go home.

LANGUAGE WORKOUT OPTION

If you want to pre-teach the language students will be using in the following activities, you may like to go to the Language Workout box now.

3 AFTER READING

- Ask students to match the questions and answers. Point out that one of the answers is not used.
- Students then listen and read and confirm their answers. Encourage students to work out the meaning of new words from the context.
- Check which answer is not used before checking the rest of the answers.

Answers

1 e 2 c 3 f 4 b 5 a d is not used

Optional activities

- ♦ Play the recording again. Pause at the points where there is a natural and obvious response needed, e.g. just before *What's wrong with him? That's terrible. What are you going to do?* and ask students to recall the response or suggest an appropriate alternative.
- ♦ Play the recording again, sentence by sentence, for students to repeat for pronunciation and intonation practice. Students then act out the dialogue in groups of three.
- ♦ Students find all the examples of *going to* in the dialogue in preparation for the next exercise.

Your response

Put students in pairs and ask them to imagine they are Pierre and discuss what they are going to say when they phone home.

4 LISTENING

- The aim is to listen for detailed information and at the same time provide further exposure to and practice of *going to*. Explain that students are going to listen to Pierre talking to Adam later. Give them time to read the statements, then play the recording. Students decide if the sentences are true or false. Encourage them to compare their answers and play the recording again if necessary.
- Check the answers.

3.03 Recording

PIERRE	*I talked to my mum and …*
ADAM	*What did she say?*
PIERRE	*Well, Dad's leg is OK – it isn't broken. He's going to leave hospital tonight.*
ADAM	*Great! When are you going to see him?*
PIERRE	*My father doesn't want me to go home early.*
ADAM	*You mean …*
PIERRE	*Yes, I'm going to stay here.*
ADAM	*Fantastic – and I know someone who's going to be very happy!*

Answers

1 False. Pierre talked to his mother.
2 True
3 False. His father doesn't want him to go home early now.
4 True
5 False. Ruby is going to be very happy.

5 SPEAKING

- Elicit different ways of saying *phone: call, ring*. Elicit the past forms. Tell students that some people phoned while they were out. Elicit *take/leave a message*.
- Explain that there are three messages and students have to decide how they are going to respond to them. Go through the first one with the class.
- Students read the messages and decide what they are going to do for each one. Be ready to explain *on your own*.
- Students then compare their answers with a partner. Make sure students speak and listen to each other and don't show each other their answers. Remind them to use *going to*. Ask two students to demonstrate with the first message.

Optional activity

Encourage confident students to say why they are going to do this, e.g. *I'm going to phone and say yes because I want to be sure it's real.*

Extension Go through the situations with the class and make sure they understand them. Then put students in groups of three and tell them to imagine they are in these situations and to discuss what they are going to do.

6 PRONUNCIATION

- In pairs, students read the words in the box to each other. Play the recording, pausing after each word for students to repeat.
- Tell students that one syllable of the word is stressed. Demonstrate with *accident*. Students predict where the stress is in the other words and listen again to check.

3.04 Recording and answers

accident ambulance barbecue holiday
hospital police programme terrible worried

Police is different because the stress is not at the beginning of the word/on the first syllable.

Optional activity

Give students long words from previous lessons, e.g. *temperature, computer, instrument, expensive, population, photograph*. If you have a Vocabulary box, use these cards. Students identify where the stress is.

7 GAME

- Tell students that this is a competition. In pairs, they guess why people are doing certain things. Do the first one with the class, eliciting a variety of possible answers. Set a time limit.
- Play the recording. Students check their ideas.

3.05 Recording and answers

1 Pierre is wearing shorts because he's going to play tennis.
2 Adam is turning on the computer because he's going to play a game.
3 Teresa is buying a ticket because she's going to see a film.
4 Mr Ward is learning Portuguese because he's going to visit Brazil.
5 Emily is running because she's going to catch a bus.

Optional activity

Game *Telepathy* Divide students into teams of three to four. Dictate the beginning of a sentence, e.g. *She is buying a hat …* Students complete the sentence individually. They must start with *because* and use *going to*. They then compare answers. If two students in a team have written the same ending, they get two points. If three students have the same ending, they get three points, etc. Keep score on the board.

8 SPEAKING

- With a less confident class, brainstorm possible activities first. Students write five things they are going to do after school.
- Focus on the example dialogue. Ask two students to read it aloud. Tell students to ask about the activities on their list. They need to find people who are going to do the same thing. Set a five-minute time limit.
- Students move around the classroom asking and answering their questions. Monitor and note any common errors of grammar, vocabulary or pronunciation.
- Ask students what the most popular after-school activities were. Write common errors on the board and ask students to correct them.
- Focus on the second example dialogue. Ask two students to read it aloud. Give students a minute to think about their answer and ask for any personal vocabulary they might need to answer. Students ask five others about their summer holidays.
- Ask if any of the students have the same plans.

Optional activity

Encourage more confident students to ask further questions, e.g. *Who are you going to go to Italy with?* and provide more information, e.g. *I'm going to Italy with my parents.*

Extension Students write sentences about what they and other students in the class are going to do after school today.

9 WRITING

- Students read the instructions. Check *epal: Is this a friend?* (Yes.) *How do you know them?* (Via email.) Point out that they can write about their friends' plans too. Set a 15-minute time limit.

Optional activity

Students include one false piece of information in their email. In pairs, students read their emails to each other and guess what is false.

LANGUAGE WORKOUT

- Ask students to look at the Language box and complete the sentences. Confident students can complete first and then check, while others can look back at exercises 2 and 3 and then complete.
- Students turn to page 120 of the Language File to check their answers.

  Answers
  I ***am*** *going* ***to*** *phone home.*
  They ***are*** *going* ***to*** *X-ray his leg.*
  You ***are*** *not* ***going*** *to be at the barbecue.*
  Is *he* ***going*** *to be all right?*
  What ***are*** *you* ***going to*** *do?*

- Highlight that
  - *going to* is used to talk about future plans and intentions
  - the form is *be* + *going to* + infinitive
  - we use contractions in spoken English *I'm going to, You're going to*, etc
  - *to* in this structure is weak and so pronounced /tə/.
  - When the main verb is *go* you can say *I'm going to go or I'm going ~~to go~~.*
- Drill the examples for pronunciation and stress.

PRACTICE

- Students do Practice exercise 23 on page 120 of the Language File.
- Go through the example with the students. Students look at the prompts and write the complete sentence.
- Check the answers by asking different students to say the completed sentences.

Answers
1 *They're going to have a barbecue.*
2 *What are you going to wear?*
3 *I'm going to wear my new jeans.*
4 *What is he going to do?*
5 *He isn't going to stay in Brighton.*
6 *Is she going to talk to him?*
7 *We aren't going to be late.*
8 *They aren't going to forget him.*

Optional activity

Back-chain sentences with *going to* to help students' pronunciation. Back-chain is drilling the end of the sentence and then adding on the earlier words, e.g. *have a barbecue, to have a barbecue, going to have a barbecue*. It helps to break down longer phrases for students while maintaining the natural intonation.

Follow-up activity

Game *Holidays* Tell students that they have won a holiday and you have a picture of their holiday destination. Hand out two copies of each picture. The holiday destinations should be diverse, e.g. a skiing resort, a deserted beach. Write the following questions on the board for the students to consider: *What are you going to take? How are you going to get there? Where are you going to stay? What are you going to do when you are there?* Tell students that someone in the class is going to the same place as they are. They mustn't show their pictures to anyone. They must move around and ask and answer the questions to find who they are going with.

HOMEWORK

Students write about the future plans of a famous person of their choice. Give an example, e.g. *Wayne Rooney is going to play for … next year. He's going to buy a house in … and he's going to learn … I'm going to watch him play.*

WEBLINK

Students can test their vocabulary through words and pictures at http://iteslj.org/v/ei

Revision and Extension p99

Language File p120

Workbook Unit 7 Lesson 1 pp78–79

Photocopiable notes p160, Worksheet p171

She loves skateboarding

Communicative aims	Language	Pronunciation	Vocabulary	Optional aids
Talking about likes and dislikes	Verb + gerund	/aɪ/ dive /ɪ/ swim	Leisure activities	Follow-up activities: large pieces of paper

WARMER 1

If you set the homework suggested, students read their descriptions to partners. The partners listen and identify the famous people.

WARMER 2

Write *Leisure activities* on the board and elicit one or two examples from the students. In pairs, students note down as many leisure activities as possible in two minutes. Ask the pair with the longest list to feed back first, and then add other ideas from other pairs. Check all students understand the words by asking them to translate them. In pairs or small groups, one student mimes an activity and the others say which activity it is.

1 OPENER

- The aim is to review activities and pre-teach vocabulary for the following exercises.
- In pairs, students match the activities with the photos. Check the answers as a class.

Answers

1 snowboarding 2 skydiving 3 skateboarding 4 knitting 5 playing the guitar

Optional activity

Write the following words on the board: *like, really like, love, hate, enjoy, don't mind, don't like*. Ask students to order them from positive to negative (*love, really like, like/enjoy, don't mind, don't like, hate*).

2 READING

- Tell students they are going to listen and read about what some famous people like doing in their free time. Ask them to note how many stars are mentioned. With a more confident class, do this as a listening exercise. With a less confident class, students read and listen. Check the answer (seven – Avril Lavigne, Johnny Depp, Cameron Diaz, Julia Roberts, Uma Thurman, Orlando Bloom, Robert Pattinson). Find out which fact they found most surprising.

3.06 Recording

See text on page 93 of the Student's Book.

3 AFTER READING

- Students read and/or listen to the text again and decide if sentences 1–6 are true or false. Ask them to make a note of the words that help them decide on their answers. Encourage them to guess the meaning of unfamiliar vocabulary from the context.
- Check the answers before students write corrections for the false sentences.

Answers

1 False. She loves skateboarding.
2 False. She likes playing video games.
3 False. He hates dancing.
4 False. They enjoy knitting.
5 True
6 False. He loves snowboarding.

Optional activity

Students close their books. Write the names of the stars on the board. Students tell each other what they remember about each person.

Your response

Have students work in pairs and think of other stars and their leisure activities.

4 PRONUNCIATION

- Focus on the examples. Play the recording. Students listen and repeat the words.

3.07 Recording

/aɪ/ *dive like ride*
/ɪ/ *swim knit sing*

- In pairs, students read the words in the box and decide which sound they contain. Play the recording for students to check.

3.07 Recording and answer

/aɪ/ *dive mind nice time write*
/ɪ/ *swim fish give sit thing*

Extension Have students work with a partner and think of four more words for each sound and write them in two lists. Then have two pairs work together and compare lists.

Optional activity

Game *Jump the line* Divide the classroom into the /aɪ/ side and the /ɪ/ side with a dividing line in the middle. Students stand on the dividing line. Read a word. If it contains an /aɪ/, they jump to that side. If it contains an /ɪ/, they jump the other way. If it doesn't contain either sound, they don't move. The student who moves the wrong way or is the last to move sits out. You could give these students the list of words to read. Alternatively, students could put their right hand up, their left hand up or their hands on their heads depending on the pronunciation. Words you could use include:
/aɪ/ *fine, nine, mine, find, dial, mobile, wife, ice (cream), exercise, seaside, lights, line, knife*
/ɪ/ *Mexico, swim, tissues, city, fifty, sister, picture, sing, cinema, visit, pizza, finger, silly, window*
Neither: *girl, birthday, train, hair*

5 LISTENING

- Tell students they are going to hear Katya and Adam talking about leisure activities. Ask them to look at the chart and predict which activities they like, don't mind and hate. Make sure they understand *don't mind.*
- Play the recording for students to check their ideas. Students compare their answers in pairs. If necessary, play the recording again.
- Check the answers by getting the students to complete the chart on the board.
- Go through the example sentences with the class. Then put students into pairs and ask them to continue making sentences about Katya and Adam using the information in the chart.

3.08 Recording

KATYA *Hey, nice one, Adam!*
ADAM *Do you want to have a go?*
KATYA *No, thanks. I hate skateboarding.*
ADAM *I love it.*
KATYA *What else do you like doing?*
ADAM *Well, I really like painting.*
KATYA *Do you? What do you paint?*
ADAM *Pictures of people. Can I paint a picture of you?*
KATYA *No, you can't! I like painting too. I like painting horses.*
ADAM *Ah – do you like riding?*
KATYA *Yes, I do.*
ADAM *I hate riding – I'm scared of horses.*
KATYA *Really?*
ADAM *What else do you like doing?*
KATYA *I enjoy swimming.*
ADAM *Hm, I don't mind swimming. When the water is warm!*
KATYA *And I like dancing – salsa, samba, you know.*
ADAM *Oh, I really hate dancing. I can't dance.*
KATYA *Of course you can! Everyone can dance!*
ADAM *Not me!*
KATYA *So you like skateboarding and painting …*
ADAM *And I like playing chess!*
KATYA *Hm, I don't mind playing chess.*
ADAM *Then let's have a game!*

Answers

	Katya	*Adam*
skateboarding	☹	☺
painting	☺	☺
riding	☺	☹
swimming	☺	😐
dancing	☺	☹
playing chess	😐	☺

6 SPEAKING

- Focus on the example question and answers. Ask several students the same question, eliciting different answers. Then ask students to interview three other students about the leisure activities in the Word Bank in exercise 1 and make a note of all the answers. Set a time limit.
- Ask several students to tell you something interesting that they learnt.

Optional activity

Encourage confident students to ask follow-up questions, e.g. *Where do you go skateboarding? Who do you play chess with?* and give more information in their answers, e.g. *Yes, I love skateboarding. I go skateboarding with my friends every weekend.*

Extension Ask students to use the notes they made to write about two of the students they interviewed.

7 WRITING

- Students read the instructions. Check understanding: *Are you writing a letter or an email?* (Email.) *What are you going to tell your epal about?* (Your likes and dislikes.) Set a ten-minute time limit.
- Monitor and note examples of good language and errors. Put these on the board and ask students to identify and correct the errors.

Optional activities

- Fast finishers can exchange their writing and check for grammar, spelling and punctuation.
- Collect in the pieces of writing and read some of them to the class (without mistakes). Students listen and identify the author.

LANGUAGE WORKOUT

- Ask students to look at the Language box and to complete the sentences. Confident students can complete first and then check, while others can look back at exercises 2 and 3 and then complete.
- Students turn to page 120 of the Language File to check their answers.

Answers
playing knitting dancing jumping doing

- Highlight that the gerund (*-ing* form) is used after *love, like, enjoy, don't mind, hate*. (The infinitive is also possible after *love, like, hate* in certain circumstances, but it's best to avoid this complication at this level.)
- Remind students about the spelling rules for *-ing* verbs, see Language File pages 117–118 under *Present continuous*.
- It might be helpful to translate the examples and draw attention to what is used instead of the gerund in the students' language.
- Drill the examples chorally and individually for pronunciation of words and sentence stress.

Optional activity

Give students a quick spelling test of words which are often incorrectly spelt in the gerund, e.g. *being, swimming, playing, studying, writing, doing, running*.

PRACTICE

- Students do Practice exercise 24 on page 120 of the Language File.
- Students complete the sentences with the correct form of the verb.
- Check the answers by asking different students to say the completed sentences.

Answers
1 playing 2 swimming 3 riding 4 cooking 5 skateboarding 6 playing 7 sailing 8 dancing

Optional activity

In pairs, students guess what leisure activities you love, like, etc. They write their predictions. Then they tell you what they have written and you confirm or correct their ideas. Find out which pair guessed the most correctly.

Follow-up activities

♦ Write this questionnaire on the board and ask students to copy it into their notebooks. Each student completes the last two questions with an activity of their choice.
How many people like playing chess?
How many people hate playing tennis?
How many people love swimming?
How many people enjoy riding?
How many people hate ___________*?*
How many people love ___________*?*
Elicit the question students need to ask. Point out that it is always *Do you like …?*, not *Do you love/hate …?* Students move round the class and interview every student about the six activities in order to find the answers. Check that everyone has the same answers in the end and, if necessary, use a show of hands to check their answers.

♦ Draw a word map on the board. Write *Leisure activities* in the centre. Elicit different categories from the class and write them on the word map, e.g. *ball games, board games, watersports, quiet activities, activities we do*. Divide students into small groups to draw their own word map on a large piece of paper or card. Encourage them to think of their own categories and add as many words as they can. Set a time limit and give bilingual dictionaries if available. The word maps can be displayed in the classroom.

HOMEWORK

Students write a paragraph about the likes and dislikes of someone in their family.

WEBLINK

For ideas about hobbies go to www.dmoz.org/desc/Kids_and_Teens/Sports_and_Hobbies

Revision and Extension p99

Language File p120

Workbook Unit 7 Lesson 2 pp80–81

Photocopiable notes p160, Worksheet p182

3 The most dangerous animal

Communicative aims	Language	Pronunciation	Vocabulary	Optional aids
Making comparisons (2)	Superlative adjectives (*-est, most*)	/f/	Animals Adjectives	Warmer 2: photos/ pictures of animals follow-up activities: blank pieces of paper; cards for Vocabulary box

WARMER 1

Read *What do the stars like doing in their free time?* changing some information to make it false, e.g. *Johnny Depp hates playing the guitar and painting.* Students shout *Stop!* when they hear incorrect information and correct it.

WARMER 2

Use pictures of animals to elicit/pre-teach animal names. Choose two animals. Students race to write a sentence comparing them, e.g. *cat, tiger: A cat is smaller than a tiger.* The first pair/team to produce a sentence which is both true and grammatically accurate wins a point. Write the comparative adjective used on the board. Students mustn't repeat this adjective. Continue with another two animals.

1 OPENER

- The aim is to pre-teach some vocabulary for the following exercises.
- Focus on the photos. Point to each photo and elicit the name of the animal. Discuss which one is most dangerous. Ask students to justify their ideas, but don't give the correct answer at this stage.

Answers

1 mosquito 2 snake 3 hippo 4 shark 5 lion

2 READING

- Tell students they are going to find out which is the most dangerous animal and the answers to four more questions. Read these out to the class or get four students to read them out.
- With a more confident class, do this as a listening exercise. With a less confident class, students read and listen. At the end, check students have understood which is the most dangerous animal (the mosquito) and elicit the answers to the other questions.

3.09 Recording

See text on page 94 of the Student's Book.

Answers

1 the cheetah 2 the sailfish 3 the falcon 4 the falcon

3 AFTER READING

- Focus on the incomplete sentences. In pairs, students predict what goes in the space. They then listen and/or read the text again to check their ideas. Encourage students to guess the meaning of unfamiliar vocabulary from the context and ignore words which are not necessary to complete the exercise. Be prepared to explain *land* (animal), *dive* (for a bird), *a bite, malaria.*
- Check the answers by nominating different students to read the sentences aloud.

Answers

1 fastest 2 fish 3 falcon, fastest
4 most 5 dangerous 6 most dangerous

Optional activities

- ♦ With a confident class, ask more questions about the text, e.g. *How fast can a cheetah run? Which are more dangerous, lions or hippos?*
- ♦ Write the following sentence beginnings on the board: *I knew that …, I didn't know that …, I'm really surprised that …* Students finish them so they are true for themselves and tell their partner.

Your response

Ask students to discuss in pairs or small groups which animals, if any, they are scared of and to report back to the class. Encourage them to say why they think many people are scared of animals which are not dangerous, such as spiders and mice.

LANGUAGE WORKOUT OPTION

If you want to pre-teach the language students will be using in the following activities, you may like to go to the Language Workout box now.

4 VOCABULARY

- In pairs, students match the words for animals in the Word Bank with the pictures. Check answers with the class. Monitor pronunciation.

Answers
1 *giraffe tiger elephant*
2 *horse cow sheep*
3 *rabbit dog cat*
4 *parrot penguin monkey*
5 *octopus whale polar bear*

5 SPEAKING

- Focus on the adjectives in the Word Bank. With a less confident class, check students understand these words by translating or using examples, e.g. *A giraffe is tall.* Ask a student to read the example sentences aloud. Elicit another example from the class. Students continue in pairs or small groups.
- Get feedback from some pairs/groups. Ask them to say one of their sentences. The class decides if they agree or disagree.

Optional activities

- Students mark the stress on the animal words.
- Encourage confident students to use the comparative as well as the superlative, e.g. *The elephant is more dangerous than the giraffe but the tiger is the most dangerous.*

6 PRONUNCIATION

- Students practise saying this tongue-twister. Play the recording. Students listen and repeat. Students practise again. Ask more confident students to try saying it for the class.

3.10 Recording
The fastest flying falcon flies faster than the fastest flying fish.

Optional activity

Students think of shorter tongue-twisters. First they need to think of an adjective, e.g. *small*. Then they need an animal and a verb that begin with the same letter, e.g. *sheep, swim*. Then they invent a sentence, e.g. *The smallest sheep swims in the sea.* The sentence doesn't need to make sense but does need to be grammatically accurate. Listen to the students' ideas and decide as a class which is best.

7 GAME

- Check comprehension of the categories in the box by giving an example, e.g. *Nicole Kidman*, and asking students to identify the category. Ask two students to read the example aloud. Remind students they can talk about the best or the worst. Encourage students to respond to each other's comments. Do they agree? Students continue in pairs.

Optional activity

Encourage confident students to justify their answers, e.g. *The best team is Manchester United because they always win. My team never wins!*

Extension Students choose four categories from the box and make sentences using *best* and *worst* for each of them. Have a feedback session in which students share their sentences.

8 SPEAKING

- Students work in pairs. Write all the names of the students in the class on the board. Student A writes down half of them on the left-hand side of a piece of paper. Student B writes down the other half. Tell them that they are going to interview the people on their list about their pets and their pets' names. They need to note the answers next to the names. Elicit the questions they need to ask: *Do you have a pet? What is it? What's it called?* Set a time limit. Students move around and interview each other.
- Students then return to their pairs and combine their information to find out which pets and which names are the most popular. Check everyone has the same answers. If not, use a show of hands to find out who is correct.

Extension Students repeat the survey with family and friends and write a short report of the results.

9 WRITING

- Ask students to write a paragraph summarising the results of the class survey. Set a time limit.

Optional activity

Students illustrate the results of their survey, e.g. as a bar or pie chart. This could then be used with the summarising paragraph for a wall display.

LANGUAGE WORKOUT

- Ask students to look at the Language box and to complete the sentences. Point out that the rules for the superlative are similar to the rules for the comparative, ie short adjectives add an ending (*est*) and longer adjectives add a word in front (*most*). Draw their attention also to the fact that the spelling rules are the same as for comparatives: *big → biggest, dry → driest.*
- Students turn to pages 120–121 of the Language File to check their answers.

Answers

*the slow**est** the hott**est** the friendl**iest***
*the **most** beautiful*

Short adjectives end in *-est* and **long** adjectives take ***most*** in front of them.

- Highlight that the superlative is used to say which is, for example, the fastest in a group of three or more. The comparative is used to compare two things or people.

Optional activities

- ♦ Get the students to cover the superlatives in the chart and remember them.
- ♦ Fast finishers can add some more adjectives and superlatives to the correct group in the chart. You could provide a list, e.g. *difficult, high, cold, happy, wet, famous, short, popular, sunny, tall, easy.*
- ♦ Ask students questions about themselves/their lives using the superlative, e.g. *Who's the tallest person in the class? What's the hottest month?* Encourage students to answer in full sentences, e.g. *The hottest month is August.*

PRACTICE

- Students do Practice exercise 25 on page 121 of the Language File.
- They complete the sentences with the superlative form of the adjectives.
- Check the answers by asking different students to say the completed sentences.

Answers

1 fastest 2 most dangerous 3 biggest
4 best 5 worst 6 most exciting

Follow-up activities

- ♦ Students work in teams. Each team writes a superlative quiz. They need five questions and they must know the correct answer. They give three possible answers for the rest of the class to choose from, e.g. *Which is the longest river in the world? A The Nile, B The Amazon, C The Rhine*. Students could pass their quizzes around, note their answers to each quiz and then add up the number of correct answers at the end. Alternatively, each team could take it in turns to read one of their questions aloud. The other teams get a point if they choose the correct answer and you keep a record of the scores on the board.
- ♦ **Game** *Back to the board* See Unit 3, Lesson 4 Warmer for instructions. Use animal words. If you are keeping a Vocabulary box, ask the students to write the words and definitions on vocabulary cards.

HOMEWORK

Students write a paragraph about 'superlative animals'. They write about at least four animals and provide some information about that animal which supports their comment, e.g. *The friendliest animal is the dog. Dogs love being with people.*

WEBLINK

Students may like to visit www.dmoz.org/Kids_and_Teens/School_Time/Science/Living_Things/Animals for more information on animals.

Revision and Extension p99

Language File pp120–121

Workbook Unit 7 Lesson 3 pp82–83

Photocopiable notes p160, Worksheet p183

Integrated Skills Messages

Skills	Learner Independence	Vocabulary	Optional aids
Reading Connecting ideas: travel website message board *Listening* Listening for details: radio phone-in *Speaking* Role play *Writing* Asking for travel information	Classroom English Vocabulary notebook Phrasebook	Travel Useful expressions	Exercise 6 Optional activity: vocabulary from Lesson 3 on small cards Follow-up activity: photos of different countries

WARMER 1

Students choose ten words from the previous lesson and make anagrams. In pairs, they exchange lists and see who can rewrite all the words correctly first.

WARMER 2

Students work in pairs or groups and list as many words as possible connected with *holidays*. They have three minutes. Ask the pair/group with the longest list to read out their ideas. Write the words on the board and then add any others suggested by other groups. Give students a further three minutes to divide all these words into categories of their choice, e.g. *weather, accommodation, things to do, transport, good holidays, bad holidays*. Ask them not to write the category headings on the paper. Pairs/groups then exchange papers and guess the categories that the other group has divided their words into.

1 OPENER

- The aim is to set the scene for the following exercises. Look at the website message board and ask the class *What is the topic?* Students should be able to answer immediately from the heading and the photos.

Answer
Travel

Optional activity

Use the photos to elicit/teach vocabulary in the text, e.g. *a whale, surf, a cowboy, a ranch*. Ask students which countries they think the photos show.

2 READING

- The aim is for students to use key words in the text to match the questions and answers.
- With a less confident class, do the first one as an example. Set a two-minute time limit for students to complete the exercise. This will encourage them to use key vocabulary rather than understand everything.
- Play the recording. Check which questions and answers match.

3.11 Recording and answers

1 *I want to go on a whale-watching holiday. But I can only find holidays in North and South America and South Africa. Where's the best place to see whales in Europe?*
E *There are plenty of good whale-watching holidays in Europe, from Greece or Spain to Scandinavia. You can even see whales – and dolphins – off the coasts of Scotland, Wales and Ireland.*
2 *My class is doing a project on India. When is the best time to travel there?*
C *It's a big country so there isn't one best time. But it's probably best from October to mid April. Summer is from March to June. There is a lot of rain from July to September. October is warm and winter is from November to February.*
3 *I love learning new skills when I'm on holiday. This year I want to learn how to surf. Where's the best place to learn? Don't say Australia or Hawaii!*
D *In Europe one of the best places is Newquay in the south-west of England. There are some good schools there and it isn't very expensive. The surf and beaches are great – it's where they have international surfing championships.*
4 *I'm going to visit my aunt and uncle in Kenya this summer and I'm worried about malaria. What's the best medicine to take? I know some malaria medicines make you feel ill. What do you suggest?*
A *You get malaria from a mosquito bite. Make sure that mosquitoes don't bite you! There are a lot of different medicines for malaria. Your doctor knows which medicine is best for the country you're going to visit.*
5 *My father works in New York and I'm going to see him this summer. I love riding and we're going to go on a cowboy ranch holiday. He says I can choose where we go. Where's the best ranch for teenagers and adults?*
B *There are lots of places to choose from in the USA. We had great fun last year at a place in Aspen in Colorado. It's a working ranch and you can help the cowboys. The riding lessons are really good and the food is excellent.*

Optional activity

Ask students which of the five holidays they would prefer and why.

3 LISTENING

- The aim is to listen for detailed information and choose the correct answers.
- Focus on the photo. Ask *Is this a television programme?* (No, a radio programme.) Explain that people call in with travel questions and the woman in the photo answers them. Students read through the summaries of the three calls and predict the answers. Point out that they need to note the website in conversation 2.
- Play the recording. Pause after each caller and allow students to compare their answers. If necessary, play the recording again.
- Check the answers by nominating students to read out the questions and answers. Ask one student to write the website on the board.

3.12 Recording

MARY *Hello, everyone. This is the travel programme phone-in. I'm Mary and I'm your travel expert today. I'm here to take your calls and answer your questions about travel anywhere in the world.*

Caller 1

SAMANTHA *Hi, my name's Samantha.*
MARY *Hi, Samantha.*
SAMANTHA *I'm calling about learning Spanish. I like learning languages and I want to learn Spanish on my summer holiday. Someone told me that Cuba is a good place to learn Spanish. Is that true?*
MARY *Yes, of course you can learn Spanish in Cuba – there are some good schools there. But for some people the best way to learn is to live with a Spanish-speaking family. Then you eat, drink and sleep in Spanish!*
SAMANTHA *Thanks very much.*
MARY *Bye!*

Caller 2

WILL *Hello. I'm Will and I'm in London.*
MARY *Hi, Will.*
WILL *My question is about the weather. When's the best time to visit Australia? I mean, what's the weather like there?*
MARY *The weather in Australia. Well, I'm sure you know that their summer is our winter – so it's always hot in December. Australia's a really big country. I think the best thing for you to do is to look at an Australian weather website. There's a great one at www.bom.gov.au That's www.bom.gov.au OK?*
WILL *www.bom.gov.au That's great. Many thanks.*
MARY *Goodbye Will.*

Caller 3

TERRY *Hello. My name's Terry and I'm calling from Manchester.*
MARY *Hello, Terry.*
TERRY *I'm going to Italy this summer for a week. It's my first visit – can you suggest places to see? I like going to museums and eating good food – I don't like beach holidays.*
MARY *You like going to museums and eating good food? Then you're going to the right country. Italy has the best food in the world and some of the greatest museums. A week isn't a long time – and Italy is a long country! So I think your best plan is to start in Naples, then take the train to Rome and then north again to Florence. That's enough for your first visit and I'm sure it isn't going to be your last!*
TERRY *Thank you very much.*
MARY *Goodbye.*

Answers

Caller 1
learn good best
Caller 2
weather Australia www.bom.gov.au
Caller 3
Italy first museums
best Start two

Optional activity

With a confident class, start by asking the students what type of programme it is. Play the introduction and check the answer. Then ask students to listen and note the three questions the callers ask. Check the answers. Finally, play the recording again and students note the answers.

4 SPEAKING

- Read through the instructions with the students. Choose one question and give students five minutes to prepare their role play, looking back at exercises 2 and 3 for help with language. You could draw attention to useful phrases, e.g. *The best way to learn is …* *It's probably best to visit in …* Students practise both roles.
- Students then change partners and try a different role-play situation. This time give a shorter time limit to prepare. Encourage them just to take a few notes. Again, students practise both roles.
- Finally, students change pairs again and do the third role play without preparation.
- Ask confident pairs to perform their role play for the class. The class listens and says whether they think the advice was good.

5 WRITING

- The aim is for students to write their own travel questions about countries they would like to visit, using the messages in exercise 2 as models.
- Encourage students to think about a place they want to visit. Why do they want to go there? What do they want to do there? Do they know the best places to visit? Do they know what the weather is like?
- More confident students write three sentences for each message. Less confident students could write two sentences.
- Students exchange their questions and correct each other's work for spelling, grammar and punctuation.

Optional activity

Students roleplay the radio phone-in again using these questions. The 'travel expert' can invent their answers.

6 LEARNER INDEPENDENCE

- The aim is to review useful classroom language. Students can then be encouraged to use these expressions, making the class increasingly an English-only zone. Asking and answering these questions in English also gives students the opportunity to use English for genuine interaction/to meet real current needs.
- In pairs, students order the words to make questions.
- Check the answers. Check students know when to use these questions, e.g. ask *What do you say when you are not sure if something is right?*

Answers

1 What do you suggest I do now?
2 What is the best way to do this exercise?
3 Can you spell it, please?
4 Is it my turn now?
5 What does this word mean?
6 How do you pronounce this word?
7 Can I use a dictionary, please?
8 Excuse me. Is this correct?

Optional activity

Write vocabulary from previous units on small cards. If you have a Vocabulary box, use these words. In pairs, one student picks up a card and asks their partner what the word means, how it is spelt and how it is pronounced. If necessary, the other student could ask to use his/her dictionary. He/She then checks it is correct with the first student. Students then reverse roles.

7

- The aim is to encourage students to group words in lexical sets (or categories) in their vocabulary notebooks rather than randomly or alphabetically. This process means that students review the meanings of the words and it also helps storage and retrieval of words from memory.
- Write the three categories on the board. Elicit an example for each.
- Students work individually and add to each category from memory. They then compare their list with a partner and add any extra words. Finally they look back through the unit and add any others that they find. Set a minimum of four words per category.

Optional activity

Fast finishers can test each other. One student gives a definition and the other says the word.

8 PHRASEBOOK

- Ask students to look through the unit, find the useful expressions and look at how they are used.
- Play the recording for students to listen and repeat the expressions.

3.13 Recording and answers

Are you OK? (Adam, Lesson 1)
What's wrong with him? (Adam, Lesson 1)
That's terrible. (Adam, Lesson 1)
What are you going to do? (Adam, Lesson 1)
What do you think? (Pierre, Lesson 1)
Please ring back. (message, Lesson 1, exercise 5)
I love it. (Example, Lesson 2, exercise 6)
I don't mind it. (Example, Lesson 2, exercise 6)
I hate it. (Example, Lesson 2, exercise 6)
What do you suggest? (Question 4, webpage)

- Students can add expressions they like to their Personal Phrasebooks. Help with translation where necessary.
- Students choose four of the questions and write their own answers, e.g. *What are you going to do? I'm going to watch TV.* Students exchange their writing and check each other's answers.

Follow-up activities

- ♦ Students work in groups. Each group chooses a country. They write three questions about travelling there, e.g. *where to go surfing, where to go for good food* and three answers. They illustrate their message board with photos of the country or drawings and the message boards are displayed around the classroom. Students walk round the classroom and read each other's message boards.
- ♦ **Game** *20 Questions* See Unit 4 Lesson 1 Follow-up activity for instructions. Ask questions about countries, e.g. *Is it big/small? Is it hot in July?*
- ♦ Students choose five words from the lesson to write on vocabulary cards. These can be added to the Vocabulary box.

HOMEWORK

Students write a paragraph about their country/a country they have visited for a travel guide.

WEBLINK

Students may like to visit this site to see webcams in different countries: www.1000cam.com

Revision and Extension p99

Workbook Unit 7 Lesson 4 pp84–85

Inspiration EXTRA!

LANGUAGE LINKS

- The aim of the exercise is to raise students' awareness of words which are similar in different languages
- Students look at the airport signs and match the words which have the same meaning. They then identify the ones that look similar.

Answers

Baggage: Bagages, Gepäck, Equipaje
Arrivals: Arrivées, Ankunft, Llegadas
Check-in: Enregistrement, Abfertigung, Facturación
Departures: Départs, Abflug, Salidas

GAME FIND SOMEONE WHO ...

- Focus on the chart. Check vocabulary, e.g. *underwater, ironing*, by translation, definition or mime.
- Tell students that they have to find someone in the class who doesn't like being underwater, someone who enjoys ironing, etc. Elicit some examples of the questions they need to ask. Remind students not to ask a negative question. With a less confident class, ask students to prepare the questions they need to ask.
- Tell students to complete the chart with eight different names. Point out that they can only use a student's name once. Tell students to shout *Stop!* when they finish. Check *How many names do you have? Are they the same or different?*
- Students move around asking and answering the questions. The student who completes the chart first wins.

Optional activity

Students add two sentences of their own to the *Find someone who …* list.

SKETCH SUPERLATIVE HOLIDAYS!

- The aim is for students to enjoy using their English while also reviewing language presented in this unit and getting valuable stress and intonation practice.
- Tell students they are going to listen to a conversation between a travel agent and a customer. Ask them to listen and say how many different holidays they talk about. With a more confident class, play the recording with books closed. Then play it again with books open. With a less confident class, play the recording once while the students follow in their books, and then once again with books closed.
- Check the answer to your question (they talk about six different holidays).

3.14 Recording

See text on page 98 of the Student's Book.

- Divide the class into two equal groups and play the recording again, with one group repeating in chorus as the travel agent and the other group as the customer. Encourage students to exaggerate stress and intonation.
- Ask the students to close their books and play the recording again. Then ask the students to work in pairs and read the sketch aloud. Choose several pairs to act out the sketch in front of the class.

Optional activity

Make an audio or video recording of students performing the sketch.

LIMERICK

- Explain that a limerick is a funny five-line poem in which the first two lines usually rhyme with the fifth line and the third and fourth lines rhyme with each other.
- Play the recording for students to read and listen. Then play the recording again with books closed.

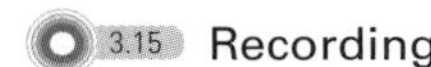

Recording

See text on page 98 of the Student's Book.

Optional activity

Students learn the limerick by heart.

REVISION

Lesson 1
Students choose from the options on page 91 of the Student's Book.

Lesson 2

Suggested answers

Katya and Adam both like painting.
Katya likes riding, but Adam hates it.
Katya likes swimming and Adam doesn't mind it.
Katya likes dancing, but Adam hates it.
Katya doesn't mind playing chess, but Adam likes it.

Lesson 3
Students' own answers

Lesson 4

Suspected answer

CALLER: *Hello, I'm Kathy and I'm calling from New York.*
EXPERT: *Hi, Kathy.*
CALLER: *I want to visit Spain next year. My question is about the weather. What is the best time of year to visit? What is the weather like?*
EXPERT: *Well, the winter is cold. Winter is from about November to February. It snows in the mountains so it's good if you want to go skiing. Summer is always very hot and all the Spanish people go on holiday in the summer, so the shops are closed. So the best time of year to visit Spain is in spring or autumn.*

EXTENSION

Lesson 1
Students' own answers

Lesson 2
If necessary, review vocabulary related to going on holiday.
Students' own answers

Lesson 3
Students' own answers

Lesson 4
Students may need to go and research this information.
Students' own answers

YOUR CHOICE!

The aim is to give students more learner independence and help them identify their preferred ways of learning. Encourage them to choose an activity that they feel less comfortable with if they want a challenge or are aware that they need practice in a particular area.
What animal am I? gives students the opportunity to practise animal vocabulary.
World Records Quiz gives students the opportunity to practise writing superlatives.

WEBLINK

Students could go to www.poetry-online.org/limericks.htm for more examples of limericks.

Language File pp120–121

Workbook Unit 7 Inspiration EXTRA! pp86–87

Food around the world

1 READING

- Ask students what food they can see in the photos. Ask *What is the relationship between the people in each photo? How old are they? What continent/country are they in? What do they eat?* Use this to pre-teach some of the vocabulary in the text, e.g. *porridge.*
- Students listen and/or read the text and match the families to the pictures. Did they guess the continents/ countries correctly?

3.16 Recording

See text on page 101 of the Student's Book.

Answers

A Japan B Mali C USA

Optional activity

Before opening their books, tell students they are going to read about 'Food around the world'. Write: *Mali, West Africa; North Carolina, USA; Tokyo, Japan* on the board. Ask *What do you think people eat in ...?*

2

- Students read the questions and answer any they can.
- They then listen and/or read again to check their ideas. Ask them to make a note of the words in the text that help them decide on their answers. Encourage students to guess the meaning of unfamiliar vocabulary from the context and ignore words that are not necessary to complete the exercise.
- Check the answers and ask students to identify where they found the answer.

Answers

1 *The Revis family and the Ukita family*
2 *Soumana Natomo*
3 *Kazuo Ukita*
4 *The Natomo family*
5 *Kazuo and Sayo Ukita*
6 *Brandon Revis*
7 *The Natomo family*
8 *Kazuo Ukita*
9 *The Natomo family*
10 *The Revis family*

3 VOCABULARY

- The aim is to encourage students to work out the meaning of vocabulary from the context.
- Ask students to find the words in the text. Encourage them to use the text to help them match the words with definitions, e.g. a stew is clearly a type of food that you make with vegetables or fish, so answer e. Be prepared to translate *grain.*

Answers

1 d 2 c 3 e 4 a 5 b

Optional activity

Put students into teams. Ask more questions on the text, e.g. *How many children does Soumana Natomo have? How old is his youngest wife?* The first team to answer correctly wins a point.

4 SPEAKING

- Students read through the prompts. Be prepared to explain/translate *healthy*. Do the first question with the class. Students continue in pairs, asking and answering the questions.
- Ask different pairs to tell the class their ideas. Ask if the rest of the class agrees with their comments.

Suggested answers

Students' own answers
The biggest family is the Natomo family.
The Revis family is trying to lose weight.
The children help with the food in the Natomo family.
Students' own answers
Students' own answers

5 MINI-PROJECT FOOD FILE

- Students read the instructions. Ask students to work in pairs and to use the prompt questions to help them.
- Set a 15-minute time limit for students to write their paragraph. Monitor and note examples of good language and errors. Put these on the board and ask students to identify and correct the errors.
- Encourage students to correct any errors and copy their texts out neatly. Then display them in the classroom for everyone to read and enjoy.

WEBLINK

Students could visit www.macmillanenglish.com/uploadedFiles/Inspiration/INSP1culture_FAW.pdf for an activity on food for special occasions.

Workbook Culture pp88–89

I'd like a cold drink

Communicative aims	Language	Pronunciation	Vocabulary	Optional aids
Making and accepting/ declining offers	*some* and *any* Countable/ Uncountable nouns *I'd like … Would you like …?*	/eɪ/ pl<u>a</u>te /æ/ th<u>a</u>nks /ɑː/ gl<u>a</u>ss	Kitchen utensils and equipment Food and drink	Warmer 2: pictures/ photos of food

WARMER 1

Game *Word association* Divide students into groups of three or four. The first student thinks of a word from the previous unit, e.g. *mosquito*. The next says a word associated with *mosquito*, e.g. *dangerous*, and so on. Students mustn't repeat words. Students can challenge each other to explain their word associations.

WARMER 2

Use pictures/photos of food to elicit food vocabulary. Write the words on the board. In pairs, students ask each other *Do you like …?*

1 OPENER

- The aim is to review and pre-teach vocabulary for the following exercises.
- Students look at the photo and describe what they can see. Ask *Who's in the photo? Where are they?*
- In pairs, students look for the items in the box. Ask one student to read out what he/she can see and ask everyone to point to it if they can see it in their picture. Check students understand the difference between *dishwasher/washing machine* and *cup/glass* by asking questions, e.g. *What do you put in the dishwasher?*

Answers

apples, a cooker, a cup, a fridge, a glass, a knife, oranges, a plate, a sandwich, a table

Optional activity

Students divide the vocabulary into three categories: food, kitchen appliances (blender, washing machine), kitchen utensils (knife, plate). They then add two more words to each category.

2 READING

- Tell students they are going to hear the conversation between Ruby, Diana and Pierre. Ask them to listen and note what they are talking about (a barbecue party).
- With a more confident class, do this as a listening exercise. With a less confident class, students read and listen. Check the answer to the question. (Ruby thinks vegetable kebabs are a good idea.)

3.17 **Recording**

See text on page 102 of the Student's Book.

3 AFTER READING

- Focus on the questions. In pairs, students make a note of any answers they already know. They then listen and read the conversation again and complete their answers. Encourage students to guess the meaning of unfamiliar vocabulary from the context. Check students have understood: *paper plate, plastic glass, sausages, vegetarian, (vegetable) kebab.*
- Check the answers by choosing different students to ask and answer the questions.

Answers

1 *No, he doesn't. (He wants a cold drink.)*
2 *Yes, he'd like some apple juice.*
3 *Yes, he does (but there aren't any).*
4 *Yes, she does.*
5 *Some paper plates and plastic glasses.*
6 *No, she doesn't.*
7 *Because she's vegetarian.*
8 *Vegetable kebabs.*

Optional activities

- 3.17 Play the recording again, line by line, for students to repeat. Students act out the dialogue in groups of three.
- With a confident class, students underline examples of *some* and *any* in the dialogue. Ask students to work out which one is used in affirmative sentences, which one in negative sentences and which one in questions.

Your response

Get the class to brainstorm good party food. If they mention particular dishes, see if they can explain how to cook them.

LANGUAGE WORKOUT OPTION

If you want to pre-teach the language students will be using in the following activities, you may like to go to the Language Workout box now.

4 VOCABULARY

- If you didn't explain the concept of countable and uncountable nouns in Unit 4, Lesson 3 (when teaching *hair*), do so now.
- In pairs, students decide if the words in the box are countable or uncountable. Point out that if they are countable, they should write both the singular and plural form. Tell students there is an equal number of countable and uncountable words.
- Check answers by asking a fast finisher to write the answers on the board. Check the plural spelling of *tomatoes* and the pronunciation of *fruit* and *vegetable*.

Answers

Countable

Singular	*Plural*	*Uncountable*
banana	*bananas*	*cheese*
chip	*chips*	*coffee*
egg	*eggs*	*fruit*
mushroom	*mushrooms*	*meat*
tomato	*tomatoes*	*tea*
vegetable	*vegetables*	*water*

5 SPEAKING

- Students read through the instructions. Ask *When do we use Is there … ?* (with uncountable nouns) *When do we use Are there … ?* (with plural countable nouns).
- Go round the class, naming students A or B. Ask two confident students to demonstrate.
- Students continue in pairs. Students then reverse roles for the second set of prompts.

Answers

Are there any books/chairs/magazines? Yes, there are.
Is there any cheese? No, there isn't.
Is there any meat? No, there isn't.
Is there any milk? Yes, there is.
Are there any vegetables/animals? No, there aren't.
Is there any bread? Yes, there is.
Are there any eggs? Yes, there are.
Are there any flowers/pens? No, there aren't.
Is there any fruit/water? Yes, there is.

Optional activity

Confident students say whether they are in the photo, and if they are, where they are, e.g. *on the table*.

Extension Students use other photos in the book for the same activity. Both students look at the photo for 30 seconds, then one closes the book and the other tests them on the things in the photo, using questions with *some* and *any*. Possible photos: page 26, 50, 66, 80. Alternatively, this could be played as a team competition with the teacher asking the questions. Insist on full answers if you play the game like this so that students practise *some* and *any*.

6 VOCABULARY

- More confident students can look at the pictures first and see how many words they already know. With less confident students, ask them to match the words in the Word Bank box with the pictures.
- Listen for pronunciation problems during feedback. Model and drill as necessary. Check *Which food can a vegetarian eat?* (You can have vegetable kebabs and there are vegetarian varieties of hamburgers and sausages.) Ask *When do you eat this type of food?* (At a party/barbecue.)

3.18 Recording and answers

1 chocolate cake 2 ice cream 3 fruit salad 4 kebabs 5 hamburgers 6 sausages 7 tomato salad 8 potatoes

7 LISTENING

- Students read through the sentences and predict the order. They then listen to confirm.

3.19 Recording

Boy *What would you like to eat?*
Girl *I'd like a hamburger and some tomato salad, please.*
Boy *Would you like some potatoes?*
Girl *Yes, please.*
Boy *And would you like some sausages?*
Girl *No, thank you. I don't want any sausages.*

Answers

1 C 2 F 3 E 4 A 5 B 6 D

Optional activity

3.19 Play the recording again, line by line, for students to repeat for pronunciation and intonation practice.

8 PRONUNCIATION

- Model and drill the three different pronunciations of the letter *a* and the example words.
- Students predict which column the words go into before listening. Play the recording once. Students compare their ideas with a partner. Play the second part of the recording for students to check. Drill each word in chorus and individually. Your students may have heard tomato pronounced with /eɪ/ as this is the US pronunciation and therefore also acceptable.

3.20 Recording and answers

/eɪ/ **plate** *make paper*
/æ/ **thanks** *apple salad*
/ɑː/ **glass** *barbecue banana*

/eɪ/ **plate** *cake crazy potato*
/æ/ **thanks** *carrot hamburger sandwich*
/ɑː/ **glass** *last party tomato*

Optional activities

- Students write a sentence which includes as many words as possible from one column.
- Divide the class into pairs/small groups. They race to think of four more words for each sound. The first pair/group to finish tells the class their words. The others then add any more words they have.

9 SPEAKING

- Focus on the food pictures in exercise 6 and ask students to choose three things to eat. Tell them they are going to act out the conversation where they ask for this food. Ask them to read the useful phrases in the box. Tell them to use the conversation in exercise 7 as a guide. Less confident students can read and adapt this conversation. More confident students can review the conversation and then work without the book.
- Ask two students to demonstrate.

Optional activity

With a less confident class, you may wish to elicit a complete dialogue and write it on the board. Students practise it. Then rub out some parts of the dialogue. Students keep practising the dialogue from memory. Eventually, remove all the dialogue.

10 WRITING

- The aim is for students to write a dialogue using the role play as a framework. Students read the instructions. Check *Where are these two people? Does B eat meat?* Set a time limit for students to write the dialogue.

LANGUAGE WORKOUT

- Ask students to look at the Language box and complete the sentences. Confident students can complete first and then check, while others can look back at exercises 2 and 3 and then complete.
- Students turn to page 121 of the Language File to check their answers.

Answers
some some any

- Go through the grammar rules with the students. Highlight that:
  - uncountable nouns cannot be used in the plural, you cannot add an *-s*
  - you use *a/an* to talk about singular countable nouns in affirmative and negative sentences and questions, e.g. *I'd like a cold drink, I don't want a hamburger. Would you like a sandwich?*
- Drill the examples for pronunciation and stress.

PRACTICE

- Students do Practice exercise 26 on page 121 of the Language File.
- They complete the sentences with *some* or *any*.

Answers
1 some 2 any 3 any 4 some 5 some 6 any 7 any 8 some

Optional activities

♦ Fast finishers think of more examples of countable and uncountable nouns.
♦ With a confident class, explain that *coffee, tea* and *water* can sometimes be countable. When they are countable they mean *a cup/glass of* …, e.g. *I'd like a coffee, please; Three coffees, please.*

Follow-up activities

♦ Each student writes down everything that he/she ate/drank yesterday, e.g. *I ate a cheese and tomato pizza and some salad.* Monitor and help with any extra vocabulary needed here. Students then move around the class and find someone else who ate these things by asking *Did you eat a pizza/any salad yesterday?* Point out that they need to find someone for each food item. It may be the same person or different people. The winner is the student who finds a match for each of his/her food items.
♦ **Game** *20 Questions* See Unit 4 Lesson 1 Follow-up activity for instructions. Ask questions about food, e.g. *Do you need any eggs to make this meal?*

HOMEWORK

Students write a description of their kitchen at home. Tell them to include some things that aren't there, e.g. *There aren't any eggs in the fridge.*

WEBLINK

Students can look at different categories, including 'kitchen' in the picture dictionary at www.pdictionary.com

Revision and Extension p111

Language File p121

Workbook Unit 8 Lesson 1 pp90–91

Photocopiable notes p161, Worksheet p184

I haven't got a games console

Communicative aims	Language	Pronunciation	Vocabulary	Optional aids
Talking about money and prices Talking about possessions	*have got* *Question: How much ...?*	/f/ /v/ /w/	Family Possessions Hobbies	Follow-up activity: Happy families cards

WARMER 1

Game *Jump the line* See Unit 7, Lesson 2 for instructions. Test the words *some* and *any*.

WARMER 2

Write the following questions on the board for the students to discuss: *Do you like shopping? What do you like buying? What's your favourite shop? How much do you spend every month? What was the last thing you bought?*

1 OPENER

- The aim is to stimulate interest in the article.
- Students look at the photos. Ask *Who are they?* and then elicit ideas from the class about which one gets the most money every week.

2 READING

- Tell students they are going to read about the two teenagers, the amount of money they have and what they spend it on. Ask them to make notes comparing themselves with Emil and Freya.
- With a more confident class, do this as a listening exercise. With a less confident class, students read and listen.
- In pairs, students discuss how they compare to Emil and Freya.

3.21 Recording

See text on page 104 of the Student's Book.

Optional activity

Ask *Do you think it's good for parents to give teenagers a lot of money?* and get students' opinions.

3 AFTER READING

- Students read the questions and choose the correct answer. Point out that one of the answers is not used.
- They then listen and/or read again to check their ideas. Encourage students to guess the meaning of unfamiliar vocabulary from the context and ignore words which are not necessary to complete the exercise.

Answers

1 f 2 g 3 a 4 h 5 c 6 d 7 b e is not used

Your response

Ask students to discuss how much they think teenagers cost their parents in their country. Encourage them to list the things that their parents pay for.

4 LISTENING

- Write some British prices on the board, e.g. *55p, £1.30, £10, £18.99* and elicit how to say them (fifty-five p, one (pound) thirty, ten pounds, eighteen (pounds) ninety-nine). Point out that there is no *and* in the number. Focus on the prices in the exercise and elicit how to say these.
- Ask students to predict how much the things in the box cost.
- Students listen and check their ideas.
- Don't go through the answers. Instead, ask two students to read the example question and answer aloud. Students continue in pairs and, in this way, check their answers with their partners.

3.22 Recording

EMILY *How much is the computer game?*
SHOP ASSISTANT *It's twenty-two fifty.*
JAKE *How much is the DVD?*
SHOP ASSISTANT *It's fifteen ninety-nine.*
EMILY *How much is the Blu-ray disc?*
SHOP ASSISTANT *It's sixteen pounds.*
JAKE *How much is the CD?*
SHOP ASSISTANT *It's twelve seventy-five.*
EMILY *How much is the poster?*
SHOP ASSISTANT *It's ninety-nine p.*
JAKE *How much is the magazine?*
SHOP ASSISTANT *It's one twenty-five.*

Answers

computer game £22.50 DVD £15.99
Blu-ray disc £16 CD £12.75 poster 99p
magazine £1.25

Optional activity

Students convert these prices to their own currency. Ask *Do you think these things are cheap or expensive?*

5 PRONUNCIATION

- Model the three sounds for the students. Ask them to identify those sounds in the sentence.
- Play the recording. Students listen and check their ideas. Play the recording again for students to listen and repeat.
- Nominate some students to say the sentence aloud.

3.23 Recording

/f/ /v/ /w/

We love watching movies – we've got twenty-five DVDs with our fifty-one favourite films!

Optional activity

In pairs, students invent another sentence including as many examples of the three sounds as possible. Ask the pair with the sentence with the most examples to dictate their sentence to the group.

6 LISTENING

- Focus on the chart. In pairs, students predict the answers.
- Play the recording and students listen to check. Allow students to compare answers, monitor and play the recording again if necessary.
- Ask two students to read the example questions and answers aloud. Elicit a few more examples from the class. Students continue in pairs.

3.24 Recording

TERESA *I haven't got any brothers or sisters – but I'd really like a sister! I've got a camera phone and I send lots of pictures to Spain! I've got a pet cat called Suzanna – that's Suzi for short. I haven't got a skateboard but I've got a hobby – painting. I'm painting a picture of Emily as a present.*

PIERRE *I haven't got any brothers but I've got an older sister – she's called Marianne. I haven't got a camera phone but I've got a skateboard at home in Geneva. I haven't got a pet but I'd love to have a dog. And I've got a hobby – it's sport. My favourite sport is basketball.*

KATYA *I've got a brother called Dima and a sister called Anna. I haven't got a camera phone because they're expensive. I've got a pet rabbit called Bunny but I haven't got a skateboard. Yes, I've got a great hobby – dancing – and I love hip-hop, jive and salsa.*

ADAM *I haven't got a brother but I've got a sister. She's called Ruby. I've got a camera phone, and I like taking pictures with it. No, I haven't got a pet. But I've got a skateboard and I go skateboarding with my friends. What about hobbies? I've got lots of hobbies, but I think my most important hobby is – girls!*

Answers

	Teresa	*Pierre*	*Katya*	*Adam*
brother	✗	✗	✓	✗
sister	✗	✓	✓	✓
camera phone	✓	✗	✗	✓
pet	✓	✗	✓	✗
skateboard	✗	✓	✗	✓
hobby	✓	✓	✓	✓

Optional activities

- Encourage confident students to make a note of more details, e.g. *What kind of pet? What hobby?*
- Students work in pairs. Student A closes his/her book. Student B talks about the information in the chart but includes some false information. Student A listens and corrects the false information. Students reverse roles.

Extension Ask students to write sentences about the characters, as in the examples.

7 SPEAKING

- Elicit questions you can ask about family, possessions and hobbies using *have got*.
- Students find out information about at least three students, about their family, possessions and hobbies. Give them time to prepare a chart similar to that in exercise 6 to note their answers.
- Tell students that they can't ask the student directly. They need to ask other students, as in the examples. Students read the example questions and answers. Ask *What do you say if you don't know the answer?* (I'm sorry. I don't know.)
- Tell students to make a note of the answers.
- Set a ten-minute time limit for students to collect their information.

Optional activity

Students check with the three people that the information they have collected is true.

Extension Students do a class survey on hobbies. They could display the information in a chart or write a short report.

8 WRITING

- Students use the information they have collected to write a short paragraph about the three students. Remind them not to write the name. Set a 15-minute time limit.
- Students exchange their descriptions and identify who they are describing. Alternatively, students could do this orally.

LANGUAGE WORKOUT

- Ask students to look at the Language box and to complete the sentences. Confident students can complete first and then check, while others can look back at exercises 2 and 3 and then complete.
- Students turn to page 121 of the Language File to check their answers.

Answers

got	*got*	*have*	*got*
not	*hasn't*	*Have*	*haven't*
has	*have*		

- Point out that:
  - *have got* is used, like *have*, to talk about possession, e.g. *I've got a guitar*, and relationships, e.g. *He's got a sister, they've got two children*.
  - you do not use contractions in short answers, *Yes, I have not ~~Yes, I've~~*.
  - *'s* can mean both *is*, e.g. *He's Irish*, and *has*, e.g. *He's got red hair*.

Optional activities

- ♦ Ask *Have your parents got a DVD player? Have you got any computer games?* Students respond with short answers. Then elicit sentences about students giving this information as prompts, e.g. *Give me a sentence: Andrea, computer games*.
- ♦ Read some sentences aloud, e.g. *He's a journalist, He's got two sisters*. Students put up their right hand if the *'s* means *is* and their left hand up if it means *has*.

PRACTICE

- Students do Practice exercise 27 on page 121 of the Language File
- They complete the sentences with the correct form of *have got*.

Answers

1 has got *2 Has, got* *3 hasn't got* *4 have got*
5 haven't got *6 haven't got* *7 have got*
8 Has, got *9 Have, got* *10 has got*

Follow-up activity

Game *Happy families* This is usually played with family sets but could be played with a different four-piece set of vocabulary, e.g. possessions: a DVD player, a mobile phone, a CD, a guitar. These words need to be written on cards. Organise students into groups. Each group has the same number of vocabulary sets as students, or if the group has five students, it needs five sets of cards. Shuffle and deal out the cards. The aim of the game is to collect a complete set. Write on the board the things that make up the complete set so the students know what they are missing. Student A asks a student in their group *Have you got (a possession)?* If the student has that card, then they must hand it over, if not, then it's another student's turn, and so on until one student completes a set and wins.

HOMEWORK

Students write a description of themselves: their family, possessions and hobbies.

WEBLINK

Students could visit www.xe.com to convert their currency into another currency. They may also like to visit www.comparecountryprices.com to find out the price of the same item in different countries.

Revision and Extension p111

Language File p121

Workbook Unit 8 Lesson 2 pp92–93

Photocopiable notes p161, Worksheet p185

3 It's different, isn't it?

Communicative aims	Language	Pronunciation	Vocabulary	Optional aids
Asking for agreement	Question tags with *be*	Intonation in question tags	Life in another country	Follow-up activity: large pieces of paper

WARMER 1

Write anagrams of different food on the board. Students race to re-order the letters to make the words.

WARMER 2

Put the following questions on the board: *When was the last time you went to a party? Whose party was it? Was there any music? Was there any food? Did you enjoy the party?* The students ask you these questions first so you can provide an example of how to answer. Students then ask and answer in pairs.

1 OPENER

- The aim is to set the context for the reading text.
- Students answer the question orally. Ask students to predict why the people feel the way they do.

Optional activity

Go through the headline of the article and the text underneath it with the class so that they understand that all the people in the photos are teenagers from other countries who are now living in the United Kingdom. Ask them to say what problems they think these teenagers might have.

2 READING

- Tell students to read the article and note down the four countries the people are from.
- With a more confident class, do this as a listening exercise. With a less confident class, students read and listen. Check answers and then ask them where the four countries are.

3.25 Recording

See text on page 106 of the Student's Book.

Answers

The people come from Azerbaijan (in Central Europe), Bahrain (in the Middle East), Peru (in South America) and Ivory Coast (in Africa).

3 AFTER READING

- Students read and listen to the article again and decide if sentences 1–8 are true, false or there is no information. Ask them to note down the words in the article that help them decide on their answers. Encourage them to guess the meaning of unfamiliar vocabulary from the context. Be prepared to translate *rich culture, connected with my culture, confident, paradise*.

Answers

1 True
2 False. (At first he didn't want to come.)
3 True
4 True
5 No information
6 True
7 False. (She has more friends in England.)
8 False. (Luis prefers Peru and wants to go back there. Inza feels freer back in the Ivory Coast.)

Optional activity

Confident students can correct the false information.

Your response

Ask students to discuss the questions and report back to the class.

4 LISTENING

- Tell students they are going to hear the conversation at the barbecue. Play the recording once for students to listen.
- Go through the questions with the class. Then play the recording again for students to note down their answers.
- Check answers.

3.26 Recording

David	*You're Katya, aren't you? I'm Adam and Ruby's dad.*
Katya	*Hello, Mr Campbell – nice to meet you!*
Adam	*It's hot, isn't it? Would you like some ice cream?*
Katya	*Yes, please. Oh, look at Pierre and Ruby!*
Adam	*They're getting on well, aren't they?*
Emily	*Hi, Teresa! Hey, what's the matter?*
Teresa	*Well, it's the end of the holiday and I … I don't want to go home.*
Emily	*I know – it's sad, isn't it?*
Teresa	*It's all right for you. You're going to stay with Katya in Moscow, aren't you?*
Emily	*Well, yes, but I'd really like to stay with you too.*
Teresa	*That's impossible this year – perhaps next.*
Jake	*Teresa, would you like something to eat?*
Teresa	*No, thanks. I'm not very hungry. Whoops – oh, I am silly, aren't I?*
Jake	*No, you aren't! Would you like another drink?*
Teresa	*Yes, please!*

Answers

1 Mr Campbell, Adam and Ruby's father.
2 Katya does.
3 Pierre and Ruby.
4 Teresa is.
5 Emily is.
6 Teresa does.

5 PRONUNCIATION

- Play the recording once and ask students to listen for the question tags.
- Students complete the sentences with the question tags in the box.
- Play the recording again for students to check their answers. Then play it for them to listen and repeat the sentences. Monitor for correct falling intonation. To help students, show intonation with a falling hand gesture, whistle the intonation if you can, or back-chain the sentences, ie model and drill the question tag on its own, then add the beginning and drill the complete phrase.

3.27 Recording and answers

1 We're enjoying the barbecue, aren't we?
2 It's hot, isn't it?
3 They're getting on well, aren't they?
4 Mr Campbell is cooking sausages, isn't he?
5 Ruby is happy, isn't she?
6 You're Katya, aren't you?
7 I am silly, aren't I?

Optional activity

Confident students can complete the sentences with the question tags before they listen to the recording.

6 READING

- Tell students they are going to do a quiz in pairs. They need to look back through the book and find the answers to these ten questions. Set a time limit. Don't check the answers at this point.
- Students look at the example dialogue. Nominate two students to read it, adding the job and a final response.
- Tell students to move around and ask different students the questions to confirm their answers. Monitor and help where necessary, making sure they are using question tags correctly.
- Check the answers with the class.

Answers

1 *He's a singer, isn't he? (Unit 1, Lesson 4)*
2 *They're in the USA, aren't they? (Unit 2, Lesson 4 and Unit 7, Lesson 4)*
3 *It's the mosquito, isn't it? (Unit 7, Lesson 3)*
4 *It's Canberra, isn't it? (Unit 1, Culture)*
5 *It's 370 years old, isn't it? (Unit 1, Lesson 2)*
6 *He's a motor racing star, isn't he? (Unit 3, Lesson 4)*
7 *They're from California/the USA, aren't they? (Unit 2, Lesson 4)*
8 *It's about 200 years old, isn't it? (Unit 1, Lesson 2)*
9 *It's getting hotter, isn't it? (Unit 5, Lesson 3)*
10 *It's by Bram Stoker, isn't it? (Unit 6, Lesson 4)*

Extension In pairs, students write five general knowledge questions. They then exchange these with another pair. They form a group of four and confirm their answers using question tags as before, e.g. *The capital of New Zealand is Wellington, isn't it? Yes, it is.*

Optional activity

In pairs, students think of five famous people/things and their nationality. Less confident students write the sentences they are going to use, e.g. *Britney Spears is American, isn't she?* Confident students just note name and nationality. Students then move around the class and check other students agree with them by using question tags.

7 WRITING

- Students read the instructions. Do an example: show students a text you have written or read it aloud, e.g. *_____ lent his camera to Adam at Devil's Dyke. ______ went to The Lanes and saw a ghost.* Students guess who it is. Encourage them to say *It's Pierre, isn't it?*
- Set a time limit for students to write their texts. They then read their text to their partner who guesses who it is about.

LANGUAGE WORKOUT

- Ask students to look at the Language box and to complete the sentences. Confident students can complete first and then check, while others can look back at the conversations and then complete.
- Students turn to page 121 of the Language File to check their answers.

Answers
aren't *isn't* *aren't*

- Highlight that
  - these question tags are not real questions, you are just checking that the person you are talking to agrees with you
  - the first part is a positive statement with the verb *be*
  - the question tag is formed with the negative of *be* and the pronoun
  - the intonation falls at the end (as in a normal sentence and unlike most questions)
  - the question tag *I am* → *aren't I?* is irregular.
- Drill the examples in chorus for pronunciation and stress.

PRACTICE

- Students do Practice exercise 28 on page 121 of the Language File.
- They complete the sentences with the correct question tag.

Answers
1 isn't he? *2 aren't they?* *3 aren't we?* *4 isn't she?*
5 isn't it? *6 aren't you?* *7 aren't I?*

Follow-up activity

Organise a maximum of eight groups. Each group chooses one of the coursebook characters and prepares a poster about him/her, including drawings, information and things that happened to them during the exchange visit.

HOMEWORK

Students write the dialogue between Ruby and Pierre and/or Diana and David Ward for the party, using the conversation in exercise 4 as a model.

WEBLINK

Students can read about other teenagers' experiences abroad at www.teenagersabroad.com/students.html

Revision and Extension p111

Language File p121

Workbook Unit 8 Lesson 3 pp94–95

Photocopiable notes p161, Worksheet p186

Integrated Skills
Invitations and thanks

Skills
Reading Connecting ideas: invitations and replies
Listening Telephone calls
Speaking Role play
Writing Thank-you letter

Learner Independence
Ways of learning in the holidays
Vocabulary notebook
Phrasebook

Vocabulary
Useful expressions

WARMER 1

If you set the homework in the previous lesson, ask students to read out their dialogues with a partner. The rest of the class listens and guesses who the speakers are, Ruby/Pierre or Diana/David Ward.

WARMER 2

Game *Word race!* Students work in pairs or groups. Tell students to write down four things you eat at a barbecue. Students race to list them. The first group to finish wins a point. Continue with other categories, e.g. four things you read, four types of shop, four family members, four verbs in the past.

1 OPENER

- The aim is to introduce the topic of the lesson. Ask the question to the class. (They are invitations and replies.)

2 READING

- The aim is for students to use key words and context clues to match the texts.
- Students read and match the invitations and replies. Then listen and check.

3.28 Recording
See text on page 108 of the Student's Book.

Answers
1 D 2 C 3 A 4 B

Optional activity

Ask more comprehension questions about the texts, e.g. *Where is Ruby and Adam's party? What time is the barbecue?*

3

- The aim is for students to read the letter in detail and notice some of the conventions of letter writing.
- Ask *Who wrote the letter?* (Katya.) *Why?* (To thank the family she stayed with.) Students read the sentences first and then read the letter to find the answers. Check students understand *miss something/someone*.

Answers
1 Mr and Mrs Fry
2 Pushkin Prospekt 4, Moscow, Russia
3 26th July
4 Second
5 Three
6 Katya's; best wishes
7 Emily's visit
8 best wishes

4 LISTENING

- Students read the summary of the first call. Encourage students to predict the answers. Play the recording once and ask students to compare their answers. Play the recording again if necessary. Check students understand *make an excuse* by asking *Does Emily really have lots of homework?*
- Repeat the procedure for the other calls. In the second call, check students have understood *accept* by asking *Does accept mean 'say yes' or 'say no'?*

3.29 Recording

Call 1

ADAM	*Hi Emily – it's Adam! How are you?*
EMILY	*OK, thanks, and you?*
ADAM	*I'm fine. Look, do you want to go to the Zero Club with me tonight?*
EMILY	*I'm not sure, Adam.*
ADAM	*There's a cool new DJ there and he plays really wicked music. Lots of soul.*
EMILY	*Soul isn't really my thing, Adam, and I've got lots of homework. Sorry.*
ADAM	*OK. Bye then.*

Call 2

PIERRE	*Hello. Is that Ruby?*
RUBY	*Speaking. Who's that?*
PIERRE	*Guess!*
RUBY	*It's you, Pierre, isn't it? Where are you? In Brighton?*
PIERRE	*No. At home in Geneva. I just wanted to ring you.*
RUBY	*It's good to hear you.*
PIERRE	*I want to ask you something. Would you like to come to Geneva with your mother? You can stay with us.*
RUBY	*Wow!*
PIERRE	*I asked my parents and they said it's OK. What do you think?*
RUBY	*Oh yes, please. I'd love to. That's great.*
PIERRE	*Ask your mum, then ring me back. OK?*
RUBY	*OK. Speak to you in a minute. Bye.*

Call 3

EMILY	*Hi Lisa. It's Emily.*
LISA	*Hiya. How's it going?*
EMILY	*Adam rang me. He invited me to the Zero Club.*
LISA	*Really? What did you say?*
EMILY	*No, of course. I like Adam but I don't want to go out with him. I made an excuse about homework. But I don't want to spend Saturday night on my own. Do you want to go to the cinema with me?*
EMILY	*What's on?*
LISA	*There's a new Robert Pattinson film.*
EMILY	*Great. What time?*
LISA	*Let's meet at seven o'clock outside the cinema.*
EMILY	*Cool – see you there.*

Answers

Call 1: tonight, wicked, no
Call 2: Geneva, family, accepts
Call 3: cinema, seven

Optional activity

With a more confident class, ask students to choose one of the conversations and re-create the dialogue. Tell them that it doesn't need to be the same as the one they heard but it needs to include the points in the summary. Ask some pairs to perform their dialogue.

5 SPEAKING

- Go through the instructions with the students. Ask them to look back at exercises 2 and 4 and write down useful language, e.g. *bring some good music, a party to celebrate …, see you there.*
- Focus on the language for inviting and accepting/ declining. Elicit a complete question, e.g. *Would you like to go to the theatre? Do you want to go to the theatre?* Model and drill for pronunciation.
- Elicit the start of the conversation: *Hi … It's … , Hi … How are you?, Fine, thanks.* Ask two confident students to demonstrate the activity.
- If possible, seat the students back-to-back to make it more like a phone conversation. Students use the prompts to make phone conversations. Have them change roles and, ideally, partners.

Optional activities

- ♦ With a less confident class, elicit a model dialogue on the board. Practise, then start rubbing out parts of the dialogue. The students continue practising it from memory. Eventually rub out all the dialogue.
- ♦ Confident students write the days of the week in their notebook. This is their diary. Tell them to complete their diary with real plans they have. They then have the phone conversations and fit the arrangements into their diaries. This could involve detailed responses, e.g. *I'm sorry, I can't. I have tennis lessons on Tuesday.*
- ♦ Ask different groups to perform their dialogues for the rest of the class.

6 WRITING

- Read the instructions with the class. Ask *Who is writing the letter? Who is the letter to? Why is she writing to them?* Encourage students to use Katya's letter in exercise 3 as a model.

Suggested answer

Dear Mr and Mrs Ward
Thank you very much for looking after me so well. I really enjoyed staying with you in Brighton.
I had an easy journey home and it's nice to see my family again. But I miss Brighton!
The three things I miss most are:
Teresa – because she was friendly to me.
Your food – I learnt a lot about British food and cooking. It's better than I imagined!
All the Brighton High School students – they were great fun, especially Adam!
I hope that you are both well. My parents send their best wishes, and we're all looking forward to Adam's visit.
With best wishes,
Jake

Optional activity

Students exchange writing and correct each other's work for spelling, grammar and punctuation.

7 LEARNER INDEPENDENCE

- The aim is to make students aware of what they can do during the holidays to maintain and improve their English.
- Nominate students to read the suggestions aloud. Elicit more specific ideas for some points, e.g. *Which English-speaking singers/bands do you like listening to? Do you hear any English on television? Where can you buy books in English?*
- Individually, students put the suggestions in order from what they think is the best idea for themselves to the least useful idea. Students compare their ideas.
- Find out which is the most popular suggestion. Ask students if they have any other ideas, e.g. look at English-language websites.

8

- The aim is to encourage students to group words in lexical sets (or categories) in their vocabulary notebooks rather than randomly or alphabetically. This process means that students review the meanings of the words and it also helps storage and retrieval of words from memory. Finding and noting favourite words is a more personalised way of reviewing vocabulary and helps with remembering words.
- Write the three categories on the board. Elicit an example for each.
- Students work individually and add to each category from memory. They then compare their list with a partner and add any extra. Finally they look back through the unit and add any others that they find. Set a minimum of six words per category.

Suggested answers

Things in the kitchen	*Food and drink*	*Favourite words*
cooker *cup* *dishwasher* *fork* *fridge* *glass* *knife* *plate* *spoon* *table* *washing machine*	*apple* *orange* *sandwich* *hamburger* *sausage* *(vegetable) kebab* *chocolate cake* *fruit salad* *potatoes* *tomato salad*	*(Students' own answers)*

9 PHRASEBOOK

- Ask students to look through the unit and find the expressions, and notice how they are used. Help with translation where necessary. Students can add expressions they like to their Personal Phrasebooks.
- Play the recording for students to listen and repeat the expressions.

3.30 Recording and answers

Hiya. (Pierre, Lesson 1)
I'm really thirsty. (Pierre, Lesson 1)
No, thanks. (Pierre, Lesson 1)
Yes, please. (Pierre, Lesson 1)
You're crazy! (Pierre, Lesson 1)
Come to our party! (Ruby, Lesson 4)
Please let me know (Invitation 4, Lesson 4)
Wicked! (Jake, Lesson 4)
See you there. (Jake, Lesson 4)

- Focus on the three dialogues. Elicit some ideas for the first space, e.g. *Would you like a cold drink? Do you want to go to the theatre tomorrow?*
- Students complete the conversations individually. Less confident students can look through the unit for ideas.
- Ask some students to read out their dialogues.

Follow-up activities

- ♦ Students work in pairs. Have them draw a 10-by-10 empty grid and write ten words from the unit in the grid. They can write them horizontally, vertically or diagonally. Students then complete the rest of the grid with random letters. Pairs exchange wordsearch puzzles and race to find the ten words.
- ♦ Choose six words from this unit, e.g. *thirsty, sandwiches, vegetarian, skateboard, skydiving, miss someone*. If you have a Vocabulary box, choose words from the box. Students work in groups to invent a short story using all six words. Set a short time limit. Ask each group to tell the class their story and take a class vote on the best.

HOMEWORK

Students write two invitations: one to invite a friend to a party at their house and one to invite a friend's parents to a barbecue with their parents. Note that the letters will be different in style. Remind students to use the examples on page 108 of the Student's Book as models.

WEBLINK

Students could revise vocabulary at www.pdictionary.com

Revision and Extension p111

Workbook Unit 8 Lesson 4 pp96–97

Inspiration EXTRA!

Optional aids

Project: photos and pictures for a project comparing two countries, scissors, glue

PROJECT HOME AND AWAY

1

- Explain to students that the aim of the project is to write file pages comparing their own country with another one of their choice. Focus attention on the example contrasting Scotland with Sweden. Divide the students into groups and appoint an 'editor' for each group. In groups, students discuss which country they would be interested in researching.

2

- Students look at the headings. They use the Internet and library books to find out information, both positive and negative, about their chosen country with regard to the items listed.

3

- Students make notes about their own country under the same headings.

4

- Students discuss their notes and decide on the three best things and two worst things about each country.

5

- Students write sentences about the best and worst things in both countries. Remind them that they can use the example as a model.
- They should read their work carefully and correct any mistakes. They can then write it out again neatly and illustrate it with photos.
- Students show their file to other groups. Display the files in the classroom if possible.

Optional activity

Students look at all the files. Take a class vote on the best. (They can't vote for their own.) Ask students to say why this is their favourite.

GAME WORD MAZE

- Students read through the instructions. Ask students to point to *fruit* and *happy*. Ask them to make a connection between *fruit* and a word in the first line, e.g. *You make juice with fruit*. Check students understand that they now need to link *juice* with a word in the next line. Students race to finish first.

Suggested answers

Fruit – juice: You make juice with fruit.
Juice – drink: I usually drink orange juice in the morning.
Drink –sandwich: I sometimes have a sandwich and a cold drink for lunch.
Sandwich – party food: Sandwiches are one type of party food.
Party food – invitation: For a party you need to prepare party food and send an invitation.
Invitation – girlfriend: If you have a party, your girlfriend will get an invitation.
Girlfriend – present: You need to buy your girlfriend a present sometimes.
Present – birthday: We normally give presents on people's birthdays.
Birthday – happy: Happy birthday!

Optional activities

- ♦ With a less confident class, review the meaning of the vocabulary. Give a definition and ask students to find the word, e.g. *Which word is a drink that you make with fruit?*
- ♦ Ask students to write their sentences connecting each pair of words.

REVISION

Lesson 1

Suggested answers

Are there any apples/books/magazines/sandwiches? Yes, there are.
Are there any bananas/tomatoes? No, there aren't.
Is there any water/bread/milk/apple juice? Yes, there is.

Lesson 2

Suggested answers

Teresa has got a camera phone/a pet/a hobby.
Teresa hasn't got a brother/sister/skateboard.
Pierre has got a sister/a skateboard/a hobby.
Pierre hasn't got a brother/a camera phone/a pet.
Katya has got a brother and a sister/a pet/a hobby.
Katya hasn't got a camera phone/a skateboard.
Adam has got a sister/a camera phone/a skateboard/a hobby.
Adam hasn't got a brother/a pet.

Lesson 3

Suggested answers

Diana Campbell is talking to David Ward, isn't she?
Steven Campbell is cooking vegetable kebabs, isn't he?
They are all enjoying the barbecue, aren't they?
Adam and Katya are standing next to Steven Campbell, aren't they?
David Ward is looking at Diana Campbell, isn't he?
Ruby and Pierre are drinking orange juice, aren't they?

Lesson 4

Suggested answer

A Hi Anna, it's Maria.
B Hi, Maria. How are you?
A Fine, thanks. Do you want to go to the theatre tonight?
B I'd love to.
A Let's meet at seven o'clock in the café next to the theatre.
B OK. See you there.

EXTENSION

Lesson 1
Possible ways of saying no.
No, thank you. I don't like …
No, thank you. I'm not hungry.
No, thank you. I don't have a plate to put it on.
No, thanks. Ask Jake. He's hungrier than me.
No, thanks. I'm vegetarian.

Lesson 2
Students' own answers

Lesson 3
Students' own answers

Lesson 4

Suggested answer

Dear Mr and Mrs Campbell,
Thank you very much for looking after me so well. I really enjoyed staying with you in Lewes.
I had an easy journey home and it's nice to see my family again. But I miss Brighton!
The three things I miss most are:
Adam – because he was friendly to me.
Your food – I learnt a lot about British food and cooking. It's better than I imagined!
All the Brighton High School students – they were great fun, especially Ruby!
I hope that you are both well. My parents send their best wishes, and we're all looking forward to Ruby's visit.
With best wishes,
Pierre

YOUR CHOICE!

The aim is to give students more learner independence and help them to identify their preferred ways of learning. Encourage students to choose an activity that they feel less comfortable with if they want a challenge or are aware that they need practice in a particular area.
Looking Backward and Looking Forward gives students the opportunity to talk and write about their experience of learning English with this book and to make plans for future learning.
Touch Something gives students the opportunity to practise their vocabulary in a game.

You may now like students to do the song *Rocket Man*. See p162 for notes and p190 for the worksheet.

Language File p121

Song – photocopiable notes p162, worksheet p190

Workbook Unit 8 Inspiration Extra! pp98–99

Units 7–8

1 Ask students who they think the best footballer of all time is. Students look at the photo and the text and find the answer given there (Pele). Students read the text again and choose the appropriate word for each space.

Answers

1 B 2 C 3 A 4 B 5 C 6 B 7 A 8 C 9 B 10 B 11 C 12 B

Optional activity

Confident students can first attempt the task without looking at the word options.

2 Students use the prompts to ask and answer questions about future plans.

Answers

1 Are Ruby and Adam going to cook dinner? No, they aren't.
2 Is Emily going to play the saxophone? No, she isn't.
3 Is Adam going to do his homework? Yes, he is.
4 Are Katya and Teresa going to buy some presents? Yes, they are.
5 Is Pierre going to paint a picture? No, he isn't.
6 Is Jake going to wear new trainers? Yes, he is.

- Students then write sentences.

Answers

Ruby and Adam aren't going to cook dinner.
Emily isn't going to play the saxophone.
Adam is going to do his homework.
Katya and Teresa are going to buy some presents.
Pierre isn't going to paint a picture.
Jake is going to wear new trainers.

3 Students match the questions and answers. Check these before students write the sentences.

Answers

1 c Adam is sitting at his computer because he's going to send an email.
2 d Teresa and Emily are standing outside the cinema because they're going to see a film.
3 a Katya is in a shoe shop because she's going to buy some trainers.
4 e Diana is buying a ticket because she's going to catch a train.
5 b Pierre and Jake are going to the sports centre because they're going to play tennis.

Optional activity

Students work in pairs. Student A closes the book. Student B says the beginning of the sentence. Student A tries to recall the end of the sentence beginning with the word *because*.

4 Students complete the sentences as in the example.

Answers

1 Katya likes drawing horses.
2 Adam and Ruby hate eating garlic.
3 Emily enjoys playing the guitar.
4 I don't mind swimming in cold water.
5 Do you like dancing?
6 We love going to the beach.

5 Students complete the sentences with superlative adjectives. With a less confident class, ask students to find/recall the superlative forms first. Check these and then ask them to choose the correct sentence.

Answers

1 most exciting 2 longest 3 biggest 4 highest 5 oldest 6 best

6 Students choose the correct word for the sentences. With a less confident class, review the rules first.

Answers

1 some 2 some 3 any 4 some 5 any 6 any

7 Students decide if the words are countable or uncountable and choose *a* or *some*.

Answers

1 some 2 a 3 some 4 some 5 a 6 some 7 a 8 some

8 Students ask and answer as in the example. With a less confident class, check the items and prices first.

Answers

1 How much is the bag? It's seventeen fifty.
2 How much is the sandwich? It's two seventy-five.
3 How much is the fruit juice? It's eighty-nine p.
4 How much is the newspaper? It's sixty p.
5 How much is the mobile phone? It's eighty-nine ninety-five.
6 How much is the jacket? It's thirty-five pounds.

9 Students put the words in the right order.

Answers
1 She has got green eyes and red hair.
2 I haven't got a lot of money.
3 Have you got any brothers or sisters?
4 She has got some new jeans.
5 Who has got the best computer game?
6 We have got all the answers right!

Optional activity

Fast finishers can find other sentences from Units 7 and 8, jumble the word order and give them to their partner to put in order.

10 Students add the appropriate question tag. Do the first one as an example with the students. When checking answers, check students use falling intonation.

Answers
1 isn't she? 2 isn't he? 3 aren't they? 4 isn't it?
5 aren't we? 6 aren't you?

VOCABULARY

11 Students complete the sentences.

Answers
1 hospital 2 fridge 3 vegetarian 4 camel
5 kill 6 pet 7 medicine 8 washing machine
9 hobby 10 knitting

Optional activity

More confident students can complete the sentences without looking at the words in the box.

12 Students match the words and definitions.

Answers
1 slow 2 malaria 3 giraffe 4 knife
5 dishwasher 6 kitchen 7 plate 8 chess

Optional activity

Students write definitions of other words from Units 7 and 8. They exchange definitions with another student and guess each other's words.

Language File pp120–121

13 Students match the verbs and words/phrases.

Answers
1 buy a ticket 2 die of malaria 3 call an ambulance
4 get on well 5 learn how to surf 6 look worried
7 spend money

LEARNER INDEPENDENCE SELF ASSESSMENT

- Explain to students that the aim of the self assessment is to encourage them to check their own progress and to take any necessary action to improve. Point out that the list 1–8 covers language from Units 7 and 8. Students tick the 'Fine' box for functional language that they feel confident using, but put a question mark in the 'Not sure' box for functional language that they have difficulties with or still cannot use confidently.
- Encourage students to look at the Language File and re-do exercises from the Workbook in areas where they have problems. They may also like to re-do exercises from the lessons and from the Revision and Extension sections in Units 7 and 8.
- Students write an example sentence for each language area in the list. You may like to elicit the grammar needed for each example, e.g. *Talk about future plans and intentions: going to* before students write sentences. Students can refer to the relevant lessons and the Language File for support.
- Ask students to compare their sentences with a partner's, and to discuss and correct any mistakes they may find. They then evaluate their own performance for each language area in terms of *Fine* and *Not sure*.
- Check their sentences so that you can note down language areas for future practice where students are uncertain.

Follow-up activity

Game *Grammar auction* Write a collection of correct and incorrect sentences on the board. Organise the students into teams. Each team has a total of £100. They can use this money to buy correct sentences. Tell them not to buy sentences that are incorrect. One team offers £5 for a sentence and if another team wants the sentence they must offer over £5 and so on until no team wants to increase the money and the sentence is sold to the team with the highest offer. The winning team is the one which buys the most correct sentences. Students then correct incorrect sentences.

HOMEWORK

Students bring their vocabulary notebooks up to date.

Students write a paragraph about a hero of their choice. He/She can be a sporting hero, a national hero or a fictional hero.

Workbook Review Units 7–8 pp100–101

1.1 Test your memory

Activity	Pelmanism card game
Language focus	Personal possessions vocabulary; the indefinite article (*a/an*)
Preparation	Photocopy one worksheet for each pair of students. Cut up the cards along the dotted lines.
New vocabulary	*watch*

Procedure

1. Divide the class into pairs and give each pair a set of cards.
2. Ask the students to write what each picture is on a blank card remembering to use *a* or *an*.
3. Do open class feedback to check the spelling and correct use of *a* and *an*.
4. The idea is that students have to find two cards that match from the two groups of cards which are spread out in front of them. Throughout the game students have to remember where possible matching cards are from having seen them in previous turns. Explain to the class that they are going to play a game of Pelmanism and demonstrate how to play with two students.
5. Word cards and picture cards are separated into two groups and placed face down on the desk. Students take it in turns to pick up one card from each group and name the picture by saying *This is a/an* ... and saying the word on the card.
6. If students pick up two cards that are different they lose their go. If they pick up two cards that match they keep the pair and have another go.
7. When all the cards are used up, the student with the most pairs is the winner.

1.2 Famous places

Activity	Information gap
Language focus	Question forms; prepositions of place; numbers and time
Preparation	Photocopy one worksheet for each pair of students. Cut it into two information cards. Bring in a photo of a famous place to show the class.
New vocabulary	*island, square*

Procedure

1. Brainstorm famous places around the world and explain to the students that they are going to talk about famous places and when they can visit them.
2. Use your photo of a famous place as an example and elicit question forms for name, location, age and time of tour. Write a simplified model on the board:

   What ... called? Where ...? How old ...? When ... tour?
3. Tell the students they are going to be given pictures of six famous places and information about three of them. Explain that they will need to ask their partner for the information about the other three places. Show them the information card and point out that the places are numbered 1 to 6. Pre-teach the words *island* and *square*.
4. Divide the class into two groups, A and B. Give each student in Group A the Student A information card and each student in Group B the Student B information card. Tell them to work with a partner from the same group to check they understand all the information on the card.
5. Ask them to find a partner from the other group. Tell them to take turns to ask questions in order to complete their information card. They mustn't show their cards to each other. If possible, make them sit back to back.
6. When they have finished, ask them to check their answers with their partner's card.

1.3 Find the family

Activity	Information gap
Language focus	Question forms; family vocabulary; numbers and dates
Preparation	Photocopy one worksheet for each pair of students and cut it along the dotted lines.

Procedure

1. Remind the students of Katya's family tree on page 17 of the Student's Book. Elicit family vocabulary, e.g. *sister, father, brother*.
2. Divide the class into two groups, A and B.
3. Show the students both worksheets and point out that all seven names are written on both pictures. Explain that Student A has some more information about three family members and Student B has some more information about three other family members.
4. Point to the picture of Tom Harris and put his information on the board. Elicit the questions needed to get that information (*Who is Tom Harris? When's his birthday? How old is he?*).
5. Give each student in Group A the Student A family tree and each student in Group B the Student B family tree. Tell them to find a partner from the other group and to take turns asking and answering questions until they have completed their worksheets. Tell them not to show their worksheets to each other until they have finished.

2.1 Spelling auction

Activity Spelling auction

Language focus Vocabulary

Preparation Photocopy one worksheet for each group of three students.

Procedure

1 Pre-teach the word *bet*. Write the word and its meaning on the board.

2 Explain to the students that they are going to play a game in groups of three. Tell them the rules:

- Each group starts with 100 gold coins.
- The group has to look at the first sentence on the worksheet and decide if all the words are spelled correctly or not. They make a group decision.
- They then bet an amount of gold coins that their answer is correct. The minimum bet is 10 gold coins. If they are confident, they should bet a large amount and if they are not confident, a small amount.
- The teacher asks each group for their answer and their bet. The correct answer is then revealed. Groups that were correct win their bet; those that were wrong lose their bet. The teacher keeps a running score on the board.
- The students now do the same for the second sentence and so on.

3 Divide the class into groups and ask each one for a team name to put on the board. Distribute the worksheets and begin.

4 When all ten sentences have been looked at, add up the scores to find the winning team. Elicit the correct spellings and put these on the board.

Key 1, 2 and 8 correct   3 photograph   4 clothes   5 brother   6 What   7 January   9 meet   10 pullover

2.2 Lost things

Activity Reading puzzle

Language focus Revision of grammar and vocabulary from Units 1–2, especially *can/can't*

Preparation Photocopy part A of the worksheet for each student in the class. Photocopy part B once for each group of eight students and cut along the dotted lines.

New vocabulary *swimming costume, swimming goggles*

Procedure

1 Put the students into groups of eight.

2 Give each student Part A and one information slip from part B.

3 Explain to the students that eight things were lost on holiday. The students have to read the clues and work out who each thing belongs to.

4 Hold up the item card pointing at the passport from Mexico and ask the students to say what is shown on the card. Then write the sentence *Richard can speak Spanish but Mike can't speak French* on the board and ask the students if they think the item on the card could belong to either of them.

5 Start the game. Looking at Part A, each student in the group tells the others which things were lost on holiday.

6 Then each student reads out his/her information slip.

7 The students match the lost items to the different people.

8 Write the names of the four people on the board and elicit the answers from each group.

9 Get all groups to agree and confirm the answers.

Key

Richard: passport and swimming goggles
Simon: saxophone and photo
Mike: football and T-shirt
Hannah: swimming costume and mobile phone

2.3 How to record music off the web

Activity Jumbled text

Language focus Imperatives; vocabulary: international computer language

Preparation Photocopy one worksheet for each group of eight students. Cut out the eight instructions along the dotted lines.

New vocabulary *mp3 player, plug in, website*

Procedure

1 Explain that students have to put instructions on how to download music from the Internet into the correct order.

2 Put the students in groups of eight. (If you have an extra student, make this student the group leader who orchestrates the activity. If you have fewer students, give some students more than one slip.) Ask them to stand in their groups in a circle.

3 Give each student in the group an instruction slip. Ask them to take turns to read out their instruction.

4 The students then arrange themselves so that they are standing in the correct order in the circle.

5 Check the order in open class.

3.1 Likes and dislikes

Activity Asking questions

Language focus *love, like, don't like, hate*; food vocabulary

Preparation Photocopy the worksheet for each student.

Procedure

1 Write these sentences on the board: *I love cheese. I like pizza I don't like eggs. I hate mushrooms.*

2 Hand out the worksheets. Explain that the students first have to look at the worksheet and decide how they feel about the different items in the left-hand column. Then they write *love, like, don't like* or *hate* in the middle column.

3 Ask the students to move around the room and state their feelings about a given item to another student, e.g. *I love pizza.*

4 The other student replies with his/her feelings about the item. If both students agree, they can write each other's name in the right-hand column.

5 The students mingle and find as many people who agree with them as possible. When they have done this, they sit down. Ask several students who loved, liked, didn't like and hated the same things that they did.

6 As a class, find out what was the most loved and the most hated food. See if they can work this out from their questionnaires. Ask individual students for their opinion and ask other students if they agree. To check, read out the list of foods and ask the students to stand up if it is the food they most love. Make a note of how many students stand up for each item. Then do the same with *hate*.

3.2 The free lesson

Activity Information gap

Language focus School subject vocabulary; *when* in present simple questions; telling time

Preparation Photocopy the worksheet for each group of three students and cut it up along the dotted lines.

Procedure

1 Brainstorm school subjects, write them on the board and practise pronunciation.

2 Write these times on the board and check that the students know how to pronounce them: *9am, 10.30am, 2.05pm* and *3.20pm*.

3 Ask the students when they have maths, English and other school subjects. Draw their attention to the question: *When do you have ...?* Write it on the board and drill it.

4 Put the students into groups of three and explain the situation: When the head teacher was telling the students the timetable, Alan, Brian and Christina were talking to each other. They didn't manage to get all the information. Fortunately, they did get some of it and now have to combine their information to find out their full timetable.

5 Give each student in each group a worksheet A, B or C. Tell them to ask each other questions to find out their full timetable. Tell them not to show their worksheets to each other.

6 When they have finished, check as a class and find out when the free period is.

Key

	Monday	Tuesday	Wednesday	Thursday	Friday
9am–10.15am	Maths	English	German	Science	English
Break					
10.30am–11.45am	Computer Science	History	Science	Maths	Art
Lunch					
12.45–2pm	French	Free period	PE (Physical Education)	Geography	Spanish
2.05pm–3.20pm	French	Science	PE (Physical Education)	Geography	Computer Science

3.3 Martina's day

Activity Running dictation

Language focus Adverbs of frequency

Preparation Photocopy the worksheet for each student.

Procedure

1 Briefly revise the adverbs of frequency covered in Unit 3, Lesson 3, making sure that the students understand the meaning of *never, sometimes, often* and *usually*.

2 Divide the class into pairs, A and B. Explain that Student B will sit and write and Student A will run and gather information.

3 Hand out a copy of Worksheet B to each pair. Ask them to guess what words might fit the spaces. They must not write anything at this stage.

4 Explain that Student A should find out from Student B what information is needed to complete Worksheet B and then go to Worksheet A and find out the information. Student A has to remember the information, go back to Student B and tell it to him/her. Student B then writes the information on Worksheet B. No shouting is allowed and only Student B is allowed to write anything.

5 Student B should do his/her best to form a question to find out the necessary information. They should do this without showing Student A Worksheet B. If necessary, write examples on the board:

How often does Martina have fruit for breakfast?
What does Martina sometimes have for breakfast?

Help the students form questions, but allow some freedom as this is not the focus of the activity.

6 Check the answers with the class, then hand out the remaining copies of Worksheet A so they can double-check the spelling.

4.1 Describe the classroom

Activity	Describing a classroom
Language focus	Vocabulary related to furniture; prepositions of place; *There is/are*
Preparation	Photocopy the worksheet for each pair of students and cut it up along the dotted lines.
New vocabulary	*bookcase, shelf/shelves*
Procedure	**1** Ask the students to describe their classroom to each other, then conduct whole class feedback and ensure that the students use correct prepositions of place. **2** Pre-teach the words *shelf/shelves* and *bookcase* and the preposition *around.* **3** Put the students into pairs and ask them to sit face to face. Tell them that they must not show their picture to their partner. **4** Explain the activity. Student A describes Classroom A to Student B who draws the furniture in the correct place in Classroom B. **5** Give the students five minutes for the activity. **6** After five minutes, the pairs should compare their pictures and check if they have made any mistakes.

4.2 He's wearing a long black coat

Activity	Memory game and matching exercise
Language focus	Present continuous affirmative
Preparation	Photocopy the worksheet for each pair of students. Cut the picture and sentences along the dotted lines. Jumble the sentences.
Procedure	**1** Put the students into pairs and distribute the picture face down. Tell them they are going to look at a picture for two minutes and that they will have to remember what they see without taking any notes. **2** Ask the class to turn over their pictures and give them two minutes to study them. **3** When the time is up, tell them to turn their pictures over again. Write *A young man* on the board and ask the students to finish the sentence (*is riding a bicycle*). Distribute the sets of cut-up sentences to each pair and ask them to match the beginnings and endings to make six sentences describing the picture. **4** Check the answers with the class.

4.3 What am I doing?

Activity	Miming
Language focus	Present continuous affirmative/questions; short answers; general vocabulary
Preparation	Photocopy the worksheet for each group of 20 students. Cut it up into strips along the dotted lines.
Procedure	**1** Elicit or pre-teach vocabulary such as *going for a walk, chewing gum* and *combing your hair* and write it on the board. **2** Explain the activity. The students are going to mime an action to the rest of the class so that they can guess what they are doing. Demonstrate by miming talking on the phone and elicit the correct sentences: *You're talking on the phone. Are you talking on the phone?* **3** Put the strips of paper face down on a desk. Each student takes one strip of paper. Make sure that they don't show it to anyone. **4** After reading their strips of paper, the students take turns to come to the front of the class and mime their activity, without using any words. They make some sounds if necessary. **5** The first student to guess correctly gets the strip of paper. The winner is the student who collects the most strips of paper.

5.1 Test your memory

Activity Memory test

Language focus Present continuous and present simple; jobs vocabulary

Preparation Photocopy the worksheet. You need one copy of Worksheet A for each student and one copy of Worksheet B for each pair of students. Cut along the dotted lines.

Procedure

1 Go through the jobs in Worksheet A with the class. Ask the students to say what duties each job might require, e.g. a waiter takes orders, serves food and drink.

2 Give out Worksheet A to the students.

3 Put the students into pairs. Explain that they are going to play a memory game. Demonstrate with a pair of students.
- Each student has a list of people and jobs (Worksheet A).
- Each pair has 20 cards placed face down in front of them.
- They have to take turns to turn over two cards and match them with one of the people on Worksheet A. For example, *Mr Brown, the waiter*, must be matched with *serves food and drink* and *is giving us a cup of coffee now*. If a student makes a match with two cards on the same go, he/she gets to keep the cards. If not, the cards are turned face down again and it is the other student's turn.
- To claim the cards, the student must say the person's name, their occupation, what they do and what they are doing now, e.g. *Mr Black is a teacher. He teaches English. He is teaching food vocabulary now.*
- The winner of the game is the student with the most cards at the end.

4 Start the game. When the students have finished, review the sentences by saying, e.g. *Mr Black is a teacher. What does he do? What is he doing now?* and eliciting the correct answers.

5.2 Whose pen is it?

Activity Information gap

Language focus Possessive 's

Preparation Photocopy the worksheet for each pair of students. Cut it in half along the dotted lines.

Procedure

1 Borrow a few items from the students and ask *Whose pen is this? Whose book is it?* etc. Elicit answers with the possessive 's, e.g. *It's Julie's pen.*

2 Tell the students they are going to make sentences from cues on their worksheet. They will then ask their partner questions to complete their worksheets. In return, they answer their partner's questions.

3 Put the students into pairs and hand out the worksheets, giving one student in each pair Worksheet A and the other Worksheet B. Give each student five minutes to write the sentences at the top of the worksheet. Check that they are doing this correctly.

4 The students then work in pairs to find out who owns what. They take turns to ask questions. When they get an answer, they draw a line between the person and the object.

5 When they have finished, they can compare answers.

5.3 Comparative crossword

Activity Information gap crossword

Language focus Comparatives

Preparation Photocopy the worksheet for each pair of students. Cut it in half along the dotted lines.

Procedure

1 Elicit the rules for making comparatives.

2 Put the students into pairs, A and B.

3 Write the adjectives *big, high, wet* and *tall* on the board. Ask Student A to read the first two to Student B. Student B replies with the comparatives. Then ask Student B to read the second two words to Student A, who replies with the comparatives of these words.

4 Explain that the students must tell their partner ten adjectives and their partner must write the comparative of each one in a crossword grid. When they have completed all ten, they should be able to find number 11.

5 Hand out Worksheet A to each Student A and Worksheet B to each Student B. Start the activity.

6 When they have finished, write all the adjectives on the board to check the answers. Get the students to come up and write the comparatives next to them.

Key

Worksheet A: 1 smaller 2 colder 3 drier 4 better 5 more difficult 6 later 7 more modern 8 hotter 9 more popular 10 worse 11 more famous

Worksheet B: 1 more important 2 lovelier 3 shorter 4 easier 5 more famous 6 longer 7 sadder 8 more expensive 9 rainier 10 sunnier 11 more modern

6.1 Who in the class?

Activity Guessing game

Language focus Past simple of *be*

Preparation Photocopy the worksheet for each pair of students. Cut it in half along the dotted lines.

New vocabulary *angry, unhappy, worried*

Procedure

1. To illustrate the activity, ask a student to guess who they think in the class was scared last night and who wasn't tired yesterday afternoon. Check with the suggested students whether the guesses were right or wrong.
2. Divide the class into two groups, A and B. Explain that they have to guess which people in the class were or weren't doing certain things at certain times.
3. Give each student in Group A Worksheet A and each student in Group B Worksheet B. Give them some time to make their guesses.
4. When the time is up, elicit questions based on the earlier examples. Write *Were you scared last night?* and *Were you tired yesterday afternoon?* on the board as models.
5. The students mingle and ask questions. They go to the people they think did the things on their worksheets. They have to tick the *Was I right?* column if they were right and put a cross in it if they were wrong.
6. Conduct quick feedback to see who made the most correct guesses.
7. Put the students in pairs, one from each group. They tell each other about their findings: how many guesses they got right and any interesting or surprising facts they found out about their classmates.

6.2 Past simple dominoes

Activity Dominoes

Language focus Pronunciation of past simple endings

Preparation Photocopy the worksheet for each group of three students. Provide scissors for each group.

Procedure

1. Draw the phonemic symbols for *-ed* endings (/d/, /t/ and /ɪd/) on the board, along with a few verbs, e.g. *call, carry, like, open, visit, play,* and ask the students to classify them according to the pronunciation of their endings. Ask them to think of two more examples for each ending.
2. Tell the students they are going to play a game of dominoes but that first they need to make the dominoes.
3. Put the students in groups of three and distribute the worksheets. Point out that the A part of each domino contains a verb in the infinitive and that on part B they must write the correct symbol for the pronunciation of the verb's *-ed* ending in the past simple. Highlight the fact that only the symbol needs to be written in the B part of each domino.
4. When they have finished, ask them to cut the dominoes out, ensuring that they remove the numbers.
5. Demonstrate the game with one group:
   - Each student is given four dominoes.
   - The youngest player goes first and lays a domino on the table.
   - The player on the left must place a domino next to the one laid down. It can be placed at either end, but the phonemic symbol must match the pronunciation of the verb's past tense ending.
   - When the player places the domino, he/she must say the verb in the past tense form. If the verb is said incorrectly or the domino is not correct, it cannot be played and the next player has a turn. The winner is the first player to put down his/her last domino.
6. Play the game and monitor progress.

6.3 Haunted hotel

Activity Information gap

Language focus Past simple

Preparation Photocopy the worksheet for each pair of students and cut it along the dotted lines.

Procedure

1. Tell the students they are going to read about a strange holiday that two friends, Jack and Jane, had last year in Cornwall in the south-west of England.
2. Write these words on the board: *storm* (n), *lightning* (n), *slowly* (adv), *cobweb* (n), *purse* (n), *burn – burnt* (v), *haunted* (adj), *strange* (adj), *frightened* (adj) and *lane* (n). Elicit or explain the meaning of these words. Ask the students to predict in pairs what they think the story will be about.
3. Review question formation using *what, how, where, who* and *when*. Write on the board *This story happened on .... (when)?* and elicit the question *When did this story happen?*
4. Divide the class into Group A and Group B. Give Worksheet A to each student in Group A and Worksheet B to each student in Group B. Tell them to work in pairs within their group to decide what questions they need to ask to get the missing information.
5. Put the students in pairs, one from Group A and one from Group B. Tell them to ask each other for the information they need to complete the story.
6. They can check answers at the end by comparing their worksheets.

7.1 What are you going to do?

Activity Board game

Language focus *going to; Why ...? Because ...*

Preparation Photocopy one game board for each group. Provide one counter per student and one dice per group.

New vocabulary *hobby, pocket money*

Procedure

1 Give each group of three or four students a game board, dice and counters.

2 Explain that the aim of the game is to get to the end of the board by saying what you are going to do and why in different situations.

3 Give a model by using an example situation: *It's Sunday. What are you going to do?* Elicit answers, e.g. *I'm going to sleep all morning. In the afternoon I'm going to play football with my friends.* Ask for a reason: *Why are you going to sleep all morning? Because I'm tired and I like sleeping!*

4 Explain the rules. The first student throws the dice and moves his/her counter on the game board. The student reads out the situation and then says what he/she is going to do. Another student asks *Why are you going to ...?* If the student can say what he/she is going to do and justify it, he/she stays on that square. If not, he/she has to move back to the previous square. If what the student says is grammatically incorrect, the other students correct the sentence and he/she moves back to the previous square. The student who gets to the finish first wins.

5 Tell the students to start the game. Monitor and act as referee.

6 When all the groups have finished, get them to tell the class about any interesting ideas and reasons.

7.2 What do you like doing?

Activity Questions and answers

Language focus Verb and gerund; hobbies/sports vocabulary

Preparation Photocopy one worksheet for each student. Arrange the chairs in the classroom in two circles one inside the other.

Procedure

1 Arrange the chairs in two circles and get the students to sit so that those in the outer circle are facing those in the inner circle. The idea is that the students in the outer circle move around and those in the inner circle stay where they are so that they speak to a number of different partners.

2 Give each student a worksheet.

3 Demonstrate the activity. Each student is going to interview other classmates about what they like doing, don't mind doing and don't like doing.

4 Write model questions on the board and elicit model answers:

What do you love doing? I love watching football games.
What don't you mind doing? I don't mind doing homework.
What do you hate doing? I hate listening to rap music.

5 Elicit a range of sports and activities.

6 Start the activity. After each pair has asked and answered the three questions, ask the students in the outer wheel to move one chair clockwise.

7 Continue until the wheel has gone one full circle, until 12 students have been interviewed or until time has run out.

7.3 Who has the fastest animal?

Activity Top trumps

Language focus Superlative adjectives; questions and answers

Preparation Photocopy and cut up a set of cards for each group.

Procedure

1 Explain and demonstrate the principles of the game *Top Trumps*. The aim of the game is to win all the cards. To win cards you have to beat the other cards. You do this by selecting a category, such as the fastest animal. All players then choose their fastest animal and the student with the one that is fastest wins all the other cards.

2 Give each pair or group a set of cards. Divide them between the students and show how the game works with one group:
- One student asks a question, eg *Who has got the fastest animal?*
- Each student chooses one of their cards. They read out the information, e.g. *I've got a tiger. It can run at 60 km per hour.*
- The student with the fastest animal says *I win. I've got the falcon. It's the fastest animal. It can fly at 440 km per hour.*
- The winning students takes all the other students' played cards.
- The game is over when one student has all the cards.

3 Start the game. Monitor and help the students when needed.

4 When the game is over, discuss some general grammatical or vocabulary issues that came up with the class.

8.1 The banquet

Activity Information gap

Language focus *Is/Are there any ...?; How much/many ... are there?*; short answers

Preparation Photocopy one worksheet for each pair and cut it in two.

Procedure

1. Put the students in pairs and get them to tell each other what they ate yesterday.
2. Pre-teach *pineapple* and *candle* by drawing them on the board.
3. Explain that each student in a pair will get a picture which is slightly different from their partner's. They can't show each other their pictures, but must ask questions about what there is/isn't and are/aren't in the pictures in order to find the differences.
4. Distribute the pictures so that one student in each pair has Picture A and the other Picture B.
5. Write the words *ice cream* and *sausages* on the board and elicit the questions *Is there any ice cream?* and *Are there any sausages?* Also elicit the answers *Yes, there is/are* and *No, there isn't/aren't* and the question *How many sausages are there?*
6. Ask the students to sit back to back and to take turns to ask and answer questions. Weaker students may need to be told that there are ten differences to find.

Key

There are ten sausages in A and 12 in B.
There is rice in A, potatoes in B.
There are five glasses in A, four in B.
There are mushrooms in A, chips in B.
There is ice cream in A, cake in B.
There is cheese in A, butter in B.
There are two candles in A, one in B.
There are bananas in A, apples in B.
There is orange juice in A, apple juice in B.
There are two pineapples in A, one in B.

8.2 Happy families

Activity Card game

Language focus *have got* (positive, negative and questions)

Preparation Photocopy one worksheet for each group of four and cut it in cards.

Procedure

1. Put the students in pairs and get them to tell each other about their families.
2. Draw a family tree on the board. Elicit family members and write them on the board. Elicit *Mr* and *Mrs* for the father and mother and teach *Miss* and *Master* for the daughter and son.
3. Tell the students that they are going to play *Happy Families* in groups of four and explain the game, demonstrating with one group if necessary.
   – All cards are dealt out so each student has five cards.
   – The students have to collect families, which consist of Mr, Mrs, Master and Miss. Write the members of the Bun family on the board as an example.
   – The students take turns to ask each other for cards. Elicit an example question and answer:
   Have you got Mr Bun the baker? *Yes, I have. / No, I haven't.*
   – The students can only ask for members of a family if they already have one member of that family.
   – If the student asked has got Mr Bun the baker, he/she must give it to the student who asked for it. That student can then have another go.
   – If the student asked hasn't got Mr Bun the baker, the student that asked for it loses his/her go and play passes to the student on the right.
   – Play continues until all the families have been collected.
   – The winner is the student with the most families.
4. Divide the class into groups of four and ask them to begin playing.

8.3 Interview with a star

Activity Information gap

Language focus Question tags

Preparation Photocopy one worksheet for each pair and cut it in half.

Procedure

1. Put the students in pairs and get them to tell each other about their favourite pop star.
2. Tell them they are going to work in pairs and that one of them is a pop star and the other a newspaper reporter. Explain that they did an interview yesterday but the reporter can't read some of his/her notes because they got wet. The reporter is pretty sure he/she can remember what the pop star said, but needs to ask some questions to check that the information is correct.
3. Show the students the interview notes. Put the first sentence *He/She is from A______a* on the board. Elicit places beginning and ending in A which could be written in the gap. Explain that both the reporter and the pop star need to complete their notes. Then the reporter will ask the pop star questions with question tags to make sure they have the same information.
4. Give out the two sets of notes, making sure that in each pair one student gets A and the other B. Tell them to complete their notes without talking to each other or showing their papers.
5. Again, using the first sentence as an example, elicit a question with a tag and the positive and negative answers:
   You are from America, aren't you? *Yes, I am. / No, I'm from Australia.*
   Point out that if the reporter has the wrong information, the pop star should say so and then give the right information.
6. Ask the students to begin. Monitor to check the use of question tags.

Together We Are Strong

Activity	Song
Language focus	Revision of language and vocabulary from Units 1–2
Preparation	Photocopy one sheet for each student. Get the recording ready. 3.31
Procedure	**1** Play the song and ask students to listen and read the words. Elicit their reactions. You may need to explain *yin and yang*, as the songwriter uses this idea to reinforce his belief that he and the person he is singing to are bound together by strong elemental forces. **2** Give students time to read through the words again and ask you any questions about vocabulary. Then focus attention on the title and ask them to discuss in pairs or small groups who they think *we* refers to. Draw their attention to the suggestions in the box, but ask for their own ideas too. Pool ideas from the class. There is no right answer. **3** Go through the choices with the class and then ask students to decide which is the main message of the song. **4** Ask students to work individually to match the words. Then compare in pairs before checking with the class. **5** Put students in pairs to discuss the question and then get them to report back to the class on their ideas.
Key	3 a 4 1 d 2 e 3 f 4 c 5 a 6 c

Raining In My Heart

Activity	Song
Language focus	Revision of language and vocabulary from Units 3–4
Preparation	Photocopy one sheet for each student. Get the recording ready. 3.32
Procedure	**1** Play the song and ask students to listen and read the words. Elicit their reactions. You may need to explain *misery* (extreme sadness). You might like to point out that many poets and singers have used bad weather as a metaphor for their feelings of sadness and suggested that the weather is in tune with their feelings. This song takes the opposite view: that the weather is in contrast to the singer's feelings. **2** Ask students to work in pairs to read the questions and choose the best answers. **3** Ask students to work individually to read the song again and choose the correct words. Check answers with the class. **4** Ask students to discuss the question in pairs. **5** Put students in pairs to discuss the question. Ask them to report back to the class on their ideas.
Key	2 1 b 2 c 3 a 3 a) is shining b) isn't c) good d) doesn't think e) is not enjoying f) isn't there 4 c

Don't You Want Me, Baby?

Activity	Song
Language focus	Revision of language and vocabulary from Units 5–6
Preparation	Photocopy one sheet for each student. Get the recording ready. 3.33
Procedure	**1** Play the song and ask students to listen and read the words. Elicit their reactions and any information that the students have understood about the people and the nature of the relationship. **2** Remind students that there are two people singing in this song and that they each have a different viewpoint on the relationship and the situation described. Ask them to read the summaries and choose the best one. **3** Ask students to work individually to decide if the statements are true or false. **4** When students have found the past simple forms, ask them to say which verbs are irregular.
Key	2 a 3 a) T b) T c) T d) F e) F f) F g) F 4 a) shook b) picked c) met d) changed e) turned f) knew (*shake*, *meet* and *know* are irregular)

Rocket Man

Activity	Song
Language focus	Revision of language and vocabulary from Units 7–8
Preparation	Photocopy one sheet for each student. Get the recording ready. 3.34
Procedure	**1** Play the song and ask students to listen and read the words. Elicit their reactions. You might like to point out that the song was written in 1972, three years after Neil Armstrong walked on the moon. It is unusual because it marks a change in attitude from astronauts being regarded as heroes to the notion that being an astronaut could become an 'everyday' occupation. **2** Ask students to work individually to decide if the statements are true or false. **3** Put students in pairs to discuss the answers to the questions. Get them to report back to the class on their ideas. **4** Ask students to discuss in pairs what they think the most exciting job and the most boring job would be.
Key	2 a) T b) F c) F d) F e) T 3 1 a 2 c 3 b 4 c 5 a

Test your memory

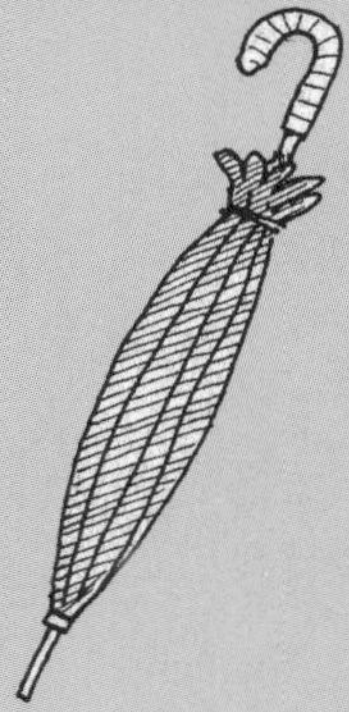

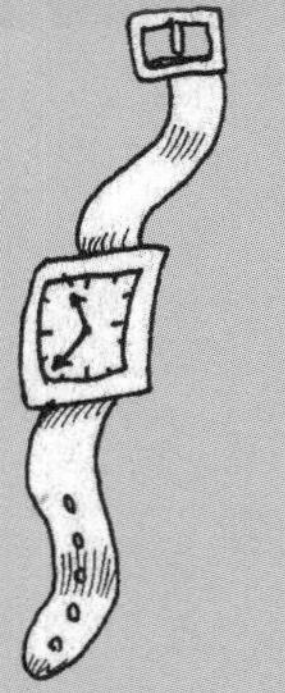

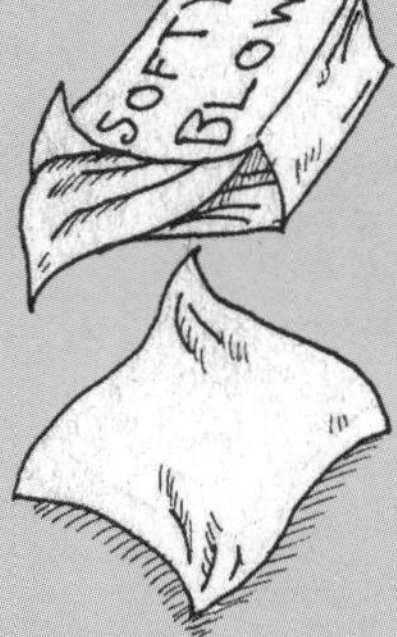

1.2 Famous places

Student A

What/called? ______ ______ ______

1

2

3

Where? ______ ______ ______

How old? ______ ______ ______

When/tour? ______ ______ ______

The Opera House

4

In Sydney in Australia
35 years old
Tour at 11.30am

The Pyramids

5

Near Cairo in Egypt
5,000 years old
Tour at 10.00am

The Kremlin

6

In Red Square in Russia
350 years old
Tour at 1.15pm

Student B

The Great Wall

1

On mountains in China
2,200 years old
Tour at 9.00am

Big Ben

2

Next to the river Thames
in England
150 years old
Tour at 8.00am

The Statue of Liberty

3

On an island in America
120 years old
Tour at 12.45pm

What/called? ______ ______ ______

4

5

6

Where? ______ ______ ______

How old? ______ ______ ______

When/tour? ______ ______ ______

Find the family

Student A

Pam Spencer
Fred's wife
2nd May
55 years old

Fred Spencer
______
______
______

Tom Harris
Mary's husband
21st January
39 years old

Mary Harris
______
______
______

Sally Spencer
Mary's sister
5th August
34 years old

Lisa Harris
______
______
______

Bobby Harris
Lisa's brother
5th December
8 years old

Student B

Pam Spencer
______
______
______

Fred Spencer
Mary's father
15th March
57 years old

Tom Harris
Mary's husband
21st January
39 years old

Mary Harris
Lisa's mother
12th April
38 years old

Sally Spencer
______
______
______

Lisa Harris
Tom's daughter
27th September
11 years old

Bobby Harris
______
______
______

Spelling auction

		correct	Not correct	Gold coins bet	Total
1	– How old are you? – I'm eighteen.				
2	That's my jacket over there.				
3	Look at this fotograph of my family.				
4	Those cloathes in that bag are very old.				
5	My borther has brown hair and blue eyes.				
6	Wat colour is your father's hair?				
7	My birthday is on the second of Janary.				
8	My sister has a new mobile phone.				
9	It is nice to meat you.				
10	How do you spell pulover?				

Lost things

Part A

Richard, Simon, Mike and Hannah each lost two things on holiday. You found:

Part B

There is one girl. Her name is Hannah.

Hannah can swim and can text her friends every day.

Richard can't run but he can swim.

Simon can read music.

Mike has two sisters and he can play football.

Richard can speak Spanish but Mike can't speak French.

Hannah has one brother and Simon has two sisters.

Mike's favourite colour is black.

How to record music off the web

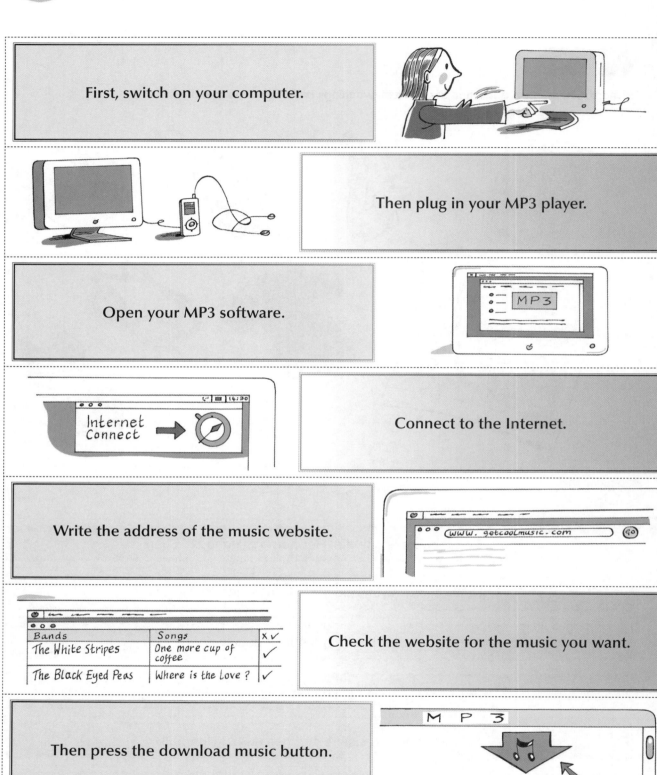

First, switch on your computer.

Then plug in your MP3 player.

Open your MP3 software.

Connect to the Internet.

Write the address of the music website.

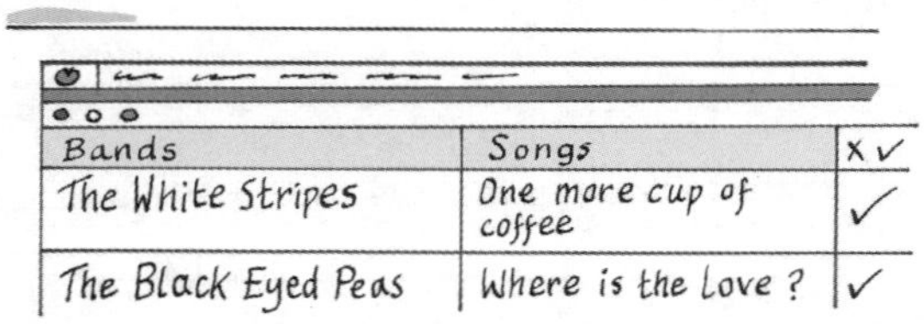

Check the website for the music you want.

Then press the download music button.

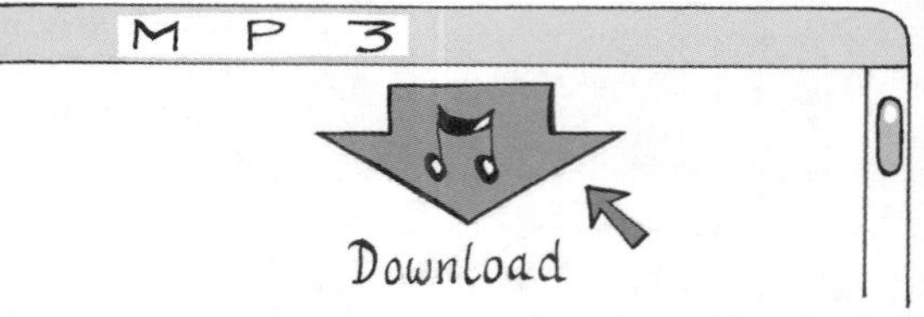

In a few minutes you can listen to your new music.

Likes and dislikes

Decide which of these things you love, like, don't like and hate. Write what you feel in the 'love / like / don't like / hate' column. Then find someone from your class who thinks the same as you. Write their name in the 'Who thinks the same as I do?' column. Try to find as many people who think the same as you.

	love / like / don't like / hate	**Who thinks the same as I do?**
carrot		
cucumbers		
Ice cream		
chips		
sweets		
bananas		
fish		
chocolate cake		
eggs		
chicken		
mushrooms		
garlic		
cheese sandwich		
Italian food		

The free lesson

A Alan's timetable

	MONDAY	TUESDAY	WEDNESDAY	THURSDAY	FRIDAY
9am–10.15am	Maths	English	German		
Break					
10.30am–11.45am		History			
Lunch					
12.45–2pm			PE (Physical Education)	Geography	
2.05pm–3.20pm			PE (Physical Education)		

B Brian's timetable

	MONDAY	TUESDAY	WEDNESDAY	THURSDAY	FRIDAY
9am–10.15am					English
Break					
10.30am–11.45am	Computer Science		Science	Maths	
Lunch					
12.45–2pm					
2.05pm–3.20pm	French				

C Christina's timetable

	MONDAY	TUESDAY	WEDNESDAY	THURSDAY	FRIDAY
9am–10.15am				Science	
Break					
10.30am–11.45am					Art
Lunch					
12.45–2pm	French				Spanish
2.05pm–3.20pm		Science		Geography	Computer Science

Martina's day

Worksheet A

Martina's day

Martina gets up at seven o'clock in the morning. She usually has fruit for breakfast but sometimes she has eggs. She never eats chocolate. She always plays tennis in the morning. She often has lunch in an expensive restaurant. Sometimes she goes shopping in the afternoon. She always goes to the gym in the afternoon. She often meets her friends for a coffee after going to the gym. In the evenings she never watches television, she usually reads a book. She goes to bed at ten pm.

Worksheet B

Martina's day

Martina gets up at seven o'clock in the morning. She ______________ has fruit for breakfast but sometimes she ______________ ______________ She never eats ______________. She ______________ plays tennis in the morning. She often has ______________ in an expensive restaurant. ______________ she goes shopping in the afternoon. She always goes to the ______________ in the afternoon. She ______________ meets her friends for a coffee after going to the gym. In the evenings she never ______________ ______________, she usually ______________ ______________ ______________. She goes to bed at ten pm.

Describe the classroom

Classroom A

Classroom B

He's wearing a long black coat

Five tourists	are standing outside the theatre.
A young man and woman	are holding hands.
Two people	are drinking coffee.
An old man	is eating an ice cream.
A young girl	is rollerblading.
Two dogs	are running.

What am I doing?

I'm dancing.	I'm reading a book.
I'm getting up.	I'm watching television.
I'm going for a walk with my dog.	I'm drawing a picture.
I'm chewing gum.	I'm swimming.
I'm driving a car.	I'm going to bed.
I'm cooking.	I'm playing tennis.
I'm using my computer.	I'm ironing.
I'm combing my hair.	I'm making a phone call.
I'm playing the drums.	I'm working in the garden.
I'm shopping.	I'm rollerblading.

Test your memory

Worksheet A

Mr Brown waiter	Mr Green firefighter	Mr White pilot	Mr Black teacher	Mr Pink musician
Mrs Brown hairdresser	Mrs Green doctor	Mrs White taxi-driver	Mrs Black model	Mrs Pink journalist

Worksheet B

serves food and drink	puts out fires	flies planes	teaches English	plays the saxophone
cuts hair	helps people who are ill or hurt	drives a taxi	wears new clothes	writes newspaper articles
is giving us a cup of coffee now	is putting out a fire at a factory now	is flying a plane from New York to London now	is teaching food vocabulary now	is practising with his band now
is drying a customer's hair now	is checking a person who's ill now	is driving someone to the airport now	is working at a fashion show now	is interviewing a famous footballer now

Whose pen is it?

Worksheet A

1 Make sentences with the words and names to help your partner solve his/her puzzle.

digital camera	Shirley	*It's Shirley's digital camera.*
bag	Anne	
book	David	
umbrella	George	
hat	Lizzie	
apple	Tony	
mobile phone	Jennifer	
watch	Bart	
key	Ian	
sandwich	Nicole	

2 Ask questions. Listen to your partner's sentences and draw lines to connect the people with their things.

Nicole Anne David George Lizzie Shirley Tony Jennifer Bart Ian

Worksheet B

1 Make sentences with the words and names to help your partner solve his/her puzzle.

digital camera	Shirley	*It's Shirley's digital camera.*
pizza	Anne	
pen	David	
sunglasses	George	
jacket	Lizzie	
laptop	Tony	
car	Jennifer	
football	Bart	
cup of coffee	Ian	
pair of jeans	Nicole	

2 Ask questions. Listen to your partner's sentences and draw lines to connect the people with their things.

Nicole Anne David George Lizzie Shirley Tony Jennifer Bart Ian

Comparative crossword

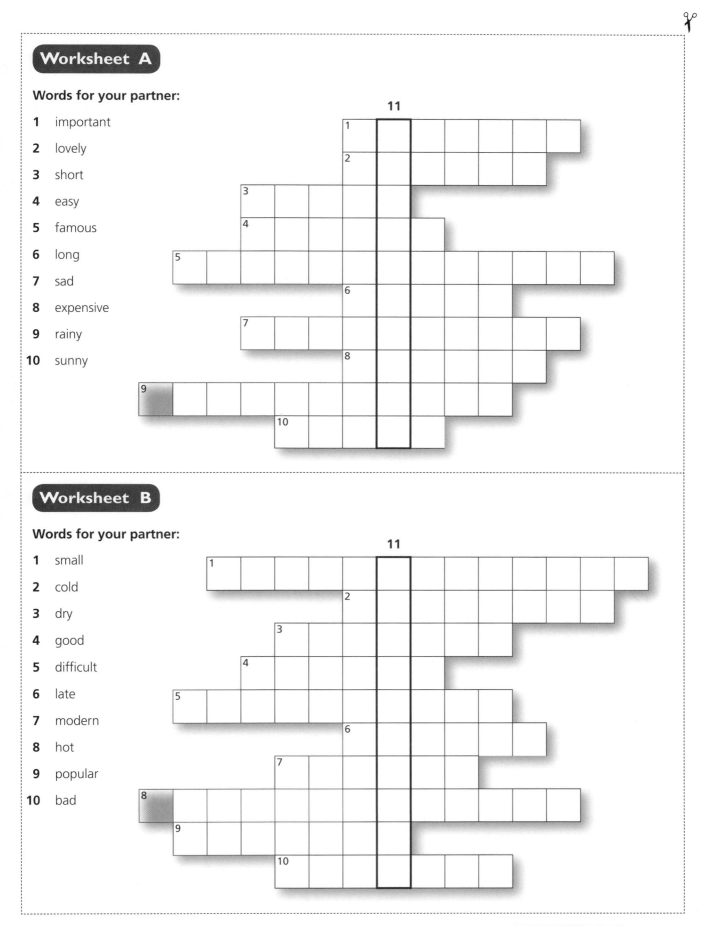

Worksheet A

Words for your partner:

1 important
2 lovely
3 short
4 easy
5 famous
6 long
7 sad
8 expensive
9 rainy
10 sunny

11

1
2
3
4
5
6
7
8
9
10

Worksheet B

Words for your partner:

1 small
2 cold
3 dry
4 good
5 difficult
6 late
7 modern
8 hot
9 popular
10 bad

11

1
2
3
4
5
6
7
8
9
10

Who in the class?

Worksheet A

Who in the class ...	Name	Was I right? Yes = ✗ No = ✓
1 was unhappy last week?	______	☐
2 was at the cinema yesterday evening?	______	☐
3 wasn't at school last week?	______	☐
4 was in the park last Saturday afternoon?	______	☐
5 was late for class this morning?	______	☐
6 was in a disco last Saturday night?	______	☐
7 was in another country last month?	______	☐
8 was happy last night?	______	☐
9 wasn't tired this morning?	______	☐
10 was at home last night?	______	☐

Worksheet B

Who in the class ...	Name	Was I right? Yes = ✗ No = ✓
1 was in another city last weekend?	______	☐
2 was happy last week?	______	☐
3 wasn't in the shower last night?	______	☐
4 was at a party last Friday night?	______	☐
5 was worried about exams last month?	______	☐
6 wasn't at school yesterday?	______	☐
7 was angry this morning?	______	☐
8 wasn't at home last night?	______	☐
9 was in a museum last Sunday afternoon?	______	☐
10 wasn't in this class last month?	______	☐

Past simple dominoes

Label	Left half	Label	Right half
12b	/t/	1a	OPEN
1b	/d/	2a	VISIT
2b	/ɪd/	3b	WANT
3b		4a	CALL
4b		5a	ASK
5b		6a	PLAY
6b		7a	NEED
7b		8a	LIKE
8b		9a	LIVE
9b		10a	START
10b		11a	WALK
11b		12a	CROSS

Haunted hotel

Worksheet A

This story happened on the tenth of December last year in Cornwall. It was a dark and rainy night. Jack and Jane were friends who wanted to go (1) ________________ (*where?*) together. They drove for six hours and the weather was terrible. It was very late when they found the hotel. It was an old building a long way from any other houses. They drove up to the hotel and knocked on the door. After a long time the door opened slowly and there was a small old man wearing old dirty clothes and he looked very white. The hall was very dark and there were a lot of (3) ________________ (*what?*) everywhere. The old man showed them to a small, cold room. They didn't like it but they were very tired so they went to bed. The beds were hard and they heard strange noises all through the night. They felt (5) ________________ (*how?*) and didn't sleep at all. They left at six in the morning and felt very happy to leave the strange hotel. They drove for (7) ________________ (*how long?*) and Jane realised that she didn't have her purse – it was in the hotel and all of their money was in it. They didn't want to go back but they needed the money so they returned to the lane where the hotel was but they couldn't see the hotel. They saw a (9) ________________ (*who?*) in a car and he stopped. 'Is there a hotel anywhere near?' they asked. He replied that the hotel wasn't there any more. It was hit by lightning in a terrible storm, caught fire and burnt down. The old owner died in the fire. 'When did it happen?' asked Jack. 'On the tenth of December, twenty years ago!'

Worksheet B

This story happened on the tenth of December last year in Cornwall. It was a dark and rainy night. Jack and Jane were friends who wanted to go on holiday together. They drove for (2) ________________ (*how long?*) and the weather was terrible. It was very late when they found the hotel. It was an old building a long way from any other houses. They drove up to the hotel and knocked on the door. After a long time the door opened slowly and there was a small old man wearing old dirty clothes and he looked very white. The hall was very dark and there were a lot of cobwebs and old pictures everywhere. The old man showed them to a small, cold room. They didn't like it but they were very tired so they went to bed. The beds were hard and they heard (4) ________________ (*what?*) all through the night. They felt very frightened and didn't sleep at all. They left at (6) ________________ (*when?*) and felt very happy to leave the strange hotel. They drove for thirty minutes and Jane realised that she didn't have (8) ________________ (*what?*) – it was in the hotel and all of their money was in it. They didn't want to go back but they needed the money so they returned to the lane where the hotel was but they couldn't see the hotel. They saw a policeman in a car and he stopped. 'Is there a hotel anywhere near?' they asked. He replied that the hotel wasn't there any more. It was hit by lightning in a terrible storm, caught fire and burnt down. (10) ________________ (*who?*) died in the fire. 'When did it happen?' asked Jack. 'On the tenth of December, twenty years ago!'

What are you going to do?

Start

Your parents want to buy you a pet.

It's your best friend's birthday.

Extra Homework! Miss a turn.

Your friend is at your house.

You're thirsty.

You're in the park.

It's raining.

You want a new music CD.

You want to have a barbecue.

It's the Christmas holiday.

You're at school.

You want a new computer game.

You're at your grandparents' house.

It's snowing.

Your grandparents want to buy you a present.

You have to stay in your room! Miss a turn.

There's a school disco tonight.

You want to have a laugh.

Ha Ha!

You want to go shopping.

You're hungry.

You are late for school.

You want a new hobby.

You want to play a new sport.

You forgot to do your homework.

You're at the beach.

It's sunny.

It's your birthday.

You have no pocket money. Miss a turn.

You want a new DVD.

It's your mum's birthday.

It's cold.

It's the summer holiday.

Finish

What are you going to do?

What do you like doing?

Friend's name	What do you love, like or enjoy doing?	What don't you mind doing?	What do you hate, dislike or not enjoy doing?

Who has the fastest animal?

king cobra

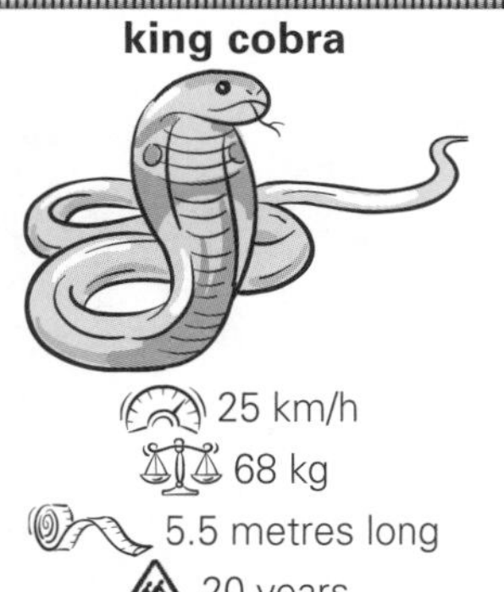

25 km/h
68 kg
5.5 metres long
20 years
kills 5 humans a year

great white shark

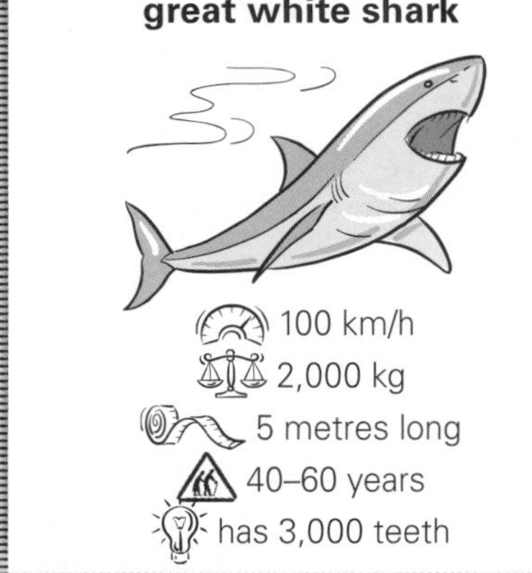

100 km/h
2,000 kg
5 metres long
40–60 years
has 3,000 teeth

hippo

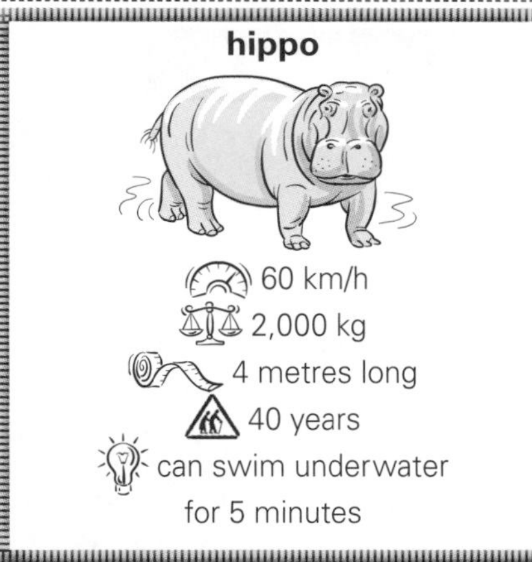

60 km/h
2,000 kg
4 metres long
40 years
can swim underwater for 5 minutes

giraffe

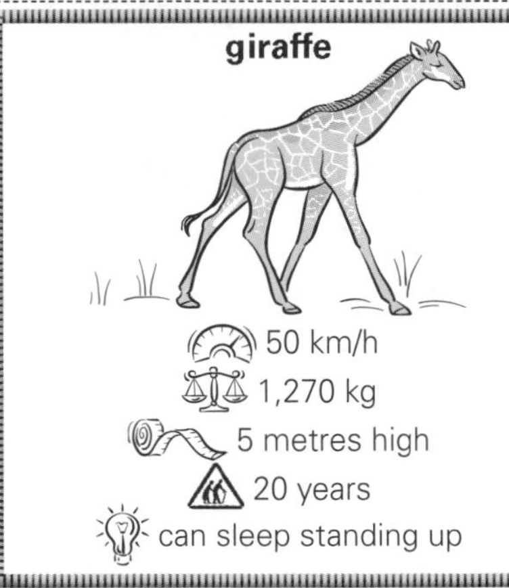

50 km/h
1,270 kg
5 metres high
20 years
can sleep standing up

tiger

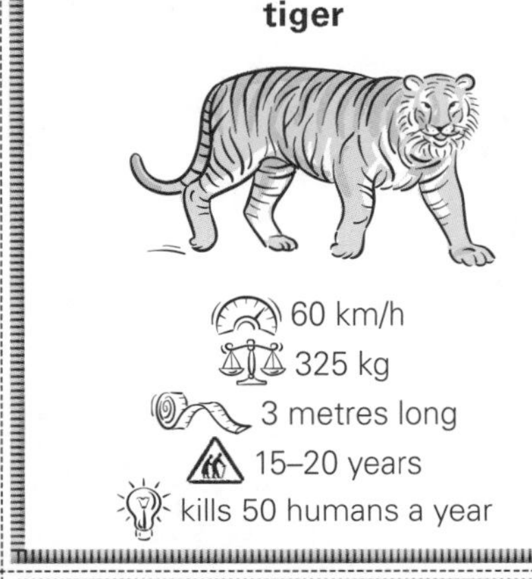

60 km/h
325 kg
3 metres long
15–20 years
kills 50 humans a year

scorpion

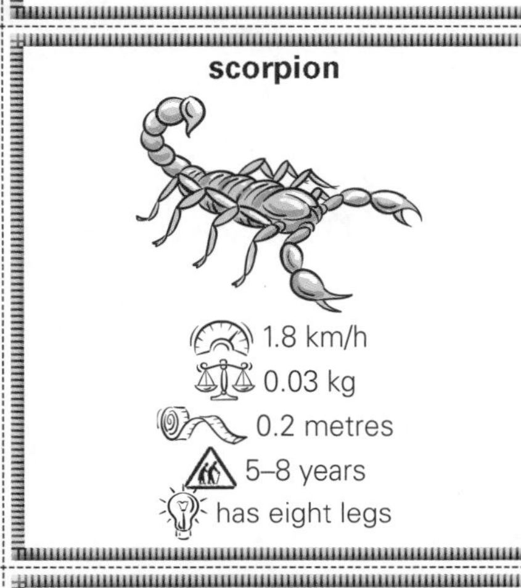

1.8 km/h
0.03 kg
0.2 metres
5–8 years
has eight legs

centipede

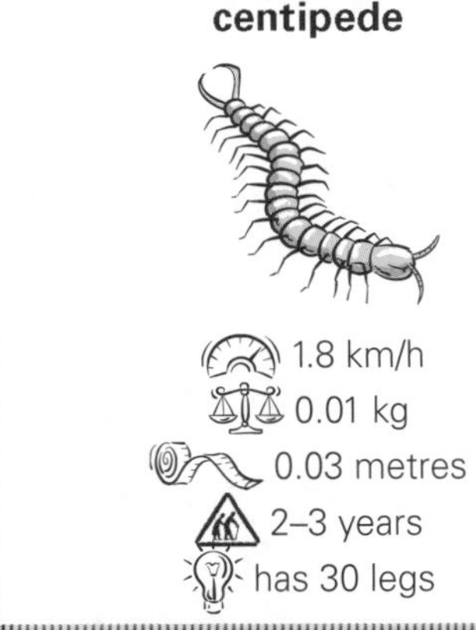

1.8 km/h
0.01 kg
0.03 metres
2–3 years
has 30 legs

tarantula

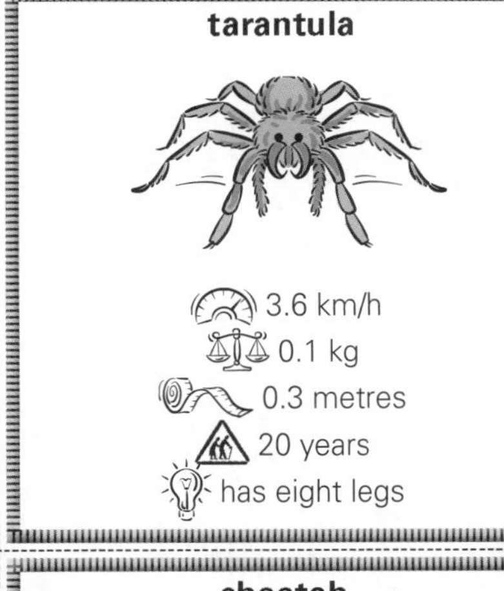

3.6 km/h
0.1 kg
0.3 metres
20 years
has eight legs

mosquito

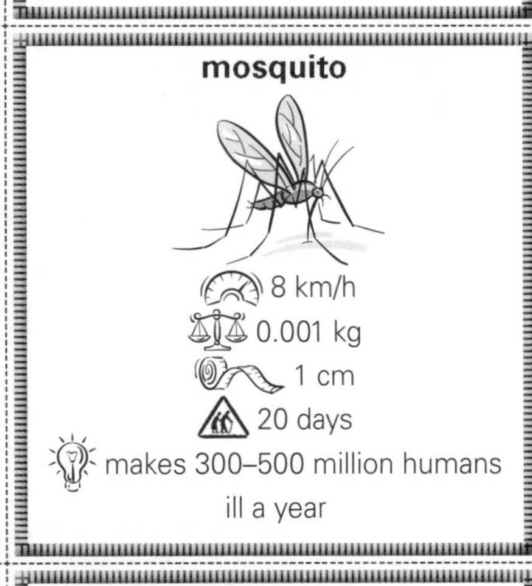

8 km/h
0.001 kg
1 cm
20 days
makes 300–500 million humans ill a year

falcon

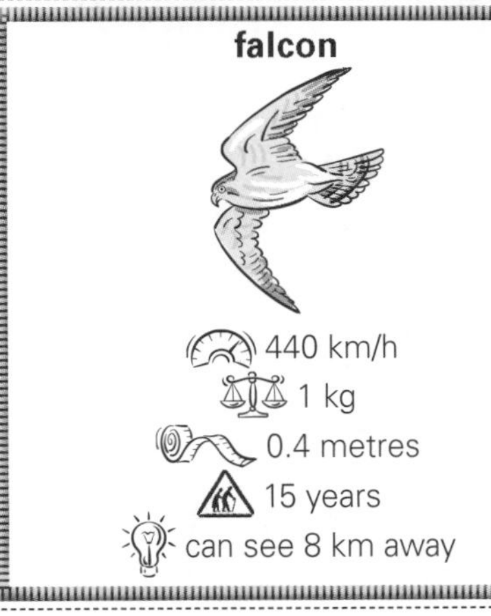

440 km/h
1 kg
0.4 metres
15 years
can see 8 km away

cheetah

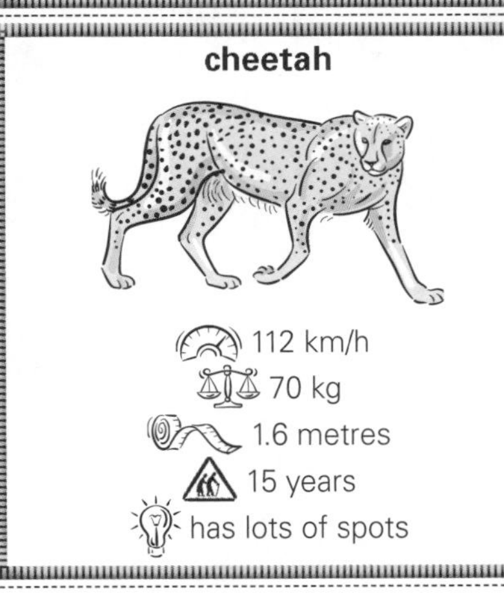

112 km/h
70 kg
1.6 metres
15 years
has lots of spots

chimpanzee

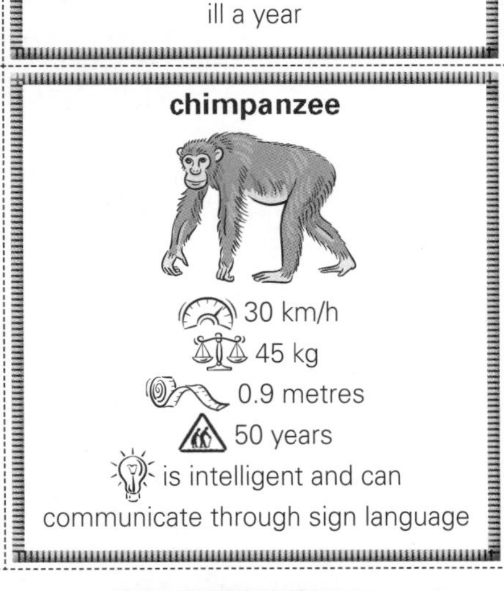

30 km/h
45 kg
0.9 metres
50 years
is intelligent and can communicate through sign language

The banquet

Picture A
WINE
WATER
ORANGE JUICE
ICE CREAM

Picture B
WINE
WATER
APPLE JUICE

Happy families

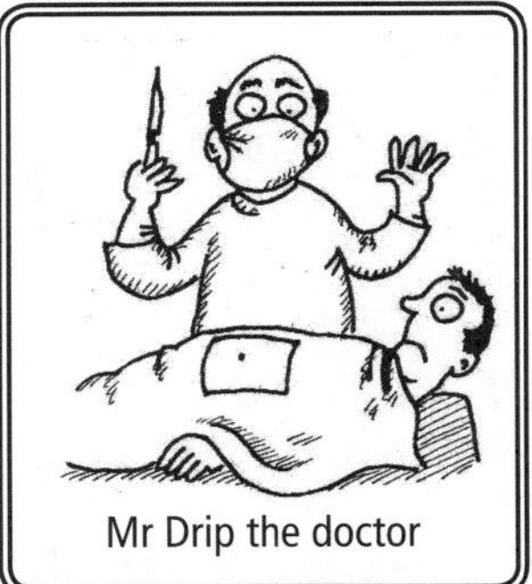

Mr Drip the doctor

Mrs Drip the doctor

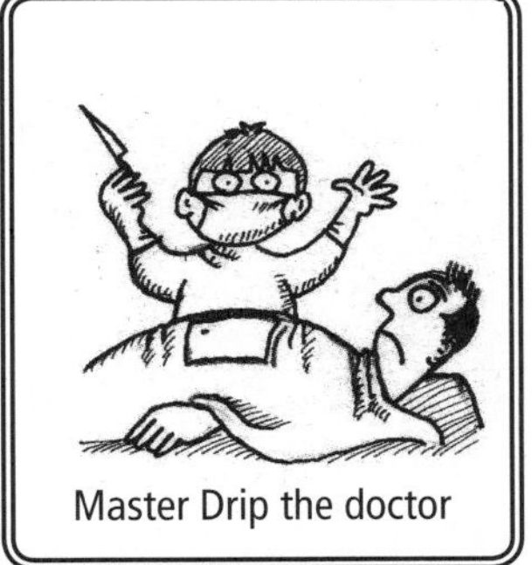

Master Drip the doctor

Miss Drip the doctor

Mr Chalk the teacher

Mrs Chalk the teacher

Master Chalk the teacher

Miss Chalk the teacher

Mr Plane the pilot

Mrs Plane the pilot

Master Plane the pilot

Miss Plane the pilot

Mr Wine the waiter

Mrs Wine the waiter

Master Wine the waiter

Miss Wine the waiter

Mr Toot the taxi-driver

Mrs Toot the taxi-driver

Master Toot the taxi-driver

Miss Toot the taxi-driver

Interview with a star

You are a famous pop star. Yesterday you had an interview for a newspaper. Today the reporter wants to check some information with you. Fill in the missing information. Then answer the reporter's questions and say if he/she has the correct information.

I am from A________________a.

I am thirty-t________________ years old.

I am in a pop group called Five S________________ .

My new song is called O________________ love.

My son is called Ja________________ .

He is fi________________ years old.

My mother is a famous ________________ star.

My favourite colour is bl________________ .

My favourite food is pi________________ .

My favourite animals are ________________ and ________________ .

You are a reporter for a newspaper. Yesterday you interviewed a famous pop star but you can't read some of your notes. You think you can remember the missing information. Complete your notes and then ask the pop star questions to see if you are right.

He/She is from A________________a.

He/She is thirty t________________ years old.

He/She is in a pop group called Five S________________ .

His/Her new song is called O________________ love.

His/Her son is called Ja________________ .

He is fi________________ years old.

His/Her mother is a famous ________________ star.

His/Her favourite colour is bl________________ .

His/Her favourite food is pi________________ .

His/Her favourite animals are ________________ and ________________ .

Song: Together We Are Strong

1 Listen to the song and read the words.

TOGETHER WE ARE STRONG

Like the river and the sea
We know that we belong
Like yin and yang through history
Together we are strong

Like ice is cold and stone is old
Like singers need a little song
If you sing for me, I'll sing for you
Together we are strong

We all know we're born alone
But then we'll see, it's easier when it's you and me

Through thick and thin, through right and wrong
Together we are strong

We all know we're born alone
But wait and see, it's easier when it's you and me

Through thick and thin, through right and wrong
Together we are strong

2 Look at the title, *Together We Are Strong*. Who do you think *we* refers to? Choose from the answers in the box or think of your own answer.

a man and a woman a father and son
Sam Moore and Sam Brown (the singers)
people in general

____

3 What is the main message of the song? Tick the correct box.

a) People are strong when they help each other. ☐
b) Nature is stronger than people. ☐
c) Everyone is born and dies alone. ☐

4 Match the words in column A with their opposites in column B.

A	B
1 thick	a) young
2 cold	b) alone
3 right	c) weak
4 strong	d) thin
5 old	e) hot
6 together	f) wrong

5 In pairs, discuss situations in which two people are better than one.

Useful information
Yin and yang: from ancient Chinese philosophy – these are the two opposite principles/forces thought to exist in everything in the universe.

Song: Raining In My Heart

1 Listen to the song and read the words.

RAINING IN MY HEART

The sun is out, the sky is blue
There's not a cloud to spoil the view
But it's raining, raining in my heart.
The weatherman says clear today
He doesn't know you've gone away
And it's raining, raining in my heart

Oh misery, misery
What's gonna become of me?

I tell my blues they musn't show
But soon these tears are bound to flow
And it's raining, raining in my heart
But it's raining, raining in my heart
And it's raining, raining in my heart

Oh misery, misery
What's gonna become of me?
I tell my blues they musn't show
But soon these tears are bound to flow
Cause it's raining, raining in my heart

Raining in my heart
Raining in my heart
Raining in my heart

2 Choose the best answers to the questions.

1 What is the weather like?
   a) It's raining.
   b) The sun is shining.
   c) It's cloudy.

2 Why does the singer say it is raining in his heart?
   a) He feels happy.
   b) He feels tired.
   c) He feels sad.

3 The words *blue* and *blues* appear in the song. *Blue* is the colour of the sky, but what are blues?
   a) feelings of sadness
   b) tears
   c) ghosts

3 Read the song again and underline the correct answer.

a The sun **is shining / isn't shining**.
b It **is / isn't** cloudy.
c The weather forecast for today is **good / bad**.
d The singer **thinks / doesn't think** the weather forecaster understands how he feels.
e The singer **is enjoying / is not enjoying** the good weather.
f He is sad because someone he loves **isn't there / is coming to see him**.

4 How would you describe the feeling of the song?

a Fun and light-hearted
b Positive and hopeful
c Sad and thoughtful

5 When you are sad, does good weather make you feel better or does it make you feel worse? Discuss with a partner.

Song: Don't You Want Me, Baby?

1 Listen to the song and read the words.

DON'T YOU WANT ME, BABY?

You were working as a waitress in a cocktail bar
When I met you
I picked you out, I shook you up and turned you around
Turned you into someone new
Now five years later on you've got the world at your feet
Success has been so easy for you
But don't forget it's me who put you where you are now
And I can put you back down too

Don't don't you want me?
You know I can't believe it when I hear that you won't see me
Don't don't you want me?
You know I don't believe you when you say that you don't
need me

It's much too late to find
You think you've changed your mind
You'd better change it back or we will both be sorry
Don't you want me, baby? Don't you want me oh
Don't you want me, baby? Don't you want me oh

I was working as a waitress in a cocktail bar
That much is true.
But even then I knew
I'd find a much better place
Either with or without you
The five years we have had have been such good times
I still love you,
But now I think it's time I lived my life on my own
I guess it's just what I must do

Don't don't you want me?
You know I can't believe it when I hear that you won't see me
Don't don't you want me?
You know I don't believe you when you say that you don't
need me
It's much too late to find
You think you've changed your mind
You'd better change it back or we will both be sorry
Don't you want me, baby? Don't you want me oh
Don't you want me, baby? Don't you want me oh

2 This song tells the story of a relationship. Choose the best summary.

a The boy is angry because the girl wants to leave him. He says that he changed her life and gave her money and success. He threatens to take it all back if she leaves. The girl wants to leave because she wants her own life. She doesn't agree that he is responsible for her success. She still loves him and enjoyed their time together but now she wants to be independent.

b The girl wants to leave because she doesn't love the boy anymore. He gave her a lot of things but she wants her freedom. They were together for five years. She now has a better job and she knows she doesn't need his help anymore. The boy is angry because he thinks she is ungrateful.

3 Mark these sentences T (true) or F (false).

a When they met, the girl was a waitress. _____
b She has a different job now. _____
c She told the boy she doesn't want to see him again. _____
d The boy wants the girl to leave. _____
e The girl agrees that the boy is responsible for her success. _____
f The girl wants to leave because she doesn't love him now. _____
g The girl has met another boy and fallen in love with him. _____

4 Find the past simple forms of these verbs in the song.

a shake _______________
b pick _______________
c meet _______________
d change _______________
e turn _______________
f know _______________

Song: Rocket Man

1 Listen to the song and read the words.

ROCKET MAN

She packed my bags last night pre-flight,
Zero hour nine a.m.
And I'm gonna be high as a kite by then.
I miss the earth so much; I miss my wife.
It's lonely out in space
On such a timeless flight.

And I think it's gonna be a long long time
Till touch down brings me round again to find
I'm not the man they think I am at home.
Oh, no no no, I'm a rocket man,
A rocket man burning out his fuse up here alone.

Mars ain't the kind of place to raise your kids.
In fact it's cold as well.
And there's no one there to raise them if you did.
And all this science I don't understand.
It's just my job five days a week.
A rocket man, a rocket man

And I think it's gonna be a long long time ...

2 Mark these sentences T (true) or F (false).

1 The singer is an astronaut. _____
2 He isn't married. _____
3 He enjoys his job because it is exciting. _____
4 He is interested in science. _____
5 He is going to be in space for a long time. _____

3 Choose the best answers to the questions.

1 Who is 'she' in the first line?
a) the singer's wife
b) the singer's girlfriend
c) the singer's boss

2 Who is with him in the rocket?
a) his wife and children
b) some scientists
c) no one

3 Why is Mars not a good place to take children?
a) It is too far away from earth.
b) It's cold and there are no people there.
c) It takes too long to get there and back.

4 How does he feel about his work?
a) It's dangerous.
b) It's exciting.
c) It's just an ordinary job.

5 Why does he say he is 'not the man they think I am at home'?
a) Being in space makes him feel like a different person.
b) He isn't as brave as his family think he is.
c) He enjoys being in space more than being at home.

4 In pairs, discuss what you think the most exciting job would be. What would be the most boring?

WORKBOOK Answers

WELCOME!

1
1 Pierre is from Switzerland.
2 David, Emily and Adam are from England.
3 Jake isn't from England. He's from the USA.
4 Is Pierre from Spain? No, he isn't.
5 Who is from Russia? Katya.

2
1 This is Roger and he's from Switzerland.
2 This is Alicia and she's from the USA.
3 This is Rafael and he's from Spain.
4 This is Ksenia and she's from Russia.
5 This is Daniel and he's from England.

3
1 I'm from Spain. She's from Spain.
2 I'm from Switzerland. He's from Switzerland.
3 We're from England. They're from England.
4 I'm from Russia. She's from Russia.
5 I'm from the USA. He's from the USA.

4
1 Are Emily and Adam American? No, they aren't. They're English.
2 Is Katya English? No, she isn't. She's Russian.
3 Is Pierre Russian? No, he isn't. He's Swiss.
4 Is Teresa Swiss? No, she isn't. She's Spanish.
5 Is Jake Spanish? No, he isn't. He's American.
6 Is David American? No, he isn't. He's English.
7 Are you English? I'm ... (students' own answer).

5
1 What is your name?
2 He is a teacher.
3 We are students.
4 I am not American.
5 Who is she?
6 They are English.
7 She is not a teacher.
8 You are at school.
9 It is nice to meet you.
10 We are not in Brighton.

6
EMILY What's **your** name?
TERESA **My** name is Teresa.
EMILY What's the name of the girl from Russia?
TERESA **Her** name is Katya.
EMILY And what's the name of the Swiss boy?
TERESA **His** name is Pierre.

7

T	H	R	E	E	Q
E	S	O	S	I	F
N	I	N	E	G	O
M	X	E	V	H	U
F	I	V	E	T	R
T	W	O	N	P	D

8
1 twelve 2 nineteen 3 thirteen 4 fifteen
5 sixteen 6 fourteen 7 eleven 8 twenty
9 eighteen 10 seventeen

9

zero	0	1	one
five	5	7	seven
twelve	12	11	eleven
sixteen	16	15	fifteen
two	2	4	four
eight	8	9	nine
fourteen	14	13	thirteen
twenty	20	18	eighteen

10
1 address 2 number 3 student 4 teacher
5 school 6 welcome 7 friend

11
1 who 2 street 3 your 4 he 5 I 6 they

UNIT 1 LESSON 1

1
1 Turner 2 spell Petrova 3 Her 4 isn't

2
1 Is this your passport?
2 Is that your umbrella?
3 Is this your ID card?
4 Is that your key?
5 Is that your wallet?
6 Is this your bag?
7 Is that your MP3 player?
8 Is that your calculator?
9 Is that your cat?
10 Is this your comb?

3
1 an 2 a 3 a 4 an 5 a 6 an 7 an 8 an 9 a
10 an

4
1 It's called a digital camera.
2 It's called an MP3 player.
3 It's called an alarm clock.
4 It's called a packet of tissues.
5 It's called a mobile phone.

5
photo – pen – comb – book – key – wallet – ticket – phone

6
1 It's a chair. 2 It's a table. 3 It's a door.
4 It's a window. 5 It's a desk. 6 It's a pencil.

7
1 What's your name?
2 Is that English?
3 What's that called?
4 It's my MP3 player.
5 Now it's your turn.
6 That's your key.
7 Where's she from?
8 What's in it?
9 Where's your passport?
10 How do you spell it?

8
1 Z 2 Y 3 I 4 H 5 R 6 K 7 O

UNIT 1 LESSON 2

1
1 F 2 F 3 T 4 T 5 T

2
1 Where's the Royal Pavilion?
2 How old is it?
3 When is the Brighton Bike Ride?
4 What time is the Brighton Bike Ride?
5 What time is it now?
6 When's the welcome party?

3
1 Those are your keys.
2 These are my friends.
3 These are your maps.
4 Those are your chairs.
5 Are those his books?
6 These are her cats.
7 Are those your pens?
8 These are my wallets.

4
1 That is the ticket.
2 This is my pen.
3 Is that your photo?
4 That is the bicycle.
5 Is this the dog?
6 This is the bottle.
7 That is my bag.
8 Is this her comb?

5

Singular	Plural
address	addresses
party	parties
visitor	visitors
copy	copies
person	people
boy	boys
photo	photos
watch	watches
city	cities
lunch	lunches
family	families
film	films
building	buildings

6
1 my things
2 – (although some nationalities have more than one surname)
3 my friends
4 –
5 –
6 a packet of tissues
7 our names
8 my keys
9 –
10 –

7
1 in 2 near 3 near 4 next to 5 on 6 in 7 on
8 next to

8
21, 24, 27 twenty-one, twenty-four, twenty-seven, thirty, thirty-three, thirty-six
15, 20, 25 fifteen, twenty, twenty-five, thirty, thirty-five, forty
24, 36, 48 twenty-four, thirty-six, forty-eight, sixty, seventy-two, eighty-four
99, 88, 77 ninety-nine, eighty-eight, seventy-seven, sixty-six, fifty-five, forty-four

9
1 sixty-six 2 seventy-three 3 eighty-nine
4 ninety-one 5 one hundred and eleven
6 three hundred and twenty
7 eight hundred and seventy-six
8 seven thousand seven hundred
9 nine thousand three hundred and fifty
10 ten thousand

10
1 It's five past six.
2 It's half past seven.
3 It's quarter to nine.
4 It's nine o'clock.
5 It's quarter past ten.
6 It's twenty to twelve.
7 It's ten past twelve.
8 It's twenty-five past one.
9 It's twenty-five to three.
10 It's ten to four.
11 It's twenty past four.
12 It's five to six.

11
building school centre eighty listen half tonight

UNIT 1 LESSON 3

1
1 sister 2 Caroline 3 grandmother 4 next to
5 Paul 6 Paul

2
1 I 2 He 3 They 4 she 5 she 6 he 7 we

3

Possessive adjectives	my	your	his	her	its	our	their

4
1 My name is Bart.
2 This is my family.
3 This is my mother.
4 Her name is Marge.
5 This is my father.
6 His name is Homer.
7 These are my sisters.
8 Their names are Lisa and Maggie.
9 This is my grandfather.
10 His name is Abe.

1 Abe 2 Marge 3 Homer 4/5 Lisa/Maggie

5
1 father 2 brother 3 daughters 4 grandfather
5 son 6 sister 7 husband 8 wife

6
April 4 August 8 December 12 February 2
January 1 July 7 June 6 March 3 May 5
November 11 October 10 September 9

7
1 the twenty-first of May
2 the ninth of July
3 the sixteenth of June
4 the second of November
5 the fourth of March
6 the thirtieth of August
7 the eighth of February
8 the twelfth of September
9 the first of April
10 the twenty-sixth of October
11 the third of December
12 the fourteenth of January

8
birthday brother daughter family father
photo February sister today twentieth

Today has the stress on the second syllable.

UNIT 1 LESSON 4

1

Emily	Adam
1 What's her surname?	1 What's his surname?
2 What's her nationality?	2 What's his nationality?
3 Where's she from?	3 Where is he from?
4 How old is she?	4 How old is he?
5 When's her birthday?	5 When's his birthday?
6 Who's her favourite singer?	6 Who's his favourite singer?

2
Students' own answers.

3

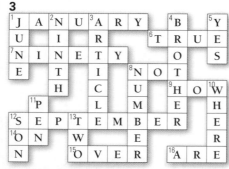

Learner independence
1 d 2 a 3 e 4 c 5 b

UNIT 1 Inspiration EXTRA!

Revision

Welcome!
1 Who / Jake
2 Where / Spain
3 What / Katya
4 What / Adam and Emily
5 Who / David Ward

Lesson 1
1 This is my ID card.
2 That is my pen.
3 This is my digital camera.
4 This is my book.
5 That is my rucksack/bag.
6 That is my key.

Lesson 2

Lesson 3
1 husband 2 son 3 sister 4 brother 5 mother
6 wife 7 grandmother 8 grandfather 9 daughter
10 father

Lesson 4
1 Where / He is from Washington in the USA.
2 What / His surname is Turner.
3 What / He is American.
4 When / His birthday is on 11th March.
5 How / He is 14.
6 Who / His favourite singer is Jay-Z.

Spelling
1 beautiful 2 building 3 photograph 4 centre
5 daughter 6 eight 7 favourite 8 friend
9 mountain 10 quarter

Brainteaser
I-T

Extension

Welcome!
1 is / is 2 Are / aren't 3 aren't / are 4 are 5 is
6 is / isn't / is

Lesson 1
a 4 b 3 c 2 d 1 e 6 f 5

Lesson 2
1 These are my bags.
2 Are those your keys?
3 What time is it?
4 It's two o'clock.
5 How old is it / are you?
6 It's 200 years old.

Lesson 3
1 The twenty-fifth of December
2 The first of January
3 The twenty-second of March
4 The fifteenth of May
5 The twelfth of August

Students' own answers

Lesson 4
Students' own answers

Spelling
1 address 2 book 3 bottle 4 guess 5 passport
6 sorry 7 spell 8 thirteen 9 umbrella 10 wallet

Brainteaser
A bottle

CULTURE

Countries around the world

1
1 Scotland 2 Northern Ireland
3 the Republic of Ireland 4 Wales 5 England

2
SCOTLAND
Capital Edinburgh
Population 5,200,000
Languages English and Scots Gaelic

WALES
Capital Cardiff
Population 3,000,000
Languages English and Welsh

NORTHERN IRELAND
Capital Belfast
Population 1,789,000
Languages English and Irish Gaelic

REPUBLIC OF IRELAND
Capital Dublin
Population 4,500,000
Languages English and Irish Gaelic

3
a2 b4 c7 d9 e8 f5 g3 h1 i6

UNIT 2 LESSON 1

1
1 F 2 T 3 F 4 T 5 T 6 F

2
1 have 2 have 3 has 4 has 5 has 6 have
7 have

3
1 Emily has a mobile phone.
2 Pierre has an alarm clock.
3 Teresa and Jake have rucksacks.
4 Katya and Emily have bottles of water.
5 Adam has a digital camera.
6 Teresa has a watch.

4
1 a jacket 2 a pair of shoes 3 a pullover
4 a pair of jeans 5 a shirt 6 a cap
7 a pair of trainers 8 a pair of trousers

5
1 Germany 2 Japan 3 India 4 South Africa
5 Puerto Rico

6
1 red 2 grey 3 black 4 white, black 5 blonde, purple 6 red, white 7 white 8 pink

7

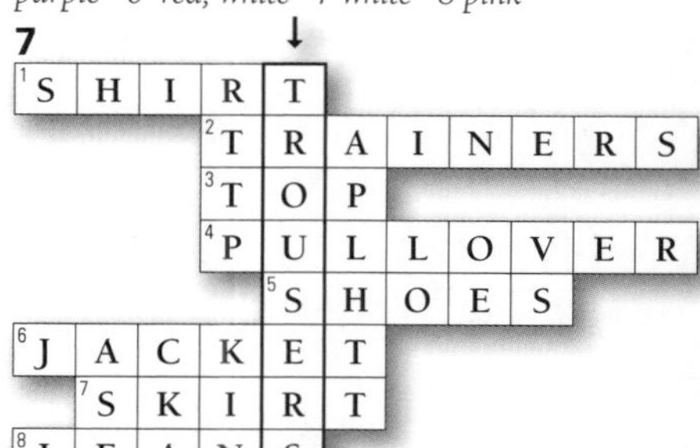

8
1 ✓ 2 ✗ 3 ✓ 4 ✗ 5 ✓ 6 ✗ 7 ✓ 8 ✓
9 ✓ 10 ✓

9
colour lovely umbrella orange jacket
mobile pullover purple trainers
trousers yellow

Umbrella has the stress on the second syllable.

UNIT 2 LESSON 2

1

1 Adam can play tennis, but he can't ski.
2 Pierre can play tennis and he can ski.
3 Pierre can't ride a horse, but he can ride a bicycle.
4 Pierre can speak four languages.
5 Pierre can't speak Russian.
6 Adam can speak English. French and Russian.

2

1 Emily can tell jokes, but she can't remember people's names.
2 Emily and Katya can speak French, but they can't speak German.
3 Adam can sing, but he can't dance.
4 Pierre can draw a picture, but he can't create a web page.
5 Teresa can sing, but she can't play an instrument.
6 Katya and Jake can't make a cake, but they can make a sandwich.

3

Students' own answers.

4

1 Can Adam ride a horse? No, he can't.
2 Can he iron a shirt? Yes, he can.
3 Can he dance? No, he can't.
4 Can he download music? Yes, he can.
5 Can he speak Spanish? Yes, he can.
6 Can he swim underwater? No, he can't.
7 Can Emily ride a horse? Yes, she can.
8 Can she iron a shirt? No, she can't.
9 Can she dance? Yes, she can.
10 Can she download music? No, she can't.
11 Can she speak Spanish? No, she can't.
12 Can she swim underwater? Yes, she can.

5

1 Katya can read music, but Jake can't.
2 Katya can play the guitar, but Jake can't.
3 Katya can't play the piano, but Jake can.
4 Katya can speak Italian, but Jake can't.
5 Katya can sew on a button, but Jake can't.
6 Katya can't remember dates, but Jake can.

6

1 and 2 or 3 but 4 and 5 or 6 but 7 or 8 but

7

1 burn a CD 2 cook a meal 3 iron a shirt
4 programme a satnav 5 ride a horse
6 lift 20 kilos 7 speak a language 8 tell a joke

8

1 cook joke people
2 guitar language question
3 light sing/sign programme
4 instrument puncture underwater
5 place create horse
6 fantastic switch watch

9

1 mind 2 this 3 dear 4 nice 5 questions 6 you
7 draw 8 light 9 behind 10 lots

10

■▪▪	▪■▪
anything	fantastic
instrument	piano
pullover	remember
bicycle	umbrella
saxophone	

UNIT 2 LESSON 3

1

1 F 2 T 3 F 4 T 5 F 6 F

2

1 Smile. 2 Don't move. 3 Come here.
4 Don't forget your jacket. 5 Don't run.
6 Press OK.

3

1 Speak English.
2 Don't be late.
3 Give him the message.
4 Don't use my phone.

4

1 Don't ask 2 don't forget 3 Go, select 4 Don't be
5 Help 6 Don't use 7 Tell 8 Keep

5

1 The, 0 2 the 3 The, 0, 0 4 the 5 the 6 The
7 the, the 8 The, 0

6

1 Now enter the phone number.
2 Here's the phone and that's the number.
3 Dial the area code.
4 The international code for Switzerland is 0041.
5 The area code for Geneva is 022.
6 Emily is on the right in the photo.

7

1 area code 2 boyfriend 3 digital camera
4 light switch 5 mobile phone 6 text message
7 laptop 8 webcam

8

1 move around 2 dial a number 3 make a call
4 keep still 5 spell a name 6 take a picture

9

Hi! Thanks for the book – it's great! See you today about 5 o'clock. Please don't forget.

10

1 ✓ 2 ✓ 3 ✗ 4 ✓ 5 ✓ 6 ✓ 7 ✗ 8 ✗

UNIT 2 LESSON 4

1

1 has 2 its 3 black 4 blonde 5 hair 6 jacket
7 have 8 single 9 film 10 songs

2

Students' own answers

3

1 M	E	2 S	S	3 A	4 G	E	5 S			6 R
O		A		7 N	O		8 H	A	V	E
9 B	10 O	Y		Y			I			M
11 I	N				12 H	E	R	E		E
L		13 B		14 T	O		T		15 A	M
16 E	17 Y	E	18 S		19 M	E		20 L		B
	E		21 O	N	E		22 C	O	D	E
	A		N					V		R
23 P	R	O	G	R	A	M	M	E		

Classroom English

1 e 2 d 3 a 4 b 5 c

UNIT 2 Inspiration EXTRA!

Revision

Lesson 1

1 has 2 have 3 have 4 have 5 have 6 has
7 has 8 have 9 have 10 has

1 shirt 2 jacket 3 shoes 4 skirt 5 pullover
6 trainers 7 cap 8 jeans

Lesson 2

Can Teresa play the saxophone? No, she can't.
Can Teresa sing? Yes, she can.
Can Emily play the guitar? Yes, she can.
Can Emily speak German? No, she can't.
Can Katya find her trainers? No, she can't.
Can Adam send a text message? Yes, he can.
Can Katya ride a horse? Yes, she can.
Can Adam dance? No, he can't.
Can Pierre cook a meal? Yes, he can.

Lesson 3

Send the picture to your mum.
Take a picture of Pierre.
Dial the international code.
Don't forget the area code.
Phone your friend later.
Come to my house at eight.
Don't use your mobile.

Lesson 4

What's your favourite band?
How many members are there?
Where are they from?
What's your favourite song?
What's their website address?

Spelling

1 black 2 clothes 3 fantastic 4 guitar 5 light
6 message 7 number 8 picture 9 purple
10 remember 11 trousers 12 yellow

Brainteaser

Alphabet

Extension

Lesson 1

1 d 2 e 3 f 4 b 5 c 6 a

Lesson 2

1 Can you sing and dance at the same time?
2 Can you speak French or German?
3 Can you play an instrument?
4 Can you remember people's names?
5 Can you make a cake or a sandwich?
6 Can you sew on a button?
7 Can you answer the Life Skills Questionnaire?
8 Can you run five kilometres?

Lesson 3

1 Go 2 Select 3 Keep 4 Press 5 Press 6 Select
7 Enter 8 Press

Lesson 4

Students' own answers.

Spelling

1 make 2 name 3 place 4 take 5 play 6 say
7 today

Brainteaser

'I' is the ninth letter of the alphabet.

REVIEW UNITS 1-2

1

1 B 2 B 3 A 4 C 5 C 6 A 7 A 8 A 9 B 10 A

2

1 watch 2 map 3 camera 4 pen 5 book
6 comb 7 mobile phone 8 guitar

3

1 C 2 A 3 B 4 B 5 A

4

1 river 2 road 3 girlfriend 4 or 5 jeans
6 band 7 lift 8 parent

Learner independence

2

1 Oh, I see. 2 Thank you very much.
3 There's something wrong.
4 Yes, of course you can. 5 Thanks a lot.
6 It's really cool.

UNIT 3 LESSON 1

1

Pizza 1 Emily Pizza 2 Katya Pizza 3 Teresa

2

1 Ruby and Adam live in a cottage.
2 Pierre lives in a flat.

3 Diana has two children.
4 We want to talk to you.
5 Ruby likes eggs for breakfast.
6 You hate cucumber.
7 The chickens live in the garden.
8 I love your jeans.

3
1 live 2 speaks 3 want 4 hates 5 likes 6 has 7 plays 8 hope

4
1 doesn't play 2 live 3 use 4 don't speak 5 don't have 6 want

5
1 Adam doesn't live in Brighton. He lives in Lewes.
2 Teresa doesn't like Lady Gaga. She likes Rihanna.
3 He doesn't want to have fish. He wants to have pizza.
4 Pierre and his parents don't have a house. They have a flat.
5 Ruby doesn't have a red top. She has a blue top.
6 Adam doesn't like tomatoes. He likes mushrooms.
7 Ruby and Adam don't live in a flat. They live in a cottage.
8 We don't want to see the fish. We want to see the chickens.

6
1 Pierre likes eggs, but he doesn't like octopus.
2 Ruby eats chocolate, but she doesn't eat bananas.
3 Emily speaks Italian, but she doesn't speak German.
4 Pierre plays tennis, but he doesn't play football.
5 Teresa and Emily hate Robbie Williams, but they don't hate Madonna.

7

A	C	U	C	U	M	B	E	R	M
Y	H	B	R	N	O	E	G	O	E
T	O	A	C	S	C	E	G	D	N
O	C	N	A	G	T	T	S	W	I
M	O	A	R	A	O	F	B	O	R
A	L	N	R	R	P	I	Z	Z	A
T	A	A	O	L	U	S	D	J	B
O	T	W	T	I	S	H	E	U	Y
M	E	Y	G	C	H	E	E	S	E
O	M	U	S	H	R	O	O	M	P

8
1 carrots 2 chocolate 3 garlic, mushrooms 4 cucumber 5 fish 6 octopus 7 banana, cheese 8 tomato 9 pizza 10 eggs

9
banana breakfast carrot chicken
chocolate cottage cucumber garden
garlic mushroom octopus tomato

UNIT 3 LESSON 2

1
1 F 2 F 3 T 4 F 5 T 6 F

2
RUBY Do you live in the city centre?
PIERRE Yes, I do.
RUBY Do you have a garden?
PIERRE No, I don't.
RUBY Do you eat eggs?
PIERRE Yes, I do.
RUBY Do you want to talk to Adam?
PIERRE No, I don't.
RUBY Do you love fish?
PIERRE Yes, I do.
RUBY Do you like octopus?
PIERRE No, I don't.

3
1 When does Adam have PE? On Wednesday at 14.10.
2 When do lessons start in the morning? At 9.00.
3 What does Adam have on Monday at 11.30? Geography.
4 When do the students have lunch? At 13.10.
5 When do lessons start after lunch? At 14.10.
6 When does Adam have computer studies? On Tuesday at 10.05.

4
1 on 2 at 3 in 4 at 5 on 6 at 7 in 8 at 9 in 10 at

5
1 at 2 in 3 from 4 to 5 from 6 to 7 at 8 at 9 after 10 before 11 from 12 to 13 After 14 in 15 On 16 after

6
1 Does Annabel walk to school every day? Yes, she does.
2 Does Annabel play basketball at break? No, she doesn't.
3 Does Annabel have a short break in the morning? Yes, she does.
4 Do they have lots of activities after school? No, they don't.
5 Does Annabel hate history? No, she doesn't.
6 Do you like sport? Yes, I/we do.
7 Do Annabel and her friends do art after school? No, they don't.
8 Do students at your school play sports? Yes, they do.

7

W	E	D	N	E	S	D	A	Y
T	H	U	R	S	D	A	Y	X
U	F	K	P	I	B	L	T	M
E	F	R	I	D	A	Y	L	O
S	N	W	J	O	L	D	W	N
D	S	U	N	D	A	Y	E	D
A	B	R	G	O	W	S	P	A
Y	S	A	T	U	R	D	A	Y

8
1 maths 2 geography 3 art 4 science 5 computer studies 6 English 7 history 8 PE 9 French

9

/uː/ do		/ʌ/ does	
blue	too	but	lunch
school	you	come	one
soon		fun	up
		love	

UNIT 3 LESSON 3

1
1 never 2 always 3 often 4 never 5 never 6 always

2
1 Adam is sometimes late for school.
2 Emily usually goes to the gym on Monday.
3 Emily never goes shopping on Sunday.
4 Pierre is always at the swimming pool on Monday.
5 Adam often plays tennis at the weekend.
6 Teresa usually does her homework in the evening.
7 Ruby is sometimes angry with Adam.

3
1 He often goes swimming on Monday.
2 He always plays basketball on Tuesday.
3 He sometimes goes to the cinema on Wednesday.
4 He usually goes dancing on Thursday.
5 He usually goes running on Friday.
6 He never goes shopping on Saturday.
7 He often plays tennis on Sunday.

4
1 Teresa never lifts weights, but Adam sometimes lifts weights.
2 Teresa usually rides the exercise bike, but Adam always rides the exercise bike.
3 Teresa sometimes goes on the rowing machine, but Adam often goes on the rowing machine.
4 Teresa often uses the running machine, but Adam usually uses the running machine.
5 Teresa always goes to dance classes, but Adam never goes to dance classes.

5
Students' own answers.

6
1 afternoon 2 computer game 3 dance routine 4 exercise bike 5 swimming pool 6 tennis court 7 timetable 8 weekend

7
1 never 2 night 3 get up 4 early 5 after 6 go

8
go: dancing, running, shopping, swimming, to bed
play: basketball, computer games, football, the guitar, tennis

9
1 ✗ 2 ✓ 3 ✗ 4 ✓ 5 ✓ 6 ✗ 7 ✓ 8 ✓

UNIT 3 LESSON 4

1
1 always 2 early 3 practises 4 goes 5 classes 6 loves 7 walks 8 sees 9 have 10 speaks

2
Sample answer
Maria Sharapova was born on 19th April 1987. She is an international tennis champion. She is from Siberia in Russia. She has long blonde hair and green eyes. Before a tournament she usually eats lots of pasta and salad. What does Maria like? She loves shopping, looking good and being with her friends. She likes fashion, singing and jazz dancing. Her favourite film is Pearl Harbor. Her favourite food is Russian food and Italian bread.

3

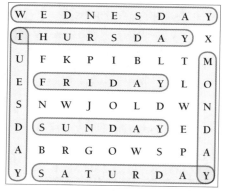

1 B	R	2 E	A	K	3 F	A	S	4 T
A		X			I			I
5 S	P	E	A	K	S		6 A	M
K		R			7 H	8 A	T	E
9 E	A	C	H			G		T
T		I				A		A
10 B	U	S	Y			M		B
A		E		11 I	C	E		L
L			12 I				13 M	E
14 L	E	S	S	O	N		Y	

Learner independence
Answers depend on students' first language.

UNIT 3
Inspiration EXTRA!

Revision

Lesson 1
1 Jake likes carrots, but he doesn't like cucumber.
2 Teresa doesn't like fish or garlic.
3 Katya doesn't like ice cream, but she likes chocolate.

Lesson 2
1 Does Babar Ali like history?
Yes, he does.
2 Does Chumki Hajra go to school in the morning?
No, she doesn't.
3 Does Adam have maths on Wednesday?
No, he doesn't.
4 Does Adam have a break in the morning?
Yes, he does.
5 Do you like history?
Students' own answer.
6 Do you have lunch at school?
Students' own answer.

Lesson 3
1 Jake usually goes to bed late at the weekend.
2 Emily sometimes has breakfast in bed on Sunday.
3 Adam and Ruby never watch TV all day.
4 Teresa and Katya often listen to music.
5 Pierre always helps in the house.

Lesson 4
1 It's on 7th January. 2 No, he doesn't.
3 In Switzerland. 4 In the morning. 5 Yes, he does.
6 Japanese food and spicy food 7 Nic
8 hip-hop, R&B, reggae, jazz and blues

Spelling
1 carr**o**t 2 chee**s**e 3 co**tt**age 4 di**ff**erent
5 di**nn**er 6 e**gg** 7 le**ss**on 8 pi**zz**a 9 ru**nn**ing
10 sho**pp**ing 11 sl**ee**p 12 swi**mm**ing
13 t**ee**nager 14 te**nn**is 15 vo**ll**eyball
16 w**ee**kend

Brainteaser
In the dictionary.

Extension

Lesson 1
1 She doesn't like cheese.
2 I speak French and German.
3 She doesn't want to talk to me.
4 They don't have a garden.
5 He wants to have pizza and chips.
6 We really don't like octopus.

Lesson 2
1 At 2 at 3 from 4 to 5 at 6 On 7 in
8 from 9 to 10 in 11 on 12 at 13 at 14 at
15 On 16 at 17 in 18 at 19 in 20 on

Lesson 3
1 usually 2 often 3 always 4 never
5 sometimes

Lesson 4
Students' own answers.

Spelling
1 ice 2 five 3 quite 4 time 5 write

Brainteaser
Banana.

CULTURE

1
1 Rebecca 2 Rebecca 3 Will 4 Rebecca and Will
5 Will 6 Rebecca 7 Will 8 Rebecca
9 Rebecca and Will 10 Will 11 Rebecca
12 Will 13 Rebecca and Will 14 Rebecca

2
1 hamburger 2 train 3 gel 4 bell 5 toast
6 shower 7 bread

3
1 True
2 False. Rebecca lives in a big house near the sea.
3 False. Will has breakfast before he catches the bus to school.
4 False. Will has two lessons before break.
5 False. Rebecca's favourite subjects are science and maths.
6 True
7 False. Will has ten lessons on Wednesdays.
8 False. There are hamburgers for lunch at Will's school.

4
Sample answer
Lucy lives in Melbourne, Australia. She is 16 and has two sisters, Ruth, 12, and Anne, 14. On weekdays she gets up at 7.15am and has a shower. She has breakfast at 7.45 and leaves home at 8.15. School starts at 8.30. Lucy's favourite lessons are art and English. School ends at 4pm. Lucy plays basketball after school. At weekends she sees her family and friends, goes to the cinema and does her homework.

UNIT 4 LESSON 1

1
1 There isn't a café on the right. There's a café on the left.
2 There aren't three tables outside the café. There are two tables outside the café.
3 There isn't a cat at the tables. There's a dog.
4 There aren't two women in the big car.
5 There isn't a train with lots of people in it. There's a bus with lots of people on it.
6 There isn't a cinema on the left. There's a cinema on the right.
7 There aren't any bicycles outside the café.

2
1 Is there a street? Yes, there is.
2 Are there any bicycles? No, there aren't.
3 Is there a bus? Yes, there is.
4 Are there any cars? Yes, there are.
5 Is there a café? Yes, there is.
6 Are there any shops? No, there aren't.
7 Is there a restaurant? No, there isn't.
8 Are there any people? Yes, there are.
9 Are there any children? No, there aren't.
10 Is there a dog? Yes, there is.

3
Possible answer
There is a bed on the right and a table on the left. There are two chairs. There is a chair next to the bed / between the bed and the table, and there is a chair on the left. There is a door on the left and on the right. There are some pictures on the walls. There is a window between the table and the bed.

4
1 How many minutes are there in an hour? There are sixty minutes in an hour.
2 How many hands are there on a clock? There are two/three hands on a clock.
3 How many days are there in a year? There are 365 (366 in a leap year).
4 How many years are there in a century? There are 100 years in a century.
5 How many numbers are there on a mobile phone? There are ten numbers on a mobile phone.
6 How many players are there in a football team? There are eleven players in a football team.

5
1 Is there an Italian one? No, there isn't.
2 Are there any open-air ones? Yes, there are.
3 Is there a new one? Yes, there is.
4 Is there a blue one? No, there isn't.
5 Are there any big ones? Yes, there are.
6 Are there any cheap ones? Yes, there are.

6

					↓				
					F				
	1 C	O	M	P	U	T	E	R	
	2 C	H	A	I	R				
			3 W	I	N	D	O	W	
4 T	E	L	E	V	I	S	I	O	N
	5 L	I	G	H	T				
	6 P	I	C	T	U	R	E		
		7 D	O	O	R				
				8 D	E	S	K		

7

■▪▪	▪■▪
teenager	attraction
cinema	fantastic
restaurant	including
everything	museum
gallery	exciting

UNIT 4 LESSON 2

1
1 John 2 Glynn and Simon 3 Laura 4 Fiona
5 Peter and Julia 6 Ian and Sally 7 Stuart
8 Mindy

2
coming cooking doing drawing getting going
having leaving making opening practising
reading running sending smiling speaking
stopping swimming

3
1 are listening 2 is talking 3 are standing
4 is raining 5 is coming 6 am looking
7 is wearing 8 is holding

4
Picture A
The girl is wearing a skirt.
The girl is eating an ice cream.
The girl is reading a book.
The waiter is standing on the left.
The waiter is holding a pen.
The waiter is wearing a T-shirt.
The boy at the table is eating pizza.
The boy at the table is wearing white trousers.

Picture B
The girl is wearing shorts.
The girl is eating a banana.
The girl is reading a magazine.
The waiter is standing on the right.
The waiter is holding a notebook.
The waiter is wearing a shirt.
The boy at the table is eating chips.
The boy at the table is wearing black trousers.

5

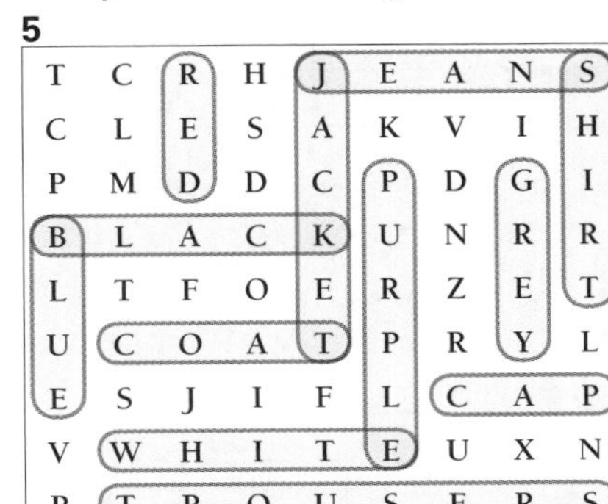

Clothes: jeans, coat, cap trousers, jacket, shirt
Colours: black, white, blue, red, purple, grey

6
1 actor grey theatre
2 eating holding learning
3 friend raining lines

4 really silly walk
5 woman famous outside
6 ghost month white

7

1 ✗ 2 ✓ 3 ✓ 4 ✓ 5 ✓ 6 ✓

UNIT 4 LESSON 3

1

1 T 2 F 3 F 4 T 5 F 6 F 7 F 8 F

2

1 Adam and Emily aren't taking photos. Katya and Teresa are taking photos.
2 Jake isn't standing next to the others. He's standing next to the shark pool.
3 The man isn't putting his foot into the water. He's putting his hand into the water.
4 The man isn't giving the sharks a drink. He is giving them some food.
5 The sharks aren't biting the man. They're taking the food.
6 Pierre isn't swimming with the sharks. The man is swimming with the sharks.

3

1 Where's she going?
2 What's he wearing?
3 What are they eating?
4 Where's he standing?
5 Where are they staying?
6 What's she drawing?
7 Where are you sitting?
8 What are they watching?

4

1 Is Diana cooking a meal? No, she isn't. She's making a sandwich.
2 Are Pierre and Adam running? No, they aren't. They're swimming.
3 Is Ruby having lunch? No, she isn't. She's eating an ice cream.
4 Are the people singing? No, they aren't. They're dancing.
5 Is the actor telling a joke? No, she isn't. She's learning her lines.
6 Are you sleeping? No, I'm not. I'm studying English!

5

			1 F		2 T	E	E	T	3 H
4 M			I		O				E
O		5 K	N	E	E				A
U			G			6 H	A	7 N	D
T			8 E	A	R			O	
9 H	10 A	I	R					S	
	R				11 F	A	C	E	
	M		12 L		E				
			13 E	Y	E				
			G		14 T	H	U	M	B

6

1 here 1 buy 3 there 4bed 5 key 6 south
7 goes 8 come 9 know 10 place

7

/ʊ/ foot		/uː/ tooth	
cook	look	choose	group
good	pull	food	soup

UNIT 4 LESSON 4

1

1 man 2 centre 3 shirt 4 trousers 5 shoes
6 left 7 window 8 houses 9 guitar 10 door
11 right 12 chest 13 bed 14 picture 15 wall

2

Sample answer

This is a painting of a girl in a café. The girl is sitting at a small table on the right. She's wearing a green coat and a yellow hat. She's drinking a cup of coffee. There's a door on the left. There's a big window behind her. It's dark outside.

3

1 R	E	2 S	T	3 A	U	4 R	A	5 N	T	6 S
I		H		C		E		O		O
7 G	H	O	S	T		8 A	F	T	E	R
H		P		O		D		E		R
9 T	O			10 R	A	I	11 N			Y
						12 N	O	13 S	E	
14 H	O	L	15 D	I	16 N	G		E		17 S
I			A		E			L		I
18 S	T	A	Y		19 W	A	L	L	E	T

Learner independence

1 d 2 a 3 e 4 c 5 b

UNIT 4 Inspiration EXTRA!

Revision

Lesson 1

1 Are there 2 Is there 3 Is there 4 are there
5 Is there 6 Are there

Students' own answers.

Lesson 2

1 are visiting 2 is taking 3 are standing
4 is raining 5 are looking 6 is eating

Lesson 3

1 Is the man selling hamburgers? No, he isn't.
2 Are the people buying fish and chips? Yes, they are.
3 Is the girl riding a bicycle? No, she isn't.
4 Is the girl wearing a helmet? Yes, she is.
5 Are the people doing exercises? Yes, they are.
6 Are the people standing on the beach? Yes, they are.

Lesson 4

Sample answers

Picture A: two beds, a desk, a wardrobe, curtains, a window, a television, magazines, books, chairs, clothes, pencils.

Picture B: a wardrobe, some posters, two beds, curtains, a window, a chest of drawers, books, a CD player, two chairs, flowers, a desk

Spelling

1 daughter 2 eight 3 ghost 4 half 5 knee
6 comb 7 know 8 light 9 listen 10 right
11 science 12 sight 13 thumb 14 tonight
15 walk 16 weight

Brainteaser

A chair or a table.

Extension

Lesson 1

Students' own answers.

Lesson 2

Sample answer

It is raining. The man is holding an umbrella. He is wearing a jacket, a tie, trousers, a white shirt and shoes. The dog is pulling the man. The cat is sitting in the tree and is smiling at the dog.

Lesson 3

1 Where are you going?
2 Are you having lunch?
3 I'm not eating anything.
4 What is she talking about?
5 The people aren't listening.

Lesson 4

Students' own answers.

Spelling

1 actor 2 calculator 3 centre 4 computer
5 kilometre 6 number 7 paper 8 photographer
9 player 10 singer 11 teacher 12 teenager
13 theatre 14 visitor

Brainteaser

A comb.

REVIEW UNITS 3-4

1

1 B 2 B 3 B 4 B 5 C 6 A 7 B 8 A 9 C 10 B

2

1 desk 2 table 3 chair 4 bed 5 wardrobe
6 window 7 door 8 light

3

1 B 2 B 3 C 4 A 5 C

4

1 comb 2 weekend 3 minute 4 football
5 tourist 6 toe 7 bad 8 flower

Learner independence

2

1 What about you? 2 How often do you come here? 3 That sounds great. 4 No, there isn't time.
5 Oh, this is silly! 6 I'm going home.

UNIT 5 LESSON 1

1

1 At 7.20, he goes swimming at the beach.
2 He meets his friends in a café at 11.45.
3 He plays tennis with Bob
4 He has dinner at home. He cooks dinner.

2

1 What time does he get up? He gets up at seven o'clock.
2 What time does he go swimming? He goes swimming at twenty past seven.
3 What time does he have breakfast? He has breakfast at half past eight.
4 What time does he go shopping? He goes shopping at quarter past ten.
5 What time does he meet his friends in a café? He meets his friends in a café at quarter to twelve.
6 What time does he play tennis? He plays tennis at half past two.
7 What time does he watch the news on TV? He watches the news on TV at 6 o'clock.
8 What time does he cook dinner? He cooks dinner at half past seven.

3

1 He's shopping.
2 He's cooking dinner.
3 He's having breakfast.
4 He's watching the news on TV.
5 He's getting up.
6 He's meeting his friends in a café.
7 He's going swimming.
8 He's playing tennis.

4

1 B 2 A 3 A 4 B 5 B 6 A 7 A 8 B 9 A
10 A

5

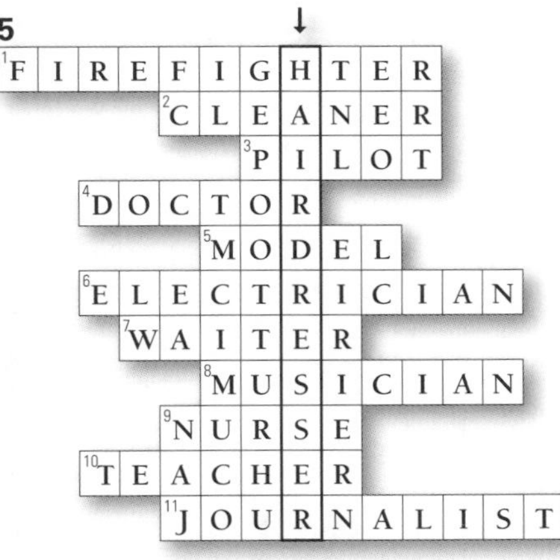

The missing word is hairdresser.

6
1 cook a meal 2 drive a taxi
3 listen to the radio 4 look after someone
5 play the trumpet 6 teach history
7 write an email

7
1 shirt 2 has 3 write 4 plane 5 code
6 three 7 one 8 ghost

UNIT 5 LESSON 2

1
1 Katya 2 Jake 3 Emily 4 Adam 5 Mr Ward
6 Pierre

2
1 Whose magazine is this? It's Katya's.
2 Whose sunglasses are these? They're Jake's.
3 Whose cap is this? It's Emily's.
4 Whose white bag is this? It's Pierre's.
5 Whose watch is this? It's Mr Ward's.
6 Whose black bag is this? It's Adam's.

3
1 Who's 2 Whose 3 Whose 4 Who's
5 Who's 6 Whose 7 Whose 8 Who's

4
1 is 2 is 3 possession 4 is 5 possession
6 possession 7 is 8 possession

5
1 hers, Her 2 his, His 3 mine, My
4 yours, Your 5 ours, Our, your/Your
6 ours/Our 7 theirs/Their

6
1 Whose phone is this?
2 I don't know.
3 It isn't mine.
4 I think it's Ruby's.
5 Who's Ruby?
6 She's Adam's sister.

7
1 earring 2 firefighter 3 hairdresser
4 police officer 5 shop assistant 6 sunglasses
7 sweatshirt 8 taxi-driver

8

■▪	▪■
bottle	around
camera	enjoy
earring	guitar
console	midday
problem	police
silver	
sweatshirt	

9
1 ✗ 2 ✓ 3 ✓ 4 ✗ 5 ✗ 6 ✓ 7 ✓ 8 ✗

UNIT 5 LESSON 3

1
1 Valencia, Brighton 2 Valencia, Brighton
3 colder 4 warmer 5 rain, drier
6 rains, wetter

2
angrier worse more beautiful bigger
more boring drier earlier better higher hotter
later luckier newer nicer foggier smaller

3
1 older 2 longer 3 shorter 4 earlier
5 sunnier 6 easier

4
1 Switzerland is bigger than Belgium.
2 Spain is smaller than Russia.
3 Athens is hotter than London.
4 Warsaw is colder than Geneva.
5 Rome is wetter than Paris.
6 Los Angeles is drier than New York.

5
sample answers
1 Spring is nicer than autumn.
2 Orlando Bloom is more famous than Robert Pattinson.
3 Winter is better than summer.
4 Science is more difficult than geography.
5 Football is more popular than volleyball.
6 Chips are more expensive than sandwiches.

6
1 windy 2 rainy 3 sunny 4 cloudy 5 snowy
6 foggy

7
1 worse 2 hot 3 easy 4 later 5 bad
6 taller/longer 7 false 8 dry 9 older
10 right/correct

8
1 nice, ice 2 drier, higher 3 later, waiter
4 daughter, shorter 5 hear, year
6 sunny, money 7 speak, week 8 nurse, worse

UNIT 5 LESSON 4

1
1 grey 2 favourite 3 personality 4 question
5 day 6 afternoon 7 Saturday 8 clothes
9 weekend 10 fun

2
Students' own answers.

3

1 C	O	2 N	F	I	3 D	E	N	4 T		5 B
R		U			I			6 E	Y	E
7 O	U	R	S		8 F	U	L	L		T
S		S		9 O	F			L		T
10 S	11 P	E	A	K	I	N	12 G		13 W	E
	I				C		A		14 O	R
15 C	A	R		16 S	U	M	M	E	R	
	N		17 B		L		E		S	
18 M	O	M	E	N	T		S	E	E	S

Learner independence

EMILY Well done, Teresa!
TERESA Thanks. Who wants to play next?
ADAM Whose turn is it?
JAKE I think it's mine.
EMILY No, it isn't yours. It's Adam's turn.
JAKE Sorry, but it isn't his. It really is mine.
ADAM Hey, what's the problem?

UNIT 5 Inspiration EXTRA!

Revision

Lesson 1
1 plays 2 is working 3 is teaching 4 have
5 am washing 6 are, going 7 flies
8 are having

Lesson 2
1 It's her cap. It's hers.
2 It's my camera. It's mine.
3 It's their computer. It's theirs.
4 They're our magazines. They're ours.
5 It's his mobile phone. It's his.
6 It's your sandwich. It's yours.
7 It's my bottle of water. It's mine.
8 It's her watch. It's hers.

Lesson 3
1 smaller 2 bigger 3 colder 4 hotter 5 drier
6 wetter 7 sunnier 8 foggier

Lesson 4
1 f 2 e 3 c 4 h 5 b

Spelling
1 autumn 2 breakfast 3 doctor 4 firefighter
5 friendly 6 higher 7 journalist 8 often
9 rainy 10 temperature 11 whose

Brainteaser
Your age.

Extension

Lesson 1
1 phones 2 are, doing 3 am listening 4 gets
5 think, is raining 6 Are, having

Lesson 2
1 Her bag 2 His packet of crisps 3 Her earrings
4 His sunglasses 5 Her watch 6 Her cap

Lesson 3
Students' own answers.

Lesson 4
Students' own answers.

Spelling
1 assistant 2 better 3 cross 4 difficult
5 earring 6 hairdresser 7 happen 8 midday
9 officer 10 small 11 summer 12 sunny

Brainteaser
The woman's son.

CULTURE

Social situations

1 b 2 l 3 d 4 g 5 a 6 j 7 e 8 c 9 i 10 k
11 f 12 h

UNIT 6 LESSON 1

1
1 He was in the café.
2 He was with Ruby.
3 He was at the gym.
4 They were on the beach.
5 He was at Emily's house.
6 They were at the cinema.

2
1 Adam wasn't in the café with Pierre. He was in the café with Emily.
2 Adam wasn't at the Sea Life Centre with his mother. He was at the Sea Life Centre with Ruby/his sister.
3 Adam wasn't in a restaurant at 12.00. He was at home.
4 Adam wasn't with Emily at 2.30. He was with Pierre.

5 Katya and Jake weren't at the gym at 4.00. They were on the beach.
6 The students weren't at Emily's house at 8.30. They were at the cinema.

3
1 Adam wasn't in the café.
2 Emily was in the park.
3 Teresa wasn't at the cinema.
4 Katya and Jake were at the supermarket.
5 Pierre was in the café.

4
1 Was Mr Ward on the beach? No, he wasn't.
2 Was Jake in the park? Yes, he was.
3 Was Emily at home? No, she wasn't.
4 Was Ruby at school? Yes, she was.
5 Were Teresa and Katya in Lewes? No, they weren't.
6 Were Pierre and Adam in the café? Yes, they were.

5
1 Was Steven in Tokyo on Monday? No, he wasn't. He was in London.
2 Was Steven in London on Tuesday? No, he wasn't. He was in Tokyo.
3 Was Steven in Tokyo on Wednesday? Yes, he was.
4 Was Steven in Beijing on Thursday? No, he wasn't. He was in London.
5 Was Steven in London on Friday? No, he wasn't. He was in Beijing.

6
1 Was President Kennedy British? No, he wasn't. He was American.
2 Was Salvador Dalí Italian? No, he wasn't. He was Spanish.
3 Was Marie Curie Belgian? No, she wasn't. She was Polish.
4 Were Lennon and McCartney American? No, they weren't. They were British.
5 Were the Incas Mexican? No, they weren't. They were Peruvian.
6 Were the Romans Spanish? No, they weren't. They were Italian.

7
1 in 2 at 3 at 4 on 5 at 6 in 7 at 8 on

8
1 ✗ 2 ✓ 3 ✗ 4 ✓ 5 ✗ 6 ✗ 7 ✓

UNIT 6 LESSON 2

1
1 c 2 c 3 a 4 b 5 d 6 a 7 c 8 d

2
1 asked 2 changed 3 cooked 4 danced
5 discussed 6 enjoyed 7 hated 8 laughed
9 looked 10 loved 11 shouted 12 smiled
13 stayed 14 talked 15 translated 16 watched

3
1 carried 2 cried 3 studied 4 worried

4
bought did flew got gave heard held knew left meant met read ran said saw sang sat spoke stole swam took taught told thought understood wrote

5
1 went 2 saw 3 took 4 asked 5 was 6 gave
7 got, swam

6
Students' own answers.

7
1 steal money 2 be strong 3 drink beer
4 eat vegetables 5 play a board game
6 sail a ship 7 wear jewellery

8
1 ✓ 2 ✓ 3 ✓ 4 ✓ 5 ✗ 6 ✓ 7 ✗ 8 ✓

UNIT 6 LESSON 3

1
1 The students didn't stay in the minibus. They left the minibus at the top of the hill.
2 They didn't cycle down into the valley. They walked down into the valley.
3 The devil didn't make the valley in the day. He made it in the night.
4 The old woman didn't switch on a light. She lit a candle.
5 She didn't put the candle by her door. She put it by her window.
6 The devil didn't think it was evening. He thought it was morning.
7 The devil didn't swim away. He ran away.

2
1 Did Pierre go shopping? No, he didn't.
2 Did Teresa go shopping? Yes, she did.
3 Did Adam and Ruby go shopping? No, they didn't.
4 Did Pierre help in the house? Yes, he did.
5 Did Teresa help in the house? No, she didn't.
6 Did Adam and Ruby help in the house? Yes, they did.
7 Did Pierre send a text message? No, he didn't.
8 Did Teresa send a text message? Yes, she did.
9 Did Adam and Ruby send a text message? Yes, they did.

3
1 Did you go to school yesterday? Yes, I did. / No, I didn't.
2 Did you have breakfast? Yes, I did. / No, I didn't.
3 Did you go to bed early? Yes, I did. / No, I didn't.
4 Did you clean your room? Yes, I did. / No, I didn't.
5 Did you borrow something from a friend? Yes, I did. / No, I didn't.
6 Did you go to the park? Yes, I did. / No, I didn't.
7 Did you wear any jewellery? Yes, I did. / No, I didn't.
8 Did you lose anything? Yes, I did. / No, I didn't.

4
1 Did Emily have a piano lesson on Tuesday? No, she didn't. She had a piano lesson on Friday.
2 Did Katya write a letter to her sister? No, she didn't. She wrote a letter to her parents.
3 Did Jake play basketball at the weekend? No, he didn't. He played football at the weekend.
4 Did Ruby and Adam cook a meal on Saturday? No, they didn't. They cooked a meal on Sunday.
5 Did Teresa get a text message from Katya? No, she didn't. She got a text message from Emily.
6 Did the students go cycling in Brighton? No, they didn't. They went swimming in Brighton.
7 Did Adam lose Pierre's MP3 player? No, he didn't. He lost Pierre's camera.
8 Did Teresa buy a present for her mother? No, she didn't. She bought a present for her father.

5
1 apologise camera worried
2 anything right wrong
3 listen later yesterday
4 angry round running
5 carried forget sorry

6

▪■	■▪
across	evening
agree	listen
explain	open
forget	visit
mistake	window

UNIT 6 LESSON 4

1
1 and 2 but 3 Then 4 and 5 but 6 Then
7 and 8 But 9 Then 10 and 11 Then
12 and

2

[1]T	E	[2]M	P	E	[3]R	A	[4]T	U	R	[5]E
E		E			E		H			X
[6]R	E	A	D		[7]D	A	R	K		P
R		N		[8]W			O			L
I		[9]W	[10]H	O		[11]R	U	N		O
[12]B	E	H	I	N	[13]D		G		[14]O	R
L		[15]I	S		O		[16]H	[17]E	R	E
E		L		[18]M				A		R
	[19]J	E	W	E	L	L	E	R	Y	

Learner independence
1 e 2 d 3 b 4 a 5 c

UNIT 6
Inspiration EXTRA!

Revision

Lesson 1
1 Was Spain the winner of the 2010 World Cup? Yes, it was.
2 Was Picasso from Spain? Yes, he was.
3 Was Venus Williams a champion at the age of 17? No, she wasn't.
4 Were the 2008 Olympic Games in China? Yes, they were.
5 Was Oprah Winfrey the first woman to win a Nobel Prize? No, she wasn't.
6 Were Tenzing and Hillary the first people on the moon? No, they weren't.
7 Was Pompeii a Roman volcano? No, it wasn't.
8 Were the Aztecs from Mexico? Yes, they were.

Lesson 2
1 came 2 sailed 3 liked 4 wore 5 ate 6 found
7 visited 8 discovered

Lesson 3
1 Did the girl wear a long red dress? No, she didn't.
2 Did the girl smile at Pierre? Yes, she did.
3 Did the girl go into a shop? No, she didn't.
4 Did Pierre run in after her? Yes, he did.
5 Did Pierre close his eyes? Yes, he did.
6 Did Pierre think the girl was Teresa? Yes, he did.
7 Did Pierre call Teresa on his mobile? No, he didn't.
8 Did Adam say Teresa was with him? Yes, he did.

Lesson 4
Students' own answers.

Spelling
1 across 2 attack 3 borrow 4 dress
5 finally 6 happen 7 jewellery 8 matter
9 shopping 10 sorry 11 terrible 12 worried

Brainteaser
Eye.

Extension

Lessons 1–4
Students' own answers.

Spelling
1 eat 2 week 3 sleep 4 leave 5 steal 6 meat
7 see 8 teenager

Brainteaser
The letter 'r'.

REVIEW UNITS 5–6

1
1 C 2 B 3 A 4 A 5 C 6 B 7 A 8 C 9 C 10 B 11 C 12 A

2
1 teacher 2 doctor 3 pilot 4 journalist 5 waiter 6 interpreter 7 musician 8 actor

3
1 B 2 C 3 B 4 A 5 B

4
1 vegetable 2 save 3 bread 4 boat 5 flower 6 Ireland 7 horse 8 terrible

Learner independence

2
1 It's time to ...
2 Whose turn is it?
3 What's the matter?
4 To be honest ...
5 What do you mean?
6 Let's forget about it.

UNIT 7 LESSON 1

1
1 She's going to buy presents for her family.
2 She's going to get a guide to London for Anna.
3 Katya's mother is going to London with Anna.
4 She's going to learn Italian.
5 He's very busy at work. He's going to go to the mountains.
6 She's going to buy some English chocolate for them.

2
1 The Black Eyed Peas aren't going to do a European tour. They're going to do an American tour.
2 The Campbells aren't going to have a pizza party. They're going to have a barbecue.
3 Ruby isn't going to play a computer game. She's going to play a board game.
4 Pierre isn't going to eat octopus for breakfast. He's going to eat eggs.
5 Jake isn't going to listen to Miley Cyrus. She's going to listen to Dizzee Rascal.
6 Teresa isn't going to go to the cinema. She's going to go to the gym.

3
1 Is Katya going to buy lots of presents? Yes, she is.
2 Is Jake going to stay in Brighton after the exchange? No, he isn't.
3 Are Ruby and Adam going to have a barbecue? Yes, they are.
4 Is the barbecue going to be on Sunday? Yes, it is.
5 Are all the students going to be at the barbecue? Yes, they are.
6 Are you going to visit Brighton next week? No, I'm not.

4
1 Why is Katya holding a cinema ticket? Because she's going to see a film.
2 Why are Jake and Pierre wearing tennis clothes? Because they're going to play tennis.
3 Why is Diana holding a bag? Because she's going to go shopping.
4 Why is Adam carrying a skateboard? Because he's going to go skateboarding.
5 Why is Emily carrying a guitar? Because she's going to have a guitar lesson.
6 Why is Ruby holding some books? Because she she's going to do her homework.
7 Why is Pierre wearing trainers? Because he's going to go running.
8 Why are Teresa and Emily carrying swimming things? Because they're going to go swimming.

5
1 call an ambulance 2 have an accident 3 speak to someone 4 look worried 5 watch a DVD 6 wear shorts 7 win a competition 8 X-ray someone's leg

6
1 ambulance 2 worried 3 message 4 barbecue 5 prize 6 DVD 7 programme 8 holiday 9 accident 10 X-ray

7
1 ✗ 2 ✓ 3 ✓ 4 ✓ 5 ✗ 6 ✗ 7 ✓ 8 ✗

UNIT 7 LESSON 2

1
1 F 2 T 3 F 4 F 5 T 6 F 5 F

2
1 I like dancing.
2 She enjoys playing golf.
3 They love sailing.
4 You enjoy cooking.
5 We like watching TV.
6 He loves painting and drawing.

3
1 Adam loves playing chess.
2 Pierre hates losing tennis games.
3 Emily loves listening to Beyoncé.
4 Pierre doesn't like ironing shirts.
5 Jake doesn't mind cooking.
6 Teresa enjoys going to the cinema.

4
1 Does Jake like dancing? Yes, he loves it.
2 Does Teresa enjoy going to museums? No, she hates it.
3 Do Teresa and Emily hate singing? No, they like it.
4 Does Pierre hate going to the cinema? No, he enjoys it.
5 Does Adam mind doing his homework? No, he doesn't mind it.
6 Do Ruby and Adam mind helping their mum? No, they like it.
7 Does Emily love running? No, she doesn't like it.
8 Does Katya like riding? Yes, she loves it.

5
1 Do you like playing chess?
2 Do you enjoy cooking?
3 Do you love dancing?
4 Do you like swimming?
5 Do you mind helping at home?
6 Do you hate cleaning your room?

(Students' own answers.)

6

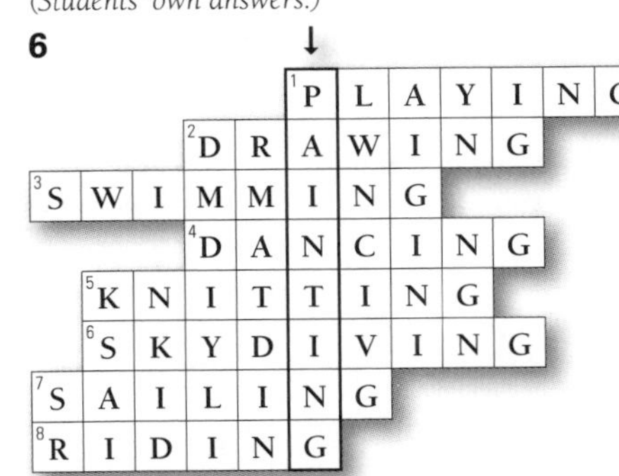

The missing word is painting.

7
1 play ice hockey 2 jump out of a plane 3 knit a scarf 4 paint pictures 5 swim with sharks 6 ride a horse 7 write songs

8
1 ✗ 2 ✓ 3 ✓ 4 ✓ 5 ✓ 6 ✗ 7 ✓ 8 ✗

UNIT 7 LESSON 3

1
1 The elephant is the biggest land animal.
2 The cheetah is the fastest land animal.
3 The whale is the biggest animal.
4 The falcon is the fastest bird.
5 The giraffe is the tallest animal.
6 The shark is the most dangerous fish.
7 The mosquito is the most dangerous animal.
8 The sailfish is the fastest fish.

2
the slowest the shortest the tallest the smallest the youngest the biggest the wettest the strangest the ugliest the most amazing the most boring the most exciting the most popular the best the worst

3
1 the highest 2 the driest 3 the sunniest 4 wettest 5 the coldest 6 the hottest

4
1 dangerous friendliest tomatoes programme
2 amazing beautiful disease malaria
3 exciting animal million flies
4 scared people level countries
5 tallest smallest football called

5

B	O	P	S	C	A	T	L	F
E	L	E	P	H	A	N	T	A
A	S	N	A	E	R	C	I	L
W	H	G	R	E	D	O	G	C
H	A	U	R	T	P	W	E	O
A	R	I	O	A	L	I	R	N
L	K	N	T	H	I	P	P	O
E	F	G	I	R	A	F	F	E

6

■ ▪ ▪	▪ ■ ▪
animal	amazing
dangerous	exciting
elephant	including
octopus	mosquito
scientist	unhappy

UNIT 7 LESSON 4

1
1 biggest 2 best 3 worst 4 cheapest 5 highest 6 high 7 sunniest 5 slowest

2
Students' own answers.

3

1 C	O	M	2 P	E	3 T	I	T	4 I	O	N
H			O		E			N		
5 E	L	E	P	H	A	N	T	S		6 I
A			U		M			7 E	8 A	T
9 P	U	L	L			10 F	A	C	T	
			11 A	12 B				T		13 U
14 G	15 O		16 R	E	D		17 M			G
	L			S			E			L
	18 D	I	C	T	I	O	N	A	R	Y

Learner independence

1 *Whose turn is it now?*
2 *Excuse me, what page is it?*
3 *Can I borrow your book, please?*
4 *What is the best way to do this exercise?*
5 *Please can you say that again?*
6 *What do you suggest I do now?*

UNIT 7
Inspiration EXTRA!

Revision

Lesson 1

1 *What is Teresa going to read? She's going to read her new magazine.*
2 *Who is Pierre going to phone? He's going to phone Adam.*
3 *Where is Katya going to go? She's going to go to the gym.*
4 *What is Jake going to play? He's going to play tennis.*
5 *What is Emily going to practise? She's going to practise the piano.*

Lesson 2

1 *Avril Lavigne doesn't hate skateboarding. She loves skateboarding.*
2 *Johnny Depp doesn't hate painting. He loves painting.*
3 *Cameron Diaz doesn't hate knitting. She loves knitting.*
4 *Robert Pattinson doesn't hate skiing. He enjoys skiing.*
5 *Johnny Depp doesn't love dancing. He hates dancing.*
6 *Orlando Bloom doesn't hate skydiving. He loves skydiving.*

Lesson 3

1 *The cheetah isn't the slowest animal. It's the fastest animal.*
2 *The falcon isn't the most dangerous bird. It's the fastest bird.*
3 *The tiger isn't the most boring animal. It's the most exciting animal.*
4 *The shark isn't the friendliest fish. It's the most dangerous fish.*
5 *The giraffe isn't the biggest animal. It's the tallest animal.*
6 *The mosquito isn't the smallest insect. It's the most dangerous insect.*

Lesson 4

Students' own answers.

Spelling

1 barbecue 2 dangerous 3 finish 4 malaria 5 competition 6 disease 7 medicine 8 scientist

Brainteaser

May.

Extension

Lesson 1

1 *What are you going to do this evening?*
2 *Who are you going to see this weekend?*
3 *Where are you going to be on Saturday night?*
4 *When are you going to visit England?*

(Students' own answers.)

Lesson 2

Teresa doesn't like skateboarding, but Jake loves it.
Teresa loves painting, but Jake doesn't like it.
Teresa doesn't mind riding, but Jake loves it.
Teresa loves swimming, but Jake doesn't mind it.
Teresa doesn't mind dancing, but Jake doesn't like it.
Teresa doesn't like playing chess, but Jake doesn't mind it.

Lesson 3

Students' own answers.

Lesson 4

Students' own answer.

Spelling

1 correct 2 excellent 3 giraffe 4 parrot 5 programme 6 rabbit 7 sheep 8 suggest 9 swimming 10 teenage 11 unhappy 12 worried

Brainteaser

When they make 22.

CULTURE

Food around the world

1

Photo a The Mendoza Family, Todos Santos, Guatemala
Photo b Costa Family, Havana, Cuba
Photo c The Batsuur Family, Ulan Bator, Mongolia

2

1 *Oyuntsetseg and Regzen Batsuur*
2 *The Mendoza and Costa families*
3 *The Mendoza family*
4 *The Costa family*
5 *The Batsuur and Mendoza families*
6 *Susana Pérez Matias and Fortunato Pablo Mendoza*
7 *The Costa family*
8 *Ramón Costa*
9 *The Mendoza family*

3

1 secretary 2 suburbs 3 warehouse 4 chemist's 5 hairdresser 6 flat

4

1 *False. Sandra Costa's sister is a hairdresser.*
2 *True*
3 *False. The Mendoza family doesn't eat fish.*
4 *False. The Batsuur family doesn't eat lots of fresh fruit.*
5 *False. She works in a chemist's.*
6 *False. Lisandra is younger than Khorloo.*
7 *True*
8 *False. Sandra Costa is younger than her husband.*
9 *True*
10 *False. The Batsuur family and the Mendoza family eat the most eggs.*

UNIT 8 LESSON 1

1

1 any 2 tomatoes 3 some, butter
4 any, some, some 5 some

2

Countable nouns		Uncountable nouns
Singular	Plural	
apple	apples	food
carrot	carrots	milk
hamburger	hamburgers	pasta
orange	oranges	porridge
mushroom	mushrooms	rice
potato	potatoes	soup

3

1 There are some apples 2 There aren't any oranges. 3 There's some fruit. 4 There are some bananas. 5 There are some glasses. 6 There's some water. 7 There isn't any milk. 8 There is a knife. 9 There isn't a spoon. 10 There is a fork. 11 There is a plate. 12 There aren't any cups. 13 There are some hamburgers. 14 There aren't any sandwiches. 15 There aren't any magazines. 16 There are some books. 17 There is a newspaper. 18 There aren't any pens.

4

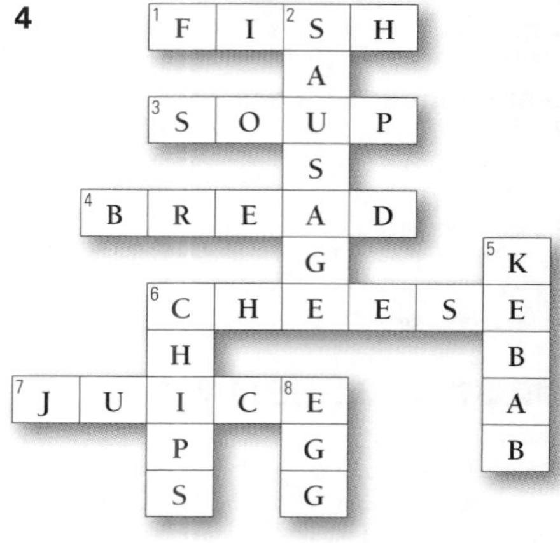

3 soup 1 fish 6 chips 4 bread 7 juice

5

1 chocolate cake 2 dishwasher 3 fast food 4 ice cream 5 tomato salad 6 washing machine

6

1 potato 2 tomato 3 cup 4 Milk 5 thirsty 6 vegetarian 7 cooker 8 Coffee 9 fridge

7

■▪▪	▪■▪
barbecue	banana
dishwasher	opinion
hamburger	potato
sandwiches	together
sausages	tomato
vegetable	

UNIT 8 LESSON 2

1

	Emily	Teresa
banana	✓	✗
bottle of water	✓	✗
CD	✗	✓
computer game	✓	✗
magazine	✓	✗
packet of tissues	✓	✓
phone	✓	✓
sunglasses	✓	✗
wallet	✓	✓

2

1 *Teresa has got a CD. Emily hasn't got a CD.*
2 *Emily and Teresa have got wallets.*
3 *Emily has got a bottle of water. Teresa hasn't got a bottle of water.*
4 *Emily and Teresa have got packets of tissues.*
5 *Emily has got sunglasses. Teresa hasn't got sunglasses.*
6 *Emily has got a computer game. Teresa hasn't got a computer game.*
7 *Emily has got a banana. Teresa hasn't got a banana.*
8 *Emily and Teresa have got phones.*

3

1 Ruby has got a brother, but she hasn't got any sisters.
2 Adam and Pierre haven't got (any) brothers.
3 Diana has got two children.
4 Teresa and Jake haven't got (any) brothers or sisters.
5 Adam has got a sister, but he hasn't got any brothers.
6 Mr Ward hasn't got (any) children.

4

1 Has Pierre got a sister? Yes, he has.
2 Has Katya got a brother? Yes, she has.
3 Has Adam got a skateboard? Yes, he has.
4 Have Katya and Teresa got pets? Yes, they have.
5 Has Pierre got a pet? No, he hasn't.
6 Have Pierre and Katya got camera phones? No, they haven't.

5

1 How much is the laptop? It's seven hundred and fifty euros.
2 How much is the mobile phone? It's one hundred and fifty euros.
3 How much is the camera? It's two hundred euros.
4 How much is the dictionary? It's thirty euros.
5 How much are the pens? They're two euros.
6 How much are the sandwiches? They're eight euros.

6

1 hobby 2 games console 3 allowance
4 DVD player 5 expensive 6 poster

7

/g/ girl	/dʒ/ orange
girl	cottage
got	sausage
good	suggest
hamburger	teenager
magazine	vegetarian

UNIT 8 LESSON 3

1

1 Yes, they are.
2 No, she isn't. She's giving plates to Pierre and Ruby.
3 No, he isn't. He's talking to Diana.
4 No, it isn't. It's a beautiful sunny day.
5 Yes, she is.
6 No, they aren't. They're sitting down at a table.

2

1 She's from Spain, isn't she?
2 His name is Babar Ali, isn't it?
3 They're in Brighton, aren't they?
4 They're at the gym, aren't they?
5 She's playing the saxophone, isn't she?
6 It's a cheetah, isn't it?

3

1 isn't it? 2 aren't they? 3 isn't it? 4 isn't he?
5 isn't it? 6 aren't they? 7 isn't it? 8 isn't it?
9 aren't they? 10 isn't he?

4

1 d 2 f 3 a 4 b 5 e 6 c

5

1 Whoops 2 ice cream 3 drop 4 dad 5 sad
6 barbecue

6

1 meet 2 well 3 something 4 please
5 hungry 6 matter 7 No 7 another

7

beginning confident connected delicious
paradise understand

UNIT 8 LESSON 4

1

1 c 2 a 3 b

2

Students' own answer.

3

[1] D	I	[2] C	T	[3] I	O	[4] N	A	[5] R	Y	
A		A		N		E		E		[6] P
[7] N	A	M	E	S		[8] W	H	A	L	E
G		E		E		S		D		N
E		[9] L	U	C	[10] K		[11] R	I	N	G
R				[12] T	E	A		N		U
[13] O	L	[14] D			Y			G		I
U		[15] A	N	Y		[16] T			[17] I	N
[18] S	K	Y			[19] W	O	R	S	T	

UNIT 8
Inspiration EXTRA!

Revision

Lesson 1

1 some 2 any 3 some 4 any 5 any 6 some
7 any 8 some 9 any 10 some

Lesson 2

1 haven't got 2 has got 3 hasn't got 4 has got
5 haven't got 6 have got 7 has got
8 haven't got 9 have got 10 haven't got

Lesson 3

1 aren't you? 2 aren't we? 3 isn't she?
4 isn't he? 5 aren't they? 6 aren't I? 7 isn't it?

Lesson 4

1 f 2 e 3 a 4 h 5 d

Spelling

1 accept 2 apple 3 arrive 4 barbecue 5 fridge 6 hobby 7 juice 8 sausage 9 skateboard
10 suggestion 11 vegetarian 12 wicked

Brainteaser

Because they've got 'keys'.

Extension

Lesson 1

Students' own answers.

Lesson 2

1 Have you got any pets?
2 Have you got any brothers and sisters?
3 Have your parents got a car?
4 Has your school got a football team?
5 Have you got a musical instrument?
6 Has your best friend got a mobile phone?
7 Have you got red hair?
8 Has your teacher got blue eyes?

(Students' own answers.)

Lesson 3

1 aren't we? 2 isn't it? 3 aren't I? 4 isn't he?
5 isn't she? 6 aren't they? 7 aren't you?

Lesson 4

Students' own answer.

Spelling

1 discos 2 euros 3 hippos 4 kilos 5 mosquitoes
6 photos 7 pianos 8 potatoes 9 radios
10 tomatoes 11 videos

Brainteaser

Lunch and dinner.

REVIEW UNITS 7-8

1

1 B 2 C 3 C 4 A 5 C 6 C 7 C 8 A 9 C
10 B 11 A 12 B

2

1 giraffe 2 octopus 3 parrot 4 polar bear
5 penguin 6 mosquito 7 cheetah 8 dolphin

3

1 A 2 C 3 B 4 C 5 A

4

1 adult 2 police 3 morning 4 penguin
5 kitchen 6 cup 7 potato 8 suggest

Learner independence

2

1 What's wrong with him? 2 What are you going to do? 3 What do you suggest?
4 Please let me know. 5 Come to our party.
6 See you there.

L.A. Adventure

L.A. Adventure encourages students to read for pleasure, while consolidating language covered in *New Inspiration 1*. Chapters 1–8 of the story correspond to Units 1–8, and Chapter 9 revises language from the whole book. The story is followed by a series of exercises testing comprehension. The story can be read in class, or teachers can set the reading as homework. Teachers may also find that students read ahead because they are keen to know the end of the story!

1 Shops!

- Write *L.A.* on the board. Ask students *What does this mean? Where is it? Is it big or small?*
- Students read the first chapter of the story on page 102. Point to the pictures and ask *What's her name? What's his name? How old do you think they are? Where are they? What time is it? Is Mark happy? Is Anna happy?*
- Students make a list of places where Mark could be. If necessary/possible, this activity could be done in students' native language.

Answers

1 Mark
2 London / England
3 Los Angeles / L.A. / America
4 3rd Street Promenade / Santa Monica / L.A.

Optional activity

Books closed. Students answer questions about the story from memory.

2 Wow!

- Ask students to recall the first chapter of the story. *What are the names of the brother and sister? Where are they? Where is Mark?*
- Ask students what they would do if they lost their brother or sister when shopping. This can be done in the students' native language. Students read the chapter on page 103 to see what Anna does.
- Point to the pictures and ask *Who is this? What can Anna see on the camera?*
- In pairs, students predict what happens next. If necessary/possible, this activity could be done in the students' native language.

Answers

1 Yes, she can. 2 No, she can't. 3 Yes, it is. 4 Yes, there are.
5 No, she can't.

Optional activities

♦ Books closed. Students answer questions about the pictures from memory, eg *Can you see a bag / a skirt / a bike / a shop in the pictures?*

♦ Students work in pairs. One is the police officer and one is Anna. They read their parts aloud. After everyone has practised, choose a confident pair to read the dialogue to the class.

3 All cars!

- Ask students questions about what happened in the previous chapter. Tell students that the next chapter is called *All cars!* Ask them to predict why it is called this. If necessary/possible, this could be done in the students' native language.
- Students read the chapter on page 104 to see if they were right. Ask *What do you think is in the bag?*
- In pairs, students predict what happens next. This activity could be done in the students' native language.

Answers

2 c 3 b 4 a

Optional activity

Books closed. Summarise the story so far but make some mistakes, eg *Mark and Anna are in London. Mark likes shopping*. Students listen. When they hear a mistake, they shout *Stop!* and correct the mistake. Alternatively, this could be a reading/writing activity.

4 He knows our faces!

- Ask students questions about what happened in the previous chapter.
- Students read the next chapter on page 105. Ask *Why do they take the van? Is it Mark's van? Why do the men take Mark?*
- Ask students what they think happens next.

Answers

1 False. Mark is eating pizza.
2 False. The men borrow a van.
3 True
4 True

Optional activity

Nominate five students to each read one of the parts in this chapter. The other students close their books while the story is read aloud.

5 It's the police!

- Ask students questions about what happened in the previous chapter. Write *paint* and a *helicopter* on the board. Tell students that these are important parts of the next chapter. Students predict why they are important.
- Students read the chapter on page 106 to see if they were right. Ask *How do the police know which van it is?*
- Ask students to imagine they are the men in the van. Ask *What do you do now?*

Answers

1 b 2 d 3 c 4 a

Optional activity

Books closed. Make some statements about the chapter. Students respond by saying if they are true or false, eg *There's blue paint of the top of the van* – false (there's red paint...), *Mark is in the van* – true.

6 I have an idea

- Ask students questions about what happened in the previous chapter. Tell students that the next chapter is called *I have an idea*. Ask them to predict who has an idea and what it is.
- Students read the chapter on page 107 to see if they were right. Ask *What is the idea? Do you think it's a good idea?*

Answers

1 It had red paint on the roof.
2 Because helicopters can't fly in car parks.
3 They painted it red.
4 Mark wrote HELP.

Optional activity

Students work in groups of three. Two are the men and one is Mark. They read their parts aloud. After everyone has practised, choose a confident group to read the dialogue to the class.

7 Can you fly?

- Ask students what happened in the previous chapter. Tell students that a bus driver is an important part of the next chapter. Students predict why he is important.
- Students read the chapter on page 108 to see if they were right. Ask *Why does the bus driver speak to the police? Why don't the men in the van stop? Where do they go?*
- Ask *What do you think is going to happen next?*

Answers

1 False. Mark and the men were in a red van.
2 False. Mark wrote HELP on the window.
3 True
4 False. The bus driver wanted the men to stop.
5 True

Optional activity

Books closed. Students say what happened in this chapter.

8 Open the door

- Ask students *What happened in the last chapter? Where was the van at the end?* Tell students that this chapter is called *Open the door.* Students predict what door this is.
- Students read the chapter on page 109 to see if they were right. Ask more questions, eg *Who tells the police they are taking a plane? Is Mark scared? Does he talk with the men on the plane? Are they friendly?*
- Ask *What do you think is going to happen next?*

Answers

1 d 2 e 3 a 4 b 5 c

Optional activity

Books closed. Students recall the story so far, from the beginning.

9 Are you all right?

- Ask students *What happened in the last chapter?* Ask *Do you think someone is going to open the door? Who or what do you think is going to go out of the door?*
- Students read the final chapter on page 110 to see if they were right. Check the answer. Ask *Is everyone all right?*

Answers

1 False. The man opened the plane door.
2 True
3 False. The pilot said Mark could have half the money.
4 True
5 True
6 False. The police officer said thank you to Mark.

Optional activities

- ♦ *Who says this?* Read sentences from different chapters of the book. Students identify the speaker. Students could continue in pairs.
- ♦ Books closed. Summarise the story but make some mistakes. Students listen. When they hear a mistake, they shout *Stop!* and correct the mistake. Alternatively, this could be a reading/writing activity.
- ♦ Students retell the whole story.

After reading activities

Write the six activities below on the board. Students choose the activities they are most interested in. The written work can be displayed in the classroom. The first activity could be videoed.

1. Choose one chapter of the story and act it out with another student / in a group.
2. Choose one chapter. Write as many questions as you can about this chapter of the story. Then give your questions to another student to answer.
3. Summarise each chapter in just one sentence.
4. Imagine you are Anna or Mark. Write your diary for the day you had an adventure in L.A.
5. Write a new ending for the story.
6. You are a film director. You are going to make a film of the story. Choose your stars and make a film poster.

Unit 1–2 CLIL Teaching notes
Maths

Code breakers!

Aims	To learn about the function of maths in code breaking.
Activities	Guessing vocabulary from pictures and from context; reading for gist and specific information; task-based learning – deciphering codes and writing alphanumerical codes.
Language	Plural nouns; basic personal questions and answers; the verb *be*; possessive adjectives; linking words: *and, but, or*; vocabulary relating to numbers, shapes and mathematical terms.
Preparation	Photocopy one worksheet for each pair.
To use	After Unit 2, either in class or as homework.
Procedure	• This CLIL spread can be given as homework or be done in pairs in class. For each activity, students can either check answers in pairs and then with the whole class, or use a monolingual dictionary to help with vocabulary if they are working at home. • First, ask students to work individually and use the words to label the pictures. Ask them to check their answers in pairs. • Next ask students to skim read the text quickly to see if their answers were correct. Check the answers with the whole class. • Ask students to read the text more carefully. Ask a few comprehension questions to check understanding: *What are the two types of codes? (transposition and substitution) In which type of code are the original letters in a different order? (transposition) In which type of code do the original letters change to different letters? (substitution) Why is it useful to know some common letters and words when you crack a code? (You can look for repeated letters or words in the message and guess what they are.)* • Now ask students to try to crack the codes on page 113. Do the first one together as a class before asking them to do the rest in pairs. Check the answers with the whole class and ask different students to write the encoded answers on the board for the class to decode. • For the project, ask students to work individually or in pairs. Ask students to prepare three to five secret codes including examples of different kinds of codes. They should also invent their own code – remind students to make it challenging but not impossible. When the students have finished, ask them to swap their codes with another pair and see who cracks the codes first.

Key

Exercise 1/2

1 *row*
2 *column*
3 *zigzag*
4 *pattern*
5 *rectangle*
6 *code*
7 *alphabetical order*

Exercise 3

1 *Message: When is lunch?*
Answer in code: Students' own answers.
Type of code: transposition
Start: column 4, row 4
Pattern: circle
Shape: square

2 *Message: What is your name?*
Answer in code: Students' own answers.
Type of code: transposition
Start: column 1, row 1
Pattern: zigzag
Shape: rectangle

3 *Message: What is your favourite colour?*
Answer in code: Students' own answers.
Type of code: substitution
Pattern: +9

4 *Message: How old is the person next to you?*
Answer in code: Students' own answers.
Type of code: substitution
Pattern: -4

5 *Message: Is this very easy?*
Answer in code: Students' own answers.
Type of code: substitution

O	R	A	N	G	E
5	6	1	4	3	2
I	S	T	H	I	S
V	E	R	Y	E	A
S	Y	A	B	C	D

Unit 3–4 CLIL Teaching notes
Drama

Theatre design

Aims	To learn about the different aspects involved in theatre design.
Activities	Guessing vocabulary from pictures and from context; reading for gist and specific information; summarising advantages and disadvantages from a text; labelling a picture of a theatre; inventing and designing the look of their own play.
Language	Present simple; present continuous; adverbs of frequency; prepositions of place; vocabulary relating to the theatre.
To use	After Unit 4, either in class or as homework.
Procedure	• This CLIL spread can be given as homework or be done in pairs in class. For each activity, students can either check answers in pairs and then with the whole class, or use a monolingual dictionary to help with vocabulary if they are working at home. • Ask students what is different about each stage, i.e. position of audience, actors, etc. Then ask them to try to match the words to the pictures. They then check their answers in pairs before skim reading the text quickly to see if they were correct. Review the answers with the whole class. • Next ask students to read the text more carefully and work in pairs to complete the table with the advantages (good things) and disadvantages (bad things) of each kind of stage. Check the answers with the whole class. • Ask students to look at the picture of the theatre and label it with the words provided. Remind them to refer back to the text if they need to. Ask students to check answers in small groups before you review them with the whole class. • For the project stage, ask students to work in groups of four. You may wish to brainstorm some ideas for a play, e.g. setting, plot, characters, etc. with the whole class first. Then ask students to discuss ideas for their play in their groups. Tell them to come up with a brief outline of their play – it is not necessary to write the script. • The second stage of the project can be as visual as the students want it to be. Tell them they can use simple line drawings, computer software or collage techniques to present their theatre design project to their classmates and explain their choices. • As an extra activity you could get students to develop and act out one scene from their play.

Key

Exercise 1

1c 2d 3b 4a

Exercise 2

Type of stage	*Good things*	*Bad things*
arena stage	*audience is close to actors*	*no scenery changes or special effects*
open stage	*audience is close to actors, scenery changes and special effects are easy too*	*audience can see other people in the audience*
end stage	*difficult scenery changes and special effects are possible, it's easy for the audience to concentrate on the play*	*audience is not close to the actors*
proscenium/traditional stage	*there is space for scenery changes and special effects at the back of the stage*	*there is an arch between the audience and the stage and many people in the audience are a long way from the actors*

Exercise 3

1 *scenery*
2 *backstage*
3 *special effects*
4 *costume*
5 *stage*
6 *actor*
7 *audience*
8 *lighting*

Unit 5–6 CLIL Teaching notes
History

The Incas

Aims	To learn about the history of the Incas and research the history of other anicent civilisations.
Activities	Predicting/guessing information; labelling pictures from context; reading for gist and specific information; identifying and categorising information from a text and completing a table; researching and writing about other people from the past.
Language	Past simple affirmative (regular and irregular verbs); vocabulary related to countries, continents, past events, expressions of time, people and lifestyles.
To use	After Unit 6, either in class or as homework.
Procedure	• This CLIL spread can be given as homework or be done in pairs in class. For each activity, students can either check answers in pairs and then with the whole class, or use a monolingual dictionary to help with vocabulary if they are working at home. • Ask students to do the true/false quiz individually. They then check answers in pairs before skim reading the text quickly to see if they were correct. Review the answers with the whole class. • Ask students to scan the text, find the four items of vocabulary and use context to match them with the pictures. Students can check answers first in pairs before you review them with the whole class. • Next ask students to scan read the text again carefully and then work in pairs to complete the table with the information from the text. Ask different pairs to share their answers with the class. • Students will need access to research materials such as books and/or the Internet for the project stage of the lesson. Ask them to work in pairs and decide which ancient civilisation they want to research. They should prepare a short description of the civilisation, using the questions in exercise 3 to help them. Remind them they can also include information about other aspects of the group's lives. Ask each pair to present their research to the class.

Key

Exercise 1

1F 2T 3T 4F 5T 6T 7F

Exercise 2

1c 2b 3d 4a

Exercise 3

Where in the world did they live?	*They lived in the Andes Mountains in South America – where Bolivia, Chile, Ecuador, Peru, and parts of Argentina and Colombia are today.*
What did they eat?	*They ate vegetables, corn and chillies.*
What was their religion like?	*They believed they were the sons of the god of the sun. They believed in gods of nature and had special objects and statues. They killed animals and humans to give thanks to their gods. They loved gold because they thought it was a present from the god of the sun.*
What clothes did they wear?	*They made clothes from alpaca and llama wool.*
What work did they do?	*They worked in the Inca leader's army, or on his land. They also built roads.*

Unit 7–8 CLIL Teaching notes

Science

Mosquitoes and malaria

Aims To learn about how malaria is transmitted, prevented and cured.

Activities Guessing vocabulary from pictures and context; predicting information about a text; reading for gist and specific information; labelling diagrams; researching and making a public health poster about how to prevent and cure malaria.

Language Adjectives; superlative adjectives; vocabulary related to animals, diseases and the human body.

To use After Unit 8, either in class or as homework.

Procedure

- This CLIL spread can be given as homework or be done in pairs in class. For each activity, students can either check answers in pairs and then with the whole class, or use a monolingual dictionary to help with vocabulary if they are working at home.
- Ask students to use the words in the box to label the pictures. Ask them to check their answers in pairs before you review them with the class.
- Then ask students to do the true/false quiz in pairs. They then skim read the text quickly to see if they were correct. Check the answers with the whole class.
- Next ask students to read the text more carefully and use the information to label the diagrams and complete the missing information in Exercise 3. Students should check their answers with another pair before you review them with the whole class.
- Students will need access to research materials, such as reference books and/or the Internet for the project stage of the lesson. Ask them to find out what the best and worst things to do are to stop people getting malaria and make a public health poster to illustrate their findings.
- As an extra activity display the posters on the classroom walls and get students to decide which ones they think are the most effective.

Key

Exercise 1

1 *medicine*
2 *mosquito net*
3 *itchy*
4 *blood*
5 *skin*
6 *sweat*
7 *saliva*

Exercise 2

1F 2T 3F 4T 5T 6T 7F

Exercise 3

a	*b*	*c*
1 *one million*	1 *mouth*	*1 a*
2 *250 million*	2 *wings*	*2 c*
3 *young children*	3 *legs*	*3 b*
4 *Central America*	4 *body*	
5 *South America*	5 *female*	
6 *Sub-Saharan Africa*	6 *blood*	
7 *South Asia*	7 *sweat*	
8 *South-East Asia*	8 *saliva*	

Audio Track List

CD 1

1.01	**Welcome**		Exercise 1
1.02			Exercise 3
1.03			Exercise 7
1.04			Exercise 8
1.05			Exercise 9
1.06			Exercise 10
1.07	**Preview, Units 1 and 2**		Exercise 4
1.08	**Unit 1**	Lesson 1	Exercise 2
1.09		Lesson 1	Exercise 4
1.10		Lesson 1	Exercise 6
1.11		Lesson 1	Exercise 7
1.12		Lesson 2	Exercise 2
1.13		Lesson 2	Exercise 4
1.14		Lesson 2	Exercise 5
1.15		Lesson 2	Exercise 6
1.16		Lesson 2	Exercise 8
1.17		Lesson 3	Exercise 2
1.18		Lesson 3	Exercise 4
1.19		Lesson 3	Exercise 5
1.20		Lesson 3	Exercise 6
1.21		Lesson 4	Exercise 2
1.22		Lesson 4	Exercise 4
1.23		Lesson 4	Exercise 7
1.24		Lesson 4	Exercise 9
1.25		Inspiration *Extra!*, Game	
1.26		Inspiration *Extra!*, Sketch	
1.27	**Culture**	Exercise 2, Countries Around the World	
1.28		Exercise 3, Countries Around the World	
1.29		Exercise 5, Countries Around the World	
1.30	**Unit 2**	Lesson 1	Exercise 2
1.31		Lesson 1	Exercise 4
1.32		Lesson 1	Exercise 5
1.33		Lesson 1	Exercise 6
1.34		Lesson 1	Exercise 7
1.35		Lesson 2	Exercise 2
1.36		Lesson 2	Exercise 4
1.37		Lesson 3	Exercise 2
1.38		Lesson 3	Exercise 4
1.39		Lesson 3	Exercise 5
1.40		Lesson 4	Exercise 2
1.41		Lesson 4	Exercise 3
1.42		Lesson 4	Exercise 8

CD 2

2.1	**Preview, Units 3 and 4**		Exercise 4
2.2	**Unit 3**	Lesson 1	Exercise 2
2.3		Lesson 1	Exercise 4
2.4		Lesson 1	Exercise 5
2.5		Lesson 1	Exercise 6
2.6		Lesson 2	Exercise 2
2.7		Lesson 2	Exercise 4
2.8		Lesson 2	Exercise 6
2.9		Lesson 3	Exercise 2
2.10		Lesson 3	Exercise 4
2.11		Lesson 3	Exercise 5
2.12		Lesson 4	Exercise 2
2.13		Lesson 4	Exercise 3
2.14		Lesson 4	Exercise 8
2.15		Inspiration *Extra!*, Sketch	
2.16	**Culture**	Exercise 2, Take two teenagers … north and south	
2.17	**Unit 4**	Lesson 1	Exercise 2
2.18		Lesson 1	Exercise 5
2.19		Lesson 1	Exercise 6
2.20		Lesson 2	Exercise 2
2.21		Lesson 2	Exercise 5
2.22		Lesson 3	Exercise 2
2.23		Lesson 3	Exercise 4
2.24		Lesson 3	Exercise 6
2.25		Lesson 3	Exercise 7
2.26		Lesson 4	Exercise 2
2.27		Lesson 4	Exercise 3
2.28		Lesson 4	Exercise 6
2.29		Lesson 4	Exercise 8
2.30	**Preview, Units 5 and 6**		Exercise 4
2.31	**Unit 5**	Lesson 1	Exercise 2
2.32		Lesson 1	Exercise 5
2.33		Lesson 1	Exercise 7
2.34		Lesson 2	Exercise 2
2.35		Lesson 2	Exercise 5
2.36		Lesson 2	Exercise 6
2.37		Lesson 3	Exercise 2
2.38		Lesson 3	Exercise 6
2.39		Lesson 4	Exercise 3
2.40		Lesson 4	Exercise 6
2.41		Lesson 4	Exercise 8
2.42		Inspiration *Extra!* Sketch	
2.43	**Culture**	Exercise 2, Social Situations Questionnaire	
2.44		Exercise 3, What do you say at a party?	
2.45		Exercise 4, What do you say at a party? continued	
2.46	**Unit 6**	Lesson 1	Exercise 2
2.47		Lesson 1	Exercise 5
2.48		Lesson 2	Exercise 2
2.49		Lesson 2	Exercise 4
2.50		Lesson 2	Exercise 6
2.51		Lesson 3	Exercise 2
2.52		Lesson 3	Exercise 5
2.53		Lesson 3	Exercise 6
2.54		Lesson 4	Exercise 2
2.55		Lesson 4	Exercise 3
2.56		Lesson 4	Exercise 5
2.57		Lesson 4	Exercise 8
2.58	**Review, Units 5 and 6, Exercise 7**		

CD 3

3.1	**Preview, Units 7 and 8**		Exercise 3
3.2	**Unit 7**	Lesson 1	Exercise 2
3.3		Lesson 1	Exercise 4
3.4		Lesson 1	Exercise 6
3.5		Lesson 1	Exercise 7
3.6		Lesson 2	Exercise 2
3.7		Lesson 2	Exercise 4
3.8		Lesson 2	Exercise 5
3.9		Lesson 3	Exercise 2
3.10		Lesson 3	Exercise 6
3.11		Lesson 4	Exercise 2
3.12		Lesson 4	Exercise 3
3.13		Lesson 4	Exercise 8
3.14		Inspiration *Extra!*, Sketch	
3.15		Inspiration *Extra!*, Limerick	
3.16	**Culture**	Exercise 1, What do families around the world eat?	
3.17	**Unit 8**	Lesson 1	Exercise 2
3.18		Lesson 1	Exercise 6
3.19		Lesson 1	Exercise 7
3.20		Lesson 1	Exercise 8
3.21		Lesson 2	Exercise 2
3.22		Lesson 2	Exercise 4
3.23		Lesson 2	Exercise 5
3.24		Lesson 2	Exercise 6
3.25		Lesson 3	Exercise 2
3.26		Lesson 3	Exercise 4
3.27		Lesson 3	Exercise 5
3.28		Lesson 4	Exercise 2
3.29		Lesson 4	Exercise 4
3.30		Lesson 4	Exercise 9
3.31	**Song**	*Together We Are Strong*	
3.32	**Song**	*Raining In My Heart*	
3.33	**Song**	*Don't You Want Me Baby?*	
3.34	**Song**	*Rocket Man*	